# CHALLENGE TO LEADERSHIP

# CHALLENGE TO LEADERSHIP

## ECONOMIC AND SOCIAL ISSUES
## FOR THE NEXT DECADE

Isabel V. Sawhill, Editor

 THE URBAN INSTITUTE PRESS · WASHINGTON, D.C.

Copyright © 1988
THE URBAN INSTITUTE
2100 M Street, N.W.
Washington, DC 20037


Distributed by arrangement with
National Book Network, Inc.
4720 Boston Way
Lanham, MD 20706


**Library of Congress Cataloging-in-Publication Data**

Challenge to Leadership: Economic and Social Issues for the
Next Decade / Isabel V. Sawhill, editor.


    p.    cm.
    Bibliography: p. 325
    Includes index.
    ISBN 0–87766–411–0 (alk. paper).
    ISBN 0–87766–412–9 (pbk.; alk. paper).
    1. United States—Economic conditions—1981–
2. United States—Economic policy—1981–    3. Economic
forecasting—United States.    4. United States—Social conditions—
1980–    5. United States—Social policy—1980–    6. Social
prediction—United States. I.  Sawhill, Isabel V.
HC106.8.C465   1988
306'.0973—dc19                      88–1289
                                                CIP

THE URBAN INSTITUTE is a nonprofit policy research and educational organization established in Washington, D.C., in 1968. Its staff investigates the social and economic problems confronting the nation and government policies and programs designed to alleviate such problems. The Institute disseminates significant findings of its research through the publications program of its Press. The Institute has two goals for work in each of its research areas: to help shape thinking about societal problems and efforts to solve them, and to improve government decisions and performance by providing better information and analytic tools.

Through work that ranges from broad conceptual studies to administrative and technical assistance, Institute researchers contribute to the stock of knowledge available to public officials and to private individuals and groups concerned with formulating and implementing more efficient and effective government policy.

Conclusions or opinions expressed in Institute publications are those of the authors and do not necessarily reflect the views of other staff members, officers or trustees of the Institute, advisory groups, or any organizations that provide financial support to the Institute.

301782

THE CHANGING DOMESTIC PRIORITIES SERIES

Listed below are the titles available in the Changing Domestic Priorities Series

# CONTENTS

# TABLES

# FIGURES

# FOREWORD

Every president of the United States in the past sixty years has entered office with a substantial agenda of urgent issues confronting him. The president to take office in 1989 may not have the most challenging assignment of all the presidents since 1931, but he certainly will confront great demands on his leadership, courage, prescience, and, alas, luck. This book, by sketching some of the (mostly) domestic issues that will inevitably find a place of priority on the incoming president's agenda, is a modest attempt to help set the agenda and weigh the approaches toward meeting the challenges.

The challenges of the 1990s and thereafter to the United States are the result of broad social, demographic, and political trends within this country and many developments beyond its shores. Some of these problems are a direct legacy of economic and social policy actively promulgated by the Reagan administration and some are not. Although the researchers who have written this book are well qualified to determine which of them belong on the doorstep of the outgoing administration and which have been the luck of the draw, that task is not the one undertaken here. Rather, they have tackled the more difficult and more important job of looking forward and projecting the character and the magnitude of what appear to them to be the unavoidable domestic issues of the next decade.

This effort is part of an eight-year Urban Institute project called Changing Domestic Priorities, which, until now has been concerned with assessing the effects of the Reagan administration's social and economic programs and policies. The project has generated dozens of books and scores of research papers. It has attracted extensive coverage in the news media and, more important, has helped shape the views of opinion leaders and policymakers about what was happening in this country and why. Social scientists and historians of the future will use the materials generated and go beyond them. Although we believe that we have played an important role in shaping the insights that will finally emerge, we claim no more than that.

This book, of a different genre, draws on different skills—those of synthesis and foresight—and will have to be assessed by different yardsticks.

If the volume provides some insight into the most pressing issues on the nation's horizon and encourages constructive action, it will have met the aspirations of its authors and the institutions responsible for their support.

William Gorham

# ACKNOWLEDGMENTS

This book represents the collaborative efforts of numerous people in addition to the individual authors. I particularly want to thank Ann Guillot for typing many drafts and keeping track of everything under extraordinary pressure, Chris Clary for overseeing the production process, Susan Hendrickson for being a "renaissance woman" capable of researching any topic, and Susan Wiener for her excellent care and feeding of all the figures and tables. I am also grateful to Priscilla Taylor for superb professional editing, to Alan Abramson for contributing his time and his ideas to chapter 1, and to Hugh Heclo and Norman Dorsen as well as many colleagues at The Urban Institute for their comments on that chapter.

The substantive chapters of the book were improved as the result of discussion and comments by members of the Changing Domestic Priorities advisory board and other scholars at a conference in the fall of 1987. Finally, essential financial support was provided by the Ford Foundation, the John D. and Catherine T. MacArthur Foundation, and the Rockefeller Foundation.

Isabel V. Sawhill

# CHAPTER 1

# OVERVIEW

Isabel V. Sawhill

> The Presidency is . . . preeminently a place of moral leadership. All our
> great Presidents were leaders of thought at times when certain historic
> ideas in the life of the nation had to be clarified. . . . Without leadership
> alert and sensitive to change, we are all bogged up or lose our way.
> —Franklin D. Roosevelt

The United States now stands at an unmarked crossroad. Behind it lies
the Reagan era, before it a number of paths into the future. The year 1988
will be a time of choosing. The choosing will, as always, be a messy and
consuming process, dominated as much by discussions of personalities and
the latest polls as by any real attention to the issues. When the issues do get
discussed, it is likely to be in one-minute bursts. This book is a modest effort
toward expanding and informing that debate.

Unlike some books of this genre, this one stops short of being prescrip-
tive. There is no platform here that will satisfy one political party or one
candidate, although some promising ideas and options are evaluated. The
book's premise is that final choices should be made in the political arena but
that information and thoughtful discussion of the issues can help. (The authors'
points of view and judgments will, of course, come through; there is no such
thing as a completely neutral analysis of the issues.)

If there is any one message that binds these chapters together, it is the
need to proceed cautiously, and with moderation, in tackling the difficult
issues facing the country. The sense of the volume is that the country needs
to avoid the quick fix, the magic bullet, the ideological solution. Government

1

has a positive role to play, but restraint is needed both in setting policy and in raising public expectations about the likely results.

This first chapter provides some overall context for the volume. It begins with a brief assessment of the Reagan years and goes on to focus on what seem to me to be the four overarching issues facing the country in the decade ahead: the nature of the U.S. role in the world, the responsibility of each generation to the next, the obligations of the haves to the have-nots, and the limits to be placed on individual freedom. The chapter also discusses the constraints likely to confront the next president in dealing with these issues and the implications of both the issues and the constraints for the *kind* of leadership needed over the next few years. It ends with a more detailed preview of the other chapters in the volume.

## The Reagan Legacy

It has been argued that there are predictable cycles and trends in political as in economic affairs—periods in which the country moves forward in one direction or another and then reacts, or simply rests.[1] But in early 1988, it was hard to predict where the nation was headed.

After fifty years of growing government activism in the United States, the liberal tide ran out in the late 1970s (earlier, if Carter is viewed as a post-Watergate anomaly); with the election of Ronald Reagan in 1980, the country took a sharp turn to the Right. The subsequent eight years have been a time of innovation. But where has it left the country, substantively and politically?[2]

Substantively, a number of problems that President Reagan inherited from his predecessors have been at least partially resolved. Inflation has declined, the economy has experienced the longest peacetime expansion on record (although the average annual growth rate of 2.5 percent has been below that for the post-World War II period as a whole). U.S. military capability has been rebuilt, and this strength has been used in negotiating an arms reduction agreement. The tax system has been overhauled in ways that are likely to promote efficiency and to distribute the tax burden for low-income families more fairly. The values of hard work, family, and private initiative have been reaffirmed. Government is no smaller than it used to be, but neither has it continued to grow.

President Reagan has also bequeathed enormous problems to his successor. During his years in office, the country has gone from being the largest net creditor to the largest net debtor nation; in a few short years, the national debt will have nearly tripled, with liabilities to foreigners projected to total $1 trillion early in the next decade. Thus, whatever prosperity has been achieved has been built on a mountain of debt that will constrain future standards of living. Inequality has increased, and the poverty rate remains higher than it was during the 1970s, in part because of Reagan administration policies.[3] Some problems have not been adequately addressed because of a preoccupation with ideological disputes (witness the confusion and controversy surrounding the AIDS Commission and the lack of action accompanying the announced war on drugs).[4] Confidence in government, which initially increased under Reagan, has been undermined by the Iran-contra revelations and by the inability of Congress and the president to forge a significant compromise on the budget. Partisanship and divisiveness appear to have increased.

On the political front, there has been talk of a Republican realignment, but the data suggest a more complex reality.[5] Conservatives have mounted a partially successful attack on liberal principles but have not substituted a new set of principles with broad appeal. Moreover, the talk of realignment assumes that political labels still have meaning during an era when more than one-quarter of all voters have no strong party identification and are likely to choose their leaders on grounds other than party—such as perceived integrity, experience, and the ability to lead. Finally, as primaries have proliferated and the candidates have increasingly relied on the media to help them reach the public, the process of choosing a president has become more open and democratic, but also less structured and disciplined. Candidates are less likely to be winnowed out because they lack experience and judgment and are more likely to be nominated or elected because they perform well on television or are able to articulate a few "new" ideas that, at least temporarily, capture the public's imagination.

Leadership is more than this. Defining it is not easy, but a firmer notion of what we should be looking for in our leaders over the next decade is worth pursuing. People's choices obviously will vary, but those choices should be made with an understanding of the principal substantive issues facing the nation, the kind of contribution that government can realistically make to resolving various problems over the next decade, and the qualities of leadership most likely to be needed during this period.

## The Defining Issues

At the broadest level, the question is, *What kind of nation do we want to be?* In a democracy, and especially in one as pluralistic as the United States, the task of grappling with this question—of articulating and shaping our shared values—falls primarily to our political leaders. It is a critical task because without these values we cease to be a nation in any meaningful sense, and we risk losing moral, if not strategic, influence in the world.

However, the question of the kind of nation we want to be cannot be answered in the abstract. Here it is approached through a review and assessment of the four major issues raised by these chapters: the U.S. role in the world, the commitments of each generation to the next, the obligations of the haves to the have-nots, and the limits to be placed on individual freedom. These are what might be called "defining issues," because the answers in each case help to establish the kind of nation we will have as we enter the twenty-first century. The answers will inevitably be shaped by history, culture, and geography, but each generation must confront them anew, integrating understandings from the past with new developments that affect our national identity and goals. The challenge for the nation and its leadership is to forge a rough consensus on the answers.

## The U.S. Role in the World

The ability of the United States to extend its influence in the world depends not only on its sense of national purpose but also on its economic and military power. In the economic arena, national self-confidence has been severely eroded. A decade ago it was assumed that American living standards would automatically rise over time, and there was little concern about the nation's long-term economic prospects.[6] The global threat to U.S. economic hegemony was simmering on the back burner, ready to boil over, but few people were watching, much less attending to, the pot. Today, in contrast, the major economic concerns are what is happening to standards of living (chapter 2), what can be done to nurture faster economic growth (chapter 3), and how the nation should respond to international competition (chapter 4).

The reason for this new interest is clear: It would be profoundly disturbing to the national psyche if, through a process of slower economic growth, we were to lose our preeminent economic position in the world. A strong economy in the United States has traditionally provided our citizens with a standard of living second to none, as well as the wherewithal to extend the nation's influence around the globe. The United States initially became the dominant economic power late in the nineteenth century when U.S. productivity surpassed that of Britain, and U.S. dominance was strengthened in the first half of the twentieth century when the European and Japanese economies were devastated by two world wars.[7] Now, with U.S. standards of living growing less rapidly than in the past and less rapidly than in other countries (see chapters 2 and 4), the specter of relative economic decline has become a reality, and concern about our ability to compete an overriding national concern. However, considerable misunderstanding exists about both ends and means in this area.

With respect to ends, the goal of maintaining a U.S. standard of living second to none is in no way inconsistent with applauding faster growth in countries with lower per capita incomes. In fact, the faster the growth of less affluent countries, the better our export markets will be, the more rapidly current income disparities among rich and poor nations will disappear, and the more political stability will be enhanced. If developing nations are able to produce low-cost goods, access to those goods can only improve the standard of living of U.S. consumers. And the continued growth and prosperity of already affluent countries that have high per capita incomes but small shares of world production (Switzerland is an example) may produce feelings of envy but would hardly seem to be a threat to the United States. Indeed, a closing of the gap in living standards between different countries is almost inevitable and probably desirable. Why should the Smiths and Jones expect to be forever richer than the Schmidts and the Tanakas?

The concern seems to be that eventually Japan (or some other industrialized country) will displace us as the major economic power. This seems unlikely, given the size of our population and the tendency of growth rates to converge over time.[8] However, there is little question that other countries have been "catching up" to the United States and that the U.S. share of world production has declined sharply.[9] And were this situation to continue, it could profoundly alter not only relative standards of living but also the balance of military power and influence around the world.

Already some observers argue that our military commitments are out of balance with our economic resources. U.S. military commitments around the world are roughly what they were at the end of World War II, when the U.S. share of world production was far larger than it is today.[10] For this reason, as well as others, a clearer definition of the vital interests of the United States around the globe is badly needed (although it was not attempted in this volume). In the absence of such a definition, as emphasized in chapter 9, decisions on how much defense spending is enough will continue to rest on quicksand. Nor can the question be avoided by assuming there are large savings to be derived from eliminating waste or inefficiency in the defense establishment. As suggested in chapter 9, given our current foreign and strategic policies, it may be possible to save $10 billion by a more "efficient" deployment of current resources, but this amounts to a mere 3 percent of the $290 billion defense budget. Thus, if our current defense commitments are viewed as inimical to our long-term economic prospects—because the defense sector is absorbing capital, highly skilled workers, and other resources that a country like Japan can devote to making its economy more productive—a more fundamental reassessment of military commitments will be needed. In addition, the goal of achieving an agreement with the Soviet Union on the

most expensive part of the nation's military arsenal—conventional forces—
could take on added importance.

This conclusion about the implications of defense spending for the economy is reinforced to the extent that the public continues to be unwilling to
finance current expenditures via higher taxes (and thus lower consumption).
Indeed, although the military build-up that began in 1981 has clearly improved
the nation's defense posture and strengthened the U.S. hand at the bargaining
table, that build-up has also contributed to current deficits and thus diminished
the nation's long-term growth prospects and ability to compete in world
markets. There is little point in winning the arms race if one loses the economic
marathon. As Britain learned at the beginning of this century, a second-rate
economic power is not likely to maintain its superpower status. The perennial
hope is that our economy will be strong enough to produce large quantities
of both guns and butter, but this may turn out to be wishful thinking.

The declining economic hegemony of the United States has still another
implication for the future. Now that purchasing power in the rest of the world
is growing rapidly and markets are increasingly linked by trade and flows of
capital across national borders, the United States has far less control over its
own economic destiny. Although mistakes in domestic fiscal policy have been
correctly blamed for the trade imbalances of the early 1980s (see chapter 4),
such imbalances could recur for any number of reasons that have little to do
with U.S. policy per se. One solution is the creation of new mechanisms for
better aligning the economic policies of different countries.[11] Yet the needed
coordination of policies among the major industrial countries conflicts sharply
with notions of national sovereignty. Unless nations are willing to enter into
some more formal arrangement under which they relinquish some of their
prerogatives in the interest of a more balanced and more stable world economy,
the principal hope is that the United States will be sufficiently strong and
respected internationally to work out more informal cooperative arrangements
with other countries. Current budget deficits have put the United States in an
extremely weak position to carry out this role. But deficits aside, any future
president must recognize the importance of providing leadership in this area
and should be prepared to do so.[12]

## Commitments to the Next Generation

For most people, the foregoing discussion will simply reinforce the
urgency of putting the U.S. economy on a stronger growth path, thereby
assuring that U.S. economic and military power and influence are maintained. But for those who find such arguments unappealing because they
appear to pit the citizens of the world against one another in a mindless

race to see who can be the richest and most powerful, there is another reason to favor growth. It is a way of bequeathing a better life to our children.

In recent years, the United States has been consuming more than it has been producing, borrowing the difference from other countries (chapter 4). Future generations will be required to set aside some of their income to service that debt. In addition, if current projections are correct, they will need to earmark a larger proportion of their income to pay for the health care and retirement of the elderly as the baby boom generation retires (chapter 6). This potential fiscal burden necessitates a fundamental reassessment of health care and retirement policies for the aged—a reassessment that must begin now so that current policies can be adjusted gradually, if need be, and future retirees can plan accordingly. At the same time, if these two commitments are not to prove unduly burdensome, the nation needs to devote a larger share of its income to savings and investment so that the next generation will be able to pay for these commitments.

What is at stake is the implicit social contract between generations, in which each generation bequeaths a higher income to its children, in return for which it expects to be supported in its old age.[13] And just as individuals who fail to save and invest for their old age may end up destitute, so an entire generation that fails to save and invest may put its own retirement income in jeopardy should its profligacy make its children poorer than they otherwise would have been and thus unwilling to finance the existing Social Security system. Conversely, with a healthy rate of economic growth and higher incomes, the requisite payroll taxes need not loom so large.

The most direct way to increase the rate of economic growth is to reduce the budget deficit, thereby freeing up savings for productive investment and augmenting the productive capacity of the economy. Other less direct steps that could be taken to increase national saving and investment—such as tax subsidies for expenditures on plant and equipment—are described in chapter 3. However, these indirect steps are likely to have small effects, and any new growth-enhancing expenditures or tax subsidies that worsened the deficit would be counterproductive.

Concern for the next generation extends well beyond a focus on the kind of productive capacity—plant, equipment, and technology—that this group is likely to inherit. It includes providing them with adequate care and education while they are young. And it entails sacrificing some current output in order to protect the environment. These, too, are investments in the future that can be part of the intergenerational compact.

In the case of education, most of the attention is now focused on improving the quality of secondary schooling at the local level—an effort in which the states have taken the lead.[14] There is also interest in compensatory or preschool education for disadvantaged children (chapter 7) and in special training programs for workers displaced from their regular jobs by trade or technology (chapter 4), both of which have been moderately successful. Much more controversial is publicly funded day care as discussed in chapter 5. However, if women are in the labor force to stay, as that chapter argues, probably no area is more ripe to become a new middle-class entitlement than child care (including universal preschool and after-school programs). If financed by an earmarked tax, it might help to correct the current tilt toward programs for the elderly and win support as an investment in America's future—that is, its children. Rethinking the current length of the school day and the length of the school year—which make little sense for employed parents and deprive our children of the opportunity to learn as much as their counterparts in some other countries—effectively joins the two issues.

But a new middle-class entitlement may not be enacted, chiefly because the entitlements that already exist are proving to be extremely expensive. Indeed, concerns about "intergenerational equity" and the growing fiscal burden associated with a graying America have already produced proposals to "means-test" existing social insurance programs, including Social Security. As a group, the elderly are now as well off as the rest of the population—and better off than families with children—a situation that suggests to some analysts that a reallocation of resources between these two groups might be appropriate.[15] To the extent that this reallocation implied a shift from consumption (by the elderly) to investment (in the care and education of children), it would be consistent with a progrowth policy and a greater commitment to the next generation.[16] However, this argument aside, it hardly seems consistent to argue for means-testing of programs for the elderly and not of programs for children, especially when growth depends so much on getting deficits under control.

Forging a new consensus on how much to invest in the future will determine what goal to set for deficit reduction, the best way to reduce the deficit (the types of outlay reductions and revenue increases that are least inimical to growth), the amount of attention to be paid to environmental issues, and the amount to spend on programs for children. Resolving this issue will sorely test our leadership, because politics is all about what one can do for people in the short run; in contrast, making commitments to the next generation often means asking people to pay the piper now. As a result, democracies are poorly equipped to invest in the future, even though their survival may depend on their doing so.

## The Two-Tiered Society

Not all the concern about children in recent years has stemmed from the fact that they represent an investment in the future. More than one out of every five children is poor. In addition, although poverty has declined among the elderly, certain subgroups, such as elderly women living alone, continue to have meager financial resources. These statistics are only some of the many that could be cited as evidence that the United States has a two-tiered society. Moreover, the tiers appear to be drifting apart. The distribution of income and earnings is more unequal than it was twenty or thirty years ago (chapter 2), the incidence of poverty is higher than at any time in the 1970s, and there is evidence of a growing underclass in urban areas (chapter 7). Finally, a more open trading system that puts American workers in competition with low-wage labor from abroad and forces the United States to specialize in knowledge-intensive goods and services may produce still more inequality (chapter 4).

What is particularly disturbing, as discussed in chapter 7, is evidence that there may be less social mobility in the United States than is commonly assumed. The problem involves not simply people who fall temporarily on hard times but also people who are born, and remain, in poverty for all or most of their lives, passing similar disadvantages on to their children. It appears that the classless society is not so classless after all. And the fact that such a large proportion of people at the bottom are black or Hispanic adds a racial dimension to the problem.

How will the nation respond? On the one hand, it is argued that allowing such divisions to persist or grow is unacceptable in a country where compassion and opportunity have become watchwords even in conservative circles, and racial integration is a widely shared goal. On the other hand, it is argued, people at the bottom must bear some responsibility for their own fate, past programs for the poor have had limited success, and too much redistribution of income through taxes and transfers can create disincentives that are debilitating to poor and nonpoor alike. Chapter 7 combines these two perspectives by arguing for a tough-minded compassion that emphasizes the responsibility of the poor to obtain an education, to work, and to support their children but does not abandon people who remain poor despite such efforts. Still a third perspective goes beyond a focus on compassion and individual responsibility to emphasize the consequences of a two-tiered society for the nation as a whole. If there is a growing underclass in America, as the data in chapter 7 suggest, this growth will impose significant social costs on the rest of the nation in the form of more street crime, higher welfare expenditures, and a growing number of young people who are ill-equipped to make productive contributions to the economy of the future. The case can be made—and has been—that certain programs, such as those that move welfare mothers into jobs or provide compensatory education to disadvantaged pre-schoolers, ultimately save money for the taxpayers or produce other public benefits. Compassion aside, the national self-interest alone would seem to dictate that such investments be made.

By merging these three perspectives or criteria—compassion, individual responsibility, and the broader national interest—it may be possible to work toward a new consensus on the obligations of the haves to the have-nots.

## Limits on Individual Freedom

Individual liberty is much prized in the United States. Billions of dollars are spent each year to defend our way of life against possible incursions from totalitarian regimes. At the same time, some limits on individual freedom are tolerated, whether it be in the form of laws against crime, the regulation of traffic, airport security checks, passports, or the imposition of taxes. Most people recognize that some limits on their personal freedom ultimately benefit them, provided that everyone else agrees to abide by the same rules. The normal mechanism for achieving such mutually beneficial agreements is government itself.

Historically, as societies have become larger, more interdependent, more technologically sophisticated, and more pluralistic, the rule of law has increasingly been substituted for less formal means of social control, leading to greater limits on individual freedom. However, Americans quite properly view such intrusions with suspicion and are concerned about new developments that threaten to expand government's reach into people's personal lives. A recent case in point is the revolution in medical technology that has transformed what used to be natural, biologically driven events into matters of human choice. Although most of the attention and controversy has centered on abortion or the "right to life," the major issue for the next several decades may be the "right to die"—that is, the right of people who are hopelessly or desperately ill or incapacitated to forgo life-sustaining treatment or even to receive medical assistance in terminating their own lives. Currently, Americans have only limited and poorly defined rights in this area as described in chapter 8, yet polls show that the public is overwhelmingly in favor of a loosening of legal restrictions on the rights of a person to choose death over life.

Meanwhile, as technology has been expanding choices, ironically and tragically, the emergence of acquired immune deficiency syndrome (AIDS) has reminded us of technology's limits, and brought with it numerous proposals to curb individual rights in the interest of containing the spread of the disease.

The debates over AIDS and the right to die (treated in chapter 8) are only two of the many that are likely to take place over the coming decade as the nation grapples with the issue of individual liberty versus the public interest. Other areas in which the issue must be confronted are abortion, school prayer, crime, substance abuse, pornography, homosexuality, surrogate motherhood, and smoking in public places to mention just a few. The importance of the issue has been heightened not only by the introduction of new technologies but also as the result of increased concern about such problems as violent crime, drug abuse, and teenage sex, which to many people symbolize social permissiveness run amok. The antidote, according to the New Right, is tougher laws and more conservative judicial appointments. Given this climate of opinion and the Reagan administration's attempt to reshape the federal judiciary in ways that would make it more sympathetic to the New Right's concerns, civil libertarians are understandably nervous.

Currently, there are two principal contending views on individual liberty versus the public interest. One school of thought includes in its definition of the public interest a society's conception of proper or virtuous behavior, and under such a definition it becomes appropriate to legislate on the basis of moral or religious principle. As an example, chapter 8 cites a California case in which a judge ruled that a quadriplegic woman should be force-fed against her wishes because, in the judge's words, ''our society values life.'' Another example is antisodomy laws. A Georgia statute, used to bring charges against a male homosexual for acts committed with a consenting male partner in his own home, was held constitutional by the Supreme Court in 1986. Community moral standards matter, in this view, and can be used to impose the majority's views on people who disagree with them.

A second school of thought holds that infringements of freedom can be justified only if they lead to clear and compelling social benefits rather than simply reinforcing the moral values of the majority. For example, the courts have long recognized society's interest in controlling the spread of communicable disease and have accepted curbs on individual liberties for this purpose. With the emergence of AIDS, this body of law and the issues it raises are now being revisited.[17]

By and large, the American tradition has been to tilt toward the second view—that is, to reject public definitions of morality but to regulate behaviors that produce demonstrable harm for the body politic.[18] It is permissible to read pornographic literature but not to sexually molest another person. It is all right to drink in one's own living room but not on the road. This kind of moral relativism, with its emphasis on social consequences, contrasts sharply with the New Right's belief in moral absolutism and the legislation of morality for its own sake. Of course, social conservatives will argue that a permissive legal system *does* have social consequences, and they have a point: the definition and measurement of social harm have always been vexing. Others see these conservative arguments as thinly cloaked and empirically weak rationales for what is better understood as a deep-seated attachment to certain values. Prayer in the schools is unlikely to produce a better disciplined or more virtuous generation of children. Where the battle is mostly symbol and hard-to-prove substance, the American tradition has, with some notable exceptions, been one of tolerance of other people's values and life-styles.[19]

This tradition suggests that limits on individual freedom are more likely to be accepted in the case of AIDS than in the case of death and dying, because the former threatens the public health whereas the latter is a much more personal matter.[20] Furthermore, moralistic legal principles may actually impede efforts to halt the spread of AIDS—by preventing the sale or distribution of clean needles to intravenous drug users, the teaching of "safer" sex in the schools, and the public certification of virus-free prostitutes.

To be sure, the guidance provided by a rejection of legal moralism and the adoption of a "social harm" criterion do not tell us *what* infringements of personal liberty are warranted in the case of AIDS.

As in many other cases, the appropriate degree of intervention is likely to hinge on the perceived effectiveness of various measures in reducing social harm (that is, curbing the disease) relative to the limits they place on individual freedom. Small infringements of freedom that produce major social benefits may be viewed as appropriate by all but the most extreme civil libertarians. Conversely, major infringements of freedom that produce few social benefits are likely to be viewed as inappropriate by all but the most socially conservative members of the population (who may even view such infringements as just recompense for amoral behavior).

A related point is that the dilemma of individual liberties versus the public interest is less of a dilemma when people voluntarily abide by certain rules—because custom, or their own moral values or sense of responsibility, pushes them in that direction. In such cases, government regulation can be avoided or at least minimized. Most people would not commit a violent crime even if it were not illegal to do so. In the case of AIDS, many observers hope that drastic measures can be avoided by encouraging at-risk populations to undergo voluntary testing and, if infected, to refrain voluntarily from sex (or unsafe sex) with uninfected persons. More generally, one way to achieve the desired benefits of government regulation while simultaneously preserving freedom is to inculcate a sense of civic duty or moral responsibility among the citizenry. The framers of the Constitution tended to believe that this was a prerequisite of self-government. And one interpretation of the public's responsiveness to President Reagan's celebration of traditional values is that the American people wanted the importance of these values reaffirmed even when they did not favor government regulation as the means of doing so.

The coming years are likely to raise this set of issues in new and unpredictable areas. The way in which such debates are resolved in courts, legislatures, and in the public's mind will help to define us as a nation. Although it would be somewhat surprising—given our history—if the public were to accept a further curbing of individual rights on grounds other than thoroughly pragmatic ones, it is also conceivable that the next decade could bring a substantial compromising of those rights in favor of a much more inclusive definition of the public interest.

## The Constraints

If one theme of this book is that there are new issues on the public agenda, a second theme is that the nation's ability to deal with these issues is more circumscribed than previously. The public likes to think that someone is in charge of their destiny—that the nation's leadership, and especially the president, can solve various problems. But the fact is that even the best of presidents operates under enormous constraints and may find that the ship of state cannot be guided from the White House deck. Indeed, in recent times many political scientists have concluded that presidential governance is, to a large extent, "an illusion."[21] President Reagan has been credited with having restored some of the power of the presidency, especially during his first term, and his example may provide encouragement to whoever follows in his footsteps. However, there are a number of reasons for thinking that the economic, fiscal, political, and technical constraints facing the next president are going to be especially severe.

### Economic Constraints

If history is any guide, a recession during the next four years is almost inevitable. With discretionary fiscal policy hobbled by large deficits and the automatic operation of various safety nets (such as unemployment insurance) curtailed by recent policy changes, the full burden of combating a recession would fall on the Federal Reserve. The Fed, however, is likely to be torn between keeping interest rates low to combat recession and keeping them high to prevent both a further decline in the value of the dollar and the higher rate of inflation that would ensue if imports were to become more expensive.

Although it would be too strong to say that we have lost control of the management of the domestic economy, our maneuvering room is seriously circumscribed. The fact that the Fed is independent of the White House, at least in theory, could make life even more frustrating for a new president. And the perception of these weaknesses by business leaders and international markets could produce an erosion of confidence that would worsen or prolong any downturn.

## Fiscal Constraints

Budget deficits have all but ruled out new spending initiatives or tax subsidies to accomplish various public purposes. Indeed, at least part of the next decade will have to be spent getting the nation's fiscal house in order, leading to a search for existing commitments that can be curtailed or new sources of revenues. In this context, chapter 9 does not flinch from putting a number of painful options on the table, although its conclusions are extremely pessimistic. Changes in spending and taxes of the sort that might conceivably be within the bounds of current political feasibility (no matter who occupies the White House) will simply not do the job. A new national consensus to do the currently unthinkable (such as raising income taxes or cutting Social Security) will have to be forged.

As serious as the deficits are, they will not remove public pressures on government to respond to various problems—leading inevitably to a search for alternative means of accomplishing national purposes. These alternatives are likely to include greater regulation, earmarked taxes and fees for particular purposes, and more emphasis on state and local initiatives and on the social responsibilities of business and private citizens (perhaps encouraged from Washington). Some of this diversification of the tools of government could prove healthy. For example, as the federal government has played a diminished role in recent years, state governments have played an unusually active and creative one in areas such as improving education, reforming welfare, and rebuilding public infrastructure.[22] In other respects, however, this search for alternatives could prove counterproductive. Competition among the states to see who can attract the most business through various subsidies could become a negative-sum game. And new regulations to accomplish social objectives (for example, mandating employers to provide health insurance) could undermine the competitiveness of American business firms and reduce employment opportunities or wages for affected workers.

## Political Constraints

Unlike a popular incumbent (Eisenhower in 1956, Reagan in 1984) or a candidate elected by a landslide (Johnson in 1964, Reagan in 1984), the next president may have little in the way of political capital to expend during his first years in office, and, given the fiscal problems just alluded to, may have difficulty accumulating it once in power. (Indeed, his popularity could deteriorate rapidly.) This problem will be compounded if the leading candidates continue to be vague about how they would handle deficits and other problems once elected, thereby depriving themselves of a mandate to govern.

In addition to the special handicaps likely to afflict the next president, other more long-standing obstacles are likely to affect the ability to govern.[23] In the first place, the fragmentation of power in the political system makes it difficult for presidents to build reliable and continuing support for their programs. Some of the fragmentation dates back to the creation of the Republic, when the Founding Fathers prescribed in the Constitution a system in which the power to take action was divided among separate institutions. Today, fragmentation also shows up in the proliferation of interest groups, the weakening of political parties, and the dispersion of power in Congress.

Besides fragmentation, presidents also confront a political environment that seems to have grown increasingly resistant to their lead. The assertiveness of Congress vis-à-vis the president is evident in statutory limits that have been placed on the president's ability to act unilaterally in the case of war-making and the impoundment of funds; in the use of all-encompassing, omnibus appropriations bills which, by effectively limiting use of the veto, further blunt the president's discretionary powers; and in congressional "micro-management" of relatively minor departmental activities. In addition, the electorate seems now in the habit of choosing a president and Congress from different parties, which adds partisan disagreements to the other sources of interbranch conflicts.

Depending on one's perspective, such checks and balances and other restraints on the presidency can be viewed either as protections from policy adventurism and abuses of presidential power or as the ultimate constraint on the nation's ability to react effectively to crises and adapt to long-term changes in economic and social conditions. Many observers now argue that structural reforms in the nation's political and governmental institutions are needed to reduce fragmentation and to strengthen the president's hand.[24]

## Technical Constraints

Government programs, once thought to be the solution to many economic and social problems, are increasingly viewed as ineffective or counterproductive. Part of the reason is that the Reagan administration's antigovernment campaign has discredited many earlier efforts, including many that were worthwhile. But this view also reflects the reality that government is not always the solution to people's problems and, in some cases, may actually do more harm than good. Earlier periods of activism are generally conceded to have raised expectations by promising to do too much, leaving in their wake greater skepticism about the efficacy of government as an instrument of national purpose. As the chapters in this book attest, there are no certain solutions to problems such as slow economic growth, the emergence of an underclass, or prevention of the spread of AIDS. Some experimentation and risk taking may be in order, and the accumulation of wisdom and experience from past efforts should ensure a higher success rate in the future than in the past. Still, it would be unwise to assume that government's ability to solve problems is only a matter of money and political will. Programmatic and organizational know-how are also critical ingredients.

## The Nature of the Challenge

By now the challenge posed in these pages should be clear. At stake is the nation's ability to retain its position of leadership in the world, to bequeath a better life to its children, to achieve a measure of social justice, and to meet new exigencies without unduly abridging individual freedoms. Meeting the challenge would be difficult in the best of circumstances, but it is made all the more excruciating by the numerous constraints likely to impinge on the next president's ability to act. No wonder a number of potential candidates have remained on the sidelines. Governing America would seem to be a no-win proposition.

But this view is too pessimistic. First, in any era, the performance of a nation is likely to come up short relative to its expectations. Indeed, one of democracy's most important attributes is its capacity for self-criticism. In an absolute sense, the United States remains a strong country, whether measured by its productive capacity, the education and enterprise of its people, its natural resources, or the resilience of its social and political institutions. The nation can take pride in its past accomplishments and be optimistic about its future opportunities.

Second, the challenges discussed in this book are long-term, whereas the constraints are, to some extent, short-term. Any recession over the next few years will inevitably give way to renewed prosperity. Deficits *can* be reduced, though it will be painful to do so. New ideas about how to tackle various economic and social problems are not in short supply; and continuing experimentation and creativity at the local level can only enhance our ability to mount more effective programs at the national level in the future. Political constraints, to be sure, are more enduring, and reform of political and governmental institutions may need to be put on the next president's agenda, although any changes that are adopted should, of course, be independent of who happens to be in power.

Finally, it is possible to make a virtue of necessity. The constraints outlined here will give us time to think about what kind of nation and government we really want and who is to pay for it, before rushing off in some new direction. The tortoise, working his way toward a national consensus on the issues discussed in this book, may be more sure-footed than the hare, even though his pace is labored and his journey too dull to please a crowd.

In making this journey, only a president can keep us on course. Members of Congress, other elected officials, and nongovernmental leaders have an important role to play but do not command the public attention or speak as unambiguously for the interest of the nation as a whole as does a president. At the same time, to be effective, presidents must work with and through these other leaders, producing in the process sustained and widespread attention to the issues facing the nation.

Leadership here does not mean possessing the laundry list of ''Boy Scout'' traits or personal qualities that people often look for in a president— integrity, experience, competence, intelligence, political skills—although these are, of course, important. Nor does it mean spending money on popular programs, promoting short-term prosperity or coming up with ''new ideas'' (whose major merit is simply that they are new). These kinds of leadership are often necessary and certainly useful for getting elected or reelected, but they are not capable of producing broad or cumulative change. That can only come from dealing with the kinds of strategic concerns—that is, the defining issues or long-term institutional problems—identified in this book.

One common characteristic of these strategic issues is that they all represent relatively long-term challenges rather than short-term crises that require immediate resolution. A second characteristic is that the solutions, in the minds of many, will require that the nation increase its commitment to what are generally thought of as politically ''weak'' claimants: the rest of the world, the next generation, the disadvantaged, and the ''public interest'' (as opposed to strong, organized special interests). Unfortunately, these two essential characteristics of the issues facing the next president can only make the job of leadership more difficult, because the press of crisis and the support of strong interests are often two of the keys to successful action.

What is called for, in this context, is what James MacGregor Burns has called ''transforming leadership,'' or the ability to motivate people to subordinate shorter-term or more specialized interests to the achievement of longer-term or higher-order goals.[25] In this sense, leadership means a president who has the wisdom to recognize and devise responses to slowly evolving problems that are not forced onto the agenda in the clarity of a crisis. It also means a president capable of restructuring the public discourse in ways that convince the public—including those who have narrow interests and those who have entirely lost interest in the political process—of the necessity and value of pursuing common goals.

Perhaps this is the wrong time in our history to expect such leadership, given the fact that the country has just been through a period of considerable innovation and may want a respite. Perhaps there is no candidate with the requisite temperament to step up to the challenge. And perhaps it is too much to ask of any one person, given the constraints mentioned earlier and the inevitable short-run crises that can beset any administration. But with these provisos, the challenge to leadership remains: without a new consensus on the issues that define us as a nation there can be no firm or sustained basis for future action, only muddle and drift.

## Summary of the Other Chapters

The issues facing the nation cannot be defined in an historical vacuum. A nation's values and the issues it considers most pertinent are bound to evolve through its history. Nor can their resolution be divorced from a working through of specific policy debates in various areas. The chapters in the remainder of this book provide the kind of historical and policy-specific context needed to begin the process of mapping an agenda for the future. The first three (chapters 2, 3, and 4) cover economic issues. The next three (chapters 5, 6, and 7) cover social issues. Chapter 8 treats the issue of individual rights versus the public interest, and chapter 9 discusses fiscal constraints and options for reducing the federal deficit.

### Family Incomes

In chapter 2, Joseph Minarik finds that standards of living in the United States are improving more slowly than in the past. In inflation-adjusted terms, the income of the typical family increased from $15,492 in 1954 to $29,458 in 1986, a near doubling in little more than a generation. However, the growth of family incomes, after averaging 3.1 percent per year between 1954 and 1973, slowed to only 0.5 percent per year between 1973 and 1986. Probing beneath these averages to see how different types of families have fared, Minarik finds that the incomes of two-earner couples have increased faster than the incomes of one-earner couples or single parents. In general, however, the slower growth of incomes after 1973 affected virtually all groups.

After examining family incomes, Minarik considers whether other, more complete measures of living standards tell a different story. For example, per capita income has grown more rapidly than family income (because people are having fewer children), fringe benefits more rapidly than cash compensation (for a variety of reasons including their more favored tax status), and consumption more rapidly than income (because people are borrowing more). For all these reasons, it could be argued that standards of living have been rising faster than indicated by conventional measures of family income. But offsetting these trends have been the growing burdens of taxes (especially payroll taxes) and of home carrying costs. These have made pretax incomes an increasingly inadequate indicator of take-home pay or discretionary spending. In addition, some of the changes that have kept per capita consumption rising (smaller families, more borrowing, more workers per family) have inherent limits. On balance, Minarik concludes that the slowdown of family income growth must be taken seriously as an indicator that standards of living are improving less rapidly than they once did.

Minarik then turns his attention to trends in the distribution of family incomes, noting that the latest figures show more inequality than at any time in the post-World War II period. Since the late 1960s, low-income families have experienced virtually no real income growth, whereas the richest 5 percent of all families experienced an increase of more than 31 percent. A common explanation for the growing inequality in family incomes is demography—in particular, the increase of one-parent families (presumed to be concentrated at the bottom of the income distribution) and two-earner families (presumed to be concentrated at the top). Minarik's research suggests that these demographic trends played little or no role, leaving growing inequality as a mystery yet to be explained.

Because income from work is by far the most important component of family incomes, Minarik also examines what has been happening to the level and distribution of individual earnings. He finds that, as was true of family incomes, slower growth and greater inequality are the predominant trends after 1970. He notes that both trends were particularly pronounced for male workers. One explanation is the large influx of inexperienced young workers into the labor force in the 1970s. Another suspect, the alleged deindustrialization of the economy, is examined and found not guilty. In fact, the pattern of industrial change over the past several decades has tended to increase male earnings and has worked to reduce overall inequality slightly.

Thus, whether family incomes or individual earnings are considered, the pattern is one of slower growth and rising inequality with, apart from the inexperience of the baby boom, no clear explanations. Inasmuch as the baby boom is now maturing, Minarik cautions against strong policy actions, especially those that aim to subsidize or protect particular sectors of the economy (e.g., manufacturing) because of their alleged importance to the level or distribution of earnings. He observes that the tax and transfer system can be used to modify the distribution of earnings if that is desired; however, it falls to Rudolph Penner in chapter 3 to take up the challenge of what, if anything, can be done about the underlying problem of slow growth that has constrained improvements in average standards of living since the early 1970s, and to Isabel Sawhill in chapter 7 to examine policies that might help those families who have been bypassed by whatever growth there has been.

## Economic Growth

The ultimate determinant of people's standard of living over the long run is their productivity. The slowdown in productivity growth in the United States after 1973 may or may not be significant in the longer sweep of history, but its immediate impact on people's standards of living impels a more searching analysis of possible causes and cures.

In chapter 3, Penner examines ten factors (the experience of the labor force, amount of investment per worker, spending on research and development, etc.) that may have been responsible for the slowdown. Studies of their relative importance do not point to any one factor as the principal culprit, and they fail to explain much of the slowdown, leaving policymakers with little guidance. Still, as Penner notes, the list of policies that might be pursued and the direction of their effects is generally known, even though there may be disagreements about the magnitude of these effects or their costs in terms of conflicts with other objectives.

Penner's menu of growth-enhancing policies includes maintaining a stable or predictable legal and institutional environment, encouraging technological change, raising the quantity and quality of labor and capital supplied to the economy, and smoothing out extreme swings in economic activity. Within this framework, Penner discusses the likely effectiveness of subsidies for research and development and public outlays for education and training. He also examines government attempts to affect capital formation through monetary policy, changes in tax law, and changes in Social Security benefits (believed by some economists to reduce private savings). However, he reserves his major attention for the impact of the federal budget deficit on future standards of living.

Assuming the reduction of the deficit by increments of $36 billion a year over the next five years (as implied by the original Gramm-Rudman-Hollings targets), he calculates that, by 1992, per capita incomes would be $115 to $285 higher, depending on the assumptions used. (Higher incomes are produced by reduced interest payments to foreigners on the national debt and by the extra earnings associated with a reallocation of national savings away from financing deficits and toward productive investment.) Over the longer run (say, a generation), the effects would be much larger. Also, viewing deficits only through the lens of economic growth misses their consequences for international flows of capital and trade and their potentially destabilizing effects on the economy over the shorter run. But achieving any of the gains from deficit reduction requires some belt-tightening (higher taxes, lower government benefits) over the coming years, and is likely to be resisted for this reason.

In the end, Penner observes that most government policies that involve a change of a few billion dollars in spending or tax concessions for the purpose of stimulating greater growth cannot be expected to have a dramatic effect on a $5 trillion economy. Moreover, nurturing economic growth may require sacrificing other objectives such as current consumption or a more equal distribution of income. Still, he argues that growth is important, not only for domestic standards of living but also for national security and the United States' economic standing in the world. So even when the benefits associated with certain progrowth policies are unclear, some risk taking may be warranted. And antigrowth policies, such as running large budget deficits in times of general prosperity, should clearly be avoided.

## International Trade

To finance the large federal budget deficits of recent years, the United States has had to borrow substantially from foreigners. The resulting foreign purchases of U.S. stocks, bonds, and other IOUs, by creating more demand for American dollars, pushed up the value of the dollar temporarily, making imports cheap and exports expensive. In chapter 4, Charles Stone argues that it was these macroeconomic events that were largely responsible for the deterioration of the U.S. trade balance in the 1980s. Contrary to much popular opinion, this deterioration is not necessarily an indication that the United States is becoming less "competitive" *over the longer run* or trade more "unfair." The trade policies of other countries, whether fair or not, have not changed much since the 1970s.

Although the trade deficits of the 1980s do not by themselves indicate a loss of fundamental competitiveness—meaning an ability to sell our goods at the level of exchange rates that prevailed before the current macroeconomic dislocation—even if the United States were to put its macroeconomic house in order, exchange rates might not stabilize around their 1980 level. Some analysts believe that poor productivity growth in the United States in the 1970s required a gradual deterioration in the international purchasing power of the dollar in order to keep trade roughly balanced during the 1970s, and that maintaining balance in the 1980s would have required a continuing deterioration in the real value of the dollar. If true, the dollar must fall well below its 1980 level before trade will be balanced, and it will have to continue to fall to keep trade balanced. Such a decline in the value of U.S. goods on world markets—by making what we import more expensive relative to what we export— would retard the growth of U.S. standards of living.

To prevent such retardation, productivity must grow at least as fast in the United States as in the rest of the world. On closer inspection, then, concerns about competitiveness boil down to concerns about economic growth, the topic addressed in chapter 3. Chapter 4 extends this earlier discussion by analyzing the role of international trade in promoting economic growth and concludes that economists' arguments that trade promotes growth remain valid in today's world economy. The latest economic research suggests that even if another country engages in unfair trade practices or provides subsidies to key industries—and even if we move away from an ivory-tower textbook world and take into account the existence of noncompetitive behavior, market dominance, and continuous technological change—the case for free trade remains strong.

This general conclusion does not mean that trade is good for everyone in the United States. Inevitably there will be gainers and losers, a topic to which Stone gives considerable attention. He notes the devastating effect of the macro shocks of the 1980s, which caused the manufacturing sector to lose about 1.6 million jobs between 1979 and 1984, jobs that paid $3,800 above the average for the economy as a whole and were replaced mainly by service sector jobs that paid $1,500 below the average.

The short-term adjustment costs imposed by shifts in trade patterns and other types of economic change have given rise to various programs to ease the pain for affected workers and firms. Stone reviews past programs and the various arguments, pro and con, for different approaches, expressing a clear preference for policies that ease the costs to workers without retarding the adjustment process itself.

Over the longer run, Stone agrees with Minarik that deindustrialization will not eliminate middle-class jobs because (union wage premiums and other market imperfections aside) wages depend not on where a person works but on the individual worker's education and ability. However, Stone predicts that trade will force the United States to specialize in products that take advantage of its technological sophistication and highly educated labor force, and that this specialization will increase the demand for skilled relative to unskilled workers. This tilt could produce socially divisive disparities in income unless education is used to upgrade the skills of people at the bottom and taxes and transfers are used to compensate for any remaining inequities.

## The Family

It is not just the economy that has been subject to wrenching change. The American family also has undergone a dramatic transformation since the 1950s. As a result of the wholesale entrance of women into the work force and rising divorce rates, the "traditional" family, consisting of a breadwinning husband and a stay-at-home wife who remain married for a lifetime, is no longer the norm. The typical family is now a married couple in which both husband and wife work, and in which the permanence of the marriage is far less certain. In chapter 5, Andrew Cherlin argues that these changes are likely to prove irreversible.

Much current concern about this transformation appropriately focuses on children. They are not party to the decisions that have caused these changes in life-style, but they may be paying the costs. Have children, in fact, been harmed by these changes in the family?

It is clear that the breakup of a marriage often causes both financial and emotional problems for children, especially in the short run. And having an employed mother also can be harmful if adequate substitute care is not provided. But with these important caveats, the evidence linking changes in the family and the rise of various social problems among children and adolescents is weak. Even the timing of various trends does not support the idea that more divorce or more employed mothers are what produced more delinquency, drug use, premarital sex, suicide, and low test scores in the 1960s and 1970s. The upward trends in most of these indicators have leveled off or reversed since the late 1970s, even though the number of employed mothers has continued to grow.

These same changes in the family have altered the lives of adults as well as children. In general, women have more income, more independence, and more self-esteem. Few, however, are receiving more help at home, with the result that employed women tend to be overburdened with child care and other household tasks and have far less time for leisure activities than their nonemployed counterparts.

Men's lives have also been transformed. According to several studies, 1950s-style marriages were good for men: they lived longer, had fewer illnesses, and enjoyed a greater sense of well-being than unmarried men. (This was less true for women.) Whether marriage continues to provide these same benefits for men in the 1980s is not clear. The easing of the burden of being the sole breadwinner may have been more than offset by the loss of services and support from employed wives. In any case, both men and women are now freer to choose a series of long-term relationships rather than one lifetime marriage, and many are doing so.

In part because people hold very different views about what should and can be done, public policy is only just beginning to catch up with these changes in such areas as the adequacy of child support after a divorce and the availability of child care for employed mothers.

One view is that policy should strongly encourage a return to the "traditional" family through, for example, much larger tax exemptions for all families with children. However, the evidence suggests that bigger tax exemptions, in addition to being very expensive, would have little effect on people's willingness to have children (or on women's willingness to stay home to care for them). Another view is that policy should ease the burdens on employed parents and their children by providing, for example, more subsidized day care. Doing this would also be expensive and might lead to an indirect transfer of income from one-earner to two-earner families, despite the fact that the latter are generally better off. However, additional supports for low-income employed parents, or at least improved targeting of existing support on this group, might be justified. And some institutional arrangements (such as the hours when schools are normally open) seem out of step with the realities of family life in the 1980s and could probably be changed at more modest cost.

## Health Care and Retirement for an Aging Population

As John Palmer notes in chapter 6, public responsibility for many of the needs of the elderly population is now more or less taken for granted in the United States. However, if current policies are continued, health care and retirement programs for the elderly population will consume an ever-increasing share of national income and government revenues over the coming decades. Social Security and Medicare expenditures, which were only 2.4 percent of gross national product (GNP) in 1965, had risen to 6.4 percent by 1985, and, even under relatively optimistic projections, will rise to 11.0 percent when the baby boom has fully retired forty years from now if current policies are continued. Were these programs to be expanded to meet the growing needs of this population for nursing home or other long-term care (not now covered except for the very poor) and catastrophic health insurance, the impending fiscal burden would be still greater. For example, the nursing home population is likely to double over the next thirty years, in part because people who would have died at younger ages in an earlier era now survive to more advanced ages, at which point they tend to need continuing care. In short, if the current commitment to financial support for the aged is maintained, and especially if it is expanded in line with the needs of the very old for care, the working-age population will be faced with rising tax burdens to pay for this support. (Indeed, as indicated in chapter 9, the major factor pushing up federal tax burdens over the past several decades has been the growth of payroll taxes needed to finance this commitment.)

How is the fiscal challenge posed by current demographic trends to be met? One view is that the burden is not, after all, very onerous. Asking the next generation of working-age people to earmark an extra 5 percent or so of their much higher real incomes for health care and retirement policies that, if maintained, will eventually benefit them as well may not be inappropriate. (It is true that the social insurance system will not be so good an overall deal for future retirees as it has been for past ones, making the intergenerational compact less appealing to those who are still very young.) A second alternative would be to move toward some form of private social insurance, encouraging people to provide for their own health care and retirement needs in old age— an option that would require current working-age people to finance both their own retirement and (if Social Security checks are not to stop tomorrow) their parents' retirement as well.

Still a third alternative, and the one that is given the bulk of the attention in chapter 6, would be to restructure current programs to make them fiscally less burdensome and better targeted toward people with the most pressing needs. Because the elderly, as a group, are now as well off financially as the rest of the population and are able to live about as well as they did during their preretirement years (in large part because of the growth of federal spending but also because more elderly have private pensions and income from assets), they should be able to shoulder more of the burden for their own health care and retirement costs. If the well-to-do elderly were to contribute more, resources would be freed up to meet the needs of those with serious health problems or low incomes. Depending on what changes were made and how they were phased in, both short-term and long-term fiscal burdens could be reduced. As Palmer stresses, however, any short-term modifications should be tailored to fit into a longer-term plan for the social insurance system as a whole, and his chapter provides the outline for this broader vision.

## Poverty and the Underclass

In 1986, 14 percent of all Americans had incomes below the poverty level. And despite the billions of dollars spent on antipoverty programs, poverty has declined little since the late 1960s.

In chapter 7, Isabel Sawhill examines these data and asks why it is that in the War on Poverty, poverty appears to have won. She concludes that antipoverty programs have worked to reduce poverty, especially among the elderly. However, the effects have been offset by demographic changes, such as the increasing proportion of households headed by women, and by the poor performance of the economy, especially the high unemployment rates of the early 1980s. Now that the unemployment rate is falling, so is the incidence of poverty; but given the post-1981 cutbacks in programs for the poor, the poverty rate is unlikely to reach the low levels achieved during the 1970s over the remainder of the 1980s.

Currently, about one-third of poor families are headed by someone who is elderly or disabled, one-third are likely to remain poor only temporarily, and the remaining one-third are what might be called the "hard-core" poor—those who live in families with chronically low incomes despite the presence of an able-bodied, nonelderly household head. Some of the hard-core poor are also members of the "underclass"—a small but rapidly growing group living in neighborhoods where welfare dependency, female-headed families, male joblessness, and dropping out of high school are so common that they appear to have become a way of life in these communities. New estimates presented in chapter 7 put the size of this population at about 1 million in 1980 and suggest that it is predominantly minority, heavily concentrated in the large cities of the Northeast and Midwest, and very poorly educated.

After examining the characteristics of the poor, Sawhill goes on to argue that policies should be designed to reflect their diverse circumstances. Some of the poor (such as those who have lost a job) need only temporary income support to help them through difficult times. The traditional safety net programs such as unemployment insurance, food stamps, and AFDC were designed for this purpose. Some of the poor (such as the elderly and disabled) need a more permanent safety net of the kind provided by Social Security or the Supplemental Security Income program. And some (such as the able-bodied chronically poor, or the underclass) need to be helped to become productive and respected members of society.

Although all these groups need help, Sawhill argues that the nation's top priority should be to stem the growth of chronic poverty and the underclass. The costs of allowing the underclass to grow unchecked include more crime, greater welfare dependency, and lower productivity among the working-age population. Children growing up in chronically poor families, and especially those living in troubled neighborhoods, may—in the absence of intervention—be doomed to repeat their parents' lives. The emergence of such a permanent underclass damages the social fabric, damage that is compounded when a majority of this population consists of minorities who are not being effectively integrated into the larger society.

To accomplish the foregoing objective, Sawhill calls for a compassionate yet tough-minded agenda that will move the chronically poor toward self-sufficiency by simultaneously attacking the three principal causes of poverty among the able-bodied poor: weak families, substantial joblessness, and poor education.

## Life, Liberty, or the Pursuit of Happiness

In chapter 8, Thomas Schelling explores some of the ways in which social objectives, individual rights, and moral and religious values conflict with one another. These conflicts are evident in debate on a wide variety of topics including gun control, abortion, surrogate motherhood, and smoking in public places. However, chapter 8 focuses on two of the many cases in which such conflicts arise: AIDS and the right to die.

Schelling first reviews the dimensions of the AIDS problem and notes that in view of the characteristics of the high-risk populations—homosexuals, prostitutes, drug abusers, blacks, and Hispanics—the potential for discrimination, privation, and even retribution in the public's response to AIDS is large.

He then explores some invasions or compromises of individual rights involved in testing for AIDS—including who has the right to test results—and notes the current lack of information on the prevalence and spread of the asymptomatic virus that is the precursor of the disease itself. He shows how such issues as whether to make clean needles more readily available to intravenous drug users, whether to test and certify prostitutes as virus-free, and whether to encourage safer sex among young people all involve a clash of social policy with moral principles. He explores at some length the potential social benefits of preventing contact between infected and uninfected persons and the kinds of discrimination and segregation—good and bad—that may occur or be imposed as a result. And he suggests that if the exponential growth of AIDS should continue and no reliable vaccine become available, a majority of the public might tolerate—or even demand—the public health equivalent of martial law to cope with this threat to their survival.

In turning to the "right to die," Schelling notes that this is one of the many issues gaining prominence in the wake of spectacular advances in medical technology that have made it increasingly easy (but costly) to keep people alive. These developments have been paralleled by increasing attention to the questions of whether, in what circumstances, and by whose decision these life-extending medical procedures can be eschewed. For example, three-quarters of the states have provided some statutory recognition of "living wills," thereby endorsing some limited and qualified "right to die."

In an attempt to help people think about the issues that must be faced if the line that circumscribes this limited right is to be better defined, he discusses five cases representing increasing orders of moral complexity. The first four cases involve allowing a patient to die naturally by removing life support systems or other treatment; the cases include persons who are legally alive but brain dead, those in a coma, incompetent persons whose suffering is clear despite their inability to communicate their preferences, and fully competent persons who wish to be allowed to die (naturally). The fifth case discussed involves competent persons who want active help in ending their own life (euthanasia or assisted suicide).

Euthanasia, even when requested by a patient, is not legal in the United States, although it is sometimes discreetly practiced by sympathetic physicians. It is legal in the Netherlands, and bills are under consideration in a few states in this country that would legalize the practice under certain conditions. Polls indicate that an overwhelming majority of the U.S. public favors legalization, and, as Schelling notes, this is a silent majority that may not remain silent much longer. However, he also stresses the profound psychological difficulties that patients and their families might experience if patients knew that the option of euthanasia was available to them. He concludes that the line between what is appropriate and inappropriate in each case may remain fuzzy whatever legislative steps are or are not taken.

## Fiscal Choices

The federal budget deficit is currently on a slowly declining path—assuming a moderately healthy economy over the next few years, no new spending initiatives, and continued reliance on the build-up of a surplus in the Social Security trust fund to finance other federal outlays. However, virtually all observers believe that a do-nothing stance entails large economic risks, leaves little maneuvering room in the event of a downturn in the economy, and provides no resources with which to respond to an international or domestic crisis, or to the problems described elsewhere in this volume.

How much and how fast the deficit needs to be reduced are matters of dispute among economists. However, a case can be made that the cuts need to total 3.6 percent of GNP relative to current policy, which, if phased in over a five-year period, would eliminate the $220 billion deficit in the non-Social Security portion of the budget in 1992. Although economically desirable, such a goal may not be politically feasible, especially when we recall that approximately 70 percent of the budget goes for defense, Medicare, Social Security, other pension programs (recently reformed), and interest on the debt.

In chapter 9, Minarik and Penner review the major options for reducing the deficit, including many that have heretofore been politically unacceptable; they come up with about $150 billion in savings—an amount that is still short of their $220 billion target for 1992. This $150 billion, which is drawn about equally from reduced spending and higher revenues, turns out to be enough to balance the overall budget but only if the Social Security trust fund surplus is allowed to finance the deficit in the non-Social Security portion of the budget.

On the spending side, the savings are achieved by cuts in defense spending that are presumed consistent with current foreign policy and strategic deterrence goals ($10 billion); increased taxation of Social Security benefits combined with a gradual fall in the ratio of benefits to preretirement income ($15 billion); reduced payments to hospitals and doctors and increased recipient premiums in Medicare ($15 billion); reform of farm programs ($6 billion); and cuts in other federal outlays, such as grants to states and localities for water, sewers, transportation, and economic development (which could save $10 billion under draconian assumptions). These deficit reduction measures, together with the savings on interest associated with them, would save a total of $71 billion in 1992.

On the revenue side, the authors come up with a combination of excise tax increases (on gasoline, alcoholic beverages, and cigarettes) and a further broadening of the income tax base beyond what was accomplished in 1986 (to include, for example, taxation of fringe benefits) for a total of $90 billion in savings. Choosing enough items from this rather painful list to yield about two-thirds of the total revenue increase, and adding the resulting savings on interest, would reduce the deficit by about $77 billion for 1992.

The authors also discuss three other major revenue-raising measures but for various reasons consider them inferior to base broadening and excise taxes. The first is a value-added or national sales tax, which, at a 5 percent rate and with necessities exempted, would raise $66 billion in 1992. The second is a slight increase in income tax rates which could raise $60 billion while still leaving rates far below their pre-1986 levels. The third is an attempt to collect the estimated $81 billion in legally owed but unpaid taxes, although the authors are skeptical that such an attempt would yield substantial revenues (net of administrative and enforcement costs).

By focusing on the large areas of the budget (such as defense and Social Security) that must be tackled if spending is to be significantly reduced and by putting all the major revenue alternatives on the table, chapter 9 makes clear the difficult political choices that must be made.

# NOTES

1. See Arthur M. Schlesinger, Jr., *The Cycles of American History* (Boston, Mass.: Houghton Mifflin, 1986); and Albert O. Hirschman, *Shifting Involvements: Private Interest, Public Action* (Princeton, N.J.: Princeton University Press, 1982).

2. See John L. Palmer, ed., *Perspectives on the Reagan Years* (Washington, D.C.: Urban Institute Press, 1986) for a more detailed review of the Reagan legacy.

3. John L. Palmer and Isabel V. Sawhill, eds., *The Reagan Record: An Assessment of America's Changing Domestic Priorities* (Cambridge, Mass.: Ballinger Publishing Company, 1984).

4. W. John Moore, "No Quick Fix," *National Journal* 19, no. 47 (November 21, 1987): 2954–59; John E. Yang, "Bigger Battle Against AIDS Severely Hampered by Smaller Fights in Congress, Administration," *Wall Street Journal*, December 28, 1987.

5. See, for example, "Opinion Roundup—The Foundations of Campaign '88: An Election Handbook," Public Opinion 10, no. 4 (November-December 1987): 21–40.

6. There was, in fact, much more concern about how to cope with the then-immediate problem of "stagflation"—a concern that by the mid-1980s had all but dissipated, as inflation and unemployment reached more acceptable levels.

7. Angus Maddison, "Growth and Slowdown in Advanced Capitalist Economies: Techniques of Quantitative Assessment," *Journal of Economic Literature* 25 (June 1987): 649–98.

8. The United States, with a population twice as big as that of the next largest industrialized economy (Japan), is likely to maintain a dominant economic position even if its per capita incomes or standards of living grow more slowly than those in other countries. The Japanese, whose per capita income has been rapidly approaching that of the United States, still produce only about two-fifths as much as the United States overall. For evidence that growth rates tend to converge, see Maddison, "Growth and Slowdown," and chapter 4.

9. Estimates of the U.S. share of the world's gross domestic product (GDP) and other comparative data on incomes are very sensitive to the way in which the incomes of different countries are adjusted for differences in purchasing power across countries. According to data from Robert W. Lipsey and Irving B. Kravis, the U.S. share of world GDP was 27 percent in 1950 and 18 percent in 1984. ("Saving and Economic Growth: Is the United States Really Falling Behind?" [New York: The Conference Board, Inc., 1987].)

10. Paul Kennedy, "The (Relative) Decline of America," *Atlantic Monthly* 260, no. 2 (August 1987): 29–38.

11. In his presidential address to the American Economic Association, Charles Kindleberger stated, "The tendency for public goods to be underproduced is serious enough within a nation bound by some sort of social contract, and directed in public matters by a government with the power to impose and collect taxes. It is...a more serious problem in international political and economic relations in the absence of international government." He went on to observe that "after about 1971, the United States, like Britain from about 1890, has shrunk in economic might relative to the world as a whole, and more importantly, has lost the appetite for providing international economic public goods—open markets in times of glut, supplies in times of acute shortage, steady flows of capital to developing countries, international money, coordination of macroeconomic policy and last-resort lending." (Charles P. Kindleberger, *American Economic Review* 76, no. 1 [March 1986]: 1–13).

12. As West Germany's former federal chancellor, Helmut Schmidt, put it, "Co-operation between North America, Japan, and the EEC is essential for a healthy world economy . . . [but] neither trilateral co-operation nor worldwide co-operation is imaginable at present without American leadership.. . . America must know: if it fails in its economic leadership, it may lose its

political leadership as well." ("Helmut Schmidt's Prescription: The World Economy at Stake," *Economist* (February 26, 1983): 30.

13. For an interesting discussion of the social contract between generations, see Phillip Longman, "Justice Between Generations," *Atlantic Monthly* 255, no. 6 (June 1985): 73–81. For an alternative view, see Eric R. Kingson, Barbara A. Hirshorn, and John M. Cornman, *Ties That Bind: The Interdependence of Generations* (Cabin John, Md.: Seven Locks Press, 1986); and Henry J. Aaron, "When Is a Burden Not a Burden? The Elderly in America," *Brookings Review* 4, no. 3 (Summer 1986): 17–24.

14. See, for example, U.S. National Commission on Excellence in Education, *A Nation at Risk* (Washington, D.C.: U.S. Government Printing Office, 1983); and *Time for Results: The Governors' 1991 Report on Education* (Washington, D.C.: National Governors' Association, 1986). For an excellent review of what has been accomplished in various states, see William Chance, ". . . the best of educations:" *Reforming America's Public Schools in the 1980's* (Olympia Wash.: Lindley Russel, 1987).

15. The alternative view is that such a reallocation would simply represent a shift in consumption from one point in the life cycle to another, and, for the working-age population, a shift from the necessity of supporting and caring for children to the necessity of supporting and caring for elderly parents.

16. Some people may prefer to let the next generation fend for itself. Winston Churchill expressed such a preference when he said, "I would like to make the people who live on this world at the same time as I do better fed and happier generally. If incidentally I benefit posterity—so much the better—but I would not sacrifice my own generation to a principle—however high or a truth however great." (Winston Churchill to Bourke Cockran, April 12, 1896, in Randolph Churchill, *Winston S. Churchill*, Companion Vol. I, Part I [Boston, 1967]; 668, as cited in Schlesinger, *The Cycles of American History*, 427).

17. Deborah Jones Merritt, "The Constitutional Balance between Health and Liberty," *Hastings Center Report* 16, no. 6 (December 1986): 2–10.

18. See Theodore J. Lowi, "Ronald Reagan—Revolutionary?" in *The Reagan Presidency and the Governing of America*, edited by Lester M. Salamon and Michael S. Lund (Washington, D.C.: Urban Institute Press, 1985), 29–56, for a more extended discussion of this point.

19. Tolerance in this case is usually interpreted to mean keeping prayer *out* of the schools in keeping with the strict separation of church and state. But arguing for tolerance when the social consequences of a behavior are minimal is a two-way street. A moment of silence or prayer at the beginning of the school day may be entirely consistent with the values of a local community and may do no particular harm to anyone else. Arguably, in cases where no ostensible harm is done, the government and the courts should protect such enclaves of traditional values just as it protects enclaves of permissive values. This argument is made by Nathan Glazer, "The 'Social Agenda,'" in *Perspectives on the Reagan Years*, edited by John L. Palmer (Washington, D.C.: Urban Institute Press, 1986), 5–30.

20. Indeed, granting people the right to die would be consistent with a reduction in health care costs—a point, to be sure, that makes some people uneasy because it could lead to subtle pressures on the old or sick to exercise this right.

21. Hugh Heclo and Lester M. Salamon, eds., *The Illusion of Presidential Government* (Boulder, Colo.: Westview Press, 1981). Although President Reagan initially confounded the experts by his strong performance during his first term, more recently the opinions of political scientists have swung back to the original belief that the presidency is a relatively weak institution. See Dom Bonafede, "Re-Rating Reagan," *National Journal* 19, no. 48 (November 28, 1987): 3065.

22. Richard P. Nathan, Fred C. Doolittle, and Associates, *Reagan and the States* (Princeton: Princeton University Press, 1987).

23. The following analysis draws heavily on material in Lester M. Salamon and Alan J. Abramson, "Governance: The Politics of Retrenchment," in *The Reagan Record: An Assessment of America's Changing Domestic Priorities*," edited by John L. Palmer and Isabel V. Sawhill (Cambridge, Mass.: Ballinger, 1984), 33–36. References to other studies that make the points

discussed here are given in that source. In addition, see Ben W. Heineman, Jr., and Curtis A. Hessler, *Memorandum for the President: A Strategic Approach to Domestic Affairs in the 1980s* (New York: Random House, 1980).

24. The proposals include strengthening political parties by giving them a greater role in the political nominating process, now dominated by popular primaries, or in financing campaigns, now dominated by wealthy individuals and special interest groups. They also include moving toward a parliamentary system by, for example, allowing sitting members of Congress to serve in the cabinet or by inaugurating team tickets that would require voters to select a president, vice president, and member of Congress from the same party. (See James MacGregor Burns, *The Power to Lead* [New York: Simon and Schuster, 1984], and Lloyd N. Cutler, "Political Parties and a Workable Government," in *A Workable Government*? edited by Burke Marshall [New York: W. W. Norton, 1987].)

25. For further discussion of these issues, see James MacGregor Burns, *Leadership* (New York: Harper & Row, 1978); John W. Gardner, *Leadership Papers* (Washington, D.C.: The Independent Sector, 1986 and 1987); Arthur Maass, *Congress and the Common Good* (New York: Basic Books, 1983); Donald K. Kinder and D. Roderick Kiewet, "Socio-tropic Politics: The American Case," *British Journal of Political Science* 2 (1981): 129–61; "Economic Discontent and Political Behavior: The Role of Personal Grievances and Collective Economic Judgments in Congressional Voting," *American Journal of Political Science* 23 (1979): 519–24; D. Roderick Kiewet, *Macroeconomics and Micropolitics* (Chicago: University of Chicago Press, 1983).

# CHAPTER 2

# FAMILY INCOMES

Joseph J. Minarik

Over the past fifteen years, the pace of growth of U.S. incomes has markedly slowed. Because standards of living have fallen short of some people's expectations and hopes, many have expressed concern about the trend in incomes. And, of course, when the public is concerned, politicians are concerned as well. So there have been a number of policy proposals to speed up income growth. These proposals range from education to taxation, industrial policies, and trade protectionism—and most have been controversial.

Other people question the significance of the income slowdown. They argue that U.S. living standards—particularly as measured by "big ticket" and new "high tech" consumption items or by alternative measures of income—are high and rising just as rapidly as before. From this point of view, the whole search for broad policy solutions to a phantom slowdown of incomes is misguided.

There is a second, related concern: that whatever the level of income, the distribution of incomes has become much less equal. Some people believe that this situation threatens to divide the nation into economic classes and to erode its unique social and political consensus and stability.

How can these concerns be evaluated? And what should policymakers do about them? This chapter examines the growth of family incomes in the United States over the past three decades. This examination shows that income growth did indeed slow down significantly after more than a decade of remarkable advancement and that although some population groups were affected somewhat less than others by the slowdown, none escaped entirely.

The second section discusses the possibility that U.S. *living standards* have moved ahead faster than measured U.S. *incomes*. It considers questions about the accuracy of the measurement of real incomes over time, the effect of taxes and housing prices on living standards, and people's habits regarding saving and borrowing. It finds that through all the ambiguities in measuring incomes and all the subjective judgments in the evaluation of living standards, the slowdown in money income looms too large to be ignored.

Next, this chapter looks at the growth of inequality in family incomes. In fact, the distribution of family incomes, as commonly measured, is now more unequal than at any time since World War II. But increasing inequality, like slowing growth in income, afflicted most major demographic groups, and no prominent demographic change can be said to have caused the entire movement toward inequality.

Finally, the chapter seeks some insight into the slower growth and greater inequality by looking at individual workers' earnings, the major source of family income. The data show that earnings have shared the trends seen in family incomes. As with family income, however, the slowdown and inequality of individual earnings have no obvious cause. In particular, the alleged "deindustrialization" of the U.S. economy has had virtually no measurable effect.

So where does all this lead? The income slowdown and the trend toward inequality have no identifiable causes; so any attempt at solving these problems (as opposed to easing their effects) will be speculative. Faster economic growth would certainly help, but there are no marked paths toward this holy grail, which the nation has been seeking for decades (see chapter 3). The nation could certainly profit from more stable macroeconomic policies, to avoid the waste of recessions and to ease business planning, but the payoff to these efforts in long-term growth is uncertain. Providing more effective education, especially for children from disadvantaged backgrounds (see chapter 8), would build a more highly skilled and productive labor force; so would training and retraining workers stuck at the bottom of the employment ladder or those hit by economic dislocations in midcareer (see chapter 4). But these are expensive, long-term policies whose ultimate payoff is unproved. Moreover, policies that seek to boost particular sectors of the economy in order to achieve growth or redistribute income are likely to slow growth and make virtually everyone worse off (see chapter 4). So an examination of the recent problems of family incomes probably inspires caution, from the risk of causing serious structural economic harm, more than it justifies policy activism.

# The Growth of Family Incomes

Most people in the United States live in families. Even though the traditional two-parent family with children has become somewhat less common, 88 percent of the population still lived in families in 1985 (compared with 94 percent in 1954).[1] Most of these people share incomes and make consumption decisions at the family level. So any generalizations about the economic status of the population must be based on the family. This section examines the incomes of the family population as a whole and then the incomes of particular kinds of families.

## The Family Population

The data on family incomes clearly show a slowdown of growth beginning about fifteen years ago. The real median income among all families increased smartly over the 1950s and 1960s (as is shown in figure 2.1).[2] In 1986 dollars, the income of the typical family increased from $15,492 in 1954 to $27,770 in 1973, a total increase of 79.3 percent. The average annual rate of growth of 3.1 percent from 1954 through 1973 compared favorably with the admittedly less precise estimates of the growth of the previous century, and was overwhelming compared with the stagnation of the 1930s.[3] Since 1973, however, family incomes have increased much more slowly. The total increase through 1986, to $29,458 in 1986 dollars, is only 6.1 percent; the annual rate of growth is much slower, 0.5 percent. The average growth over the period was reduced by the deep recessions of 1974-75, 1979-80, and 1981-82; but even in the intervening recoveries, the growth of family incomes did not match the average for the 1960s.

The ultimate cause of this downturn in U.S. economic fortunes is still uncertain (see chapter 3 for a complete discussion). It may even be assuming too much to look to the 1970s for the cause of the economic slowdown. As was pointed out earlier, the economic performance of the 1950s and 1960s was extraordinarily good—perhaps too good to be sustainable. The performance in the early post-World War II years may have been boosted by a supply of physical capital, technology, and labor that could be extracted from the economy only under the pressures of the war and the release of pent-up demand in the postwar years. It is therefore conceivable that the 1970s and the 1980s, without their extreme cyclicality, are more typical of long-run growth prospects than the admittedly more appealing 1950s and 1960s.

Whatever the cause of the income slowdown of the 1970s, its implications were far-reaching. The drop in economic growth raised questions about the performance of the economy and about U.S. competitiveness in the world

FIGURE 2.1

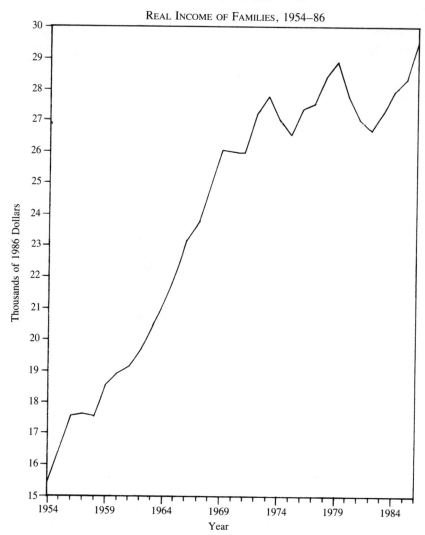

REAL INCOME OF FAMILIES, 1954–86

SOURCE: U.S. Bureau of the Census, "Money Income of Households, Families, and Persons in the United States," *Current Population Reports*, Series P-60, nos. 156 and 157 (Washington, D.C.: U.S. Government Printing Office, 1987).

market. And partly as a result of these concerns, economic policy took some new and unorthodox turns, including the massive experiment in fiscal stimulation of the supply side of the economy in the early 1980s. It is still uncertain whether trade protectionism will follow. Clearly, the slowdown in growth can test the U.S. self-control to reject actions with superficial appeal but substantial long-term costs.

## Family Composition and Incomes

Different types of families felt the income slowdown to different degrees. This section looks at several large demographic groups whose relative incomes shifted significantly. These groups also changed in their relative proportions of the population, thereby affecting overall income growth. (See chapter 6 for a discussion of the economic status of the elderly, a prominent demographic group not discussed in this chapter.)

**Two-Earner Married Couples.** Almost 55 percent of all married women were in the labor force in 1986, about double the percentage of 1954.[4] Thus, most married couples now have two earners. Furthermore, the economic status of two-earner families has improved relative to that of traditional one-earner couples. As might be expected, the incomes of two-earner couples are generally greater than the incomes of one-earner couples (the median for two-earner couples in 1986 was $38,346, for one-earner couples, $25,803). But the incomes of two-earner couples have also grown faster than those of one-earner couples since the 1950s, especially since the mid-1970s; in fact, the incomes of one-earner couples have declined in real terms from the early 1970s (see figure 2.2).[5] The stagnation of the incomes of one-earner couples, among whom the single earner is typically the husband, suggests that the rapid relative growth of the incomes of two-earner couples is coming from the wives.[6]

Nonetheless, income growth for two-earner couples still slowed noticeably in the 1970s. From 1954 to 1973, the incomes of two-earner couples grew, on average, by 3.1 percent per year; after 1973, however, their income growth slowed to 0.7 percent per year. Thus, two-earner families as a group may have survived the income slowdown better than others, but they did not avoid it entirely. And because two-earner couples fared the best of all large demographic groups, the income slowdown was obviously pervasive and not caused by some particular demographic change.

**One-Parent Families.** Divorce rates have steadily increased since the early 1960s; there were 9.5 divorces per 1,000 married women in 1954, but 21.3 in 1983.[7] As a result, the population of one-parent families has expanded. One possible cause of this trend is that the greater financial independence of

FIGURE 2.2

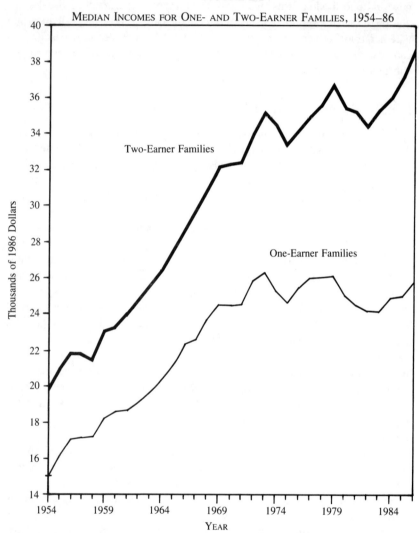

MEDIAN INCOMES FOR ONE- AND TWO-EARNER FAMILIES, 1954–86

SOURCE: See figure 2.1.

women, built on increased education, work experience, and access to better-paying occupations, has facilitated the termination of unsatisfactory marriages.[8] Ironically, although the increase in divorce may have been caused to some extent by the greater financial independence of women, the divorce boom itself has caused frequent financial hardship for women and their children. If simply because a one-parent family has only half the potential adult wage earners, a divorced woman and her children have lower economic prospects than a two-parent family has. The lesser earnings prospects of women compared with men makes the status of most one-parent families still worse.

The incomes of female-headed families are, in fact, low—a median of $13,647 in 1986, compared with $32,805 for husband-wife families. Furthermore, whereas the incomes of husband-wife families have grown at least modestly, aided by the earnings of working wives, one-parent families headed by women have had virtually no growth in real incomes since the early 1970s (see figure 2.3). (Statistics on the much smaller number of one-parent families headed by men show that their real incomes also have not grown since the 1970s).

**Black Families.** The gap between the incomes of white and black families has been another concern, and the aggregate data yield little comfort. The incomes of black families continue lower than those of whites, with only slight progress in narrowing the gap: in 1954, incomes of black families were 56 percent of those of whites, on average; in 1986, they were 57 percent. However, the average income of all black families conceals some significant changes within the black population. Two-parent black families have closed a substantial part of the gap between their incomes and those of comparable white families. In 1968 (when the Census Bureau first computed the statistic), black two-parent family median income was 72 percent of that of comparable white families, but by 1986 the black median income was 80 percent of that of whites. The slower progress in closing the gap between the incomes of all black and all white families reflects the rapid growth in the number of black one-parent families.[9]

**Conclusion: Demographic Change and the Income Slowdown.** The data show that different groups of families have had markedly different experiences, over all of the past three decades but particularly since the income slowdown of the 1970s. The income gap between two-earner couples and other families has widened over the past decade; one-parent families, and even traditional one-earner married couples, are relatively worse off. But even two-earner couples as a group suffered a slowdown in the growth of their incomes, so the slower growth was pervasive.

FIGURE 2.3

MEDIAN INCOMES FOR HUSBAND-WIFE AND FEMALE-HEADED FAMILIES,
1954–86

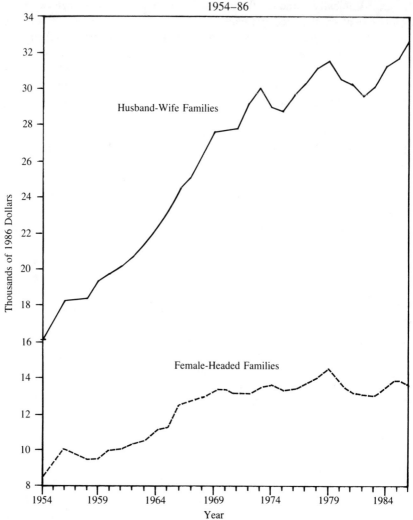

SOURCE: See figure 2.1

The demographic changes of the 1970s clearly influenced overall family income growth, but computations with the 1970 and 1980 censuses show that there would have been an income slowdown even without them. If the proportion of families headed by women had remained the same over the 1970s but all other changes followed their actual course, average real family income would have declined by a total of 4.2 percent instead of the actual 6.0 percent—still far worse than the growth of almost 30 percent over the 1960s. The increase in the number of two-earner couples pushed the other way; it reduced the income slowdown by about 1.8 percentage points total, a significant amount, but small in relation to the size of the slowdown. Had both these factors been constant, real family incomes over the 1970s would have declined by 6.1 percent—only 0.1 percent different from the actual experience.[10]

Finally, the differences in incomes among the various demographic groups cannot explain the income slowdown. Thus, the growth in the real median income of two-earner couples (0.7 percent per year) from 1973 to 1986 was less than the growth of the real median income of all families (3.1 percent per year) from 1954 to 1973. So even if all other families had enjoyed the same income growth as two-earner couples, there would still have been an income slowdown. The problems of the 1970s were pervasive, and they did not result from the changing composition of the family population.

## Incomes Versus Living Standards

Data on family incomes point unambiguously toward slower growth of living standards in the 1970s and 1980s. Other data, and some anecdotal observation as well, might suggest that this measurement exaggerates any slowdown in the growth of actual living standards. One question is how we measure income; another is whether living standards qualitatively differ from incomes and have grown at a different rate. The upshot of the analysis is that although money incomes, as measured thus far in this chapter, are not a complete measure of well-being, they are at the very least a harbinger of future living standards that cannot be ignored. Thus money incomes remain an important economic indicator.

### Per Capita versus Family Income

Over the past ten years, the measure of per capita personal income, as presented in the national income and product accounts, has grown faster than median family income as measured by the Census Bureau (see figure 2.4).[11] This disparity has raised doubts about whether there really has been an income slowdown.

FIGURE 2.4

MEDIAN FAMILY INCOME VERSUS PER CAPITA PERSONAL INCOME,
1954–86

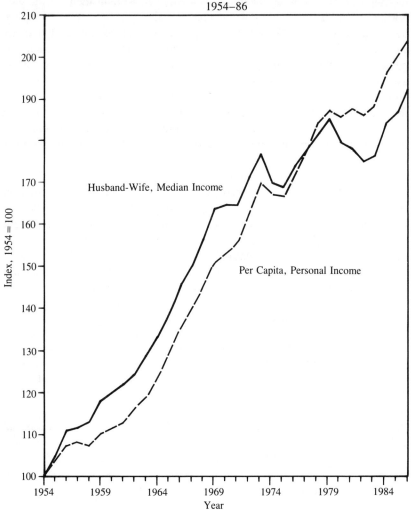

SOURCES: See figure 2.1 and *Economic Report of the President, January 1987*, tables B-3,
B-22, and B-30.

Much of the quantitative difference between these two measures in recent years arises from the choices of parents to have fewer children. For a given income, smaller families clearly need to spread their resources less thinly than larger families, thereby raising well-being. Smaller families also mean a reduction in the ratio of dependent to working persons in the population, and this reduction increases per capita income (and potential per capita consumption as well). People can disagree as to whether the reduction of average family size was an economic choice intended to raise living standards or a decision unrelated to economic values (or both, to varying degrees, among different families). Ultimately, however, the reduction in childbearing has a limit; and if that choice has become an important means of raising living standards, and income growth continues slow, it bodes ill for the future. And the slowdown of growth of money incomes clearly reduces the living standards that families can achieve at any given family size, so a measure of per capita income cannot supersede a measure of money income (though it certainly can supplement it).[12]

## Income in Kind

There is a further and entirely separate issue in the usual comparison of per capita income and family income. Per capita personal income (as commonly measured from the national accounts) includes noncash fringe benefits (such as employer-paid life and health insurance premiums) and in-kind government transfers (including food stamps and medical services under Medicare and Medicaid), whereas the Census Bureau's measure of money income does not; and fringe benefits (perhaps for tax reasons) and government in-kind transfers have been increasing faster than money incomes. Fringe benefits and in-kind transfers clearly add to the well-being of families and thus should be counted in income; but there are real questions about how to value them. The value of fringe benefits and in-kind transfers to individual workers and families is subjective and typically less than their full cost. (Fringe benefits usually come in predetermined combinations, so workers cannot choose exactly the benefits that they want. Furthermore, given that fringes are exempt from federal income tax, it is not surprising that workers would accept fringe benefits that they would not buy with their own after-tax dollars.) It would be preferable if data on money income could include in-kind income, but the best available data indicate that doing this would explain only part of the slowdown in growth of family incomes;[13] and there are other desirable additions to our income measurement base that would push in the other direction, as the following section illustrates.

## Taxes

Taxes are not deducted from census money income, but the frustration over the slow increase in living standards since the early 1970s may be due to increases in taxes as much as to decreases in the rate of growth of money incomes. Taxes are a wedge between income and potential consumption. Because taxes are largely uncontrollable and because many people do not perceive a link between taxes paid and government services received, taxation has aroused popular protest in recent times. The "tax revolt" of the late 1970s, largely directed against states and localities, and the favorable response to the large tax cuts proposed by "supply-side economics" in the early 1980s, attest to this frustration.

Despite periodic tax cuts, the federal individual income tax burden on families with average incomes has increased (because inflation eroded the personal exemption and the standard deduction and pushed taxable incomes into higher rate brackets). For example, a typical family of four with an income at one-half the median paid no income tax in the early 1950s but had an income tax burden of about 6 percent by the late 1960s; in the 1970s and 1980s taxes were cut and then returned to the 6 percent level (see table 2.1).[14]

TABLE 2.1

INCOME TAX BURDENS ON FAMILIES AT MULTIPLES OF THE MEDIAN INCOME, SELECTED YEARS, 1954–88
*(Percent)*

|       | Multiple of the Median Income | | |
|-------|------|------|------|
| *Year* | *0.5* | *1* | *2* |
| 1954 | 0   | 6.2  | 12.0 |
| 1959 | 1.0 | 8.8  | 13.7 |
| 1964 | 2.2 | 8.2  | 12.5 |
| 1969 | 5.8 | 11.0 | 15.6 |
| 1974 | 5.7 | 10.2 | 15.3 |
| 1979 | 4.6 | 11.2 | 17.6 |
| 1980 | 5.4 | 11.6 | 18.3 |
| 1981 | 6.3 | 12.3 | 19.2 |
| 1982 | 5.9 | 11.3 | 17.6 |
| 1983 | 6.0 | 10.6 | 16.3 |
| 1984 | 6.3 | 10.6 | 16.2 |
| 1985 | 6.4 | 10.6 | 16.3 |
| 1986 | 6.5 | 10.7 | 16.5 |
| 1987 | 4.4 | 8.6  | 14.1 |
| 1988 | 4.3 | 9.0  | 14.3 |

SOURCE: Author's calculations.

The tax rate on median-income families almost doubled between the early 1950s and 1981, while the burden on families that had twice the median income increased by more than half over the same years. All these families got some relief from the 1981 tax cuts, but for the family at half the median income the relief evaporated in bracket creep by 1984. The Tax Reform Act of 1986 cut taxes more substantially, especially for the lowest-income families (financed by increasing taxes on corporations).

Another major change, however, was the increase in the Social Security payroll tax in both absolute terms and relative to the income tax. Over the entire period, but especially since the 1970s, the payroll tax has been a growing burden on typical families (see table 2.2). For example, whereas the income tax burden on median-income families increased by 1.9 percentage points, or less than one-fourth, between the 1959 and 1986, the total (income plus payroll) tax burden increased by 7.0 percentage points, or more than half.

Even with the relief from the new tax law, the long-term effect on disposable incomes of income taxes, and especially income plus payroll taxes, remains large. Real median family income grew by 103.7 percent between 1954 and 1986; but income net of income and payroll taxes grew only 81.4 percent—still appreciable, but clearly reduced by the tax bite. The drain of taxes was particularly painful over the 1970s and early 1980s, when pretax income growth slowed; from 1969 to 1986, gross income grew by 18.7 percent, but income net of total taxes grew by only 14.3 percent.

Thus, if the slowdown of real incomes was an affront, the growth of taxes only added insult to injury. Clearly, taxes collected in the 1970s and 1980s have not kept the federal deficit in check, and the outlays toward which these taxes went did benefit the population; nonetheless, the tax factor must be considered in any assessment of family well-being. The role of the payroll tax is especially controversial. Workers are buying future annuities through their payroll taxes, and so that tax is not an unmitigated drain even on lifetime cash incomes. But payroll taxes have taken an increasing share of current incomes, and some people question whether the current burden has become excessive. This issue cannot be assessed without obtaining a more comprehensive view of the Social Security system and the status of the elderly (see chapter 6), and of Social Security in the context of the budget (see chapter 9).

So although the absence of in-kind receipts from measures of cash income tends to understate living standards, the absence of taxes in such measures tends to overstate living standards.

TABLE 2.2

EFFECTIVE INCOME AND PAYROLL TAX RATES, AND DISPOSABLE INCOME FOR FAMILIES OF FOUR, SELECTED YEARS, 1954–88

| Multiple of the Median Income | 1954 | 1959 | 1969 | 1979 | 1986 | 1988 |
|---|---|---|---|---|---|---|
| Median income | | | | | | |
| Income (1986 dollars) | 16,108 | 19,390 | 27,627 | 31,586 | 32,805 | 33,747 |
| Effective income tax rate (percent) | 6.2 | 8.8 | 11.0 | 11.2 | 10.7 | 9.0 |
| Effective payroll tax rate (percent) | 1.7 | 2.1 | 3.7 | 6.1 | 7.2 | 7.5 |
| Disposable income (1986 dollars) | 14,848 | 17,280 | 23,559 | 26,125 | 26,937 | 28,189 |
| One-half median income | | | | | | |
| Income (1986 dollars) | 8,054 | 9,695 | 13,815 | 15,793 | 16,403 | 16,874 |
| Effective income tax rate (percent) | 0.0 | 1.0 | 5.8 | 4.6 | 6.5 | 4.3 |
| Effective payroll tax rate (percent) | 2.0 | 2.5 | 4.8 | 6.1 | 7.2 | 7.5 |
| Disposable income (1986 dollars) | 7,893 | 9,352 | 12,350 | 14,098 | 14,165 | 14,879 |
| Twice median income | | | | | | |
| Income (1986 dollars) | 32,216 | 38,781 | 55,254 | 63,172 | 65,610 | 67,494 |
| Effective income tax rate (percent) | 12.0 | 13.7 | 15.6 | 17.6 | 16.5 | 14.3 |
| Effective payroll tax rate (percent) | 0.8 | 1.1 | 1.9 | 3.3 | 4.6 | 4.8 |
| Disposable income (1986 dollars) | 28,070 | 33,064 | 45,585 | 49,994 | 51,793 | 54,611 |

SOURCE: Author's calculations. Items may not add to totals because of rounding.

## Housing

Another notable drain on perceived living standards is the increasing carrying cost of owner-occupied housing, which has arisen from the combined and compounded effects of increases in home selling prices, increases in typical mortgage debt (to cope with the price increases, buyers reduced their down payments), and a long-term increase in interest rates (although rates have eased from their peaks in the mid-1980s).[15] Mortgage durations were extended to keep monthly payments in line, but even so, carrying costs increased. The typical thirty-year-old man purchasing the median-price home under typical mortgage terms would have incurred carrying costs equal to 14 percent of his income in 1949, 16 percent in 1959, 21 percent in 1973, and 44 percent in 1983.[16] This escalation of the carrying cost of housing bore particularly heavily on younger families; many had trouble assembling funds for down payments, and many found monthly payments unmanageable. For those who already owned homes, the increases in selling prices simply added to their wealth, albeit in a form that some felt unwilling to realize. Furthermore, the inflation of the 1970s increased the money incomes of then-current homeowners but did not increase their monthly payments, thereby sparing their budgets the strain that beset renters.[17] Ironically, for people who did stretch their budgets to buy homes, the slowdown of inflation in the 1980s means that there will be less growth of nominal incomes to relieve the pressure of fixed-dollar mortgage payments (although slower inflation has allowed favorable refinancing and has held down payments under adjustable-rate mortgages).

The increase in home carrying costs is substantial in relation to the relatively slow growth of incomes in the 1970s and 1980s. In fact, the increase in the carrying cost of a newly purchased median-priced home as a percentage of income is several times larger than the increase in the combined income and payroll taxes of a family with the median income, and similarly larger than the increase in after-tax income. Thus, it is important to put the housing and tax issues into perspective when thinking about the federal budget deficit. Reducing the deficit through tax increases beyond those reflected in tables 2.1 and 2.2 would have an obvious and direct negative effect on family incomes. But the large increases in carrying costs on homes should give some hint of the leverage on family well-being now held by interest rates. Should continuing large deficits dissuade foreign lenders from holding a large and growing U.S. government and private debt, the resulting increase in interest rates and downward pressure on the market values of existing homes, not to mention the macroeconomic consequences, could dwarf the effect of an increase in taxes.

As an example, the median income of two-parent families in 1988 (when the Tax Reform Act of 1986 is fully phased in) should be about $36,500, and the federal income tax for a typical family of four at that income level will be about $3,270. Suppose that there were a tax increase to raise $100 billion to close the federal budget deficit and, as a worst case for the typical family, that this were collected through a 25 percent across-the-board increase in the individual income tax. The typical family would pay roughly $820 per year more in taxes; but that amount is about equal to the additional interest on an $80,000 home mortgage from an increase of only one percentage point in the interest rate. Obviously, these figures represent the potential outcomes in only the broadest terms; but they should suggest the vulnerability of many families to continuing budget deficits and the contingencies they involve.

Reflecting changes in home prices and carrying costs in the measurement of real incomes has been notoriously difficult.[18] To represent the effects on the entire population, a price index should take account of the benefit of appreciation of existing homes for current owners as well as the burden on potential buyers; and it should recognize that few consumers buy a home at any given time. However, any price index conveying the average effects in this sense cannot depict the enormous distributional effects between owners and nonowners of the changes in the housing market.

## Inflation, New Products, and Quality Change

There are still further questions about whether incomes adequately represent living standards over time, or whether simple dollar figures give a distorted picture. Of several problems in this connection, perhaps the most important is measuring inflation in a period of technological change. When prices change and products do not, inflation is a simple concept. But when products are improved or entirely new products appear, it is no simple matter to quantify the effect on the purchasing power of a dollar of income. Some people argue that the rapidfire introduction of new and radically different products (home computers and videocassette recorders—VCRs—for example) and the substantial improvement in quality of others (such as automobile tires and home appliances) have caused an exaggeration of the measure of inflation and an understatement of real family incomes. If the prosperity of the 1950s and 1960s was measured in known commodities like houses and automobiles but the prosperity of the 1970s and 1980s came in radically new computers and VCRs, Americans' well-being might well be mismeasured by dollar incomes today. But measuring the quality of homes and automobiles was difficult in the 1950s, as changes in features made the end products different. And as the current generation has computers and VCRs, so earlier generations had new products like televisions, telephones, and radios to confound their measures of real income. So technological change in the products Americans buy may or may not make the measurement of real incomes today any less accurate than it was twenty or thirty years ago, and no definitive judgment is likely.

## Consumption versus Income

Consumption is certainly an important element in almost everyone's perception of personal well-being. It is easy to ignore consumption and dwell on income, under the implicit assumption that spending out of income is more or less constant; but in recent years, consumption behavior has changed significantly. Between 1973 and 1986, personal consumption expenditures have increased from 88.2 percent to 92.9 percent of personal income; people are saving less, and spending more, of their incomes.[19] If people measure their standards of living by how much they consume, rather than how much they earn, spending 4.7 percent more of the income they have is a perfect substitute for 4.7 percent more income.[20] Thus, over the past thirteen years, Americans' willingness to spend more of their incomes has compensated for about 0.4 percent per year less income growth—compared with actual growth of the median family income of 3.1 percent per year from 1954 to 1973, and 0.5 percent per year from 1973 to 1986. Americans therefore have increased their consumption since 1973 almost as much by decreasing their rate of saving as by increasing their incomes.

It is conceivable that many people have reconciled themselves to a lower level of saving and feel better off spending more today; and that is a useful insight into current living standards. Although this strategy prevents decreases in consumption in the short run, it inevitably must reduce wealth and consumption over the longer term, and certainly runs risks for retirement. So using consumption, rather than income, as a quantitative measure of well-being would make sense only if the focus were solely on the present; if long-term consumption is the issue, it is essential to look at measures of income.

## Conclusions

There are some real measurement issues in the assessment of incomes and living standards. The breadth of the measure chosen can make a significant difference in measured income; both in-kind income and taxes would noticeably affect census money income—in opposite directions. But none of these factors detracts from the common money income measure as an indicator of well-being. Its accuracy as a measure of income is reasonable, because omitted factors do not lean preponderantly one way. And income does act as a long-term constraint on living standards, even if changes in behavior can have measurable effects in the short run. Thus, the slowdown in growth of money incomes must be taken seriously.

## The Distribution of Family Incomes

The statistics on median incomes considered so far are indicative of the situation of the typical family or household. Nonetheless, as the divergent paths of the median incomes of different kinds of families and households indicate, there has been a range of experience. Thus, statistics on the distribution of incomes among families might or might not show a systematic trend of improvement or deterioration in the status of those above or below the typical income level.

The most common presentation of the distribution of income among families is through the shares of total income of each quintile (fifth), and also the top 5 percent, of families ranked by income. These income shares have been fairly stable over time (see table 2.3). Nonetheless, there was a modest movement toward greater equality of incomes (greater shares of total income received by lower quintiles, and smaller shares by upper quintiles) in the 1950s and 1960s, and a reversal of this trend in the 1970s and early 1980s. The latest figures show a postwar extreme in the inequality of the shares of income at the top and bottom of the distribution, with the share of the middle quintile at its postwar low.[21]

Two alternative views of this change in the distribution of income are perhaps even more striking. One is to consider the average real incomes within each quintile and the top 5 percent of the population. As figure 2.5 shows, the bottom quintile has enjoyed no real income growth since the late 1960s (in 1986 dollars, the average income in the lowest quintile in 1969 was $8,181; in 1986, it was $8,033). For the second quintile, the picture was not quite so bleak, but total real income growth since 1969 was only about 4 percent (or less than 0.2 percent per year). In contrast, the average real income of the top 5 percent of families grew by more than 30 percent (or about 1.6 percent per year). Even for the highest-income families, there was a slowdown starting in the early 1970s, but the growth of incomes at the bottom of the scale slowed even more.

Yet another perspective is to consider the size of the dollar shifts of income that these changes in quintile shares imply. Thus, between 1969 and 1986, the bottom quintile of families lost 1 percent of total money income. This represents a shift of about $22.5 billion, or roughly $1,750 per family. Over the same period, the second quintile lost more than 1.6 percent of total

TABLE 2.3

PERCENTAGE SHARE OF MONEY INCOME RECEIVED BY EACH QUINTILE AND TOP 5 PERCENT OF FAMILIES, RANKED BY INCOME, SELECTED YEARS, 1954–86

| Year | Lowest Quintile | Second Quintile | Middle Quintile | Fourth Quintile | Highest Quintile | Top 5 Percent |
|------|------|------|------|------|------|------|
| | | | *Percentage Distribution of Aggregate Income* | | | |
| 1954 | 4.5 | 12.1 | 17.7 | 23.9 | 41.8 | 16.3 |
| 1959 | 4.9 | 12.3 | 17.9 | 23.8 | 41.1 | 15.9 |
| 1964 | 5.1 | 12.0 | 17.7 | 24.0 | 41.2 | 15.9 |
| 1969 | 5.6 | 12.4 | 17.7 | 23.7 | 40.6 | 15.6 |
| 1974 | 5.5 | 12.0 | 17.5 | 24.0 | 41.0 | 15.5 |
| 1979 | 5.2 | 11.6 | 17.5 | 24.1 | 41.7 | 15.8 |
| 1980 | 5.1 | 11.6 | 17.5 | 24.3 | 41.6 | 15.3 |
| 1981 | 5.0 | 11.3 | 17.4 | 24.4 | 41.9 | 15.4 |
| 1982 | 4.7 | 11.2 | 17.1 | 24.3 | 42.7 | 16.0 |
| 1983 | 4.7 | 11.1 | 17.1 | 24.3 | 42.8 | 15.9 |
| 1984 | 4.7 | 11.0 | 17.0 | 24.4 | 42.9 | 16.0 |
| 1985 | 4.6 | 10.9 | 16.9 | 24.2 | 43.5 | 16.7 |
| 1986 | 4.6 | 10.8 | 16.8 | 24.0 | 43.7 | 17.0 |

SOURCE: See figure 2.1.

FIGURE 2.5

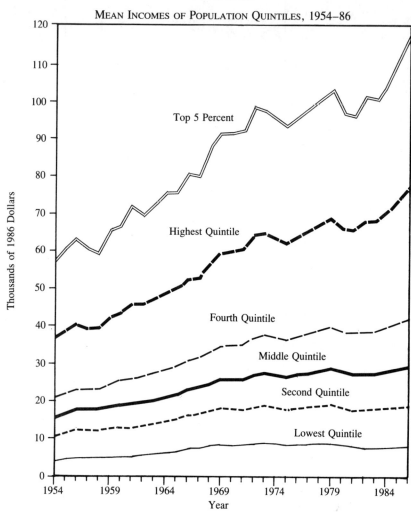

MEAN INCOMES OF POPULATION QUINTILES, 1954–86

SOURCE: See figure 2.1.

income and the middle quintile 0.9 percent. In contrast, the top 5 percent of families gained 1.4 percent of aggregate income, or almost $10,000 per family.[22] As in the case of the income slowdown, it is natural to search for causes; and again, the obvious candidates disappear under careful examination. The growing proportion of minority families could not have been the cause, because the trend in income distribution of white families taken alone has been toward greater inequality. The trend toward family dissolution and the growing number of one-parent families clearly contributed but could not have been solely at fault, because the trend in income distribution among husband-wife families alone was toward inequality over the same period.[23] Nor was the greater number of two-earner couples responsible, even though those families typically had incomes above the average. First, after 1970, when the shift toward greater inequality began, the number of two-earner couples exceeded the number of one-earner couples; so after that date, families sending a second spouse into the labor force were becoming more like the typical family, not less. Furthermore, the inequality of the income distribution among two-earner couples increased far less than that for all husband-wife families. So quantitatively, the shift toward second earners in families was in fact an equalizing influence and worked against the overall trend toward greater inequality.[24] One possible explanation is the decline in the real value of government transfer payments, particularly Aid to Families with Dependent Children, since the period of state and local fiscal stringency in the late 1970s.[25]

Thus, there is no clear villain in the shift toward greater inequality of family incomes, just as there was none in the slowdown of income growth. These unfavorable developments were pervasive and broadly based. Any further investigation must get to the roots of movements of family incomes.

## Individual Earned Incomes and the Family

In the United States in 1986, 73 percent of personal income was derived from wages and salaries and self-employment.[26] This simple arithmetic suggests that the level and the rate of growth of earned income, which have varied over time, are the strongest determinants of family incomes.

### The Level of Individual Wages

The behavior of wages can be analyzed most closely through observations of individual workers in surveys taken by the Bureau of the Census.[27] The annual mean real labor incomes of all workers and full-year workers grew by more than one-quarter over the 1960s but by less than 5 percent from 1969 through 1979 (see table 2.4). Growth thus far over the 1980s has been little improved. Growth in labor incomes for men slowed even more than growth for women over the 1970s, and women have enjoyed much greater wage growth thus far over the 1980s. This contrast between the modest progress of female workers and the relative stagnation of male earnings agrees with the findings of other studies.[28] Even the progress of female earnings slowed significantly in the 1970s, however, and so the mystery of slower income growth among families clearly extended to individual earnings as well.

**Possible Explanations of the Slowdown in Wage Growth.** The causes of the wage growth slowdown of the 1970s are naturally a matter of great interest. The fundamental inquiries look to the chief indicators of the productivity of an individual worker or of the work force as a whole—experience and education.

Beginning in the mid-1960s, as the baby boom began to come of working age, younger workers rushed into the U.S. job market; at the same time, women entered and reentered the labor force in unprecedented numbers, carrying relatively limited labor force experience with them. Young and inexperienced workers typically start at the bottom of the occupational ladder and work their way upward as they gain experience, become more productive, and find their ultimate roles in the job market. The U.S. economy performed quite well in expanding the bottom of the ladder so that so many of those labor market entrants could find places (although some did not). This broadening had the expected effect of increasing the number of low-paying jobs and pulling down average labor incomes. (In contrast, the major nations of Europe, whose labor forces grew rapidly over the same period, had less of a slowdown of wages but also much less growth in the number of jobs—and hence, more rapidly rising unemployment.) Young workers in the 1970s and 1980s faced still further difficulties in the frequent and sharp recessions of that period and the decline in investment per worker, which combined to reduce incomes and make starting a career more difficult. (See chapter 3 of this volume.)

In fact, the rapid influx of young workers could reduce incomes in two ways. One would simply be by making lower-paid young workers more numerous. Another, somewhat subtler, linkage would be for the baby boom to increase the competition among younger workers seeking entry-level jobs, causing their wages to be bid down even lower relative to those of the rest of the working population. This latter "crowding" effect would compound the simple "relative wage" effect to reduce average incomes even more.[29]

Both the "crowding" of young workers and their increasing proportion of the work force held down aggregate wages over the 1970s and the early 1980s. The relative proportion of male and female workers who were under

TABLE 2.4

MEAN ANNUAL EARNINGS OF INDIVIDUALS BY SEX AND WEEKS WORKED, SELECTED YEARS, 1959–86
(*In 1986 dollars*)

| Year | Women and Men, Number of Weeks Worked | | Women, Number of Weeks Worked | | Men, Number of Weeks Worked | |
|---|---|---|---|---|---|---|
| | At least One | At least Fifty | At least One | At least Fifty | At least One | At least Fifty |
| 1959 | 13,376 | 17,316 | 7,143 | 10,164 | 16,818 | 19,883 |
| 1969 | 17,028 | 22,088 | 9,641 | 13,302 | 22,107 | 26,022 |
| 1979 | 17,793 | 22,920 | 10,822 | 14,545 | 23,259 | 27,910 |
| 1986 | 18,733 | 23,545 | 12,767 | 16,325 | 23,708 | 28,621 |

SOURCES: U.S. Bureau of the Census, public use samples (1 in 1,000), 1960, 1970, and 1980; *Current Population Survey*, public use samples, 1980 and 1987.

age thirty increased steadily through 1979, from about one-fifth to more than one-quarter of those employed for the full year (see table 2.5). Furthermore, the earnings of young workers relative to those of middle-aged workers declined—from 68 percent to 54 percent for men, and from 94 percent to 77 percent for women. The shifting of the age distribution and the bidding down of the wages of young workers thus had a substantial depressing effect on the overall level of earnings.[30]

Working in the other direction was the increasing educational attainment of the population. Education is generally assumed to make workers more productive, and the marked increase in years of schooling over time should therefore have a positive effect on earnings. Table 2.6 shows a significant shift in the population toward greater educational attainment; the share of the work force without a high school education fell enormously from 1959, and the percentage with at least a college education more than doubled.[31] Further computations indicated that the increasing educational attainment of the population more than offset the unfavorable shift of the age distribution.[32]

Male workers may also have been crowded by female workers entering the labor force. As women made inroads into hitherto male-dominated occupations, they could have bid down the earnings in those categories, thus reducing the earnings of men. At the same time, because those occupations offered higher wages than those largely occupied by women, women's earnings could have increased more rapidly. This pattern would explain the more rapid growth of female than male earnings. It is difficult to say what role this influence played in the male wage growth slowdown, especially because the movement of women into traditionally male occupations has been limited.[33]

Other attempts at explaining the wage growth slowdown look beyond individual worker productivity to the shift in the allocation of the labor force among industrial categories, where ''deindustrialization'' is claimed to have forced workers from relatively high-paying manufacturing jobs into relatively low-paying service jobs. However, it is difficult to explain why workers should be paid differently in different sectors of an efficiently operating economy if their productivity is the same. From this point of view, shifts of the labor force among industries or occupations should not adversely affect aggregate earnings. The wage data confirm this benign view of ''deindustrialization.'' The wage growth slowdown covered a broad front of industrial categories and was not confined to any particular sector among either men or women; so a decline in employment in any one sector could not explain slow overall growth. Further quantitative analysis shows that undoing the change in the industrial composition in the labor force over the 1960-80 period would have actually reduced mean labor earnings among men. A similar analysis indicates that shifts among occupational categories reduced earnings

TABLE 2.5

PERCENTAGE DISTRIBUTION OF FULL-YEAR WORKERS AND AVERAGE ANNUAL REAL LABOR EARNINGS, BY AGE GROUP, SELECTED YEARS, 1959–86

| Age Group | Men | | | | Women | | | |
|---|---|---|---|---|---|---|---|---|
| | 1959 | 1969 | 1979 | 1986 | 1959 | 1969 | 1979 | 1986 |
| **Under 30** | | | | | | | | |
| Percentage of workers | 17.8 | 21.8 | 27.1 | 25.6 | 21.6 | 26.2 | 32.3 | 28.8 |
| Earnings as a percentage of the earnings of 40- to 49-year-olds | 68.3 | 64.9 | 58.0 | 53.9 | 94.3 | 89.1 | 86.7 | 76.7 |
| **30–39** | | | | | | | | |
| Percentage of workers | 27.4 | 23.2 | 26.8 | 30.5 | 21.9 | 17.8 | 23.8 | 28.9 |
| Earnings as a percentage of the earnings of 40- to 49-year-olds | 97.4 | 94.2 | 89.8 | 86.5 | 101.3 | 96.8 | 104.7 | 100.3 |
| **40–49** | | | | | | | | |
| Percentage of workers | 25.2 | 24.6 | 19.8 | 21.1 | 26.2 | 23.8 | 18.8 | 21.4 |
| Earnings as a percentage of the earnings of 40- to 49-year-olds | 100.0 | 100.0 | 100.0 | 100.0 | 100.0 | 100.0 | 100.0 | 100.0 |
| **50–59** | | | | | | | | |
| Percentage of workers | 18.8 | 20.0 | 18.0 | 15.1 | 20.1 | 21.8 | 17.0 | 14.2 |
| Earnings as a percentage of the earnings of 40- to 49-year-olds | 94.3 | 94.4 | 98.0 | 93.7 | 100.0 | 96.7 | 100.2 | 91.4 |
| **60 and over** | | | | | | | | |
| Percentage of workers | 10.9 | 10.3 | 8.3 | 7.7 | 10.2 | 10.4 | 8.1 | 6.6 |
| Earnings as a percentage of the earnings of 40- to 49-year-olds | 79.4 | 77.0 | 78.6 | 78.3 | 84.9 | 90.3 | 86.0 | 71.4 |

SOURCES: See table 2.4.

TABLE 2.6

PERCENTAGE DISTRIBUTION OF FULL-YEAR WORKERS AND AVERAGE ANNUAL REAL LABOR EARNINGS, BY EDUCATIONAL ATTAINMENT, SELECTED YEARS, 1959–86

| Education Level | Men | | | | Women | | | |
|---|---|---|---|---|---|---|---|---|
| | 1959 | 1969 | 1979 | 1986 | 1959 | 1969 | 1979 | 1986 |
| Less than high school | | | | | | | | |
| Percentage of total | 50.6 | 38.2 | 22.2 | 15.3 | 43.8 | 32.7 | 19.1 | 10.9 |
| Earnings as a percentage of the "College completed" group | 52.6 | 53.4 | 59.0 | 49.3 | 57.8 | 54.5 | 59.5 | 47.3 |
| High school completed | | | | | | | | |
| Percentage of total | 38.2 | 47.1 | 55.8 | 57.3 | 50.0 | 59.9 | 67.6 | 67.1 |
| Earnings as a percentage of the "College completed" group | 69.1 | 67.2 | 72.5 | 67.8 | 77.7 | 68.9 | 74.4 | 66.9 |
| College completed | | | | | | | | |
| Percentage of total | 8.3 | 10.3 | 14.4 | 17.9 | 5.2 | 6.1 | 10.1 | 16.3 |
| Earnings as a percentage of the "College completed" group | 100.0 | 100.0 | 100.0 | 100.0 | 100.0 | 100.0 | 100.0 | 100.0 |
| Some graduate school | | | | | | | | |
| Percentage of total | 3.0 | 4.4 | 7.6 | 9.5 | 1.0 | 1.3 | 3.2 | 5.7 |
| Earnings as a percentage of the "College completed" group | 115.8 | 128.8 | 123.7 | 126.1 | 124.1 | 124.4 | 128.6 | 129.9 |

SOURCES: See table 2.4.

modestly over the 1960s but increased earnings equally modestly over the 1970s.[34]

Also noteworthy over the entire period was a slow but steady erosion of the margin between the earnings of whites and nonwhites. Nonwhite men made significant relative progress over the 1960s; and in the 1970s and 1980s, when white incomes were stagnant, nonwhite incomes continued to grow at a modest pace. Among women, incomes of whites and nonwhites have become virtually equal.

## The Distribution of Earnings

As with the distribution of family income, the distribution of earnings has become less equal since the early 1970s; but the problem is confined to males, particularly those who worked less than the full year.[35] The list of potential causes of the growing inequality of earnings is much the same as that for the earnings growth slowdown. Younger workers tend to have a more unequal earnings distribution (as well as earnings below the average for the entire population), and the growing proportion of young workers in the population has tended to increase overall inequality. But well-educated workers tend to have more equal earnings, and the increasing educational attainment of the population has offset the unfavorable shift in the age profile of the population. Furthermore, because women's wages became more nearly equal to men's wages, and black wages became more nearly equal to whites' wages, the growing numbers of black and female workers did not increase the overall inequality of earnings.[36]

A more controversial suspect is the deindustrialization hypothesis; it is sometimes alleged that the decline of employment in the manufacturing sector has pushed workers into a service sector with a few high-paying jobs and many low-wage, dead-end jobs. Again, it is hard to explain why there would be a vastly different distribution of earnings among workers with similar skills. And again, the data fail to support a hypothesis of increasing earnings inequality because of industrial change. The increase in inequality occurred in virtually every industrial and occupational category, and the shift of workers among industries and occupations tended, if anything, to reduce overall inequality only modestly.[37]

**Summary.** Thus, again, the changes in incomes and inequality over the 1970s and 1980s have no clear cause. Greater inequality was not the sole result of demographic change, although the unfavorable shift in the age distribution with the entry of the baby boom into the labor force did contribute. Deindustrialization, or structural change in general, appeared to play no role. Instead, earnings were distributed less equally across the population and within most subgroups. And just as there is no clear cause for this trend toward inequality, so is there no obvious way to reverse it.

## Conclusions

What has been happening to U.S. living standards? Why? What does it portend for the future? And what, if anything, should be done about it?

It seems clear that there has been a marked slowdown in the growth of incomes and that incomes have been distributed less equally—both at the individual level, as earnings from labor, and as total family incomes. These unfavorable shifts have followed a period of unprecedented favorable move-ment toward both faster growth and greater equality. Certain groups have been spared some of the effects of the recent bad news. Women's earnings have been less adversely affected than men's, and racial minorities' incomes than whites' (although both women and minorities continue to receive less income than men, and one-parent families have fared especially poorly). Two-earner married couples have fared markedly better than others, but even their incomes have grown more slowly than in the 1950s and 1960s.

In some respects, this income growth slowdown might be doubted; mea-surement issues are critical. Fringe benefits and in-kind government transfers, not typically measured in family income, have grown more rapidly than money incomes and thus reduce any measured income growth slowdown—but they come nowhere near eliminating it. And in-kind benefits are valued by their recipients less highly than cash. Furthermore, there are other factors not included in cash income—notably the growing tax burden—that work in the other direction. So income measurement problems, although real, do not alter the basic conclusion that the growth of family incomes has slowed.

The population at large has clearly somewhat cushioned the effect of this income growth slowdown. People have tried to maintain their consump-tion by borrowing more; but this strategy has limits—and long-term costs. Families have reduced the number of children they have, and so their resources need not be spread so thinly; but this strategy has limits as well. Although these behavioral changes have postponed the effect of the income growth slowdown, there is no question that reduced income growth over time would impose a constraint on living standards.

Why have these marked changes in the level and distribution of incomes occurred? There is no definitive answer. The pace of income growth of the 1950s and 1960s could well have been unsustainable, resting largely on historical accident and the enormous prior sacrifices of war. If so, it would be a mistake to lament the passage of that era—and much more to the point to seek the greatest possible prosperity under the new circumstances. One factor that has certainly cost our economy growth, whether from the pace of the 1950s and 1960s or from some lower level, is the changing age profile of the population. The growing number of young workers in the 1970s both expanded a low-paid part of the work force and bid down wages on a broader front. The U.S. economy did well to accommodate these workers—the European economies fared less well, with more unemployment—but there was discernable downward pressure on wages. Conversely, the growing numbers of women and minority workers, and the alleged process of deindustrialization, had no measurable effect in reducing earnings and making them less equal. It is clear that personal choice played a role in the behavior of incomes, as marital dissolution created one-parent families who fared poorly, but greater labor force participation by married women boosted their families' incomes.

What do these developments portend for the future? If the income growth slowdown is driven largely by the unfavorable age profile, it is being undone as the baby boom matures. If the process of generational crowding and the bidding down of wages works in reverse, greater wage equality and faster growth may follow; but this unique circumstance is impossible to forecast with certainty. If the demographic trends driven by personal choice (particularly the greater marital dissolution and labor force participation of married women) continue, they will have their effects on the level and distribution of family incomes; but these effects have thus far largely been offsetting.

And what can be done if income growth continues slow and inequality continues to increase? There are two basic choices: treating the symptoms and treating the disease. Attacks on the symptoms through tax and transfer policies are widely understood. Indeed, the Tax Reform Act of 1986 was an important start in this direction, with significantly reduced taxes for low-income working families and a more progressive distribution of the overall tax burden (especially taking into account the increase in the corporate income tax, which many economists would agree is borne primarily by upper-income persons through their ownership of business capital). Interest continues to build in welfare reform, certainly motivated at least to some degree by the evidence of growing inequality.

Common sense usually suggests that it is better to treat the disease than the symptoms; the exception is when the disease is not well understood and when some of the potential treatments carry high risks and the others have limited remedial value at best. The generic prescription for more rapid growth of family incomes is faster and more stable growth of economic output and productivity; but, as is argued in chapter 3, economists have a limited understanding of the causes of growth and limited ability to promote growth and smooth the business cycle. Furthermore, the income growth slowdown quite likely rests, at least to some degree, on a lack of employable skills among a significant portion of the population. Improved and extended education—from preschool through adulthood—should build up those skills and thus have a payoff in income growth. However, it is uncertain how successful such efforts can be with adults—or even children well into the primary grades; and it is also uncertain how effective education is for even young children who have no prominent model of the reward to education and all too many models of the rewards to illicit behavior. Thus, education policies are expensive and largely unproved—their effect would be evident only in the very long run.

It is in focused attempts to increase and equalize incomes in the marketplace that our understanding is weakest and the potential damage by radical, errant policies is greatest. The only identifiable downward influences on incomes are beyond our reach. We cannot speed the maturing of the baby boom, and any policy intervention against the increase in marital dissolution would swim against the tide of individual choice.

But policy restraint is most needed with regard to allegations about structural change in the economy. Policies to subsidize or protect particular sectors because of their alleged importance to the distribution of earnings would not enhance efficiency or accelerate growth; rather, they would distort the allocation of resources and reduce real incomes for most of the population while delivering subsidies to a select group. Thus, the challenge to policy in the coming years may be largely to resist bogus treatments that would move our economic symptoms from one part of the economy to another, while worsening the underlying disease.

NOTES TO CHAPTER 2

1. U.S. Bureau of the Census, *Statistical Abstract of the United States, 1987* (Washington, D.C.: U.S. Government Printing Office, 1986), table 55, p. 42; table 61, p. 45; *Statistical Abstract of the United States, 1956*, table 2, p. 5; table 47, p. 47.

2. Presentation of income data over time raises two methodological issues: the choice of a statistical measure and the correction for inflation. The measure used here, the median income, is the income received by the middle-ranking, fiftieth-percentile, family. It is thus the best measure of the change in the situation of the typical family. Correction for inflation in U.S. income statistics has been a problem because of difficulties with the official Consumer Price Index (CPI). The CPI was widely suspected of overstating the rate of increase of the cost of homeownership over the inflationary period of the 1970s, as discussed in Alan S. Blinder, "The Consumer Price Index and the Measurement of Recent Inflation," *Brookings Papers on Economic Activity* 2 (1980): 539-65. The CPI methodology for measuring changes in the cost of homeownership was accordingly revised effective in 1983. Ironically, the old methodology, which probably overstated the increases in homeownership costs during the period of rising interest rates in the 1970s, was removed before it could make a compensating overstatement of the decline in cost during the period of falling interest rates in the 1980s. Thus, the CPI is not only inconsistent because of this important change in methodology, it is also biased upward because of the timing of the change. Hence its use probably understates real incomes. The Bureau of

Labor Statistics created an experimental measure of inflation in consumer prices, with the cost of homeownership based on the cost of renting an equivalent home. This price index, called the CPI-X1, was computed for the years from 1968 through 1982, when the CPI itself was revised to use this methodology. Combining the CPI-X1 (when available) with the regularly published CPI creates a price index with less distortion of the cost of homeownership, and thus a more accurate deflator for creating measures of standards of living. It is this latter index that is used in this chapter.

3. Council of Economic Advisers, *Economic Report of the President, January 1987* (Washington, D.C.: U.S. Government Printing Office, 1987), table 41.

4. *Statistical Abstract of the United States, 1987*, table 653, p. 382; see chapter 5 for a complete discussion.

5. Of course, statistics on family incomes for two different years do not imply that the same families are represented in each year; some families form or are dissolved between the two years, and others change from one- to two-earner status or vice versa. The statistics thus represent only the group of two-earner married couples in each particular year.

6. Women have made modest progress in entering relatively high-paying occupational categories that are largely dominated by men (Suzanne M. Bianchi and Daphne Spain, *American Women in Transition* [New York: Russell Sage Foundation, 1986], chapter 5). This progress, though modest, would increase the earnings of women as a group by more than the overall average rate of wage growth, and thereby could contribute to the more rapid growth of incomes of two-earner couples. Thus, the median earnings of full-time, full-year female workers, which hovered at about 60 percent of the earnings of comparable males for many years, reached 68 percent in 1985 (Nancy S. Barrett, "Women and the Economy," in *The American Woman 1987-88*, edited by Sara E. Rix [New York: Norton, 1987], 102, 124). It also seems likely that female workers' economic progress and married women's labor force participation proceeded hand-in-hand in a selective process. In 1954, the gap between the median income of one-earner couples and that of two-earner couples was so small (under $5,000 in 1986 dollars and less than $1,300 in 1954 dollars, or about 32 percent of the median for one-earner couples) that it seems likely that wives' work was often either casual employment or a response to low or reduced earnings on the part of the husband. As working wives became more common and accepted, however, it seems likely that wives of higher-earning men would work and that wives would enter the labor force less as a short-term response to financial stress and more as part of the building of a more lucrative career. Thus the gap between one-earner and two-earner incomes grew (to more than $12,500 in 1986 dollars, or almost 49 percent of the median income of one-earner couples).

7. *Statistical Abstract of the United States, 1987*, table 123, p. 80; *Historical Statistics of the United States, Colonial Times to 1970* (Washington, D.C.: U.S. Government Printing Office, 1976), 64; see chapter 5 of this volume for a discussion.

8. Other possible factors include financial stress through slower economic growth and the strains of combining working and family life for women. And of course, once marital dissolution became more common, divorce became more socially acceptable (Bianchi and Spain, *American Women in Transition*, chapter 1).

9. Frank S. Levy, *Dollars and Dreams: The Changing American Income Distribution* (New York: Russell Sage Foundation, 1987), 199.

10. Computations from the 1970 and 1980 census public use sample microdata files, by the author. This comparison between census years extends from 1969, a business-cycle peak, to 1979, another peak year.

11. National income and product accounts data are collected by the Bureau of Economic Analysis, Department of Commerce. As commonly measured using the published CPI, census family income is biased downward (see note 2 above). The family-income curve in figure 2.4 already has this bias corrected. Per capita personal income is deflated with the personal consumption expenditures deflator of the national income and product accounts, which is not subject to the home-cost bias of the CPI.

12. Another aspect of demographic change can distort per capita income. The maturing of the baby boom has added an increasing proportion of relatively low-wage workers to the labor

force. But the addition of these low-wage workers to the population can raise per capita income, even while it indicates a reduction of potential living standards among individuals and families. Consider the example of a population of families with average incomes of $20,000, single people with average incomes of $10,000, and enough children that average per capita income is $5,000. If a young adult leaves home to form his own household and earns an income of $7,500, it will raise per capita income even while it reduces the average income of unrelated individuals (and thus, presumably, average living standards). The final section of this paper suggests that this phenomenon has in fact distorted measured per capita income; young workers' incomes have fallen relative to the overall average. So a measure of per capita income can distort reality and is at best one piece of information about living standards.

13. For example, the Labor Department's measure of average hourly compensation including fringe benefits has its own slowdown, though less than that of cash wages, beginning in 1973. *Economic Report of the President, January 1987*, table B-43, p. 294.

14. Note that the median real family income rises over time, and so the tax burdens at a constant fraction of the median income are those on a rising, not a constant, level of real income.

15. The median home price in 1986 dollars increased from $79,232 in 1976 to $93,750 in 1982; first-time buyers reduced their down payments from an average of 18.0 percent in 1976 to 11.4 percent in 1985; and interest rates peaked in the midteens in the early 1980s (*Statistical Abstract of the United States, 1987*, tables 1293 and 1295, p. 716). It is likely that the median-price home in later years was larger or otherwise "better."

16. Frank S. Levy and Richard C. Michel, "An Economic Bust for the Baby Boom," *Challenge* (March-April 1986): 37.

17. Frank S. Levy and Richard C. Michel, "The Economic Future of the Baby Boom," The Urban Institute, Washington, D.C., processed, December 5, 1985; and Levy, *Dollars and Dreams*.

18. See note 2 above.

19. *Economic Report of the President, January 1987*, table B-25, p. 274. In fact, saving has decreased even more than consumption has increased, because reduced savings have increased households' interest expenses—a wedge between the national income accounts measures of personal consumption and personal saving.

20. Assuming, for sake of simplicity, that all income is spent on the margin.

21. There are three important qualifications about the statistics shown in table 2.3. First, the Census Bureau has always limited the maximum amount of income reported in its surveys to protect the confidentiality of the respondents. Over time, these maximum dollar amounts have been increased to keep pace with the growth of incomes. For income year 1985, the maximum dollar amount was increased from $99,999 to $299,999. This had the effect of significantly increasing the measured share of total income of the highest quintile and the top 5 percent of the population; without this change, the measured percentage of income going to the highest 5 percent of the population in 1985 would have declined by 0.2 percent instead of increasing by 0.7 percent, and the share of the highest quintile would not have changed instead of increasing by 0.6 percent. There is no question that the figures with the higher maximum stated incomes are more accurate, or that there has been a gradual trend toward inequality from the 1960s; however, the changes in that dollar ceiling do distort the measured movements of the income distribution over time and have certainly exaggerated the increase in inequality from 1984. Another important qualification of such income distribution statistics is that the same families do not remain in the bottom quintile (or the top quintile) year after year; there is mobility in the U.S. income distribution. Thus, if the share of income in a particular quintile declines from one year to the next, it is not to say that one identical group of families were relatively worse off in the second year than in the first. And finally, the omission of in-kind income and of taxes from census money income, as described earlier, affects the measured distribution of income as well as its measured growth. Frank Levy has concluded, however, that the omission of these forms of income has not led the measured trend of inequality to depart significantly from its actual path (Levy, *Dollars and Dreams*, 194-95).

22. This calculation from the official statistics is affected by the censoring of upper-income data described in note 21 above. In 1986 dollars, the maximum income reported in census statistics in 1969 was about $150,000; in 1986, it was $300,000. Thus, the share of income received by lower-income taxpayers in 1969 was understated, and the swing between 1969 and 1986 was correspondingly overstated. U.S. Department of Commerce, Bureau of the Census, *Current Population Reports*, Series P-60, *Money Income of Families and Individuals*, various numbers.

23. Joseph J. Minarik, "The Growth and Distribution of Incomes in the United States," Urban Institute Working Paper, Washington, D.C., 1988.

24. This is true in part because, over much of the period, two-earner couples were responding to economic hardship or low earnings on the part of the primary worker, as is discussed in note 6 above. Therefore, although some spouses of high-wage men entered the labor force and increased their families' incomes to a modest degree in percentage terms, other spouses of low-wage men entered the labor force and increased their families' incomes considerably in percentage terms. Levy, *Dollars and Dreams*, 161-62.

25. U.S. Congress, House Committee on Ways and Means, *Background Material and Data on Programs Within the Jurisdiction of the Committee on Ways and Means* (Washington, D.C.: U.S. Government Printing Office, March 6, 1987), 636-46; Levy, *Dollars and Dreams*, 182-91. A counterargument is that these transfers have created a dependent population that has swelled the lower end of the income distribution. Charles Murray, *Losing Ground: American Social Policy 1950-80* (New York: Basic Books, 1984).

26. *Economic Report of the President, January 1987*, table B-24, p. 272.

27. This analysis uses responses to the 1960, 1970, and 1980 decennial censuses, and to the 1980 and 1987 *Current Population Surveys*, to follow labor incomes (wages, salaries, and incomes from self-employment). The advantage of using these individual observations is that they can be manipulated and analyzed in any conceivable subgrouping, and according to any of an array of individual characteristics. The annual *Current Population Survey* obviously gives the latest possible year of data; the 1960 census is the earliest pertinent set of data on individual households.

28. Barrett, "Women and the Economy," 100-49; Richard B. Freeman, "The Effect of Demographic Factors on Age-Earnings Profiles," *Journal of Human Resources* 14, no. 3 (1980): 289-318; W. Norton Grubb and Robert H. Wilson, "The Distribution of Wages and Salaries, 1960-1980: The Contributions of Gender, Race, Sectoral Shifts and Regional Shifts," Lyndon B. Johnson School of Public Affairs, University of Texas at Austin, processed, 1987; Peter Henle and Paul Ryscavage, "The Distribution of Earned Income Among Men and Women, 1958-77," *Monthly Labor Review* 103 (April 1980): 3-10; Robert Z. Lawrence, "Sectoral Shifts and the Size of the Middle Class," *Brookings Review* 3 (Fall 1984): 3-11.

29. Martin D. Dooley and Peter Gottschalk, "Earnings Inequality among Males in the United States: Trends and the Effect of Labor Force Growth," *Journal of Political Economy* 92, no. 1 (1984): 59-89; Freeman, "The Effects of Demographic Factors"; Finis Welch, "Effects of Cohort Size on Earnings: The Baby Boom Babies' Financial Bust," *Journal of Political Economy* 87, no. 5, part 2 (1979): S65-S97.

30. Possibly noteworthy were two exceptions to this general pattern. First, the earnings of both male and female workers in their thirties declined relative to the earnings of workers in the peak earning age group (those in their forties) over the 1960s, despite rapid economic growth and despite the fact that the former age group became a smaller part of the labor force over that period. Perhaps this situation was caused by increased competition from the growing population of workers in their twenties. Second, the relative earnings of workers in their twenties have continued to decline thus far in the 1980s, even as their numbers as a proportion of the labor force have begun to decline. Again, this situation might be explained by the large relative size of the adjacent cohort of workers (in this instance, workers age thirty to thirty-five).

31. The payoff to greater education clearly fluctuated with the economy and was reduced temporarily in the 1979-80 recession, when the incomes of less-educated groups increased relative to those with a college degree.

32. Minarik, "The Growth and Distribution of Incomes in the United States."

33. Barrett, "Women and the Economy"; and Bianchi and Spain, *American Women in Transition*, chapter 5.

34. Minarik, "The Growth and Distribution of Incomes in the United States."

35. This finding coincides with Freeman, "The Effects of Demographic Factors"; Henle and Ryscavage, "The Distribution of Earned Income Among Men and Women"; Lawrence, "Sectoral Shifts"; and Grubb and Wilson, "The Distribution of Wages and Salaries." Both James Medoff, "The Structure of Hourly Earnings among U.S. Private Sector Employees, 1973-84," December 1984, Harvard University and National Bureau of Economic Research Discussion Paper, processed, and Marvin H. Kosters and Murray N. Ross, "The Influence of Employment Shifts and New Job Opportunities on the Growth and Distribution of Real Wages," in *Contemporary Economic Problems: Deficits, Taxes, and Economic Adjustments*, edited by Phillip Cagan (Washington, D.C.: American Enterprise Institute, 1987), using data on usual hourly earnings for all full-time workers, find no increase in inequality. One important issue not easily addressed is the growing number of working-age men who have no earnings at all; labor force participation among men twenty years old and over declined from 88 percent in 1954 to 79 percent in 1986 (*Economic Report of the President, January 1987*, table B-36, p. 286), and the number of black men ages twenty-five to fifty-five who had no earned income increased from 5 percent in 1969 to 11 percent in 1978 (Frank Levy, "Changes in the Employment Prospects for Black Males," *Brookings Papers on Economic Activity* 2 [1980]: 513-37). Including such persons in the analysis, which is not done in this study, would show a greater trend toward inequality.

36. Minarik, "The Growth and Distribution of Incomes in the United States."

37. Ibid.

# CHAPTER 3

# ECONOMIC GROWTH

Rudolph G. Penner

Economic growth is a mysterious phenomenon. There was very little of it through most of human history, but with the advent of the Industrial Revolution, our planet was forever changed. Once growth began, each generation of young people expected to be better off than their parents, but as growth has slowed in the United States and other countries those hopes have been jeopardized. The economic and social effects of this disappointment, although difficult to predict, cannot be desirable.

## The Characteristics of Modern Growth

Simon Kuznets has identified six characteristics of the new era.[1] First, per capita production and population began to grow at a very rapid rate on a sustained basis. The rate of growth of per capita production in the developed world between 1850 and 1960 was about ten times the estimated rate for the previous nine centuries. Because the rate of population growth was more than quadruple that of the earlier period, the rate of growth of total production rose by more than forty times.

While the author was director of the Congressional Budget Office, the CBO staff prepared "Economic Growth, Capital Formation, and the Federal Deficit," chapter 3 in *The Economic and Budget Outlook: Fiscal Years 1988–1992*, January 1987. This article benefited greatly from that effort, and I wish to thank the CBO staff, working under the direction of William Beeman, for that indirect assistance.

Second, productivity began to soar. The fact that per capita production grew even faster suggests higher productivity growth rates for labor, but the productivity of capital and land also began to grow at a much faster rate.

Third, the structure of the economy began to change rapidly. At first, manufacturing replaced agriculture; then, services rose relative to manufacturing. The size of individual units of production began to rise, and there was a shift from small, personal, individual proprietorships to more impersonal, larger organizations.

Fourth, the structure of society was also altered. It became more urbanized and more secular as the church lost its dominant role.

Fifth, the economies of the developed world reached out internationally, both peacefully and militarily, as colonies were established and trade and capital flows grew rapidly.

Sixth, the geographic area that is directly experiencing modern economic growth is severely limited. In 1973 when Kuznets wrote, Japan was the only country without a European heritage that had reached a high level of economic development. Since then we have witnessed rapid progress in newly industrialized countries such as South Korea and Taiwan, but large areas of Africa and Asia remain underdeveloped and the gap between rich and poor nations continues to grow.

It is not easy to explain why the Industrial Revolution began or why Britain was the the first country to experience it. But the emergence of modern science and the related explosion of innovative activity clearly played an important role. That role was self-sustaining as increases in productivity provided a surplus that could be partially reinvested in further scientific endeavors. Other sources of growth will be investigated as this analysis proceeds, but it is hard to imagine economic growth of any significance without technological change.

## The Importance of Growth

Most economists find it hard to believe that anyone has to be convinced of the benefits of growth, but society has witnessed numerous no-growth movements and Luddite attacks on new technologies through the ages. Such movements generally lose their fervor when, for brief periods of time, the economy experiences zero growth as a result of the business cycle. Once tried, zero growth quickly loses its appeal.

If total product grows at a 3 percent annual rate, it increases almost twentyfold over a century. At a 2 percent annual rate, per capita output or standards of living increase seven times over the same period. Because of the power of compounding, even small differentials in growth over much shorter periods of time imply significant changes in living standards. For example, if per capita output grows 2 percent rather than 1.5 percent for thirty years—approximately one generation—measured living standards will be about 16 percent higher.

Measuring total product is difficult. For lack of a better standard, the gross or net national product (GNP, NNP), adjusted for the effects of inflation, is generally used as a measure of total product. In a market economy, the worth of an individual product is recorded at the relative price at which it is traded in the marketplace. Thus, a lifesaving drug is valued at its market price, even though people who benefit from it would be willing to pay much more to have it available. At a more mundane level, new products, such as videocassette recorders, or improvements in the quality of old products probably add more to the quality of life than is indicated by the growth in the real GNP. The problems of measuring growth multiply in a planned economy, where the prices of goods are often set by the state, and it is not clear how a free market would value them.

The production of goods for the marketplace can also have bad aspects that are not recorded by the GNP. Pollution and the other health and safety hazards that accompany the production and consumption of goods and services do not have market prices and thus are not subtracted from traditional measures of living standards. Conversely, when some of the surplus provided by growth is used to improve the quality of the environment, health, or safety, the ensuing benefits are not recorded either.

Although severe measurement problems exist, they probably should not be overemphasized. If the unmeasured harm that sometimes accompanies measured growth could be quantified, it would be highly unlikely to alter the conclusion that sustained, measured growth provides a vast improvement in the quality of life. The unmeasured benefits of growth are enormous, and measured growth provides us with the wherewithal to deal with its bad aspects.

Although standards of living are usually measured by product per capita or consumption per capita, it is important to note that the growth of total product is also of considerable importance. For example, it determines the economic sacrifice necessary to achieve a given level of military power. Imagine that two countries start by devoting 6 percent of their GNP to defense spending, and assume that they are equally efficient in using these resources. If GNP grows at 3 percent in one country and at 2 percent in the other, the latter country will have to devote about 8 percent of its GNP to defense, or one-third more, after thirty years in order to keep up militarily. The relative size of a country is also important economically. A large country is more likely to have some monopoly power in international trade and so, in theory, can alter the terms of trade in its favor. This power gives it an advantage in international negotiation over trade and other policies.

Whatever the merits of growth, the fact is that we have become used to it. Many of our institutional arrangements depend on growth, and some were designed when it seemed realistic to be more optimistic about our growth prospects than can now be warranted. Among these arrangements, the most important is Social Security, which depends on each successive generation's having a higher per capita income so that an equal proportional transfer to older generations provides a positive rate of return on the contribution that workers made during their working lives.

## Growth as a Messy Process

Economists have become the butt of many jokes because, in attempting to explain reality, they are prone to assuming away the most difficult and interesting problems. Economic growth is commonly studied as though the economy is always in equilibrium. All economic actors are assumed to possess all existing technological and organizational knowledge, and all compete vigorously to maximize personal gain. Something that disturbs the system, such as an innovation, creates a new equilibrium path, whose characteristics can be described and contrasted with those of the old path. Sometimes the nature of the path between the equilibriums is studied, but more often it is not.

It has to be admitted that the growth process is messier than indicated by the traditional growth models favored by the profession. Growth may be inherently a disequilibrium rather than an equilibrium process. Technology marches forward erratically, and economic actors do not learn the latest techniques instantaneously. The process through which knowledge is created, spreads, is exploited, and sometimes overexploited is probably one of the most interesting aspects of growth—an aspect studied in some detail by Schumpeter.[2] Identifying the cultural and religious characteristics of a society that foster innovation, the spread of knowledge, saving, and work may be more intellectually interesting than identifying economic conditions that alter equilibriums, but it is also much harder.[3]

But the problem with messy processes is that they are difficult to understand. Although the few economists who have taken unconventional approaches to the study of growth have succeeded in being intellectually provocative, they have generally failed to produce insights that are both intellectually appealing and empirically verifiable. Without empirically verifiable propositions regarding growth, it is impossible to evaluate government policies designed to foster the process.

Although models that assume that economies are always in equilibrium may miss much that is important to economic growth, they do provide a precise organizational framework for studying what is important economically. Social variables may be inherently more important to growth than economic variables, but they are usually less amenable to government influence.

Richard Nelson has argued that this traditional approach of the economist is reminiscent of the drunk who looks for his lost watch under the lamppost, not because he lost it there, but because the light is better. His criticism may be well taken. The economy may be constantly subjected to such severe shocks from changes in economic and social variables that it never has a chance to approach the type of equilibrium growth path described by economists. In these circumstances, studying equilibriums and possible government actions to change them is beside the point. Although this is clearly a problem, it may not be so serious as it seems. To the contrary, if one examines two hundred years of modern economic growth, the remarkable thing about the trend line is its stability. Even an event as traumatic as the Great Depression appears as only a minor interruption in the almost inexorable upward trend in production at fairly stable growth rates.

A more perplexing implication of the Nelson analysis is that noneconomic forces may change in a way that alters the relative importance of the contribution to growth made by economic variables or of the nature of the interactions among them. Government may make a strong effort to change a variable that is no longer so important as it once was.

Economists must rely on social institutions' changing more slowly than economic variables do, which is usually the case (although economic analysis often misses some important noneconomic changes). But economists know more than they are usually given credit for (which is not much), and although they may occasionally make serious mistakes, the basic presumption of the following analysis is that traditional economic analyses of growth provide useful insights for policymakers hoping to influence growth. The light shone on the problem is often dim and a great deal of groping is necessary, but it is all that we have.

## How Much Growth is Enough?

If the usefulness of traditional analysis is conceded, it becomes meaningful to ask whether some equilibrium growth paths are superior to others or whether higher paths are always better.[4] The private market does reward private persons for taking actions that are conducive to growth: Savings earn a rate of return, higher wages result from harder work and investments in education, and innovations usually produce royalties or higher profits. It is generally believed, however, that the rewards given individuals are insufficient to provide enough growth. Government taxes income, and that reduces the reward to work, saving, and innovative activities. Moreover, it is often difficult for innovators to keep the full return on their discoveries because, despite the patent system, innovations can often be easily copied without the full return's being paid to the innovator.

Consequently, there is theoretically some rationale for government actions that encourage growth. It is therefore necessary to ask how vigorous these growth-inducing policies should be. All have costs.

The growth path can be raised by increasing capital formation, work effort, and the rate of technological change, and by improving the quality of the existing labor force and stock of capital. But, assuming that society is satisfied with the overall level of economic activity in the short run, there is no way to increase growth-related activities without reducing something else that society values. Government policies can be designed to increase savings and capital formation, but only by reducing consumption. That will hurt in the short run. People losing immediately may be persuaded that they will be rewarded with higher living standards eventually,[5] but it can take a very long time before consumption is restored to previous levels, and the main benefit probably accrues to future generations rather than to the generation making the sacrifice.[6]

Thus, growth-inducing policies are likely to impose costs on the present generation so that future generations can live a better life. Moreover, some in the present generation will lose more than others. Many of the policies favorable to growth are unfavorable to persons in the lower part of the income distribution. Consequently, society frequently faces a conflict between pursuing what it deems an equitable income distribution and attaining a higher growth path. Such choices cannot be made solely on economic grounds. A considerable dose of ethics is involved.

The analysis of growth policies becomes even more complicated when considered in an international setting. To the extent that the living standards of current and future generations of Americans are of interest here, it is necessary to be concerned with the creation of U.S.-owned wealth, whether it is located at home or abroad. Consequently, it should not be a matter of concern if a successful U.S. prosaving policy drives down U.S. rates of return to the point that some U.S. savings flow abroad. As long as the savings are not being pushed abroad by taxing savings invested at home at a higher rate, that is how the return to U.S. wealth and therefore future U.S. living standards will be maximized. If more than living standards—questions of U.S. military power, for example—are of interest, the size of total U.S. production may become important, and the location of U.S.-owned wealth becomes an issue. Similarly, policies that attract foreign capital to the United States raise U.S. production and U.S. living standards to the extent that American labor becomes more productive, but the increase in U.S. incomes is less great than the increase in U.S. production because foreigners have the right to the return on their capital even though it is located in the United States. Therefore, when growth policies are considered, it is always important to ask whether it is the growth of U.S. production or of U.S. incomes that is important. In a world of internationally mobile capital, they are two very different things.

## The Slowdown in Growth

As already mentioned, the United States has experienced a distinct slowdown in the pace of economic growth since 1973. Although this slowdown coincides with the onslaught of the energy crisis, various analysts assign different values to the importance of the rise in energy prices in explaining the break in the growth trend. In any case, the economy grew at a 3.7 percent annual rate in the period 1948 to 1973 and only at a 2.4 percent rate from 1973 through 1986.

The slowing of growth coincided with a particularly high rate of growth for the labor force and employment. Thus the slowdown in output per hour worked was even more dramatic than the slowdown in the growth of total output; as a result, wage growth was depressed. (The implications for the level and distribution of family income were discussed in chapter 2.)

Although there is little agreement as to the quantitative impact of different variables in explaining the growth slowdown, most economists begin with the same list of culprits:

1. As already noted in chapter 2, the members of the baby boom of the 1940s and 1950s began entering the labor force in large numbers in the 1970s, and the labor force on average became younger, less experienced, and presumably less productive over the decade. Simultaneously, women began entering the labor force in large numbers, also lowering the average experience level.

2. The earlier shift of workers from low-productivity agriculture to higher-productivity manufacturing slowed markedly after the mid-1960s. Most analysts assign some weight to this factor, but it involves a logical inconsistency. Although the techniques of growth accounting assume economic equilibrium, this factor, to be important, requires a disequilibrium—in that it

must be assumed that the marginal product of labor was persistently lower in agriculture than in other sectors prior to the mid-1960s.

3. Because the labor force grew rapidly and net investment was relatively low, the ratio of capital to labor grew less rapidly after 1973 than it had in the earlier period.

4. As already noted, energy prices rose rapidly in the mid- and late 1970s. Important structural changes were imposed on the economy, and some of the capital stock produced for an era of low energy prices became economically obsolete. Again, a large part of the problem involved adjusting to a disequilibrium before reaching a new, lower equilibrium growth path for the long term.

5. New regulations were imposed that reflected society's growing concern about the quality of the environment, health, and safety. The regulations often required investments or new activities whose product was not included in the measured GNP.

6. The economy experienced three significant recessions between 1973 and 1986, and unemployment remained at levels that were higher than those typical in the postwar period. The intensity with which the capital stock was used may have been lowered, and the labor force may have permanently lost valuable experience and changed its expectations in a way that lowered productivity.

7. The inflation rate was high and fluctuated greatly, as did the foreign exchange value of the dollar. Because of the interaction between inflation and the tax and regulatory system and because of the effects of the dollar's value on exports and imports, significant structural changes were imposed on the economy—changes that imposed substantial adjustment costs and made some of the capital stock economically obsolete.

8. From the late 1960s to the middle 1970s there was a slowdown in government-financed research and development expenditures related, in part, to the slowdown in spending on defense and the space program. As a result, beneficial spillover effects to the rest of the economy may have been reduced.

9. Increased crime and dishonesty directly imposed costs and required unproductive, preventive expenditures.

10. The rise in energy prices encouraged the exploitation of relatively unproductive energy sources; more generally, productivity in mining declined as the richest ores were depleted.

The literature that attempts to identify the quantitative importance of the individual factors listed above has been summarized by Wolff and others, whose results are shown in table 3.1. A common finding is that after accounting for all factors that are amenable to quantitative analysis, a considerable part of the slowdown in growth remains unexplained. Not having a

TABLE 3.1

ESTIMATES OF THE IMPORTANCE OF SELECTED FACTORS
IN THE PRODUCTIVITY SLOWDOWN

| *Factor and Researcher* | *Periods Compared* | *Percentage of Slowdown Attributed to Factor* |
|---|---|---|
| Capital formation | | |
| Capital-to-labor ratio growth | | |
| Denison (1979) | 1948–73/1973–76 | 4 |
| Kendrick | 1948–66/1973–78 | 21 |
| Clark | 1948–65/1965–73 | 35 |
| Nadiri | 1948–74/1974–78 | 38 |
| Tatom | 1950–72/1972–79 | 39 |
| Norsworthy and Harper | 1948–65/1965–73 | – |
| | 1965–73/1973–77 | 49 |
| Norsworthy, Harper, and Kunze | 1948–65/1965–73 | – |
| | 1965–73/1973–78 | 71 |
| Denison (1982) | 1948–73/1973–81 | 8 |
| Vintage effect | | |
| Kendrick | 1948–66/1973–78 | 10 |
| Clark | 1948–65/1965–73 | 14 |
| | 1965–73/1973–78 | 9 |
| Pollution and regulation | | |
| Denison (1979) | 1948–73/1973–76 | 13 |
| Kendrick | 1948–66/1973–78 | 16 |
| Denison (1982) | 1948–73/1973–81 | 6 |
| Energy price effect | | |
| Denison (1979) | 1948–72/1972–76 | 3 |
| Norsworthy, Harper, and Kunze | 1965–73/1973–78 | 16 |
| Hudson and Jorgenson[a] | 1948–72/1972–76 | approx. 20 |
| Labor quality | | |
| Hours worked (efficiency-adjusted) | | |
| Denison (1979) | 1948–73/1973–76 | 10 |
| Denison (1982) | 1948–73/1973–81 | 6 |
| Age-sex composition | | |
| Denison (1979) | 1948–73/1973–76 | 3 |
| Denison (1982) | 1948–73/1973–81 | 1 |
| Education | | |
| Denison (1979) | 1948–73/1973–76 | – 12 |
| Denison (1982) | 1948–73/1973–81 | – 3 |

(continued)

TABLE 3.1

ESTIMATES OF THE IMPORTANCE OF SELECTED FACTORS
IN THE PRODUCTIVITY SLOWDOWN
(CONTINUED)

| Factor and Researcher | Periods Compared | Percentage of Slowdown Attributed to Factor |
|---|---|---|
| Research and development | | |
| Denison (1979) | 1948–72/1972–76 | 3 |
| Griliches | 1965–73/1973–77 | 10 |
| Kendrick | 1948–66/1973–78 | 13 |
| Nadiri (whole economy) | 1948–74/1974–78 | 17 |
| Nadiri (private economy) | 1948–74/1974–78 | 37 |
| Output composition (resource allocation) | | |
| Denison (1979) | 1948–73/1973–76 | 13 |
| Kutcher, Mark and Norsworthy | 1947–66/1966–73 | 23 |
| Norsworthy, Harper, and Kunze | 1948–65/1965–73 | – |
| | 1965–73/1973–78 | 24 |
| Thurow | 1948–65/1965–72 | – |
| | 1965–72/1972–77 | 45–50 |
| Wolff | 1947–67/1967–76 | 48 |
| Nordhaus | 1948–65/1965–71 | 77 |
| Denison (1982) | 1948–73/1973–81 | 12 |

SOURCE: Edward N. Wolff, comment on paper by Edward F. Denison, "Accounting for Slower Economic Growth: An Update," in *International Comparisons of Productivity and Causes of the Slowdown*, edited by John W. Kendrick (Cambridge, Mass.: Ballinger, 1984, 50–51).

a. Percentage contribution based on Denison's estimate of a 2.97 percentage-point decline in overall productivity growth.

satisfactory explanation for the slowdown, of course, makes it very difficult to say what should be done about it.

Table 3.1 shows that different researchers differ widely as to the importance of the falling capital-to-labor ratio in explaining the growth slowdown. Economists' ignorance on this point is particularly troublesome, because the government possesses a number of policy instruments that are relevant to capital formation—direct public investment, tax incentives, and the budget deficit—and it is important to know whether it is worth using them.

A key conceptual issue involves the relationship between investment and the pace of technological change. Is new investment necessary to exploit new knowledge, or can it be exploited by rearranging the existing capital stock and labor force? If new investment is necessary, the return to policies that stimulate investment will be very much higher than if it is not. Exactly the same questions can be raised with regard to investments in human capital that also may be necessary to use new knowledge.

It is difficult to think of any innovation that does not require some investment in physical or human capital for its implementation. Some economists, like Denison, who treat technological change as though it is independent of investment, would not deny this point but would make the more subtle argument that investments implementing innovations are likely to be highly profitable and probably will be undertaken regardless of small changes in economic conditions or government policies. Thus, variations in aggregate investment are likely to be caused by variations in marginally profitable investments that have little to do with implementing technical change. But marginally profitable innovations exist as well, and if they require new investment to implement them, the choice whether to proceed could be quite sensitive to economic conditions and policies that affect the cost of capital.

It is, however, impossible to document this phenomenon empirically. Denison argues that if there were a strong relationship between investment and technological change, the capital stock would rapidly become technologically obsolete. This obsolescence would be manifested by much higher scrappage rates and by lower prices for secondhand capital goods than are actually observed.

Capital can become economically obsolete even if it is not technologically obsolete. The vast rise and fall of energy prices in the 1970s and 1980s and the large rise in imports in the 1980s are examples of phenomena that may reduce the productivity of old capital that is not suited to new conditions.[7] Such economic obsolescence could have played a role in the productivity slowdown, but again it is difficult to find evidence supporting this hypothesis in scrappage data or in secondhand markets.

Many economists have suggested that a slowing of technological change— whether related to or independent of the pace of capital formation—may have played a considerable role in the growth slowdown. But technological change is impossible to measure directly, and the evidence remains murky. There is some inconclusive indirect evidence, however. The rate of growth of industry spending on research and development (R&D) slowed in the 1970s, and that may have affected the pace of technological change with some time lag. More recently, beginning in 1980, industrial R&D has again begun to soar, but the number of patents issued peaked in 1972 and has yet to show any signs of responding to increased R&D activity.[8]

After an enormous amount of research by excellent scholars, however, the growth slowdown of the 1970s and early 1980s remains partially unexplained. Such a mystery tempts one to ask whether growth is being measured properly and whether the slowdown may be an illusion. It is particularly interesting that the trend in productivity growth in manufacturing and agriculture has remained the same since the 1950s, whereas the slowdown has been particularly acute in sectors such as mining, construction, and services.

In mining, the slowdown has a ready explanation. The richest deposits of minerals have been exploited over time, and the energy crisis encouraged the exploitation of less productive sources of oil. In construction, the issues are more complicated, but a change in the mix of the product may have played some role. It is, for example, much easier to construct an interstate highway across the wheat fields of Kansas than through the middle of a city—a more common activity in recent years.

In services, the issues are even more complex because of the diversity of activities found in the sector. In financial services, there has been an explosion of new products ranging from new financial instruments to automated teller machines. The efficiency impact of such innovations is devilishly difficult to estimate. In the retail trades, where measured productivity has been plummeting recently, changes in taste may be completely confounding the statistics. For example, if shoppers suddenly demand the services of a real live butcher behind the meat counter in the supermarket and are willing to pay for it in the form of increased meat prices, the relevant statistics will show increased inflation, more labor input to sell the same amount of meat, and a consequent fall in retail productivity. The increased service to the consumer is given no value by current accounting techniques.

But it is not enough to claim measurement problems—they have always existed. It is necessary to show that they have somehow become worse since 1973, and that is more difficult. It may be that productivity improvements are inherently more difficult to measure in the service industries and that their growing share of GNP has made the measurement problem more serious, but it takes a major act of faith to attribute the growth slowdown entirely to measurement illusion.

Richard Nelson has suggested a more profound measurement problem.[9] Because growth accounting is done by weighting the contribution of various factors by their share in national income, it assumes that the economy is always in equilibrium. To the extent that growth is a disequilibrium process, with new knowledge spreading slowly and the economy slow to adjust to external shocks, the traditional approach may yield a misleading picture of what is really important. Nelson also believes that the traditional approach, by treating different factors separately, misses some important interactions among them, such as the relationship between education and the creation and application of new technology—and pays insufficient attention to the characteristics of the changing institutional framework within which the factors operate. Testing Nelson's hypotheses can be done only at the most micro of levels and unfortunately such research has not progressed very far.

## Government Policy and the Sources of Growth

If so little is known about the reasons for the recent slowdown in growth, it might be concluded that government is helpless to do anything about it. But this conclusion would overstate the importance of the disagreements just described. While it is impossible to assign precise quantitative significance to various explanations, scholars generally agree on the list of variables that may have played a role and on the direction of the effects of changing the variables on the list. Because changing a variable by changing a government policy generally imposes some cost, in that some other policy goal cannot be pursued as vigorously, what is not known is the precise rate of return received by enduring that cost. In other words, policymakers must make their decisions under conditions of great risk and uncertainty, but this is common in matters of public policy. Indeed, policymakers are paid mainly to make decisions of this type.

In what follows, government policies that affect variables important to growth—the legal and institutional environment, technological change, and the quantity and quality of labor and capital—are examined in detail. The importance of short-term stabilization policy is also discussed briefly. In all cases, the uncertainty and the cost of progrowth policies are stressed. It is difficult to maintain a proper balance between stressing the importance of nurturing growth and fully describing the difficulties and uncertainties involved in formulating appropriate policies. The intent is not to suggest that policy should remain paralyzed. It is to suggest only that policymakers remain cautious. There are no easy answers, but that does not mean that difficult and uncertain policies should not be tried—as long as the risks are well understood.

### The Legal and Institutional Environment

In a mixed economy like that of the United States, the growth of the economy is largely the result of trillions of private decisions, as individuals and firms respond to the economic and social incentives facing them. A mixed market economy cannot function without private property and contract rights enforced by the state. Indeed, the most important thing that the government does may be to establish the legal and institutional rules of the game within which the growth process proceeds. The rules must be predictable, and any erosion of the rule of law must be viewed with alarm.

Enforcing the rules of the game can be costly, and the costs can rise significantly with any new threat to public order. For example, investments in increased airport security are costly not only to those making them but to millions of inconvenienced passengers as well. Overinvesting in maintaining public order can be as inefficient as underinvesting.

Changes in the rules of the game can also impose large efficiency costs. For example, the replacement of the old rule of caveat emptor with the new rule of product liability has undoubtedly raised production costs significantly.

But regardless of intense debates over the desirability of particular rules, many rules are necessary for the efficient functioning of a free-market economy, and government must enforce those rules. It is hard to imagine two things more incompatible than growth and anarchy.

Mancur Olson has analyzed a different institutional problem that may be of some significance.[10] He argues that as economies age, special interest groups become gradually more powerful and better entrenched. In an effort to acquire an ever higher proportion of national income for their own constituents, they successfully push the government to adopt policies inimical to the overall public interest and so retard economic growth.

In a democracy, it is difficult for government to inhibit public interest lobbying. Indeed, it may be preferable to encourage as much lobbying as possible. When every conceivable special interest group is represented, their efforts will offset one other. We may be rapidly approaching that stage in the United States.

## Technological Change

There is a broad consensus that the supply of innovations would be deficient in a completely free market, because innovators find it extremely difficult to capture the full worth of their innovation. Because it is relatively easy to copy new ideas, and copying reduces the reward to the innovator, there is a rationale for government subsidization of innovators. Part of the subsidy is often indirect. The ideal of perfect competition is often abandoned, and monopoly power is granted to the innovator by issuing a patent.

Hirshleifer[11] has questioned the conventional wisdom, arguing that successful innovations typically have two effects: they increase overall productivity and they alter the distribution of income. Innovators who exploit their prior knowledge of distributional effects can capture more than the full worth of their innovations. For example, Eli Whitney was foolish to engage in his ultimately futile effort to enforce his patent for the cotton gin. As soon as he understood the distributional implications of his invention, he should have devoted his efforts to buying cotton land on margin and selling sheep land short. The fact that Eli Whitney died penniless casts some doubt on the practicality of this argument, but the Hirshleifer argument is highly provocative and deserves more analysis.

However, the conventional wisdom has prevailed and government is an active participant in the innovative process. In fiscal 1986, the federal government spent $53.1 billion—about 5.4 percent of the total budget—on R&D activities and facilities. Of this amount, almost two-thirds was spent by the Defense Department, but some of that may have had beneficial side effects on the private sector. Between 1976 and 1986, defense R&D grew at an annual rate of 13.4 percent, whereas nondefense R&D, growing at 4.5 percent, fell short of the rate of inflation by about 1.5 percent per year. Nondefense R&D is one of the few nondefense spending areas favored by the Reagan administration in its 1988 budget, where it recommends a 12.3 percent increase between 1986 and 1988 compared with an assumed cumulative price increase of about 7 percent.[12]

It is, of course, very difficult to judge the effectiveness of government spending for R&D. The conventional wisdom holds that that it is most important to subsidize basic research where the returns are particularly uncertain and difficult to capture. The Reagan administration has followed this strategy and recommends more than a 20 percent increase in defense and nondefense basic research spending between 1986 and 1988.

Although government spending on R&D is often considered sacrosanct and discussed as though no amount is too much, it must be remembered that R&D funds are as difficult to allocate effectively as any other sort of public spending. Like other spending, R&D funding is susceptible to special interest group pressures and often goes into the pork barrel along with water projects and other public investments.

In addition to the subsidies provided by direct spending, research activities receive important tax benefits. Although research expenditures are in the nature of an investment, in that they pay off over a long period of time, the tax law allows them to be deducted from taxable income immediately. This is equivalent to eliminating the immediate income tax burden on the return to the investment. In the corporate sector, the returns are eventually taxed by the personal income tax when they show up as dividends or capital gains.

Increases in spending for research and experimentation (R&E) over a base of past spending receive a tax credit of 25 percent. Combined with expensing, this credit has the effect of making the after-tax return to qualified expenditures higher than the before-tax return, that is, a negative tax is levied.

The credit was put on an incremental basis in order to reduce the tax subsidy to outlays that would have been made without the credit. Of course, many of the subsidized increases would have occurred anyway, and some firms whose R&E outlays are declining might have been induced to cut spending less if they had qualified for the credit. As it is now structured, the credit sometimes has the perverse result of reducing a firm's R&E spending one year so that more of its spending qualifies for the credit in future years.

Because the effectiveness of the current credit has been so often questioned, the Tax Reform Act of 1986 narrowed its scope somewhat and renewed it only through 1988. Whether it should be renewed beyond that date raises three issues. First, how much of an R&E subsidy is enough? That is to say, is expensing sufficient or is more of a subsidy warranted? Second, if more than expensing is warranted, should it be done on the tax or expenditure side of the budget? Third, if tax subsidies are desirable, can the current credit be redesigned to be more effective, or is a completely different approach desirable?

These issues cannot be resolved here, but a few points can be made. First, the answer to the question "How much is enough?" depends on the social rate of return to the R&E that is likely to be stimulated per dollar of subsidy. Estimating the social rate of return to further R&E spending is no easy trick, but people who attempt it tend to obtain very high estimates.[13] This result seems to imply that further subsidies are warranted, but a subsidy must be so designed that it does not take too many dollars of subsidy to stimulate an additional dollar of R&E spending. It is hard to design a subsidy system that does not end up subsidizing much spending that would have occurred in the absence of the subsidy. Economists call subsidies for activities that would have taken place anyway "windfalls," and, because they do not absorb any resources directly, they are often considered to be costless transfers of income from the public sector to recipients. But it must be remembered that these transfers have to be financed, and the taxes levied or debt issued to finance them do have costs; these costs are considered in some detail later.

If an additional subsidy is provided, it is not easy to decide whether it should be on the tax or spending side of the budget. The tax subsidy related to expensing is easy to administer because it does not require the explicit differentiation of R&E outlays from other expenditure items. Once a tax credit is provided, such differentiation becomes necessary and numerous definitional problems are raised. In the first instance, the taxpayer makes the decision, and it is not practical to challenge all the dubious choices that are made. As a result, many expenditures that receive a subsidy are sufficiently dubious that such subsidization would not be tolerated in an outlay program. In an outlay program, the decision regarding which firms and projects to subsidize would have to be made bureaucratically, and such decisions are vulnerable to political interference and considerable waste as well. It is often alleged that outlay subsidies are scrutinized more carefully and more frequently than tax subsidies, but it is hard to give this argument much weight with regard to the R&E credit, which has been reconsidered and debated frequently during its short life.

If the subsidy remains on the tax side, there is good reason to consider changing its design. For example, the credit could be provided to all spending as opposed to incremental spending. The perverse incentives inherent in the present structure would be eliminated, and firms whose spending would otherwise decline would receive an incentive to curb the decline or reverse it. For the subsidy to remain revenue neutral, however, the rate of credit would have to be lowered. A lower marginal incentive would be available to more firms, and some spending may be subsidized that would have occurred anyway. But there is a strong possibility that a credit of this type would be more cost-effective.

Totally different tax subsidies also could be considered. For example, equipment and structures related to R&E are now depreciated like any other investment, but they could be expensed. Administrative questions would abound, however, in deciding such things as how to handle equipment used both for research and regular production.

## The Quantity and Quality of Labor

Labor is the most important contributor to the growth of total output, accounting for approximately three-quarters of national income. An extraordinary number of studies have attempted to document the effects of government policies on the quantity and quality of labor, and the research efforts of the past cannot be done justice here.[14] Although there is much disagreement regarding the overall sensitivity of labor supply to tax and transfer programs, it is possible to make a few generalizations about recent results. First, whatever the sensitivity of the overall supply of labor, the response to changes in economic incentives seems to be greater among secondary workers—employed wives and teenagers—than among adult men. Second, as econometric techniques have become more sophisticated, researchers have tended to find stronger responses to economic incentives. The results of such work are still, however, regarded as being highly controversial.[15]

Tax policy viewed in isolation is hardest to contend with because the theoretical effects of increasing income taxes are ambiguous. An increase in the tax rate reduces the reward from extra work and so would be expected to reduce effort. But higher tax rates also make taxpayers poorer and so would be expected to reduce their consumption of all sorts of good things, including leisure time. Put another way, taxpayers have to work harder to achieve their former living standard, and this may spur greater work effort. The fact that the two theoretical effects may cancel out does not mean that tax policy is unimportant. If both effects are very strong, a proportional tax system raising the same income as one that is more progressive may significantly raise work effort.

Transfer programs that depend on income do not possess the same ambiguity as taxes. They convey income to the recipients, thus making them more likely to consume more leisure, and, because benefits fall as private income rises, they reduce the reward to extra effort. Again, recent research suggests that the strongest negative labor supply effects occur among employed wives and teenagers.

The results just referred to view tax and transfer policy in isolation, but the proceeds from higher taxes must be used for something—to finance greater spending, reduce the deficit, or reduce some other tax. Similarly, increases in transfers must be financed. It can be said with considerable confidence that increased income taxes used to finance income-dependent transfers reduce work effort. The reward for extra work is reduced by both the increased taxes and the increased transfers, but overall income levels remain unaffected initially. Therefore, there is no overall change in people's ability to afford leisure. (This result could be contradicted only if taxpayers and transfer recipients reacted very differently to changes in their standards of living.) Tax increases used to finance government purchases of goods and services or to reduce debt or some other tax have a more ambiguous effect. It is necessary to know the labor supply effect of the other side of the policy decision before reaching any conclusion.

All this clearly suggests that society often faces a conflict between improving economic efficiency and growth and achieving a socially acceptable income distribution. This conflict is present in all ideologies. Even the most conservative and fervent proponents of growth advocate retaining the income tax, although they would make it less progressive. But even a proportional income tax is less efficient than a head tax, and no one advocates the latter.

Although there is always a conflict between efficiency and equity, and economists possess no expertise in choosing how the two goals should be balanced, economists can identify policies that impose especially high efficiency costs in order to achieve modest redistributions of income. For example, very high marginal tax rates are probably self-defeating. They inspire illegal tax evasion, and legal tax avoidance becomes very costly to society as people pursue occupations not because they are productive, but because they provide the greatest opportunities for sheltering income. Moreover, with very high marginal tax rates, political demands to create new tax loopholes become more intense and are more likely to be successful.

Over time, the top federal marginal income tax rate in the United States has come down significantly. From 91 percent in the 1950s and early 1960s, it was reduced to 70 percent by the 1964 tax cut; it was lowered further to 50 percent by the 1981 tax cut (it had risen briefly because of the Vietnam War surtax). Now, as a result of the 1986 tax reform, the highest rate is 33 percent. Although a few people call for even lower rates, the United States has clearly come a long way in the pursuit of economic efficiency for higher-income groups. The rates affecting most other taxpayers have not changed so much. The inflation of the 1970s pushed the middle class into higher tax brackets and undid the benefits of the 1964 marginal rate cuts for many. The 1981 cuts attempted to offset most of the effects of past inflation and indexed the tax rate structure. The effects of the more recent tax reform on the middle classes are more complicated and less easy to characterize, but many low-income taxpayers were taken off the tax rolls altogether. The main point is that, whatever problems remain, they have greatly diminished over the years, and the momentum for further marginal rate cuts in the income tax is unlikely to be strong.

Nevertheless, there are still instances in which the cumulative marginal rates resulting from a combination of the federal income tax, state, and local income taxes, the payroll tax, and benefit reductions under transfer programs can be very high, and this problem always deserves attention. The worst instances result from discontinuities, which economists refer to as notches. For example, in most states, only recipients of welfare qualify for Medicaid. People working their way off welfare may face a loss in Medicaid benefits far exceeding their additional wage for an implied marginal tax rate far in excess of 100 percent. The budget cost of reducing such penalties is often very high, but so may be the gains in economic efficiency.

There are other instances in which efficiency gains can be purchased without budget cost and with little effect on income distribution. For example, many economists believe that the unemployment insurance system raises the unemployment rate by subsidizing temporary layoffs. In the absence of such a system, employers and employees would have more of an incentive to agree to spread work out more evenly throughout the year. A policy change that would more carefully align the payroll tax paid by a firm with its employment history would reduce such inefficiency.

It might be asked whether it is counterproductive to search for policy reforms to increase the supply of labor when so many people are unemployed. That line of argument misses the point of the sort of reform discussed earlier. Some portion of the unemployed population is unemployed because of disincentives created by public policy. This portion is likely to become relatively more important as the overall unemployment rate falls. At some point the overall unemployment rate cannot be further reduced without causing inflation. A major reason for trying to make labor markets more efficient is to lower the unemployment rate at which this occurs. Then policymakers can aim for a lower employment rate over the entire business cycle. Although efforts to increase the supply of labor might temporarily raise the measured unemployment rate, any short-term loss that results would be overwhelmed by gains in the long term.

Studies of economic growth emphasize the quality of labor input as well as its quantity. Government's main effect on the quality of input is thought to stem from the quantity and composition of its spending on education and training. But the importance of government laws and regulations also should be noted. They determine what sort of labor can be used (e.g., child labor laws) and how it can be used (e.g., occupational health and safety rules); more generally, they establish the legal framework within which explicit and implicit contracts are negotiated between employers and employees.

The bulk of public spending for education occurs at the state and local levels of government. The federal government plays only a minimal role in aiding elementary and secondary education, but a slightly more important relative role in higher education.

Denison estimates that the improved education of the labor force contributed 0.53 percentage point of the 3.59 percent annual rate of growth of the nonresidential business sector in the 1948–73 period, and 0.61 percentage point of the 1.80 percent annual growth rate in the 1973–81 period. In other words, the slowdown would have been 4 percent greater had it not been for the improved contribution of education.

The Denison finding refers to the beneficial effect of educational expenditures. To calculate the rate of return to expenditures on education or to decide whether it would be worthwhile to increase those expenditures in the future, it is necessary to relate benefits to costs. The rate of return to education is often measured by the increase in compensation experienced as one invests more in schooling. There is some controversy as to whether education actually increases the productivity of the person educated or simply serves as a filtering device, identifying people with ability by forcing them to leap various educational hurdles. In the latter role, education still performs an economically valuable service for employers, but there may be cheaper ways of gaining the same information—and it might be argued that employers should bear more of the cost themselves by taking more risks with new hires.[16]

Conversely, measuring the rate of return to education by focusing solely on the associated increase in compensation may miss many of its social benefits even when those benefits are judged solely by the contribution of education to economic growth. If a higher educational level makes a worker better able to create or apply new techniques, there may be a link between educational investments and the pace of technical change—a link that may not be identified by analyses such as that of Denison, who treats the two inputs as completely separable. The greater contribution of better-educated persons to the pace of technological progress may not be capturable in their compensation for the same reasons that the returns to new technology are not entirely capturable.

If, however, it is decided that a greater social investment in education is warranted, many issues remain to be resolved. For example, what sort of educational expenditure is most productive?[17] What level of government should make the investment—federal, state, or local? Should aid be focused on the student or on the educational institution? Space limitations prevent such issues from being explored here.

In addition to supporting formal education, the government has invested in job-training programs over the years, especially for disadvantaged and displaced workers. Evidence on the success rate of such programs is mixed and difficult to summarize briefly.[18] Generally, the programs seem to have had greater success in training women than men, but some programs, such as the Jobs Corps, seem to have provided high returns for both sexes. Evaluations suggest that the income of participants was raised, but the increased income seems to have resulted from improving the employability of individual workers rather than from improving their productivity. That is to say, participants seemed better able to get and hold jobs and so worked more hours, but at about the same rate of pay as before. Clearly, government must proceed with care in the training area, making sure that programs are well designed. Considerable experimentation would seem desirable before embarking on full-blown program initiatives.

## The Quantity and Quality of Capital

Table 3.2 illustrates recent trends in savings and investment in the United States since the 1950s. Gross investment relative to GNP is only slightly less in the 1980s than it was in earlier periods. Gross savings have, however, declined more significantly. Before 1979, the United States, on average, supplied savings to the rest of the world, but more recently we have become dependent on foreign savers to finance our investments. That means, of course, that they will reap a higher proportion of the return to capital located in the United States; in other words, Americans will not retain the full benefit of the continued high levels of investment.

TABLE 3.2

GROSS AND NET INVESTMENT AND SAVINGS AS A PERCENTAGE OF GROSS AND NET
NATIONAL PRODUCT BY DECADE, 1950–86

| Years | Gross Investment | Gross U.S. Savings | Gross Foreign Savings | Net Investment[a] | Net Savings[a] |
|-------|------------------|--------------------|-----------------------|-------------------|----------------|
| 1950–59 | 16.1 | 16.0 | −0.2 | 8.1 | 8.0 |
| 1960–69 | 15.6 | 16.3 | −0.6 | 7.8 | 8.6 |
| 1970–79 | 16.7 | 16.7 | −0.2 | 7.7 | 7.9 |
| 1980–86 | 15.9 | 14.4 | 1.5 | 5.3 | 3.5 |

SOURCE: U.S. Department of Commerce, Bureau of Economic Analysis.
  NOTE: As a percentage of GNP, gross U.S. and foreign savings should, by definition, add up
        to gross investment. Rounding and a statistical discrepancy prevent this from occurring,
        however.
   a. As a percentage of NNP.

Over the years, depreciation has grown relative to gross investment, as investments in shorter-lived assets have become more prevalent. Consequently, net investment has declined more significantly in the 1980s, and net saving has dropped precipitously, largely because of the enormous federal budget deficit. Whether it is important to focus on gross or net investment is a matter of some controversy. Some economists question recent measures of depreciation as upwardly biased. Furthermore, gross investment is of considerable importance if investment is accepted as being important to the pace of technological change. Then a rapid turnover of the capital stock suggests that its average quality is improving rapidly. But if the productivity of investment is better measured net of depreciation, the decline of net investment then becomes more alarming. Whatever concept is used for investment, the more rapid decline of gross and net domestic savings implies that Americans own less of the capital stock, and that is also a matter of concern.

Numerous government policies influence saving and investment decisions. Federal, state, and local governments directly influence the pace of capital formation through their decisions regarding the appropriate amount of public capital formation. At the federal level, the rate of nondefense physical capital formation has declined significantly since the mid-1960s. In 1965, direct spending on such capital formation amounted to 0.45 percent of the GNP. By 1986, the figure had fallen to 0.27 percent. Capital formation indirectly supported by grants to state and local government fell from 0.74 to 0.63 percent of the GNP over the same period. In absolute real terms, net federal investment in fiscal 1986 was little different from its levels in the early 1970s. State and local investment fell from about 3 percent of the GNP in 1964–65 to about 2 percent in 1984–85.

Of course, the fact that such investment has declined relatively reveals little about the rate of return to further public investment in the 1980s. Some of the decline is related to reduced public investment in water projects or classic pork-barrel projects that were not thought to have a high rate of return in the first place. Another portion of the restraint is related to the virtual completion of the interstate highway system, a major public works project of the late 1950s and 1960s. Nevertheless, many economists argue that the public infrastructure has been deteriorating in recent years and that the decline in public investment is related to the budget pressures imposed by growing entitlements more than to a lack of socially profitable public investment opportunities.

The government influences the demand for private investment through its effect on aggregate demand in the economy, monetary policy's influence on interest rates, and tax policy's effect on rates of return. Economists agree that changes in the quantity of sales or demand are very important in influencing a firm's investment decisions, but there is considerably more controversy about the quantitative importance of changes in the cost of capital. However, most economists assign the cost of capital some importance, and most policy debates relate to the government's role in altering that variable.

The real interest rate is crucially important to the cost of capital; its influence is strongest for longer-term investments. Real interest rates can be influenced in the short run by monetary policy, but economists disagree about whether they can be influenced over the longer term—how the longer term should be defined.

The most interesting policy debates of recent years have involved the role of tax policy in influencing the cost of capital. Tax policy is important in determining what the rate of tax should be on capital income, at what rate investments can be depreciated for tax purposes, and whether an extra incentive in the form of a tax credit or other subsidy should be provided for investment expenditures.

Between 1954 and 1986, depreciation deductions became more and more generous; there was a downward, if fluctuating, trend in the corporate and other marginal tax rates, and an investment tax credit was periodically provided for equipment investment. Particular types of investment, such as that in multifamily dwellings for low-income renters, received especially generous tax treatment. In general, whenever it was deemed desirable to stimulate investment, incentives were provided directly to new investment by accelerating depreciation deductions and providing an investment tax credit rather than by lowering the tax rate on capital income, which would lower the tax burden on both old and new investment. The strategy was to provide the biggest bang for the buck by encouraging new investment while not losing tax revenues resulting from investments made in the past.

Obviously, the degree to which this strategy could be effective was limited. For some new investments the tax burden became negative, that is to say, the after-tax rate of return exceeded the before-tax rate of return. But this was true only if investors had sufficient income against which to deduct the various tax incentives or if deductions and credits could be sold to other parties in the form of tax shelters. Some enjoyed the whole panoply of incentives, while others lost them. A large number of distortions and inequities developed, and the response was the Tax Reform Act of 1986.

Depreciation deductions were made less generous, the investment tax credit was eliminated, and limitations were imposed on the creation of tax shelters. At the same time, corporate and personal tax rates were lowered. The net effect, however, somewhat raised the effective tax rate on new investment. The federal income tax system taxes capital income more heavily than wage income, because much capital income is taxed first by the corporate tax and then by the personal income tax when corporate profits are distributed as dividends or realized as capital gains. When the total tax system, including payroll taxes and state and local sales taxes, is examined, it becomes less clear whether capital or labor bears a heavier tax burden, but tax reform probably increased the burden on capital compared with the previous level.

Some economists believe that tax reform will significantly reduce the capital stock in the future and reduce the potential growth of the United States.[19] Others point to the fact that, as a result of tax reform, different types of capital will be taxed more equally. Consequently, investments are more likely to be made where they are socially most productive rather than where they obtain the greatest tax benefits. Although the capital stock may well be lower in the future, it will be more efficiently allocated and this improved allocation will offset the reduced amount.

Since Hobbes wrote more than two hundred years ago, arguments have been made for not taxing capital at all. The arguments are partly ethical (that it is fairer to tax people on what they extract from the economy as roughly measured by their consumption than on what they contribute as roughly measured by their income) and partly economic (a consumption tax would be more conducive to saving and investing and therefore to economic growth). Consumption taxes are often opposed as too burdensome on low-income groups, but it is possible to design consumption taxes to be quite progressive.[20] Therefore the question of what should be taxed can be debated separately from questions of how the tax burden should be distributed. Nevertheless, the tax reform debate clearly reached the conclusion that capital income should be taxed at quite a high rate. An implicit decision was made to sacrifice some economic growth on the ground that total income, including that from capital, was a better indication of the ability to pay taxes than consumption alone. The argument over where the greatest tax burden should lie—consumption versus investment, capital versus wage income—is sure to break out anew whenever tax increases or decreases are debated in the future.

Analyses of the effect of the tax-transfer system on saving are as complex as analyses of the effect on work effort. As with work effort, the taxation of the income from saving has two opposite theoretical effects. If it is assumed that all saving is to finance future consumption, a tax on the income from saving is like an excise tax on future consumption. On the one hand, it favors present consumption over future consumption and so discourages saving. On the other hand, it reduces all consumption and so may increase saving if there is a tendency to reduce present more than future consumption in response to a loss of income. Put another way, a tax on the income from saving may encourage it because one has to save more in order to achieve any given consumption level in the future. The same argument can be made if the goal of saving is to leave a larger estate or for any other purpose. But a tax on saving cannot be analyzed in isolation. The funds raised by the tax must be used for something. If the funds are used to reduce a consumption tax, we can be sure that the effect will be to lower saving. If they are used to reduce the deficit, the effect is more complicated and will be discussed later. If the funds are used to finance a transfer payment, the total effect depends on the type of transfer.

The most important transfer payments involve retirement systems, and the most important retirement system is Social Security. There has been extensive debate about the effect of Social Security on private saving behavior. If, in its absence, children would support retired parents, it probably does not affect saving significantly. Payroll taxes simply substitute for payments from children to parents. If it is instead a substitute for private pension systems, its effect is probably more important. The current Social Security system— being largely a transfer of payroll taxes from the young to the old—does not provide real savings for the economy. There is currently a surplus of payroll tax receipts over pension payments, and that surplus is invested in a trust fund. But the fund is much smaller than it would have to be to fund Social Security fully, and, besides, the surplus is used to finance the deficit in the rest of the government's budget. A private pension system would, on the other hand, require real saving on the part of participants in order to fund it.[21]

It is possible that that Social Security and other government pension plans substitute for intergenerational transfers and private pension plans. That is, government pensions may provide higher benefits than those provided by voluntary transfers from children to parents, thus having some effect on saving, but not so much as if they substituted only for funded private pensions. This implies, however, that increases in benefits would have a large impact on private saving even though the system as a whole does not. As is so often the case, empirical research does not provide clear evidence of the effects of Social Security and other pension plans on saving. Studies can be found to support any conceivable prejudice.[22]

The lack of unambiguous evidence on the effects of the tax-transfer system on saving and investment decisions is sufficiently frustrating by itself, but the issue is confounded even more when international factors are taken into account. It was earlier noted that efforts to increase investment in the United States may draw in savings from abroad, whereas efforts to encourage saving may contribute to capital outflows from the United States.

The one policy variable that most economists believe has a clear effect on national savings is the federal budget deficit. Even here there is some dissent, however. Robert Barro believes that taxpayers are rational enough to see that increases in the budget deficit will increase their future tax bills because interest payments and debt repayment will rise in the future. They will, therefore, increase their saving to prepare for these future liabilities.[23] Thus increases in private saving offset increases in public dissaving. A glance at the evidence would seem to suggest that the Barro hypothesis is without foundation because, according to the national income accounts, private savings as a percentage of income have declined while the federal deficit has soared. Barro would reply, however, that capital gains on stocks, bonds, and real estate make up the difference, and these are not counted as savings by the national income accounts.

Nevertheless, the Barro argument has not won many followers in the economics profession and for the sake of the arguments made here, it will be assumed that private saving behavior is not directly affected by changes in the federal deficit.

Others have debunked concern about the deficit on the ground that government accounting techniques are misleading. They argue that once the deficit is adjusted for such things as the effects of inflation, government assets, and changes in contingent liabilities represented, for example, by the promise to pay future Social Security benefits and to make up losses on government-guaranteed debt, the deficit appears much less alarming.[24] To gain a full understanding of the importance of such adjustments, it is necessary to understand the behavioral impact of the variable underlying the adjustment. For example, if the deficit is adjusted to reflect the extent to which inflation erodes the real value of the outstanding public debt, it is of considerable interest to know whether holders of the debt save more to make up this loss. If they do not, the traditional national income accounting version of the deficit may be a better measure of the behavioral impact of government dissaving on the economy. But it may still be advisable to examine an adjusted deficit to estimate the change in the real claims of debt holders on the federal government.

Such issues cannot be explored in detail here and are not important to analyses of the effects of *changes* in the true deficit. It is here assumed that the changes in fiscal policy to be discussed do not affect government investment in human or physical capital or in contingent liabilities. The effects of inflation are noted as the analysis proceeds.

The cost of the deficit is lowest if it can be financed by selling government debt to foreigners. The rate of capital formation in the United States is not directly altered and the rate of return on such borrowing is lower than the rate that would be paid to foreigners investing in private U.S. securities.

Suppose that the federal deficit is reduced in $36 billion increments for five years starting in fiscal 1988; that is, the 1988 deficit is reduced by $36 billion from where it would be otherwise, the 1989 deficit is reduced $72 billion, and so on.[25] Given this policy, $540 billion less in public debt would be outstanding by the end of 1992 than would be the case if no deficit reduction had occurred. If, in the absence of deficit reduction, all the extra debt had been sold to foreigners, interest payments abroad would be roughly $37 billion higher.[26] Avoiding that cost would raise the growth rate of U.S. incomes by only about 0.1 percent per year between 1987 and 1992. This does not sound like much, but it is equivalent to a gain of more than $115 in per capita income in 1987 dollars.[27]

Nevertheless, if the assumptions underlying this calculation turned out to be realistic, budget deficit reduction may not look very appealing to the typical American. The implied nominal rate of return to spending cuts or tax increases is only 6.8 percent, and this would be lowered further if, in 1992, foreigners had to pay U.S. taxes on their U.S. interest income. Most Americans pay a much higher rate of interest when they borrow, and many can earn a higher rate on their savings. Therefore, under the assumptions used thus far in this analysis, Americans may be quite pleased to have government borrow from foreigners on their behalf.

However, the proposed calculation undoubtedly understates the benefits of deficit reduction. It is quite unrealistic to believe that deficit cuts would reduce foreign holdings of U.S. public debt dollar for dollar. To the extent that the foreign sector financed the rise of the budget deficit in the early 1980s, much of the financing was indirect. Foreigners bought private U.S. securities and other assets, while Americans, who might otherwise have purchased those assets or invested abroad, bought U.S. public debt instead.

If the budget deficit is reduced in the future, foreign purchases of private U.S. assets and U.S. public debt are likely to be lowered. Because the rate of return paid in private assets exceeds that paid on the public debt, the rate of return to budget deficit reduction is likely to be higher than the 6.8 percent just suggested.

More important, there is no guarantee that foreigners will be willing to continue financing the U.S. budget deficit, either directly or indirectly. In 1987, foreigners apparently lost confidence in U.S. policies, and foreign private investment in the United States virtually evaporated. Foreign central banks stepped in and purchased U.S. securities in order to support the dollar, effectively taking over the financing of our deficit. But that practice is unlikely to continue, and to the extent that foreigners reduce their total lending, real interest rates will rise and real investment will be reduced in the United States. If budget deficit reduction can be used in the future to mitigate the fall in U.S. investment, the benefits of deficit reduction rise significantly.

The exact magnitude of the benefits depends, of course, on the importance of investment to economic growth—a matter of some academic dispute as noted earlier. If, in the extreme, it is assumed that little technological progress is possible without investment, it is reasonable to assume a nominal rate of return to investment of about 16 percent.[28] If it is further assumed that each dollar of deficit reduction allows a dollar extra of investment, the total implied increase in 1992 current dollar GNP is $92 billion.[29] The rate of growth of the economy is increased by 0.2 to 0.3 percent between 1987 and 1992 and, measured in 1987 dollars, the gain in per capita income is more than $285.

The assumptions used to derive this figure probably overstate the benefits of deficit reduction, whereas the assumptions underlying the earlier estimate of $115 per capita, when foreign investors were assumed to underwrite the entire deficit, probably understate the benefits. Earlier in the 1980s when foreigners were more willing to invest in the United States, the lower figure might have provided a better notion of the gain to be derived from reducing the deficit, but now that foreigners have become more reluctant to finance our deficit, the benefits to future deficit reduction may be growing rapidly.

As the analysis is extended further into the future, the benefits derived from reducing the deficit grow slowly but eventually become much higher. Each addition to income means that the country can save and invest more. This allows more production and yet more savings and investment. These indirect effects of deficit reduction are trivial in the short run and were ignored in the calculation of 1992 benefits, but over the decades they accumulate and become highly significant.

In the examples just described, it was assumed that the 1992 deficit reduction was $180 billion or almost 3 percent of GNP. If, in future decades, the budget deficit could be lowered by 3 percent of GNP, the GNP would be raised (1) by roughly 4 percent in the very long run, say a generation, assuming that deficit reduction reduces foreign borrowing by a like amount, or (2) by about 17 percent, assuming that the entire deficit reduction is translated into increased U.S. capital formation.[30]

Although the benefits of deficit reduction are substantial in the long run, it must be reemphasized that they take a long time to accrue. To obtain them, Americans have to sacrifice in the short run by giving up consumption. It may take more than twenty-five years for the nation to regain the consumption levels enjoyed before deficit reduction. This fact illustrates why it is so difficult to sell deficit reduction politically. The most important gains are not enjoyed by this generation; it is our children and grandchildren who will benefit most.

But it may be misleading to focus so much analysis on future economic income. As the growth of U.S. production is lowered in the long run by the budget deficit, the U.S. role in the world is sure to change. The United States will not be able to afford so much military strength, and, if other countries gain in size relatively, U.S. bargaining power in trade and other policy matters will be diminished. To the extent that the United States becomes more dependent on inflows of foreign capital, its domestic policies will have to be framed to please foreign investors more than Americans. So, unless the United States gets its fiscal house in order, these more subtle costs may eventually make direct economic costs pale in comparison.

## Stabilization Policies

This chapter has focused on long-term factors that influence the U.S. ability to grow; that is appropriate because growth is inherently a long-term phenomenon. But the long term consists of a series of short terms, and short-term business cycles have a lasting effect on long-term growth. Most obviously, investment suffers during recessions, and it is doubtful that booms completely compensate. Recently, it has been argued that there is a comparable effect on human capital formation, as periods of high unemployment deprive the labor force of training opportunities and may affect long-term incentives to work.[31] Such factors suggest that the need to endure relatively high rates of unemployment during the 1980s in order to squeeze out the inflation of the late 1960s and 1970s may have been costly indeed to the U.S. long-term growth prospects.

The world probably would be a better place if the business cycle were eliminated, but, unfortunately, nobody knows how to do that. The ability to forecast the economy is wanting. Even after a problem is recognized, new policies take a long time to formulate and will affect the economy only after a considerable time lag. There is a significant chance that a cyclical problem will have cured itself before anticyclical policies have an effect. As a result, stabilizing policies may, in fact, turn out to be destabilizing.

These problems will not prevent governments from trying to counter the business cycle from time to time. The cause of long-term growth will be furthered if such policies are undertaken with moderation and with full recognition that it is possible to do more harm than good.

## Summary and Conclusions

This paper began with the statements that economic growth was a mysterious process and that significant growth is a fairly recent phenomenon in human history. There is much that is unknown about it quantitatively, in that nobody knows how much various factors affect it. Much, however, is known qualitatively about growth. It is clear that technological change is very important, as are improvements in the quantity and quality of the capital stock and the labor force. Much less is known about the importance of interactions among these basic factors. All this suggests a need to diversify government policies. Technological change is clearly vital to the growth process, but focusing all government subsidies on research and development would be highly risky. The fact that physical and human capital investment may be complementary to technological change suggests the need to consider those variables as well.

When judging government policies with respect to their implications for growth, policymakers tend to focus on their effect on the growth rate. This is not the right way to approach the problem. Most government policy changes have a one-time effect, moving the growth path upward or downward. Once the change has occurred and has been adjusted to, which may take a very long time, the economy is likely to grow at the same rate as before the change, but along a higher or lower path. The worth of a policy should be determined by calculating, as precisely as possible, the rate of return to any expenditure of funds or tax concessions or deficit reduction. Here economists' ignorance regarding the quantitative importance of the factors underlying growth can be a major handicap, but often the effects of small policy initiatives can be computed more accurately than the effects of some grand macro change. Of course, the cost of a progrowth policy often involves more than money. Some other goal of government policy such as income redistribution may have to be sacrificed, in which case a policy will be evaluated very differently by people of differing ideologies.

In examining the growth or antigrowth policies of the federal government in the United States, the most important thing to remember is that total federal government spending absorbs less than one-quarter of the GNP, and most of that spending is determined largely by its effects on things other than the level of the growth path. A change of a few billion dollars in spending or tax concessions more directly related to growth would represent a major policy change from a political point of view but could not be expected to have a dramatic impact on a GNP of $5 trillion. Nevertheless, the dollars expended may earn a high percentage rate of return, which would make the policy initiative worthwhile, but it is important to remain cautious about claiming too much for such policies.

Perhaps the most important role that government plays in the United States is in creating the legal and institutional environment for the innumerable private decisions that are really important in determining the overall growth rate. That environment has two levels. At one level, the government establishes legal and institutional rules of behavior. A mixed market economy cannot function unless property rights and contracts are enforceable. More philosophically, it is hard to imagine our economy's performing successfully without a considerable dose of personal freedom to move about and to pursue new ideas.

At another level, the overall tax, transfer, and regulatory system has a significant influence on the economic incentives that shape individual decisions. Here conflicts with other goals of public policy are most likely to arise. Although the cliché about a rising tide that floats all ships is largely true, the exceptions are too numerous to be ignored. Some ships are sunk, although that rarely happens. A more likely case is one in which individuals or groups expected to sacrifice in the cause of growth find that it is a very long time before they regain their previous status and then surpass it. The rate of return to them may be positive, but it is so low that they would not make the investment voluntarily. Thus in growth policy as in other areas of public policy it is impossible to avoid interpersonal comparisons when formulating initiatives.

Many of the progrowth initiatives identified in this paper would add to public spending or reduce tax revenues. Policies fostering private investment in research and development have the promise of providing particularly high rates of return. Some training and education programs also look promising, although it is necessary to be selective and some experimentation may be warranted. More generally, it may be argued that our tax system is too burdensome on capital and not burdensome enough on consumption. But new programs, whether involving spending increases or tax incentives, must be financed. It would be foolish to finance such initiatives by increasing the budget deficit, because it is known with considerable confidence that such action would be destructive to growth. It would also be dangerous to finance new policies with tax or spending changes that carry a substantial risk of reducing capital formation elsewhere or of creating new disincentives to save or to work.

In conclusion, it is hard to exaggerate the importance of nurturing growth with public policy. Many of our institutional arrangements, especially pensions, depend on continued growth, and many were designed in an era when it was common to assume more growth than now seems likely to materialize. The effects of small changes in the growth path on future living standards can be enormous, and the role of the United States in the world economy and its ability to defend itself depend on the size of its economy relative to the economies of other nations. Although it is extremely difficult to estimate the rate of return to progrowth policies with any precision, this is an area in which some risk taking may be warranted. Certainly, government actions that are likely to be antigrowth, such as maintenance of a huge budget deficit, should be corrected as soon as possible.

NOTES TO CHAPTER 3

1. Simon Kuznets, "Modern Economic Growth: Findings and Reflections," in *Population, Capital, and Growth: Selected Essays* (New York: W. W. Norton, 1973), 167–71.

2. Joseph A. Schumpeter, *Capitalism, Socialism, and Democracy*, 3d ed. (New York: Harper and Row, 1950).

3. This section owes much to Richard R. Nelson, "Research on Productivity Growth and Differences," *Journal of Economic Literature* 19, no. 3 (September 1981): 1029–64.

4. Note that the discussion refers to the growth *path* and not the growth *rate*. It is an important distinction. In simple growth models, the equilibrium growth rate is determined by the rate of labor force growth plus the rate of technological change. Some policies alter the level of the growth path, but not the equilibrium growth rate. As the economy moves from a lower to a higher equilibrium path, the growth rate is obviously increased, but only in the short run.

5. In simple growth models, it is possible to identify the national saving rate that maximizes per capita consumption in the long run. See Edmund Phelps, "The Golden Rule of Accumulation: A Fable for Growthmen," *American Economic Review* 51, no. 4 (1961): 638–43. It is generally believed that U.S. saving rates are far below consumption-maximizing levels. See Edward M. Gramlich, "How Bad Are the Large Deficits?" in *Federal Budget Policy in the 1980s*, edited by Gregory B. Mills and John L. Palmer (Washington, D.C.: The Urban Institute Press, 1984), 52–59.

6. See Ryuzo Sato, "Fiscal Policy in a Neo-Classical Growth Model: An Analysis of the Time Required for Equilibrating Adjustment," *Review of Economic Studies* 30, no. 1 (February 1963): 16–23.

7. See Martin N. Baily, *Brookings Papers on Economic Activity*, vol. 1 (Washington, D.C.: Brookings Institution, 1981), 1–50.

8. For a review of the literature, see Martin N. Baily, "What Has Happened to Productivity Growth?" *Science* 234 (October 24, 1986): 443–51.

9. Richard R. Nelson, "Where Are We in the Discussion? Retrospect and Prospect," in *International Comparisons of Productivity and Causes of the Slowdown*, 397–410.

10. Mancur Olson, *The Rise and Decline of Nations: Economic Growth, Stagflation, and Social Rigidities* (New Haven: Yale University Press, 1982).

11. Jack Hirshleifer, "The Private and Social Value of Information and the Reward to Inventive Activity," *American Economic Review* 61 (September 1971): 561–74.

12. *Special Analyses, Budget of the United States Government, FY 1988*, Special Analysis J (Washington, D.C.: U.S. Government Printing Office, 1987).

13. For a review of the literature, see Congressional Budget Office, *Federal Support for R&D and Innovation*, Washington, D.C., April 1984, table 1, 29–30.

14. Excellent reviews of the literature relevant to tax and transfer programs can be found in Barry Bosworth, *Tax Incentives and Economic Growth* (Washington, D.C.: Brookings Institution, 1984), chapter 5; and in Robert H. Haveman, "How Much Have the Reagan Administration's Tax and Spending Policies Increased Work Effort?" *The Legacy of Reaganomics*, edited by Charles R. Hulten and Isabel V. Sawhill (Washington, D.C.: The Urban Institute Press, 1984), 91–126.

15. A prime example is Jerry A. Hausman, "Labor Supply," in *How Taxes Affect Economic Behavior* (Washington, D.C.: Brookings Institution, 1981), 27–83. This particular study finds such high responses that Haveman regards them as being unrealistic; see "How Much Have The Reagan Administration's Tax and Spending Policies Increased Work Effort?," 111.

16. For a critical discussion of such hypotheses, see Richard Layer and George Psacharopoulos, "The Screening Hypothesis and the Returns to Education," *Journal of Political Economy* 82, no. 5 (September-October 1974): 985–98.

17. Eric A. Hanushek, "Conceptual and Empirical Issues in the Estimation of Educational Production Functions," *Journal of Human Resources* 14, no. 3 (Summer 1979), 351–87.

18. For a more adequate summary, see Michael L. Wachter, "The Training Component of Growth Policies," in *Removing Obstacles to Economic Growth* (Philadelphia: University of Pennsylvania Press, 1984), 41–69; and Laurie J. Bassi and Orley Ashenfelter, "The Effect of Direct Job Creation and Training Programs on Low Skilled Workers," in *Fighting Poverty: What Works and What Doesn't*, edited by Sheldon Danziger and Daniel Weinberg (Cambridge, Mass.: Harvard University Press, 1986).

19. Lawrence H. Summers, "A Fair Tax Act That's Bad for Business," *Harvard Business Review* (March-April 1987): 53–59.

20. U.S. Treasury, *Blueprints for Basic Tax Reform*, Washington, D.C. January 17, 1977.

21. Robert J. Barro, *The Impact of Social Security on Private Saving*, with a reply from Martin Feldstein (Washington, D.C.: American Enterprise Institute, 1978).

22. See Henry Aaron, *Economic Effects of Social Security* (Washington, D.C.: Brookings Institution, 1982), chapter 4.

23. Robert J. Barro, "Public Debt and Taxes," in *Federal Tax Reform: Myths and Realities*, edited by Michael Boskin (San Francisco: Institute for Contemporary Studies, 1978).

24. Robert Eisner, *How Real is the Federal Deficit?* (New York: Free Press, 1986); and Laurence J. Kotlikoff, "Budget Deficits, Stripped of Delusions," *Wall Street Journal* (November 4, 1987): 36.

25. Given the CBO baseline, this would imply a small surplus in 1992 in the overall budget, but a small deficit would remain in the non-Social Security part of the budget.

26. This calculation assumes an average interest rate on the debt of 6.8 percent, which is roughly consistent with recent CBO interest rate projections.

27. The assumed inflation rate is 4 percent. The calculation of benefits is, of course, greatly oversimplified. The macro economic effects of deficit reduction on short-term economic activity, the exchange rate, and the U.S. trade balance are not considered. Moreover, different people would be affected very differently by spending cuts and tax increases, and so may gain much more or less than the average amount of $115. As interest is paid abroad, less would also be saved in the United States and this would further reduce U.S. growth. However, this indirect effect on growth is trivial in the short run.

28. See Gramlich, "How Bad Are the Large Deficits?", 60. He assumes a real rate of 11.4 percent, and this analysis assumes an inflation rate of 4 percent.

29. The cumulative deficit reduction of $540 billion in the 1988–92 period allows an increase in the capital stock valued at $571 billion by the end of 1992, as inflation increases the nominal value of investments made earlier. The increase in the capital stock lowers its rate of return somewhat, and the productivity and wages of workers increase. Total production rises $92 billion. Of that amount, $91 billion is simply the nominal rate of return (0.16) multiplied by the addition to the capital stock ($571 billion). An additional $1 billion accrues because infra-marginal additions to the capital stock have a slightly higher marginal product than 16 percent. No allowance is made for the depreciation of capital added in the 1988–92 period so as to increase the upward bias inherent in this example. A standard Cobb-Douglas production function underlies the calculations.

30. It can be shown mathematically that foreign borrowing of a steady 3 percent of the GNP would eventually result in a foreign debt-to-GNP ratio equal to 0.03 divided by the growth rate of GNP. If, as a crude approximation, it is assumed that the rate of return on the foreign debt is equal to the growth rate of GNP (there is a weak tendency for this equality to be satisfied over long periods of history), payments to foreigners will also equal 3 percent of GNP. But then payments will reduce U.S. income and savings. In a typical Cobb-Douglas growth model, this indirect effect would be worth about another 1 percent of GNP. The estimate that assumes that deficit reduction is translated into real capital formation is based on a Cobb-Douglas growth model in which the capital share is 25 percent and deficit reduction increases the national savings rate from 5 to 8 percent of GNP. The low capital share implies that technological change is not embodied in the capital stock and so may result in an understatement of the gains.

31. See O. J. Blanchard and L. H. Summers, "Fiscal Increasing Returns, Hysteresis, Real Wages and Unemployment," *European Economic Review* 31, no. 3 (April 1987): 543–60.

# CHAPTER 4

# INTERNATIONAL TRADE

## Charles F. Stone

The United States has been the world's dominant economic power since the end of World War II, but that dominance now appears to be diminishing. Other nations have grown faster and made inroads into markets traditionally dominated by U.S. industry, especially in manufacturing. This loss of economic dominance has raised fears that America is "deindustrializing" and that many Americans will see their standard of living fall as "good" manufacturing jobs are replaced by "bad" service sector jobs. Other nations are perceived as taking advantage of the openness of U.S. markets while denying the United States access to their own. Many people now believe that the United States must respond with activist trade policies of its own if the slow economic growth and increasing inequality in earnings that have plagued the economy since the early 1970s are to be reversed.

Others dismiss international competition and changes in the industrial structure of the economy as nothing to worry about. They view trade as an important source of economic growth and barriers to trade as a serious impediment to growth. They believe that the quality of the labor force—and its flexibility and adaptability to changing market conditions—plays a far more important role in generating a satisfactory standard of living than does the preservation of any particular industrial or occupational structure.

This chapter explores the relationship between the growing internationalization of the U.S. economy and its ability to deliver a high and rising

The author would like to thank Frank Schiff and Richard Cooper for useful comments and suggestions for improvement.

standard of living to most Americans. Although the findings here tend to refute the propositions that trade is bad for America or that the economy is becoming deindustrialized, this chapter does identify some problems associated with the structural changes that are likely to occur in an increasingly competitive world economy. The chapter also examines policies that would allow the nation to achieve the advantages associated with adjusting to international competition while protecting most Americans from large reductions in their earnings stemming from forces beyond their control.

It is hard to talk about the impact of international competition on the U.S. economy without talking about the most visible signs of that impact—the trade deficit and the loss of jobs in industries hurt by trade—and this is done in the first part of the chapter. However, as discussed in that section, these short-term dimensions of the trade problem have more to do with how macroeconomic policy has been conducted in the United States and abroad than with any fundamental decline in U.S. competitiveness.

The question of whether the United States has a long-term competitiveness problem is addressed in the second part of the chapter. This section takes a particularly hard look at the argument that the realities of international competition require a rethinking of the United States' traditional commitment to free trade and concludes that free trade remains in the national interest even in a world of large trade deficits, rapid technological change, and policies by other governments that interfere with free trade.

The last part of the chapter addresses the skeleton in the closet of free-trade advocates—the fact that free trade makes some people worse off than they would be if they were protected from international competition. This section identifies areas in which the government could mitigate some of the hardships of people hurt by the U.S. adjustment to international competition without interfering unduly with the adjustment process itself.

## Short-Term Dimensions of the Trade Problem

Although imports and exports have never been so large a share of the gross national product (GNP) in the United States as they have been in most other countries, their importance has markedly increased since the end of World War II. In 1950, trade (as measured by the average of imports and exports) represented about 5 percent of GNP, but by 1980 it represented about 12 percent of GNP (figure 4.1). Although merchandise imports began to grow more rapidly than merchandise exports during the 1970s, exports of services and earnings on U.S. investments abroad grew fast enough to maintain a net export surplus through 1982 (figure 4.2).[1]

FIGURE 4.1

IMPORTS AND EXPORTS, 1950–86

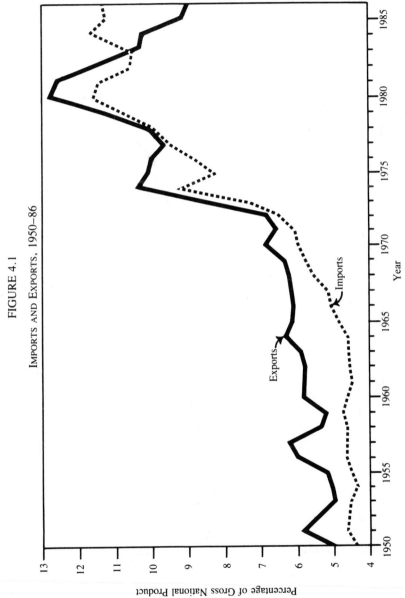

SOURCE: National Income and Product Accounts.

FIGURE 4.2
TRADE AND THE DOLLAR, 1972–86

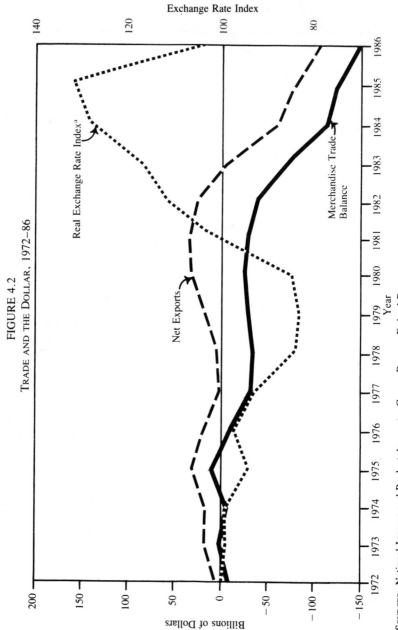

SOURCES: National Income and Product Accounts, Census Bureau, Federal Reserve.
a. Measured by the right scale, with a base year of 1972 = 100.

Thereafter, however, the trade situation deteriorated rapidly, and U.S. imports now exceed U.S. exports by well over $100 billion a year. Between 1982 and 1986 the United States went from being the world's largest creditor nation to being its largest debtor, and the debt continues to mount. In less than ten years, the U.S. international debt may approach $1 trillion; $50 billion a year will be required simply to meet the interest payments on this debt.

## Macroeconomic Origins of the Trade Deficit

What caused this trade deficit and what does it mean for the economic well-being of the typical American? One popular explanation is that the United States is losing the battle to remain competitive in world markets because of slow growth in productivity and a decline in the quality of U.S. products. Another is that unfair trade practices abroad have boosted foreign exports to the United States while limiting imports from the United States. But the productivity slowdown began in the 1970s, well before the trade deficit worsened (U.S. productivity actually has grown faster than foreign productivity in recent years); and any advantage afforded foreign producers by their countries' trade policies, whether or not these policies have been fair, has changed little since the 1970s. Furthermore, a loss in competitiveness from poor growth in productivity or poor product quality would normally be expected to cause the dollar to depreciate by enough to keep exports and imports in balance. Yet the deterioration of the U.S. trade balance was preceded by a sharp appreciation of the dollar, and the trade deficit has not disappeared despite the dollar's subsequent decline (figure 4.2).

Statistical studies of the causes of the trade deficit rank the behavior of the dollar as the most important cause. In one representative study, for example, three-quarters of the deterioration in the trade balance between 1980 and 1986 is attributed to changes in the dollar and the rest to differential growth rates between the United States and its trading partners that have caused the demand for foreign products in the United States to grow more rapidly than the demand for U.S. products abroad.[2] Other investigators using a similar methodology have found roughly the same breakdown between changes in the dollar and relative growth rates.[3] However, one recent study attributes only a third of the deterioration in the trade balance to the dollar and another third to differential growth rates, leaving about a third as an unexplained residual. This residual may reflect a fundamental loss of competitiveness—or it may simply indicate that the lagged effects of the dollar's decline since 1985 have not yet been reflected fully in the trade balance.[4]

Whatever their exact apportioning between the dollar and differential growth rates, these studies clearly identify the trade deficit as primarily a macroeconomic phenomenon. They do not, however, account for why the dollar has behaved as it has or why domestic demand has grown more rapidly in the United States than in the rest of the world. The explanation for these developments favored by the Reagan administration and its supporters is that the Reagan economic recovery program has so revitalized this country that there has been a strong influx of foreign saving to take advantage of burgeoning investment opportunities in the United States. As a matter of balance-of-payments arithmetic, a net inflow of foreign capital must be offset by a trade deficit. Thus, according to this interpretation, the trade deficit was an inevitable by-product of the strong dollar—a by-product that resulted when foreigners increased their demand for U.S. assets. Nor is the foreign debt associated with such a trade deficit viewed as a burden to future generations, because debt used to finance productive investment is easily repaid from the income generated by that investment.

The problem with this interpretation of the trade deficit is that there has been no investment boom. As a share of national income, investment is about the same as it was in the previous peak year of economic activity, 1979 (figure 4.3). Now, however, more than half of net investment in the United States is being financed by foreign borrowing rather than domestic saving, and the income that will be generated by that investment will accrue as interest payments to foreigners rather than as income to U.S. citizens. Thus, the line showing investment net of foreign borrowing in figure 4.3 gives a truer picture of the investment that raises the U.S. standard of living than the line showing actual investment. It seems evident that the future is being shortchanged as never before.[5]

These observations suggest that the United States has been enjoying a consumption binge rather than an investment boom. This view is consistent with a widely accepted interpretation of the origin of the trade deficit that links it to the federal budget deficit. According to this interpretation, upward pressure on interest rates associated with increased federal government borrowing and a restrictive monetary policy attracted a flood of foreign saving, and the trade deficit was the inevitable by-product of the strong dollar associated with these capital flows. The data in table 4.1 support this interpretation. They show that domestic spending in the United States rose above domestic income between 1980 and 1986 and that none of this spending increased the proportion of income spent on investment.

Although these data suggest a strong link between federal budget deficits and the trade deficit, critics of this interpretation correctly point out that there is no historical correlation between budget deficits and trade deficits. In fact,

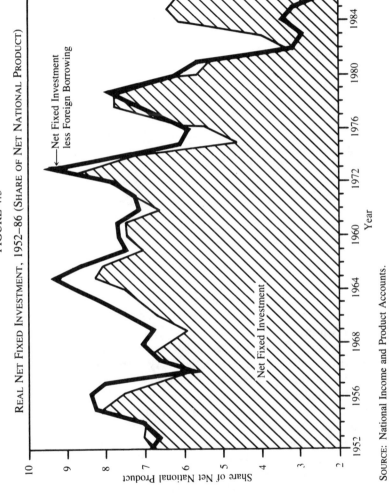

FIGURE 4.3

REAL NET FIXED INVESTMENT, 1952–86 (SHARE OF NET NATIONAL PRODUCT)

SOURCE: National Income and Product Accounts.

TABLE 4.1

THE COMPOSITION OF DOMESTIC SPENDING AND GNP, 1960–86

*(Percentage of GNP)*

| Item | Average 1960–80 | 1980 | 1986 | Change 1980–86 |
|---|---|---|---|---|
| Consumption | 62.8 | 63.4 | 66.1 | 2.7 |
| Government purchases (including state and local) | 20.3 | 19.4 | 20.5 | 1.1 |
| Investment | 16.0 | 16.0 | 15.8 | −0.2 |
| Total domestic spending | 99.1 | 98.8 | 102.5 | 3.7 |
| Net exports to the rest of the world (investment in) | 1.0 | 1.2 | −2.5 | −3.7 |
| Total domestic income (GNP) | 100.0 | 100.0 | 100.0 | 0.0 |
| Addendum: National saving (GNP less consumption and government purchases) | | | | |
| Federal budget deficit | −1.1 | −2.2 | −4.8 | −2.6 |
| Other national saving[a] | 18.0 | 19.4 | 18.2 | −1.2 |
| Total national saving | 17.0 | 17.2 | 13.4 | −3.8 |

Source: National Income and Product Accounts.
NOTE: Entries may not add to total because of rounding.
a. Includes personal saving, business saving, and state and local government surpluses.

the original concern with large budget deficits was that they would be inflationary or that they would crowd out private investment. What was overlooked was how sensitive international capital flows had become to interest rate changes. Without international capital flows, the clash between an expansionary fiscal policy and an anti-inflationary monetary policy would have produced much higher interest rates and much less domestic investment; with them, the stimulus to U.S. spending from large federal budget deficits was able to spill over into the world market without creating inflation and without crowding out investment.[6]

An explanation that focuses exclusively on U.S. macroeconomic policy goes a long way toward explaining the deterioration of the U.S. trade balance, but the trade problems caused by U.S. macroeconomic policy were aggravated by developments in the rest of the world. First, as shown in the statistical studies mentioned earlier, other things being equal, if other industrial countries had pursued more expansionary policies, U.S. exports would have grown more rapidly and the trade deficit would have been about one-third lower. (There is a question, however, about whether, given the rapid expansion in

U.S. demand, the rest of the world could have expanded demand as well without risking inflation.) Second, the U.S. trade deficit was increased by a loss of exports to debt-burdened developing countries. Once again, however, U.S. macroeconomic policies were an important cause of the rise in interest rates that was instrumental in precipitating the debt crisis. These observations reinforce the conclusion that if the United States had pursued more balanced macroeconomic policies, the U.S. trade deficit would be substantially smaller than it is.

## Reducing the Trade Deficit

This analysis indicates that the key to an orderly reduction in the trade deficit is a reduction in the federal budget deficit. Until the fundamental imbalance between total domestic spending and total domestic income is corrected, any attempt to reduce the trade deficit through import restraints and export promotion is doomed to failure. As long as a substantial imbalance remains, any benefits that some industries derive from trade restraints will be offset by losses in other industries.[7] A fall in the value of the dollar and a reduction in the trade deficit unaccompanied by a reduction in the federal budget deficit—as might occur if the rest of the world were to lose confidence in the dollar and stop lending to the United States—would lead to higher interest rates, a decline in domestic investment, and possibly a recession.[8]

Attempts to get countries like West Germany and Japan to stimulate their economies, and measures to relieve the debt burden on less developed countries, will do little to improve the U.S. trade deficit unless the United States also takes appropriate actions to restrain its own spending. However, if the United States does begin to restrain its domestic spending, other countries will have to expand theirs—and there will have to be debt relief—to offset the contractionary effects on the world economy that will follow from the actions of the United States.

One of the most important lessons learned from the international macroeconomic instability of the past several years is that sovereign nations in a highly interdependent world economy have less freedom than they think to pursue independent macroeconomic policies. If similar instability is to be avoided in the future, the leading trading nations must coordinate their macroeconomic policies to bring domestic policy objectives into line with international policy constraints.[9]

## The Burden of International Debt

No matter what policies are pursued in the future, past trade imbalances have left an enduring legacy in the form of a large foreign debt. Figure 4.4

FIGURE 4.4

NET U.S. INTERNATIONAL INVESTMENT POSITION, 1970–95

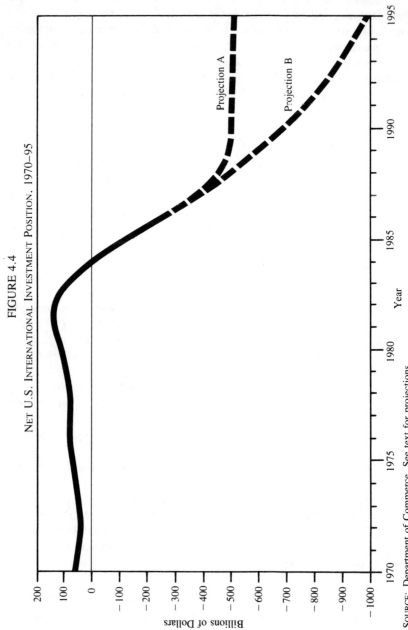

SOURCE: Department of Commerce. See text for projections.

shows that although the United States was a net international creditor until 1982, subsequent trade deficits produced a net external debt of nearly $300 billion by 1986. No one can reliably project how the U.S. trade balance will behave over the next several years, but figure 4.4 shows that even if the current account is brought into balance in 1990, the external debt of the United States will exceed $500 billion (Projection A, which assumes a current account deficit of $120 billion in 1987, $80 billion in 1988, and $40 billion in 1989). The figure also illustrates a somewhat more pessimistic scenario (Projection B) in which the current account deficit is reduced by $10 billion a year between 1987 and 1995 and the external debt approaches a trillion dollars and is still growing. Assuming a 5 percent interest rate, financing the debt will entail a $50 billion a year drain on U.S. income. To reduce the debt, the United States would have to run a balance of payments surplus for a number of years, and doing this would entail an even larger drain on income.

Under Projection B, the United States would still have a current account deficit of $40 billion in 1995; with interest obligations of $50 billion a year, this implies a $10 billion a year surplus in noninterest goods and services. How much the dollar might have to fall to achieve this surplus is not known. One recent study provides evidence that a steady decline in the real purchasing power of the dollar (the terms of trade) was required to keep the current account roughly in balance during the 1970s.[10] If a continuing steady decline in the terms of trade would have been required to maintain a current account balance in the 1980s as well, the dollar must do more than simply reverse its appreciation to 1985 to balance the current account. It must fall further still if the surplus of Projection B is to be achieved. There is some evidence that there is less need for a steady decline in the U.S. terms of trade now than there was in the 1970s (once the level required for current account balance is reached), but no one really knows how much more, or even whether, the dollar will have to fall before the United States can begin to stabilize and then reduce its external debt. The longer the underlying causes of the trade deficit remain uncorrected, however, the greater will be the build-up of external debt and the sharper will be the decline in the U.S. terms of trade required for correction. Neither is good for the future standard of living.

## Trade and Jobs

Many people see the trade problem as primarily a jobs problem. They view the loss of jobs to imports as a serious threat to long-term standards of living in the United States; they are especially alarmed by the losses of the past several years. However, at the same time that imports have surged and the trade deficit has widened, overall employment in the United States has grown and the unemployment rate has come down. The reason is that the growth in aggregate output and employment depends much more on the growth in aggregate demand allowed by monetary and fiscal policy than on the composition of that demand, and growth in aggregate demand has generated more than enough jobs in the rest of the economy to offset the loss of jobs to imports. Moreover, it is unlikely that the Federal Reserve Board would have allowed overall aggregate demand to expand much more rapidly than it did during this period without the help against inflation afforded by competition from imports. Thus, the changes in the pattern of output and employment associated with the trade deficit do not appear to have had an important effect on overall job growth in the economy, but they have affected the kinds of jobs that have been created and lost.

Table 4.2 shows that if trade patterns had remained as they were in 1979, there would have been 1.6 million more manufacturing jobs in 1984 and correspondingly fewer jobs in the rest of the economy.[11] Table 4.3 shows that the typical job lost as a result of changing trade patterns paid $3,800 above the average for the economy as a whole, whereas the typical job that replaced it paid $1,500 less than the average for the economy as a whole. Clearly, many workers who lost their jobs during this period faced a poor

TABLE 4.2

TRADE AND DISTRIBUTION OF JOBS, 1979–84

| Industry | Employment Change Due to Trade, 1979–84 (FTE Jobs) | Share of 1984 Employment (Percent) |
|---|---|---|
| Agriculture, forestry, fisheries | −45,000 | −3.1 |
| Mining | 117,000 | 12.3 |
| Construction | 99,000 | 2.3 |
| Durable goods manufacturing | −1,110,000 | −9.8 |
| Nondurable goods manufacturing | −525,000 | −6.9 |
| Transportation, communications, utilities | 120,000 | 2.4 |
| Wholesale and retail trade | 821,000 | 4.3 |
| Finance, insurance, real estate | 123,000 | 2.2 |
| Services | 385,000 | 2.1 |
| Government | 15,000 | 0.1 |
| Total | 0 | 0 |

SOURCE: Author's calculation. Actual full-time-equivalent (FTE) employment in 1984 is from National Income and Product Accounts less the author's estimate of what FTE employment would have been in 1984 with the same total employment in the economy and 1979 trade patterns.

TABLE 4.3

THE EFFECT OF CHANGING TRADE PATTERNS ON EMPLOYEE COMPENSATION, 1984

| Item | Industries Losing Jobs | Industries Gaining Jobs |
|---|---|---|
| Size of job shift (millions of FTE jobs) | − 1.7 | 1.7 |
| Total 1984 employment (millions of FTE jobs) | 17.9 | 73.2 |
| Average compensation per FTE in shifted jobs (dollars) | 28,086 | 22,793 |
| *Addendum*: | | |
| Total employment (millions of FTE jobs) | NA | 91.1 |
| Average compensation per FTE (dollars) | NA | 24,306 |
| Job shifts as share of total .employment (percent) | NA | 1.9 |
| Change in average compensation due to shifts (dollars) | NA | − 100[a] |

SOURCE: Author's calculations.

a. Difference between compensation in jobs gained and compensation in jobs lost ($22,793–$28,086) multiplied by total number of jobs shifted (1.7 million) divided by total employment (91.1 million) = − $100 per job.

NA = Not applicable.

prospect of finding comparable jobs paying comparable wages. Surveys of dislocated workers conducted by the Bureau of Labor Statistics (BLS) in 1984 and 1986 show, for example, that about a million experienced workers a year lost their jobs between 1979 and 1985 (many of them for reasons other than import competition, of course) and that although two-thirds of them subsequently found new jobs, many of them experienced a substantial cut in wages.[12] Similarly, new entrants into the labor force faced a lower probability of finding a job paying above-average compensation than they would have with more balanced trade.

Nevertheless, employment shifts attributable to trade represented less than 2 percent of all jobs in the economy in 1984, and if the net changes in wages attributable to these shifts had been spread evenly across all workers, they would have amounted to a loss of barely $100 per worker (five cents an hour for full-time workers) in 1984 compensation. A crude calculation suggests that the average worker experienced a short-term increase in purchasing power of about $200 in 1984 because of the strong dollar that caused these employment shifts.[13] To the extent the trade problem is a jobs problem, it is a jobs problem for particular workers. The problems these workers face should not be minimized, and they are discussed later in this chapter, but for the economy as a whole, neither the total number of jobs nor average real earnings have been much affected by changes in the pattern of output and employment associated with the trade deficit.

## Summary

In summary, the trade deficits of the 1980s stemmed from macroeconomic policy decisions both here and abroad, much more than from unfair foreign competition or a deterioration in underlying competitiveness. The combination of large federal budget deficits and an anti-inflationary monetary policy in the United States, together with a slowdown in growth abroad and an increase in foreigners' willingness to lend to the United States, allowed U.S. spending to grow faster than U.S. income. However, none of this extra spending boosted investment as a share of GNP above historical levels. Rather, current consumption (including government purchases of goods and services) rose above levels that would have been sustainable without an influx of foreign saving, and the United States began to build up a large foreign debt.

Moreover, none of this extra spending boosted output and employment in manufacturing in this country. U.S. consumers bought more manufactured goods, but they bought them from foreign producers. Domestically, the extra spending generated by the macroeconomic policies of the 1980s boosted output and employment in the service industries. These changes in the pattern of output and employment had little effect on total employment or the average wage, but they very much affected the kind of jobs that were created and lost, and thus affected the distribution of earnings. Some workers lost high-paying jobs they would have retained with more balanced trade, but other workers with different skills had an easier time finding a job.

In the short term, the average worker probably enjoyed modest net benefits from an overvalued dollar, but as the foreign debt becomes more burdensome and the dollar declines, these benefits will erode and the true costs of the macroeconomic policies of the early 1980s will be felt. Manufacturing output and employment will be stimulated by a decline in the dollar, but the purchasing power of U.S. wages generally will be depressed. The longer the United States continues to borrow to support current consumption, the greater will be the drain on future income.

But suppose the United States puts its macroeconomic house in order? Will it be able to compete, or have the problems related to the overvalued dollar in fact masked an underlying deterioration in competitiveness that will require a steady decline in the U.S. terms of trade with the rest of the world beyond what will be required to pay for the debts that have been accumulated so far? Put another way, if the United States had not incurred large budget and trade deficits during the 1980s, would its long-term growth prospects have suffered nonetheless from increasing foreign competition?

## Trade, Competitiveness, and Long-term Growth

To be competitive with foreign producers and pay U.S. workers the highest wages in the world, U.S. producers must achieve superior productivity or product quality. Any slippage in this productivity or product quality advantage represents a "competitiveness problem" because it threatens the wage premium enjoyed by U.S. workers. The standard of living in the United States suffers whether competitiveness is restored by an explicit reduction in U.S. wages or by a decline in the value of the dollar that reduces the international purchasing power of U.S. wages. Few sophisticated proponents of the view that the United States has a competitiveness problem would go so far as to say that international competition has reduced or will reduce the standard of living below what it would be if the country did not trade at all. The question really is whether the gains this country has traditionally enjoyed from trade are eroding, and, if they are, whether there is anything that can be done about it.

Those who argue that the United States has a competitiveness problem assert (1) that the U.S. gains from trade are eroding because an indifference to maintaining international competitiveness on the part of U.S. producers and policymakers has allowed foreign producers, often with the help of their governments, to increase their share of world trade; and (2) that U.S. competitiveness and gains from trade will continue to decline unless the government turns away from free trade and embraces the same kinds of policies other countries have used to defend and promote the competitiveness of their industries. Advocates of free trade dispute each of these assertions, but before their arguments are considered here, it is worth looking at the decline in U.S. dominance of world trade in its historical context.

### The Loss of U.S. Economic Hegemony

The United States emerged from World War II as the world's preeminent economic power, enjoying a near monopoly on the production of many capital-intensive or technologically sophisticated manufactured goods. However, as Europe and Japan began to rebuild their industrial bases, it was almost inevitable that this monopoly position would be eroded. As other industrial countries developed innovative capabilities similar to those of the United States and work forces with similar education and training, it was only natural that their productivity and standards of living would rise toward those of the United States. Figures 4.5 and 4.6 show that West Germany and Japan in particular have closed the gap between themselves and the United States in both per capita income and manufacturing productivity, but that they have not yet surpassed the United States in either measure.

Of course, in the nineteenth century, Britain was the dominant world economic power; several other industrialized countries subsequently caught up to and surpassed Britain in their material standards of living. No one can be certain that the same is not in store for the United States, but it has not happened yet; and there may be a real difference between the pace of economic growth that other countries have been able to achieve in rising toward parity with the United States and the pace of economic growth that they will be able to sustain once rough parity is achieved. Recall from the previous chapter that hard work and productive investment in physical capital, human capital, and knowledge are the key contributors to rising living standards. It is almost surely easier to promote hard work and deferred gratification (saving) when the goal is to move into the class of wealthy nations than it is to maintain those incentives once a country has become wealthy. Also, more dramatic advances in productivity can be achieved by countries that can imitate others' technological advances than by countries that must push out the frontiers of technology themselves. William Baumol, for example, draws such an implication from his analysis of data on long-term historical trends in productivity growth in sixteen industrial countries, which show that productivity levels have tended to converge over time, with the countries starting out the farthest behind growing the most rapidly.[14]

These observations suggest that fears that other nations will surge past the United States and leave it in their dust are almost certainly misplaced—as long as the United States provides a reasonable environment for promoting growth along the lines outlined in the previous chapter. The United States should not expect to be by far the richest country in the world or to dominate world trade as it did in the 1950s or even the 1960s. To do so would require that it consciously try to keep other nations poor. The question remains, however, as to whether the U.S. standard of living will grow most rapidly under a free-trade policy regime or whether the United States would be better off protecting or promoting key industries in the face of mounting international competition.

FIGURE 4.5

TRENDS IN PER CAPITA GDP, 1950–85

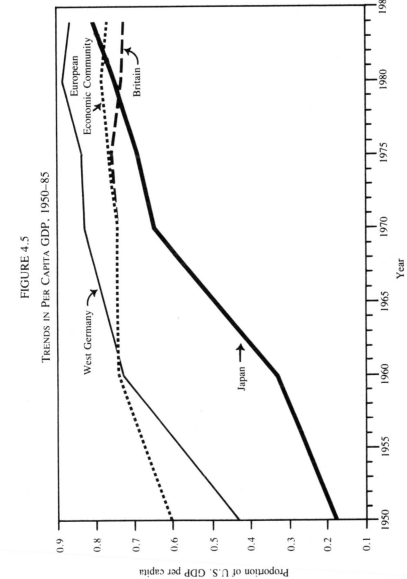

SOURCE: Adapted from Angus Maddison, "Growth and Slowdown in Advanced Capitalist Economies," *Journal of Economic Literature*, June 1987.

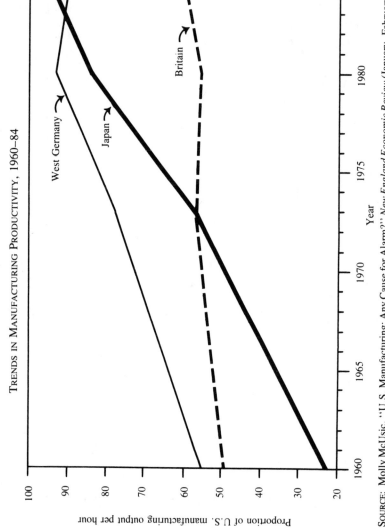

FIGURE 4.6

TRENDS IN MANUFACTURING PRODUCTIVITY, 1960–84

SOURCE: Molly McUsic, "U.S. Manufacturing: Any Cause for Alarm?" *New England Economic Review* (January–February 1987):10.

## The Gains from Trade and the Costs of Protectionism

Economists since Adam Smith have argued that trade enhances the wealth of nations and that barriers to trade reduce the wealth of nations. Politicians, however, have always recognized that some people are hurt by trade and that trade restrictions can be good politics even if they are bad economics. Thus, despite a general recognition of the value of trade and notwithstanding the substantial trade liberalization that has taken place since the end of World War II as a result of successive rounds of multilateral trade negotiations, no major trading country practices free trade. Trade restrictions abound, and pressures for further government interference with the free flow of goods in international trade have been growing in the United States and elsewhere. Economists explain this as a shortsighted yielding to special interests that are hurt by trade, but critics of free trade argue that the U.S. adherence to free-trade policies in a world in which U.S. trading partners pursue import-restricting and export-promoting policies reduces the U.S. standard of living below what it would be if the United States engaged in similar practices.

Such conclusions receive little support from conventional economic analysis, which shows that when standardized products are produced and sold in competitive markets, no country can gain at the expense of another by subsidizing its exports or restricting its imports.[15] A country that adopts such policies hurts itself and may hurt its trading partners, in comparison with conditions of free trade, but there is no countermeasure that one nation can take against another nation's protectionist policies that will not hurt the first nation still further. Export subsidies transfer income from the country granting the subsidy to its trading partners. More of the export good is sold, but at least part of the subsidy is captured by foreign consumers. Tariffs reduce the volume of trade, hurting both countries, but a retaliatory tariff compounds the felony by reducing trade still further.

The implication of this analysis is that a country maximizes its national income by pursuing free trade, no matter what policies its trading partners pursue. Although workers and shareholders in firms that face increasing import competition would be better off if they were protected from this competition, the overall gains from protecting those who would be adversely affected by free trade are smaller than the overall losses to the rest of the economy, because protection introduces income-reducing inefficiencies into the economy.

Hufbauer and Rosen estimate, for example, that in 1984 special trade protection in eighteen industries cost U.S. consumers $54 billion in higher prices and introduced inefficiencies that lowered national income by $7 billion. Of the income lost by consumers, $40 billion was transferred to workers and firms in the protected industries, and another $7 billion accrued as tariff revenue to the government. However, because some protection took the form of voluntary export-restraint agreements rather than tariffs, foreign producers captured $7 billion of the income lost by U.S. consumers. This, along with the $7 billion in inefficiencies mentioned earlier, resulted in a net loss to the U.S. economy of $14 billion. Moreover, protection appears to have had a regressive effect on the distribution of income. Some low-income workers benefit from protection and some high-income consumers are hurt. On balance, however, the costs to consumers from protection are more concentrated among lower-income groups than are the benefits to producers.[16]

Although protectionism may be good politics, it is bad economics. It would be better to design a set of policies to compensate those who are hurt by trade out of the net gains from trade than to forgo those net gains by invoking protectionism. That the country's trading rivals might choose to favor some sectors of their economy at the expense of their overall national income is not a good argument for the United States to do the same.

Defenders of free trade must recognize, however, that although trade maximizes national income at any moment in time, it does not guarantee that the gains from trade will grow over time. One important determinant of how the gains from trade behave over time is the relationship between productivity growth in the United States and abroad and the U.S. terms of trade. For example, rising agricultural productivity worldwide is increasing the supply of agricultural products and reducing their prices. Countries that are net importers of such agricultural products gain unambiguously from these productivity advances, but countries like the United States that are net exporters will see some of the gains from expanding volume offset by declining export prices. In the case of manufactured goods, when rising productivity in the countries of the Pacific Basin allows them to sell the United States standardized consumer products at ever lower prices, the U.S. terms of trade (and hence its gains from trade) improve, other things being equal. Conversely, when rising productivity allows other countries to replace U.S. exports of machinery or high-tech products in their own or third-country markets, the U.S. terms of trade and gains from trade fall, other things being equal.

Thus, conventional economic analysis does not support the conclusion that trade always enhances growth. It does, however, support the conclusion that some trade is always better than no trade and that, even when foreign productivity growth erodes the gains from trade, protectionist policy intervention cannot offset these harmful effects.

## New Arguments for Protection

Economists' conclusion that a policy of benign neglect is the best response to the trade practices of other governments or strong growth in productivity abroad strikes many people as evidence of how out of touch most
economists are with the real world. Critics take great delight, for example,
in pointing out how unrealistic the model is from which economists derive
their conclusions. In contrast to the competitive markets of the economics
textbook, many real-world markets are characterized by oligopolistic market
structures in which the exploitation of economies of scale in production,
product differentiation, and the development and introduction of new products
are much more important than price competition in the rivalry among firms
for market share and profits.

Recently, however, new developments in the theory of international trade
have begun to bridge the gap between academic thinking and the concerns
of businesses, workers, and policymakers by incorporating more realistic
assumptions into the analysis of trade and protection.[17] Under textbook competitive conditions, patterns of trade are determined by comparative cost
differences across industries in different countries, and the gains from trade
are based on a country's ability to export goods that it can produce cheaply
and to import goods that would be expensive to produce domestically. Maximum gains are achieved under free trade because all countries' production
patterns are structured as efficiently as possible. However, when comparative
advantage in international markets derives from the ability to exploit economies of scale or to develop new products or new production techniques,
some gains from trade may derive from the monopolistic exploitation of such
advantages. From a cosmopolitan standpoint, free trade continues to be the
policy that maximizes average standards of living throughout the world; but
from a nationalistic standpoint, tariffs and export subsidies may be useful
tools for protecting existing national monopoly advantages and for developing
new ones.

These academic ideas have provided ammunition for proponents of more
activist "strategic" U.S. trade policies. Advocates of free trade cannot dismiss
arguments about the harm to the U.S. from foreign government trade practices
or the benefits from selected tariffs and export subsidies so readily in situations
where comparative advantage is based on the monopolistic exploitation of
special advantages as they can when markets are competitive. Nevertheless,
in the context of actual U.S. trade patterns, as distinct from theoretical possibilities, arguments that the United States should adopt strategic trade policies
remain unconvincing.

Before large trade deficits emerged in the 1980s, the United States enjoyed a strong and growing net export position in agricultural products, especially wheat and soybeans; in chemicals; and in machinery and other technologically sophisticated products. It experienced a rising net import position in oil, textiles, steel, cars, and TVs and other consumer products. Although trade balances have worsened in almost all industries in recent years as a result of the macroeconomic policies discussed earlier, these relative strengths and weaknesses have been maintained. In line with its relative abundance of arable land, capital, skilled labor, and technological expertise, the United States has tended to specialize in the production of goods and services that employ those factors of production most heavily. It has relied on imports for standardized products that can be produced more cheaply abroad.

New arguments for protection seem particularly inappropriate with respect to U.S. imports, because the gains of foreign producers are based primarily on cost advantages that cannot be exploited monopolistically and are therefore passed on to U.S. consumers in the form of lower prices. True, imports have cost jobs in some U.S. industries, but, as discussed earlier, they have not caused employment in the economy as a whole to suffer. Nor is the overall economy hurt by the loss of high-paying jobs in industries like automobiles and steel. During the 1970s the wages of steelworkers and autoworkers rose dramatically relative to their productivity and relative to the wages of other workers in the economy. To the extent the high wages paid in these industries represent monopoly profits captured by workers at the expense of shareholders, other workers, and consumers, they represent a transfer of income within the U.S. economy rather than a net addition to income. In fact, the benefits that consumers in general enjoy from access to lower-priced (and often better quality) steel and automobile imports more than offset the costs to workers who lose their jobs in these industries and must accept lower-paying jobs elsewhere in the economy.

National defense is another argument frequently offered as a reason for protecting some industries. Certainly, the steel industry will shrink in the face of growing international competition, but it is unlikely to disappear. Furthermore, if U.S. steel capacity should threaten to fall below the amount deemed necessary to meet national defense needs, it would be more efficient to subsidize steel production directly through the defense budget than to provide import relief.[18] Nor is steel production an important source of productivity growth the loss of which would threaten overall technical progress in the economy. Similarly, long-term growth in the standard of living would hardly seem to depend on whether Americans produce all, half, or none of the textiles, TVs, or VCRs that they consume.

Foreign governments may be subsidizing their steel, automobile, and consumer goods industries and giving them an ''unfair'' advantage over U.S.

producers, but the extent of such subsidization is less than is generally believed. Furthermore, as far as consumers are concerned, any advantage to foreign producers from such subsidies is no different from the "unfair" advantage tropical countries enjoy in the production of bananas and coffee, that the Organization of Petroleum Exporting Countries (OPEC) enjoys in the production of oil, or that the United States enjoys in the production of wheat because of climate and natural resource endowments. The fact that foreign governments have encouraged their industries to produce certain kinds of goods is not ipso facto evidence that the United States is harmed by such a development.[19] Particular workers and particular firms may be hurt, but the nation as a whole derives long-term benefits from lower import prices, whether they are due to artificial subsidies or natural cost advantages.

There are, however, some circumstances in which foreign trade practices can cause short-term disruptions in U.S. labor markets that it would be preferable to avoid. For example, Japan's determination to become a major exporter of steel after World War II and the more recent expansion of steel capacity in newly industrializing countries, together with a sharp drop in the rate of growth of demand for steel worldwide following the OPEC price increases of the 1970s, have produced a surplus of steel-making capacity in the world. As a result, countries try to keep up their own capacity utilization and employment by charging low prices for exports ("dumping") and limiting imports. This "beggar thy neighbor" policy of trying to export unemployment aggravates problems in relatively open economies like the United States. Dumping is, however, against U.S. trade law, and international trade agreements allow the imposition of countervailing duties to prevent it. Furthermore, true dumping of surplus production can cause short-term disruptions but not permanent long-term harm.

As for U.S. exports, it is lamentable that protectionist agricultural policies around the world limit U.S. agricultural markets, and other countries should be encouraged to do themselves a favor and buy more of their food and feed from the United States. (The United States, by the same token, should do itself a favor and remove barriers to imports of sugar and other agricultural products that are now protected.) The fact that restraints on foreign demand for U.S. products are artificial does not, however, justify export subsidies to U.S. producers selling standardized products in competitive markets.

A better case for worrying about the trade practices of foreign governments can be made in the case of high-tech goods like semiconductors. There is little question that the Japanese targeted their semiconductor industry for special treatment and that U.S. semiconductor manufacturers were denied free access to the Japanese market. It is probably also true that U.S. semiconductor manufacturers have made lower profits than they would have without Japanese competition, although rivalry among domestic producers and the entry of more domestic producers could equally well have eroded profitability. However, unless U.S. semiconductor manufacturers shrink to insignificance and there are no entrants in the future, the Japanese will continue to face strong competition and will find it hard to raise prices to monopoly levels. Achieving a dominant position in a market through government subsidy represents a Pyrrhic victory for the Japanese unless they can earn a return large enough to justify the subsidy.[20]

In many respects, proponents of an activist trade policy are resurrecting somewhat tarnished ideas from the industrial policy debate of a few years back. Put more charitably, they are adding a new gloss to an old, and in principle, legitimate argument for protection—the infant industry argument. Whether couched as competitiveness, industrial policy, or infant industry protection, their main argument is that there are some industries that are so important to promoting economic growth but so vulnerable to failure, especially in the early stages of new-product development, that they should receive targeted government support in the form of tariffs or subsidies until they have grown large enough and strong enough to survive on their own without that targeted support.

The main objections that have been raised against the adoption of strategic trade policies center on the enormous difficulty of translating the theoretical case for intervention into practical policies that do more good than harm. First, as shown in the discussion of U.S. imports and exports, it is difficult to identify clear, practical instances in which the theoretical conditions under which intervention would be appropriate apply. Second, the decision about what industries to target requires considerable guesswork about inherently unknowable future developments, and the cost of guessing wrong can be quite high because resources that would otherwise have been more profitably employed have been diverted into the targeted industry. The private market, too, is vulnerable to misforecasting the future, so the question becomes whether the potential myopia of myriad decision makers in the private market is more of a problem than the risk that a government relatively remote from the action will put all of its eggs in the wrong basket. Finally, and perhaps most important, decisions about what industries to target will almost inevitably become political decisions rather than economic decisions, increasing the likelihood that criteria other than those that underlie the case for intervention will be applied.

The United States should expect to face increasing international competition in areas of traditional U.S. strength, including high-tech products, in coming years. However, substantial opportunities will remain for mutually beneficial intraindustry trade between the United States and other countries, in which one country specializes in one product line and another country in a different product line within the same broad industry group.[21]

The general policies to promote growth discussed in chapter 3 will allow the United States to take advantage of these opportunities and remain a strong international competitor in the most technologically sophisticated products. Although the United States may need to adopt strategic trade policies in some situations, these need to be analyzed case by case; no general competitive strategy can or should be developed. Tough talk and the threat of imposing trade restrictions are useful if they encourage other countries to open their markets, but the game must be played very carefully lest it degenerate into the mutually destructive imposition of further restrictions.

## Summary

In summary, imperfect competition, economies of scale, technological change, and product differentiation have led many people to question the strong conclusions of traditional models of international trade, which urge benign neglect in the presence of active trade intervention by the U.S. trading partners. However, the case for free trade remains strong even under real-world conditions, suggesting that there should be a presumption against protectionist policy intervention even in the presence of "unfair" foreign competition.

This argument does not imply, however, that the United States should be unconcerned with its international competitive position—it should; but general policies to promote growth are to be preferred to specifically trade-oriented policies. Nor does it imply that the United States should be unconcerned with the effect of trade on the distribution of income or with the short-term side effects of pursuing appropriate long-term policies.

## **Distributional Consequences of International Competition**

A theme that has run through this chapter is that international competition is good for the average American, but it may not be good for all Americans. Over the long term, the pattern of production encouraged by international competition will raise the market value of some skills relative to others, and the wages paid for low-valued skills may fail to rise in line with overall economic growth. In the short term, changes in the pattern of demand may cause some experienced workers to lose their jobs and have difficulty finding comparable jobs. If the costs to individual workers of adjusting to international competition are not identified and proper policy responses developed, groups that are adversely affected may resist change; if they are successful politically, the potential gains from trade will not be realized fully, although overall they may be much larger than the costs to those who must adjust.

## Trade, Deindustrialization, and the Distribution of Income

To many people, the most important distributional consequence of the growing internationalization of the U.S. economy is the loss of "good" manufacturing jobs and their replacement by "bad" service sector jobs. Fears are expressed, for example, that unless manufacturing is protected from import competition, the United States will become a nation of hamburger stands and that most new jobs will be undesirable, dead-end "McJobs." Most high-tech "MacJobs" are thought to be worse than the manufacturing jobs they replace, and those that are thought to be better are thought to require technical or managerial skills that place them beyond the reach of the typical worker. Even if average incomes rise over time, few Americans would look favorably on a situation in which the number of middle-class jobs that have traditionally represented economic success in this country was declining.[22] But is such a prospect in the offing?

Probably not. Studies cited in chapter 2 provide little evidence to support the hypothesis that middle-class jobs are disappearing. People who argue that they are disappearing infer long-term consequences from short-term shocks that have hit high-wage jobs disproportionately, and they give insufficient attention to the more basic forces that ultimately shape the distribution of earnings.

Certainly, the 1980s were hard on Smokestack America. Battered by back-to-back recessions and a strong dollar, manufacturing employment fell sharply from its 1979 peak and has yet to recover to that level. However, manufacturing employment as a share of total employment has been declining for a long time, and recent employment shifts attributable to trade represent relatively minor deviations from this trend (figure 4.7). Manufacturing output, in contrast, is higher than it has ever been and the share of output accounted for by manufacturing has hardly changed over the past forty years. With higher productivity growth than other sectors of the economy, manufacturing industries have been able to expand output in line with overall economic growth while the number of manufacturing jobs has fallen. Although manufacturing employment may eventually surpass its 1979 peak, these trends are likely to continue, and most of the new jobs generated in the economy will not be manufacturing jobs.

If viewed only from the perspective of existing wage patterns, such a shift might seem to imply a worsening in the distribution of earnings, because many of the manufacturing jobs that will be lost will be high-paying unionized

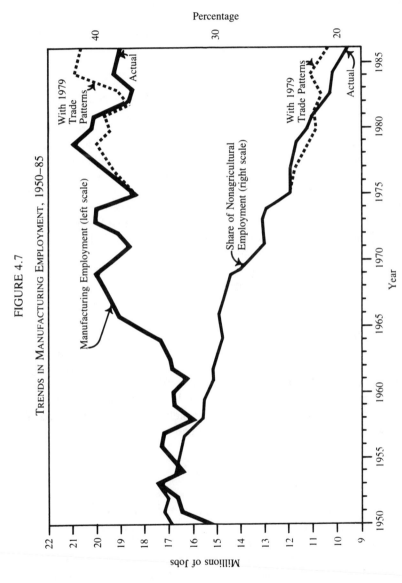

FIGURE 4.7

TRENDS IN MANUFACTURING EMPLOYMENT, 1950–85

SOURCE: Bureau of Labor Statistics in *Economic Report of the President, January 1987,* table B-40 and author's calculations.

jobs in sectors like steel. Furthermore, the short-term employment shifts associated with the changing trade patterns of the 1980s have reinforced the belief that high-wage jobs are disappearing and being replaced by low-wage jobs (recall table 4.3). Over the long term, however, the distribution of earnings depends much more on the distribution of skills and educability in the population than it does on the industrial or occupational composition of employment opportunities.

International competition will encourage the United States to increase production of goods and services that take advantage of its large capital stock, skilled labor force, and technological sophistication, while discouraging the production of standardized manufactured goods that employ relatively unskilled workers. These developments, in turn, will increase the demand for skilled labor and reduce the demand for unskilled labor. Although the characteristics and skill requirements of "good" jobs will change, so, too, will the characteristics and skills of workers—unless there is a widespread failure of the educational system to provide tomorrow's workers with the basic reading and reasoning skills that tomorrow's good jobs will require.

Barring such a failure, most workers can expect to enjoy a higher standard of living in an economy open to international competition than in one protected against such competition. However, competition from standardized products produced with cheap foreign labor, the relocation of U.S. operations abroad, and direct competition from immigrants will tend to keep the earnings of workers in the U.S. economy who lack the skills to get mainstream jobs from rising in line with general economic growth. Although a widening of the earnings gap between skilled and unskilled workers may accompany the growing internationalization of the U.S. economy, improvements in the educational system—especially improved education of disadvantaged students—can reduce the number of potentially disadvantaged workers, and changes in the structure of taxes and income security expenditures can reduce the risk that socially divisive income disparities will emerge.

## The Short-Term Costs of Adjusting to International Competition

Although these long-term distributional consequences of the growing internationalization of the economy are important, the more immediate concern of most workers is how international competition affects their own earnings and job security. When shifting patterns of comparative advantage lead to shifting patterns of demand for different goods and different kinds of workers, some workers, including well-paid, experienced workers, will lose their jobs and face little prospect of getting them back. Some of these dislocated workers may move readily to other jobs, but other workers with investments in specific skills, union wage premiums, community or family ties, or a lack of knowledge of alternatives will move less readily, especially if the only prospects they see entail lower earnings than they enjoyed in the past. It will be small comfort to them to know that the nation as a whole is benefiting from the changes that are causing them hardship.

One reason for worrying about these dislocated workers is that the American sense of fair play argues against letting a small group bear relatively large individual costs so that the rest of us can enjoy relatively modest individual benefits. A second, pragmatic reason is that it is easier politically to adopt appropriate free-trade policies if there is some protection for persons who might otherwise be hurt by such policies. Finally, and perhaps most important, excessive unemployment associated with dislocation is costly and wasteful.

A certain amount of frictional unemployment is necessary and desirable while workers search for jobs in which they will be most productive, but dislocated workers may be prone to excessive spells of unemployment. For one thing, older, experienced workers may have little knowledge about how to search for a new job. For another, workers with skills that are no longer in demand may need to be retrained to be employable at reasonable wages, but they may be ignorant of retraining opportunities. Finally, workers dislocated from relatively high-paying jobs may remain unemployed too long, hoping to get their old jobs back, before accepting the fact that their market value has depreciated. Excessive unemployment translates into lost output and lower national income, which diminish the gains from trade. Policies that reduce structural unemployment and encourage adjustment in a cost-effective way are good for the individual workers and good for society because they raise national income and reduce unemployment insurance and other transfers.

How serious is the dislocated-worker problem? Surveys by the Bureau of Labor Statistics mentioned earlier in this chapter provide the most comprehensive data on dislocated workers in the 1980s. According to these surveys, the number of adult workers with three or more years of job tenure who lost their jobs because of a plant closing or move, nonseasonal slack work, or the abolition of their shift or position averaged about a million a year between 1979 and 1985 (table 4.4). However, when the definition is restricted to workers who experienced more than five weeks of unemployment, the count of dislocated workers drops to about 800,000 a year; and when the definition is restricted to those who experienced more than the twenty-six weeks of unemployment typically covered by unemployment compensation,

TABLE 4.4

CHARACTERISTICS OF DISLOCATED WORKERS, 1979–85

| Characteristic | 1984 Survey (1979–83) | 1985 Update (1979–84) | 1986 Survey (1981–85) |
|---|---|---|---|
| Total (millions of workers) | 5.1 | 5.1 | 5.1 |
| Percentage full-time | 92.5 | 92.5 | 94.7 |
| Percentage age 25–54 | 70.6 | 70.6 | 77.0 |
| Labor force status at time of survey | | | |
| Percentage employed | 60.1 | 67.3 | 66.9 |
| Percentage unemployed | 25.5 | 12.4 | 17.8 |
| Percentage out of the labor force | 14.4 | 20.4 | 15.3 |
| Unemployment experience, number of workers with— | | | |
| More than 5 weeks of unemployment | 3.9 | NA | 3.5 |
| More than 26 weeks of unemployment | 2.2 | NA | 1.9 |
| Distribution of earnings change among previously full-time workers reemployed full-time on date of survey (percentage) | | | |
| Earnings loss greater than 20 percent | 27.4 | 17.9 | 27.5 |
| Earnings loss less than 20 percent | 14.1 | 15.6 | 12.9 |
| Earnings gain less than 20 percent | 25.2 | 24.5 | 24.5 |
| Earnings gain greater than 20 percent | 23.5 | 34.9 | 26.8 |
| Not reported | 9.8 | 7.1 | 8.3 |
| Total | 100.0 | 100.0 | 100.0 |
| Number of reemployed workers (millions) | 2.3 | NA | 2.7 |
| Percentage of all dislocated workers | 44.5 | NA | 51.8 |

SOURCE: Bureau of Labor Statistics.
NA = Not available.

the number drops still further to 540,000 a year. By this most narrow definition, only about one worker in twenty who experienced some unemployment each year was a dislocated worker who experienced excessive unemployment.

Table 4.5 provides information about dislocated workers at the industry level. These data show that the dislocated workers of the 1980s have come disproportionately from goods-producing industries. Although the dislocated worker population included a large number of service sector workers, they represented a small proportion of all service sector workers. Furthermore, as shown in table 4.5, employment opportunities in the ser-

TABLE 4.5

DISLOCATED WORKERS BY INDUSTRY

| | Dislocated Workers | | | | Percentage Change in Total Employment 1979–84 |
|---|---|---|---|---|---|
| | In Thousands | | As a Percentage of 1979 Jobs | | |
| Industry | 1979–84 | 1981–86 | 1979–84 | 1981–86 | |
| Agriculture | 100 | 141 | 6.6 | 9.3 | −3.8 |
| Mining | 151 | 177 | 13.2 | 15.4 | −17.7 |
| Construction | 481 | 359 | 10.8 | 8.1 | −4.3 |
| Manufacturing | | | | | |
| Durables | 1,685 | 1,707 | 13.4 | 13.5 | −10.1 |
| Nondurables | 824 | 883 | 10.3 | 11.0 | −5.6 |
| Services | 1,831 | 1,858 | 3.1 | 3.1 | 10.0 |
| All industries | 5,072 | 5,125 | 5.8 | 5.9 | 4.8 |

SOURCE: Bureau of Labor Statistics.

vice sector were expanding much faster than employment opportunities in the rest of the economy, making it easier to reabsorb dislocated workers. In contrast, an absolute decline in the number of manufacturing jobs made it especially difficult for dislocated manufacturing workers to be reemployed in comparable jobs.

This was a difficult period for dislocated workers. Every year from 1980 through 1986 was characterized by a weak overall labor market. The problems of manufacturing workers were aggravated by dislocations due to trade, notwithstanding the impact of trade restraints in key industries like steel, textiles, and automobiles. The transportation and communications industries were being restructured as a result of earlier deregulation initiatives.

Despite these difficulties, about 60 percent of the workers identified in the 1984 survey as becoming dislocated between 1979 and 1984 were reemployed in 1984 and more than two-thirds were reemployed a year later. Similarly, two-thirds of those identified in the 1986 survey as becoming dislocated between 1982 and 1985 were reemployed in 1986. A majority of those who were reemployed received wages at least as high as the wages they received in their previous job (table 4.4). However, many workers who lost their jobs received little or no advance notice that they would lose their jobs and little or no job counseling or placement assistance from their employers, which probably contributed to the fact that many remained unemployed for a long period of time or dropped out of the labor force entirely.[23] Also, a substantial minority of dislocated workers who subsequently found new jobs had to accept wages that were less than 80 percent of the wages they earned in their original jobs. Finally, many of the dislocated workers who experienced large adjustment costs were experienced male workers with good technical and general job skills whose prolonged unemployment is particularly costly to the economy.

Is the dislocated worker problem growing? Unfortunately there are no data comparable to those from the Bureau of Labor Statistics surveys for earlier periods, and so indirect evidence must be used to put the experience of the early 1980s into historical perspective. First, both the unemployment rate and economists' estimates of the unemployment rate consistent with stable inflation rates have shown an upward trend since the early 1950s. Furthermore, increases in unemployment in recent years have been concentrated among mature men, job losers, and the long-term unemployed; these increases do not seem to be readily attributable to measurement problems, demographic shifts, or cyclical factors.[24] However, measures of potential dislocation such as the number of workers in contracting industries or actual job losses in contracting industries show considerable variability over time but no upward trend once business cycle effects are removed. If increasing dislocation due to structural change is an important factor that has contributed to the long-term rise in the average unemployment rate, it does not show up in these data.

Thus, dislocated workers seem to represent a small but important minority of all workers, and economic factors that contribute to dislocation seem to have been particularly severe in recent years.[25] It is impossible to know for certain whether the macroeconomic problems of the early 1980s have masked newly emerging structural problems, but at least some of the dislocation identified in the BLS surveys would not have taken place without the extreme pressure put on manufacturing by the trade and exchange rate developments discussed earlier in this chapter. If the economic recovery continues and the budget and trade deficits are brought under control, the dispersion of employment changes across industries is likely to be reduced. Manufacturing losses will be reduced and gains in the service sector will be smaller.

Although patterns of comparative advantage associated with increasing international competition will probably change gradually, so that much adjustment can be accomplished through natural attrition, the dislocated-worker phenomenon will not vanish entirely, and there may be episodes in the future when it is as serious as it was in the early to mid-1980s. The United States was not particularly prepared to deal with the problem then, and it would be prudent to be better prepared in the future.

## Policies Toward Dislocated Workers

The United States has never had a systematic program to deal with the problems of dislocated workers. Unemployment insurance is meant to provide a financial cushion against income losses during temporary spells of unemployment, but it was not designed to promote adjustment of unemployed workers into other industries. In fact, unemployment insurance is generally viewed as detrimental to adjustment because it weakens the financial incentives to look for a new job. Employment and training programs have tackled the general problem of dislocated workers and other programs have specifically targeted workers dislocated by trade, but these programs have shown little consistency over the years in their levels of funding or in the kinds of workers targeted for assistance.

**Employment and Training Programs.** During the past twenty-five years, the United States has had three different employment and training regimes. The Manpower Development and Training Act (MDTA), which operated from 1962 to 1973, was originally designed to address the problems of structural unemployment among adult workers, but it evolved into a program in which two-thirds of training positions went to youth and disadvantaged workers. The Comprehensive Employment and Training Act (CETA), which replaced MDTA in 1973, was the nation's major employment and training program until it expired in 1982, but it never served many dislocated workers. Title III of the nation's current employment and training program, the Job Training Partnership Act (JTPA), provides funds to state governments, which they must partially match, to support local projects specifically targeted toward dislocated workers.

Assistance under Title III may be provided in the form of training, job placement, worker relocation assistance, or support services (such as child care or transportation). States may administer projects directly or they may distribute funds to local organizations, including unions or employers. States were slow to take advantage of JTPA, and fewer than 100,000 people a year were served by JTPA through 1984, compared with the nearly 500,000 dislocated workers a year who experienced prolonged bouts of unemployment. More workers have been enrolled in JTPA programs since 1985, but the program still fails to reach most dislocated workers. Moreover, JTPA is serving a somewhat higher proportion of women, minorities, younger workers, and better-educated workers than it is the older white men who constitute an important fraction of the dislocated-worker population.

According to a survey by the General Accounting Office, through March 1985, Title III projects had placed a higher percentage of participants (69

percent) at a higher average hourly wage ($6.61) than earlier employment
and training programs. However, most participants failed to find jobs with
wages comparable to the jobs they had lost, and the average wage earned by
program participants was well below the average wage of $8.52 paid to private
sector, nonsupervisory workers. The major service provided was job placement assistance (to 80 percent of participants); fewer than half of all participants received training, and fewer than a quarter received support services.[26]

Critics of employment and training programs properly point out that
evaluations of these programs, especially those of MDTA and CETA, do not
reveal whether the programs have provided benefits sufficiently large to justify
their costs; but the record of past programs is not universally dismal and the
verdict on JTPA is not yet in. Advocates of such programs can find examples
of successful and creative programs, and the diversity fostered under Title
III of JTPA may reveal more.

Programs offering a full range of training and job search assistance do
seem to be successful, at least in the short term, for highly motivated workers
in strong local labor markets.[27] Job search assistance seems to be more cost-
effective than training, and basic education seems to be as necessary as
vocational training. Programs seem to be reasonably successful in enabling
participants to compete more effectively for existing jobs and to achieve more
stable employment, although not generally at higher hourly wages or in more
highly skilled positions than they held before the training. Programs that reach
dislocated workers early, ideally before they have actually been laid off, seem
to be far more successful than programs that serve workers who have already
been unemployed for some time. However, questions remain as to whether
the earnings gains afforded program participants last long enough to justify
program costs, whether the workers who are successfully placed are those
who would have done reasonably well even without the program, and whether
these programs have effectively lowered the number of unemployed workers
rather than simply given program participants an advantage over nonpartic-
ipants in the competition for jobs.

**Trade Adjustment Assistance.** In addition to general employment and
training programs, the United States has had a program of Trade Adjustment Assistance (TAA) targeted on workers dislocated by trade. TAA was
established as part of the Trade Expansion Act of 1962, expanded and
liberalized under the Trade Expansion Act of 1974, and then scaled back
substantially in 1981 as part of the Reagan budget cuts. Until 1969, no
workers received aid under the strict eligibility criteria; but between TAA's
liberalization in the mid-1970s and its peak funding in 1981, $3.9 billion
was paid out to 1.3 million recipients. TAA was designed to help workers
in industries where the Labor Department certified that imports made an

important contribution to unemployment and to assist firms and communities where the Commerce Department made a similar certification. Workers were eligible for both generous cash allowances (70 percent of weekly wages for up to seventy-eight weeks), and services such as job search, counseling, training, and relocation subsidies. These services were little used, but they were all that remained of the program after 1985, when funding for all cash payments was stopped.

TAA is now widely judged to have been a failure. Few people were served initially, and a large number of those who were served ended up returning to their old employers—which suggests that the program was serving persons facing temporary layoffs rather than those facing true dislocation. There is little evidence that TAA promoted adjustment, and many of the workers who received assistance were high-wage workers who returned to high-wage jobs. This experience with TAA calls into question the general approach, when designing a program, of focusing on the cause of a job loss rather than its consequences. Adjustment assistance programs are needed for workers who face a permanent job loss and difficulty finding a job, regardless of the cause of the job loss. Workers facing temporary earnings losses caused by import competition do not, in principle, have a greater claim on assistance than those facing temporary earnings losses for other reasons, who are eligible only for unemployment compensation.[28]

**Special Protection for Industries Harmed by Imports.** TAA is one example of how concern with dislocated workers has often focused on dislocation associated with imports. A second example is the establishment of an "escape" clause in U.S. trade law that provides a procedure whereby industries that believe they have been harmed by imports can petition for relief through tariffs, quotas, or some other form of protection. Responsibility for determining whether injury has indeed occurred and for recommending relief rests with the U.S. International Trade Commission (USITC), an independent federal agency. The president must then determine whether to take the recommended action.

In important instances, however, such as President Reagan's negotiation of a voluntary automobile export-restraint agreement with the Japanese, the escape clause mechanism has been circumvented and special protection has been given to particular industries through other means. This special protection has been very costly, especially when measured in terms of jobs preserved in affected industries. For example, Hufbauer and Rosen estimate the annual costs to consumers per job preserved to be $42,000 in textiles and apparel, $105,000 in automobiles, and $750,000 in steel. These costs are several times the likely dislocation costs that workers in these industries would face if protection were removed.

In contrast to the escape clause, which provides a standardized administrative procedure for determining injury and setting a remedy, congressionally mandated or presidentially negotiated protection is explicitly political and the benefits to the few from greater protection get far more attention in the political arena than the costs to the many. Also, the political process tends to produce nontariff forms of protection, because the costs to consumers are less transparent, even though the social costs of nontariff barriers are higher than the costs of tariffs when foreign producers and importers capture what would otherwise be tariff revenue. The protection afforded steel and textiles and apparel, for example, is equivalent to what would be afforded by a 30 percent tariff, but little government revenue flows from this protection.[29] Finally, special protection granted outside the escape clause procedure tends to last longer than escape clause protection. For example, Hufbauer and Rosen estimate that the average duration of escape clause relief is about four years, whereas textile protection of one sort or another has been in effect since 1957, and steel protection of one sort or another has been in effect since 1969.

Like Trade Adjustment Assistance, special protection for industries harmed by imports has turned out to be an expensive and ineffective way of dealing with dislocation due to trade. Rather than providing workers, firms, and communities with breathing room while necessary adjustments are made, special protection has fostered the illusion that no adjustment need be made.

## New Directions for Policy

An important theme of this chapter is that adjustments in the structure of the economy will be needed if the United States is to profit fully from expanding world trade. Unfortunately, President Reagan has allowed special protection to spread while he has been in office, and many recent congressional initiatives have contained protectionist elements that would impede rather than foster effective adjustment.

For example, proposals to impose trade restraints on countries whose trade surplus with the United States is "too large" fail to recognize the underlying macroeconomic causes of the U.S. trade deficit. The proposed actions would be ineffective in reducing the trade deficit, would impose costs on consumers, and would confer benefits on producers without regard to the degree of dislocation they might be experiencing. Proposals to make it easier to get relief through the escape clause by weakening the standards needed to prove injury or by removing the president's discretion in implementing the USITC's recommendations would legitimate the spread of costly special protection. Proposals to make relief from imports conditional on an industry's submitting an acceptable plan for restructuring would be useful if they encouraged contracting industries to make an orderly adjustment, but it is more likely that political concern with preserving existing patterns of production and employment would cause resources to be wastefully reinvested in industries that should shrink.

Advocates of free trade who recognize that the complete elimination of all protection is not a politically acceptable alternative to protectionism have suggested reforms of the escape clause that would promote free trade in the long term while giving industries breathing room to adjust in the short term.[30] These proposals would make relief more certain upon demonstration of injury than it is now (without weakening the standards required to show injury), but they also would make relief more certain to expire after a fixed period of time during which protection is phased out. Also, no relief other than tariffs would be granted. Such a policy not only would make the costs of protection more apparent than they are when nontariff relief is granted, but also would generate government revenue that could be used to fund adjustment assistance programs to help affected workers find new jobs, compensate them for permanent income losses, and reduce the burden on communities with large numbers of dislocated workers. Representative calculations by proponents of such proposals indicate that relief could be provided at far less cost than the relief now provided through special protection. The conversion of existing special protection to tariffs would be worthwhile regardless of whether the escape clause mechanism is revamped.

As a means of heading off protectionism, programs that focus on trade-impacted industries have some appeal, but many dislocated workers are from industries in which technological change or slow growth in demand are the causes of dislocation and trade is of little or no importance. These workers' claim to adjustment assistance is as strong as the claim of workers dislocated by trade. There is nothing like the escape clause that would give their industries breathing room to adjust, but adjustment assistance payments and employment and training programs could provide workers with a financial cushion against large income losses while helping them to find work elsewhere.

By far the most effective policies for minimizing the costs of adjusting to structural dislocation are aggregate macroeconomic policies that promote growth and high employment. Poor overall economic performance greatly reduces the effectiveness of programs whose goal is to place dislocated workers in new jobs, no matter how well designed those programs are. And the flexibility and adaptability of the private market should not be underestimated.

Individual workers, firms, and communities bear a substantial responsibility for their own welfare, and private market negotiations provide maximum freedom to develop suitable arrangements for carrying out these responsibilities. If, for example, the pace of economic change is indeed accelerating and fears of dislocation are increasing, firms may find that in order to attract and keep the best workers they will have to promise advance notification of plant closings or layoffs, portable pension and health insurance coverage, in-house job search assistance, generous severance pay, and the like. Workers, in turn, may find that, to get jobs providing these benefits and to allow their firms to be competitive, they will have to accept lower guaranteed wages and more flexible working conditions. Average compensation need not be reduced by such arrangements, but the proportions of that compensation accounted for by straight wages, nonwage benefits, and profit sharing will change.[31]

Thus, employment and training and adjustment assistance programs should be designed to fill gaps in the market adjustment process, and care should be taken that they do not supplant or unduly subvert private market efforts. Toward this end, programs should have relatively strict eligibility standards, and the employment and training component should be designed so that there is a reasonable expectation that it will reduce structural unemployment rather than simply redistribute the incidence of unemployment. If the mistakes of TAA are to be avoided, any adjustment assistance payments meant to compensate for permanent earnings losses need to be targeted on workers with the largest losses and the greatest difficulty becoming reemployed.

As mentioned earlier, evaluations of employment and training programs have found that they are much more effective if they reach affected workers early— even before they have been laid off or before their plant has closed. Also, these programs seem to be more effective when business is closely involved in their implementation. These findings suggest the desirability of nurturing the development of organizations like the Private Industry Councils (PICs) now required in JTPA programs to bring business and community leaders together in a cooperative effort to prevent excessively disruptive dislocation and to promote adjustment where plant closings or layoffs cannot be avoided. Another potentially useful innovation would be the creation of rapid response teams similar to those that seem to have been successful in Canada in bringing technical assistance to communities facing a plant closing or other dislocation of a significant fraction of their labor force. The diversity of local approaches fostered under JTPA has the desirable feature of encouraging the development of innovative solutions to the dislocated-worker problem. The federal government has an oversight role, but it should also serve as a clearinghouse and disseminator of successful ideas developed at the local level and as a provider of technical assistance to communities that need help in mounting an effective program.

Although businesses have opposed legislation that would require firms to give advance notice of plant closings or large layoffs, there seems to be a

synergy between advance notice, rapid intervention, and successful adjustment. In fact, companies that have voluntarily implemented advance notice,
severance, and job-search assistance programs seem to have been rewarded
with improved employee morale and continuing good productivity.[32] Of course,
too-rigid regulations requiring firms to give advance notice or mandating
severance pay could do more harm than good by raising firms' perceived
costs of expanding employment or restricting the ability of workers and firms
to reach mutually agreeable arrangements regarding what proportion of compensation should be wages and what proportion should be insurance against
peremptory dislocation. However, the value of advance notice in aiding adjustment suggests the desirability of encouraging business to give such notice
whenever feasible. Although some early legislative initiatives to mandate
advance notice were overly rigid and provoked predictable business hostility,
some of business's worst fears appear to have been allayed in currently
proposed legislation. Any legislation passed in this area should be flexible
enough to allow for some diversity of circumstances among firms without
being so watered down as to be meaningless.

Employment and training programs will be most successful if they can
expect to place workers in new jobs with pay comparable to what they were
earning in the jobs they lost; but such an expectation is not always realistic.
The provision of cash payments to compensate for permanent earnings losses
may, therefore, be politically necessary to enhance the attractiveness of ad-
justment-oriented programs over protectionist alternatives, but it would be
desirable to find a way to compensate for earnings losses and at the same
time encourage adjustment. As an example of what might prove useful,
workers could be allowed to continue to receive unemployment compensation
for a fixed period of time after accepting a new job, with the size of the
continuing payment tied to the gap between earnings on the new job and
earnings on the lost job.

Not everyone believes that an expanded federal government effort is
necessary to combat the dislocated-worker problem. To some, a policy of
benign neglect is as appropriate in dealing with the short-term distributional
consequences of adjusting to international competition as it is in dealing with
foreign governments' policies to promote their own industries. Such an approach is appealing if one believes strongly (1) that the dislocated-worker
problem of the early to mid-1980s was a transitory phenomenon related to
recession, an overvalued dollar, and the introduction of greater competition
to monopolistic industries with excessive union wage premiums; (2) that under
more normal circumstances workers and firms adapt reasonably quickly and
efficiently to changing economic conditions; and (3) that little in the record
of past government efforts to tackle the dislocated-worker problem inspires

confidence that the political process can develop cost-effective programs to deal with any residual dislocation.

This view is probably too optimistic with respect to the market and too pessimistic with respect to the government. There is always a danger that otherwise worthwhile federal government programs will fall prey to bureaucratic inefficiencies or pork-barrel politics that expand their size and dilute their effectiveness, but carefully targeted programs crafted along the lines just discussed seem to offer a reasonable hope of buffering adjustment costs while still promoting adjustment.

Policies discussed thus far deal with the problems of experienced workers facing dislocation. However, if the United States is indeed entering a new era of international competition in which earnings disparities between skilled and unskilled workers might widen, more radical policy approaches may be appropriate to allow workers at the bottom of the income distribution to share in the economy's growth. If the United States is to take maximum advantage of the opportunities afforded by trade and technology to grow and prosper, firms must be free to pay workers according to the value of what they produce and workers must be willing to accept jobs in accordance with their skills. At the same time, however, workers willing to work hard full-time must earn enough to enjoy a satisfactory standard of living. Proposals to raise the minimum wage or to require firms to provide health insurance or other fringe benefits run the risk of simply raising prices or reducing employment opportunities if the costs imposed on firms are not justified by the workers' productivity.

The most straightforward way to let market wages signal where people can be employed most efficiently yet still reduce income disparities is to introduce greater progressivity into the tax and transfer system. Of course, if marginal tax rates are too high or social insurance benefits are too generous, incentives to work, save, and invest may be undermined. Conversely, too great a disparity between the standard of living available to those with mainstream jobs and the standard of living available to those whose lack of education and training keeps them from getting such jobs can be harmful as well. In return for a more open market economy in which their incomes will be as high as possible, workers with the best mainstream jobs would be expected to pay more in taxes. Those with the worst jobs would be compensated with an expanded social safety net.

Consider, for example, a scheme in which more progressive tax rates are combined with (1) a broadening of the tax base to make fringe benefits paid by employers taxable as ordinary income to the worker and (2) an expanded social insurance program in which refundable tax credits are allowed for purchases of health insurance, supplemental retirement saving, or education and training. The expenditures qualifying for credits would replace the fringes now provided only in "good" jobs. Such a scheme would function as a targeted negative income tax. Workers with low incomes would receive a subsidy (perhaps as "negative" withholding in their weekly paycheck) for favored expenditures; those with higher incomes would be net taxpayers despite the credit.

Such a system imposes no requirements on employers to provide a certain minimum set of benefits, and it imposes no obligation on workers to purchase these benefits. It does, however, provide good incentives in the form of a tax credit (stronger than a deduction), and the refundability provision allows for payments to households with particularly low earnings if such purchases are made. Because the system imposes no obligations on employers, it encourages an efficient wage structure based on the value of output produced. As many necessities become cheaper and as workers at all wage levels gain the greater income security such a program provides, differences in earnings among different jobs will translate into differences in discretionary spending. Low-wage jobs will allow for fewer restaurant meals, fancy vacations, luxury automobiles, and housekeeping services than high-wage jobs, but they will not signify an inability to meet a minimal satisfactory standard of living. In this way, differences in wages can still encourage people to acquire the education and training necessary to get good jobs, but the difference between a high-wage job and a low-wage job will represent a greater or lesser ability to enjoy discretionary expenditures rather than the difference between a satisfactory and an unsatisfactory standard of living.

The point of this discussion is not to argue for this or any other specific plan, but rather to suggest that a new view of the role of the government and of the market may be appropriate if the United States is to be as successful as possible in adjusting to international competition.

## Summary

Structural adjustment to foreign competition is, on the whole, both necessary and desirable if the standard of living in the United States is to be as high as possible. Most workers should be able to acquire the education and training that will allow them to get good jobs and to share in the rising standard of living afforded by expanding world trade, but international competition may make some workers worse off than they would be if the United States adopted more protectionist policies. Workers with the least education and training face the risk that competition from cheap foreign labor will keep their wages from rising in line with growth in the rest of the economy. More highly trained workers face the risk that shifting patterns of comparative advantage will cause some of them to lose high-paying jobs and have difficulty finding comparable jobs. Reform of existing programs can promote more efficient adjustment to changing labor market conditions while providing greater protection to individual workers, but the nation might wish to consider more radical changes in the structure of taxes and transfers to make sure that most Americans will share in the country's growth.

## Conclusions

This chapter has explored the relationship between the growing internationalization of the U.S. economy and its ability to deliver a high and rising standard of living to most Americans. Although skepticism has been expressed that the United States is becoming deindustrialized or losing its ability to compete in world markets, complacency is not in order. The typical American will experience a higher standard of living if the economy is open to technological change and foreign competition than if it is resistant to change, but there is some risk that a substantial minority will fail to participate in economic growth and that others will risk being displaced from good jobs. Some economists believe that these risks simply constitute the price that must be paid for economic growth. It has been argued here, however, that considerations both of fairness and of efficiency require that the country improve policies to help the people bearing the short-term costs of adjusting to economic change and to offset the effects of any tendency for the distribution of market wages to become more unequal.

NOTES FOR CHAPTER 4

1. The Balance of Payments Accounts (BPAs) of the United States record transactions between U.S. residents and foreign residents in a double-entry bookkeeping system. The difference between merchandise exports and merchandise imports in these accounts is reported monthly and gets the most attention as a measure of the country's trade deficit. The balance on goods and services is a more comprehensive measure of current trade flows, because it includes transactions in services (such as travel, transportation, and insurance) and the difference between U.S. income earned abroad (such as interest on holdings of foreign bonds) and foreign income earned in the United States (such as interest on foreign holdings of U.S. securities). In theory, net exports recorded in the National Income and Product Accounts (NIPAs) are identical to the balance on goods and services recorded in the BPAs, but there are differences in the actual series because of differences in the treatment of some items. The current account balance, which adds unilateral transfers from U.S. residents and the U.S. government to foreign residents and governments, is the most comprehensive measure of current trade flows. Overall, the BPAs must balance, hence any current account deficit must be offset by a surplus in the accounts measuring capital transactions. Capital account transactions that can finance a current account deficit include increases in U.S. liabilities to foreigners or reductions in foreign liabilities to U.S. residents and sales of foreign assets by U.S. residents or purchases of U.S. assets by foreigners.

2. W. L. Helkie, and P. Hooper, "The U.S. External Deficit in the 1980s," in Ralph C. Bryant, Dale W. Henderson, Gerald Holtham, Peter Hooper, and Steven A. Symansky, eds., *Empirical Macroeconomics for Interdependent Economies* (Washington, D.C.: Brookings Institution, forthcoming.)

3. For a discussion of the results from several econometric models, see Ralph C. Bryant, and Gerald Holtham, "The U.S. External Deficit: Diagnosis, Prognosis, and Cure," in *Empirical Macroeconomics*; and C. S. Hakkio, and R. Roberts, "Has the Dollar Fallen Enough?" *Economic Review*, Federal Reserve Bank of Kansas City, July-August 1987.

4. See P. R. Krugman, and R. E. Baldwin, "The Persistence of the U.S. Trade Deficit," *Brookings Papers on Economic Activity* (1987), 1, as well as the comments by other participants.

5. Assuming the labor force remains constant, national income rises with the capital stock. Although most of the benefits of foreign investment accrue to the foreign investors themselves, small spillover benefits accrue to U.S. workers from the larger capital stock afforded by foreign investment.

6. Even without international capital flows, a crowding out of private investment could have been avoided if higher interest rates induced a substantial increase in private saving; but most estimates of the interest sensitivity of private saving provide little hope for optimism on that score. Private saving actually fell somewhat during the 1980s despite a sharp rise in real interest rates.

7. The initial impact of trade restraints would be to shift demand from foreign producers to domestic producers. If there were considerable slack in the economy, domestic output and employment might be able to expand, and the gap between domestic spending and domestic production (and hence the trade deficit) could shrink. More realistically, however, if the economy were close to high employment or if the Federal Reserve Board were worried about restraining inflation, the initial stimulus to domestic output and employment would lead the Fed to tighten the money supply to keep aggregate output and employment from rising above their target levels. Such monetary restraint would result in higher interest rates and an appreciation of the dollar that would hurt interest-sensitive and trade-related industries by the same amount that protected industries were helped. The problems of trade-related industries would be exacerbated if foreigners retaliated with tariffs of their own.

8. It is not inevitable that domestic investment would be crowded out by the budget deficit, but see note 6 above. Nor is a recession inevitable: in theory, the rise in net exports could exactly offset the fall in investment, keeping aggregate output and employment nearly the same as before the plunge in the dollar; but this situation would require a combination of good policy and good luck.

9. See Bryant and Holtham, "The U.S. External Deficit," for a discussion of the need for cooperation to correct the U.S. trade deficit in an orderly fashion.

10. Krugman and Baldwin, "The Persistence of the U.S. Trade Deficit." The terms of trade measure the constant-dollar value of imports that can be bought per constant dollar of exports and are calculated by dividing the price index for exports by the price index for imports. The U.S. terms of trade had to decline in the 1970s to keep U.S. goods competitive with foreign goods because foreign productivity was growing more rapidly than U.S. productivity.

11. These estimates are for full-time-equivalent employees as reported in the National Income and Product Accounts before the June 1987 revisions. They are derived from an input-output analysis described in appendix A of Charles F. Stone and Isabel V. Sawhill, "Labor Market Implications of the Growing Internationalization of the U.S. Economy," Research Report RR-86-20 (Washington, D.C.: National Commission for Employment Policy, June 1986). Briefly, the change in employment in each sector attributable to changes in the pattern of trade between 1979 and 1984 was estimated by subtracting from actual employment in each sector in 1984 an estimate of what employment in that sector would have been in 1984 if the proportion of output needed to produce exports and the percentage change in output required to replace imports in each sector had remained the same as they were in 1979, assuming the same growth in total employment as took place between 1979 and 1984.

144                                                CHALLENGE TO LEADERSHIP

12. See *Displaced Workers*, 1979-83, Bulletin 2240, U.S. Department of Labor, Bureau of Labor Statistics, July 1985, and "Reemployment Increases among Displaced Workers," U.S. Department of Labor Press Release USDL 86-414, October 14, 1986.

13. If the dollar is assumed to have been 40 percent lower than it was, merchandise imports in 1984 to have been about $200 billion, and only one-fourth of the dollar appreciation to have been passed on to consumers in the form of lower prices, the gain from changing trade patterns would be 10 percent of $200 billion spread over 91 million full-time-equivalent workers, or $220 per worker.

14. William J. Baumol, "Productivity Growth, Convergence, and Welfare: What the Long-Run Data Show," *American Economic Review*, December 1986.

15. Conventional economic analysis does recognize that if a country enjoys market power by virtue of its size in any particular market, it may be able to improve its terms of trade by imposing a tariff (or an export tax, as OPEC did with oil in the 1970s). However, such a strategy will be successful only if other countries do not respond with tariffs of their own. If they do, everyone ends up worse off than they would be under free trade.

16. See G. C. Hufbauer and H. F. Rosen, *Trade Policies for Troubled Industries* (Washington, D.C.: Institute for International Economics, March 1986), tables 2.2 and 2.4; S. Hickock, "The Consumer Cost of U.S. Trade Restraints," *Quarterly Review*, Federal Reserve Bank of New York, Summer 1985; and W. E. Cline, *The Future of World Trade in Textiles and Apparel* (Washington, D.C.: Institute for International Economics, September 1987).

17. See, for example, P. Krugman, ed., *Strategic Trade Policy and the New International Economics* (Cambridge, Mass.: MIT, 1986).

18. See R. Z. Lawrence and R. E. Litan, *Saving Free Trade: A Pragmatic Approach* (Washington, D.C.: Brookings Institution, 1986) 17-18.

19. For a critique of targeted industrial policies, see *Industrial Change and Public Policy*, A Symposium Sponsored by the Federal Reserve Bank of Kansas City, 1983, especially P. Krugman, "Targeted Industrial Policy, Theory and Evidence," 123-76. For a concise discussion, see R. D. Norton, "Industrial Policy and American Renewal," *Journal of Economic Literature*, March 1986, 33-36. Krugman's discussion of Japanese targeting of steel is particularly telling.

20. There is some evidence that Japan's dominance in steel and consumer electronics has been just that, and the same may be true for semiconductors. See Krugman's discussion in the Kansas City Federal Reserve Symposium, and K. Yamamura, "Caveat Emptor: The Industrial Policy of Japan," in Krugman, *Strategic Trade Policy and the New International Economics*, for cautionary accounts about the success of Japanese industrial policy.

21. Summarizing a detailed theoretical examination of how the introduction of imperfect competition and increasing returns alters the conclusions of traditional trade models, Helpman and Krugman conclude:

> Our analysis in this book then suggests an overall presumption that trade remains beneficial in a world characterized by economies of scale and imperfect competition. Indeed, the presumption is for extra gains, over and above, the conventional gains from trade. (E. Helpman, and P. Krugman, *Market Structure and Foreign Trade* [Cambridge, Mass.: MIT, 1985], 265)

22. See B. Bluestone and B. Harrison, *The Deindustrialization of America* (New York: Basic Books, 1982); B. Bluestone, and B. Harrison, "The Great American Job Machine: The Proliferation of Low Wage Employment in the U. S. Economy," a study prepared for the Joint Economic Committee of the U.S. Congress, December 1986; R. B. Reich, "Industrial Policy," *New Republic*, March 31, 1982; R. Kuttner, *The Economic Illusion* (Boston: Houghton Mifflin, 1984); L. Thurow, "Losing the Economic Race," *New York Review of Books*, September 27, 1984; and A. Etzioni, *An Immodest Agenda* (New York: New Press, 1983) for a representative set of views on deindustrialization, the decline of the middle class, and the loss of competitiveness.

23. See U.S. General Accounting Office, *Plant Closings: Limited Advance Notice and Assistance Provided Dislocated Workers*, GAO/HRD-87-105, July 1987, for evidence on the notice and assistance given to workers whose plants were closed.

24. See L. H. Summers, "Why Is the Unemployment Rate so Very High Near Full Employment?" *Brookings Papers on Economic Activity* 2 (1986).

25. See M. H. Kosters, "Job Changes and Displaced Workers: An Examination of Employment Adjustment Experience," in P. Cagan, ed., *Essays in Contemporary Economic Problems* (Washington, D.C.: American Enterprise Institute, 1986), 302.

26. U.S. General Accounting Office, *Dislocated Workers: Local Programs and Outcomes under the Job Training Partnership Act*, GAO/HRD-87-41, March 1987.

27. See Stone and Sawhill, "Labor Market Implications."

28. The original rationale for TAA was that workers suffering economic losses from a deliberate policy decision to liberalize trade were entitled to some compensation for having the rules of the game changed on them. In the absence of a deliberate and disruptive policy change, however, losses due to changing patterns of international competition are no different from losses arising from changing patterns of domestic demand or technological change.

29. Both tariffs and quotas restrict imports and raise the price of the protected good. A tariff raises the price directly, and the increases in domestic supply and reductions in domestic demand that follow from the price increase reduce the demand for imports. A quota restricts the quantity directly, but prices must rise to bring demand into line with the now-smaller supply. Thus, it is always possible to estimate the tariff that would have an equivalent effect in reducing imports to any given quota. The tariff yields government revenue, whereas the price increases associated with quotas increase the profits of those who are able to buy or produce at the world market price and sell at the higher, protected, domestic price.

30. See, for example, Hufbauer and Rosen, *Trade Policies for Troubled Industries*; and Lawrence and Litan, *Saving Free Trade*.

31. For a discussion of some preliminary movements toward innovative employment arrangements, see Committee for Economic Development, *Work and Change: Labor Market Adjustment Policies in a Competitive World*, CED, 1987, especially chapter 3.

32. Ibid.

# CHAPTER 5

# THE FAMILY

Andrew Cherlin

When Samuel H. Preston, in a widely cited article, wrote about "the earthquake that shuddered through the American family in the past 20 years," he was expressing both amazement at the scope of the change in the family and uneasiness about the results.[1] This chapter examines two dramatic changes that have transformed the family lives of average Americans over the past few decades: the great increase in work outside the home among married women with young children and the sharp rise in divorce. Many observers are concerned about the consequences of these two trends for children, their parents, and society as a whole. The concern extends to politicians and policymakers, who now issue position papers and draft legislation on family-related matters that a generation ago would have been thought too private for public debate.

This chapter focuses on the "typical" family with children under age eighteen in the broadly defined middle-class.[2] Relatively little attention will be paid to the intertwined problems of poverty, family structure, welfare policy, and the so-called underclass—an important set of issues, to be sure, but one that is discussed in chapter 7. Nor is much attention paid here to the

My thinking on these issues was greatly stimulated by the participants at a small conference on family policy held at The Urban Institute under the auspices of the Changing Domestic Priorities Project on June 15 and 16, 1987. The participants included Mary Jo Bane, Gretchen Condran, Cynthia Fuchs Epstein, Frank F. Furstenberg, Jr., Paul A. Jargowsky, Marie Oser, Carolyn C. Rogers, Harold Watts, and Nicholas Zill.

problem of caring for aging parents, although this, too, is an emerging concern, as noted in chapter 6.

# Family Changes

In any consideration of the changes in divorce and the employment of married women that have occurred since the 1950s, it is important to remember that the decade of the 1950s was probably the most unusual one for family life in this century. For example, it was the only period in the past 150 years in which the birthrate rose substantially; in the 1950s young adults married at earlier ages than in any twentieth-century decade before or since, and the increase in divorce was unusually low.[3] Although many people think of the 1950s family as "traditional," the falling birthrates, rising divorce rates, and increasing age at marriage of the 1960s and 1970s were more consistent with long-term historical trends.

## Marriage and Divorce

Since the 1950s there has been a steady, upward movement in age at marriage. In 1960 the median age at marriage for women was 20.3; in 1984 it was 23.0. As a result, 57 percent of women ages 20 to 24 in 1984 had never married, compared with 28 percent in 1960.[4] Similar increases in marriage age have occurred for men. Moreover, there has been a sharp increase in the number of unmarried couples living together—from about a half-million in 1970 to about 2 million in the mid-1980s. These two phenomena—the postponement of formal marriage and the rise in cohabitation—have led some observers to question whether the institution of marriage is weakening. But studies suggest that for most young adults, cohabitation is a stage in a courtship process that still leads to marriage. Moreover, the overwhelming majority of men and women will eventually marry, probably 85 to 90 percent of all women and a higher percentage of all men.[5] Although these percentages are lower than those in the unusual 1950s, they suggest that marriage remains a central aspect of adult life.

What has occurred, nevertheless, is an increase in marital disruption. Between the early 1960s and the mid-1970s, the divorce rate roughly doubled. Since then, however, the divorce rate has been on a plateau—albeit a high-altitude one. At current rates, about half of all first marriages would end in divorce. And because a majority of persons who divorce will marry again, perhaps one-third of all persons who entered adulthood in the 1970s will eventually marry, divorce, and remarry.[6] The causes of the rise in divorce are not well understood, but they include the increasing economic independence of women, societywide attitudinal shifts, and possibly the relatively unfavorable labor market position of the large numbers of young men from the baby boom generation.

As a result of these changes in marriage and divorce, the family life course of adults and children has changed greatly since the 1950s. Instability and diversity have increased for adults and children. In 1985, 23 percent of all families with children under age eighteen were maintained by a single parent, usually the mother. Most of the growth of single-parent families is due to the rise in divorce, with the rise in the proportion of births occurring out of wedlock being a second factor. If current rates continue, about half of all children would spend some time in a single-parent family before they reach age sixteen. And of those children whose parents divorce and remarry, about half would experience a second disruption before they reach sixteen.[7]

## Women's Labor Force Participation

A related change in the family since the 1950s is the great rise in the number of married women in the labor force. Unlike the trends in marriage, divorce, and family size, which have followed a roller-coaster pattern of ups and downs, the march of mothers into the labor force has been steady and relentless. Even during the family-oriented 1950s married women were increasingly taking jobs outside the home. By 1986, 61 percent of currently married women with children under age eighteen were in the labor force compared with 41 percent in 1970 and 24 percent in 1950. Among currently married women with children under age six, the labor force participation rate stood at 54 percent in 1986, compared with 30 percent in 1970 and 12 percent in 1950.[8] During the 1950s the sharpest increases occurred among mothers of school-age children; in the 1960s and 1970s mothers of preschoolers had the highest rate of increase; and in the 1980s mothers of very young preschoolers have had the highest increases. By 1986, half of all mothers with children age one or younger were in the labor force.[9] Thus, in the post-World War II years women have moved from a pattern in which paid work was either forgone upon marriage or interrupted until the children were in school to a pattern of nearly continuous paid work. About 76 percent of married female workers with children ages six to seventeen work full-time, and 61 percent of those with children under age six work full-time.[10] The greater prevalence of part-time work among women than among men has implications, to be discussed later, for the kinds of child care programs that might be designed.

What brought about this momentous change in women's lives? The first point to note is that because a similar trend has occurred in every developed country, explanations that focus on factors specific to the United States, such as the policies of particular administrations or peculiar characteristics of American postwar culture, are inherently suspect. What we have seen represents no mere shift in American attitudes. Nor can we ascribe this change to short-term macroeconomic conditions. Married women's labor force participation increased in the 1950s and 1960s even though inflation rates were low and productivity and men's wages were rising steadily.

What has happened is that the "cost" of staying home, in terms of forgone earnings, has increased for mothers. That is, women now face better employment opportunities and enjoy higher wages than in the past. To be sure, women workers still earn less, on average, than men. But the important point is that women can expect to earn more than they used to. The demand for women workers has been fueled by the expansion of the service sector, where many occupations have become typed as women's jobs. Moreover, with lower birthrates and longer life expectancies, women can no longer expect that child care responsibilities will occupy most of their adult lives.

This is not to say that attitudinal shifts and financial pressures had no effects. At some point during the past few decades, being an employed mother became socially acceptable, perhaps even expected. At some point, enough couples may have bought houses by pooling two incomes to drive prices beyond the easy reach of single-earner couples. But the movement of married women into the paid labor force is an ineluctable trend that is deeply embedded in the growth and development of the United States and all other industrialized nations. It is a movement that may become even stronger as projected labor force shortages make women an increasingly important component of the supply of workers. And as such, it is difficult to see how this movement, which has continued unabated for decades, can be reversed.

The conclusion that working mothers are not going to return home—that, on the contrary, their attachment to the labor force is likely to grow—has profound implications for public policy. Although there are still some people who mourn the loss of the single-earner, "family wage" system so common in the 1950s and who believe its reinstatement would be beneficial, the evidence suggests that the prospects for reinstatement are slim. There will be no return to the 1950s, barring cataclysmic disruptions such as depressions and world wars. Yet social adjustments to this change—in the hours of work and school, for example—are occurring slowly. Right now societal ambivalence about working women prevents these adjustments from occurring more rapidly, although most observers agree, whether enthusiastically or grudgingly, that mothers are in the labor market to stay.[11]

# Children, Mothers, and Fathers

What are the consequences of the changes in divorce and employment for the lives of children and their parents? The question of whether children have been harmed is crucial, because society has an interest in the rearing of the next generation. Our government has long regulated the rearing of children in ways almost no one would question any more, such as the way they must be educated and the extent to which they can work for wages. If changes in the family can be shown to have significantly harmful effects on children, then reasonably broad support for government intervention might develop. Moreover, to some extent adults freely choose their family situations and can therefore be assumed to benefit from those choices. For example, at least one ex-spouse is presumably happier after a divorce; many, if not most, employed mothers derive satisfaction from their work, and all derive income. Of course, there are important constraints on adults' decisions about work and family roles. But children can be said to have no choices at all, and it is not clear that they fully share the benefits that their parents may gain from a divorce, from a job, or even from additional income. If certain costs are being imposed on children by recent family changes, some public intervention on their behalf might be justified.

## Children's Lives

Two important questions about the consequences for children need to be answered: Has the well-being of children declined? And can these declines, if any, be linked to family-related behaviors such as the growth of single-parent families or the employment of mothers? Unfortunately, the evidence on these issues is far from definitive, and reasonable people might make differing interpretations. Nevertheless, the following conclusions seem warranted: In some important respects, children are less well off than two decades ago. But only a portion of the decline in the well-being of children can be attributed to increasing marital instability; and little or none of the decline can be clearly linked to the increasing number of mothers working outside the home.

With respect to family income, on average, children are better off than they used to be. After adjusting for inflation and changing family size, the mean family incomes of children increased 46 percent between 1962 and 1983. But during the same period, the gap widened between the family incomes of poorer children and of better-off children.[12] Overall, the rise in marital disruption worsened the economic position of children by increasing the number of single-parent families; but the growth in number of mothers who work outside the home—by increasing the number of two-earner families—helped. The analysis of family incomes in chapter 2 suggests that in the aggregate these two trends have had more or less offsetting effects.

The economic harm to children from parental divorce occurs because fathers generally earn more than mothers, but children remain with their mothers in about 90 percent of divorces. In the first year after divorce the living standard of women drops, on average, 30 percent whereas the living standard of men actually rises 10 to 15 percent.[13] The drop is sharpest for women and children in families that are relatively well off before divorce. This pattern suggests that middle-class families in which the husband has high earnings and the wife's labor market experience is limited suffer the largest declines. For example, in one national survey, the Panel Study of Income Dynamics (PSID), white children in families with predivorce incomes above the median experienced a 38 percent decline in living standards in the year after the divorce. Nevertheless, few better-off children plunge below the poverty level as a result of divorce. Yet for children in families that are just getting by, a parental divorce often means a fall into poverty. Among white children in the same study who were in families with predivorce incomes below the median, 14 percent were poor before the divorce, but 41 percent were poor in the year after the divorce. And although this dramatic increase in poverty lasted only a year or two for most, five years later 18 percent of these children were still poor.[14]

In principle, fathers could compensate their ex-wives and children by providing adequate child support payments. But child support payments tend to be low and unreliable. In a 1985 Bureau of the Census survey, only 48 percent of mothers who were supposed to receive child support payments reported receiving the full amount, 26 percent received partial payment, and 26 percent received nothing.[15] In addition, the average amount received is modest (about $2,200 per year), and child support awards are rarely indexed for inflation.

Many divorced women, especially those who are relatively young and less educated, improve their economic position by remarrying. The addition of a male income has a substantial effect; five years after the divorce, women in the PSID study who had remarried had a standard of living nearly equal to that of divorced men or intact married couples. Yet even for women who remarry, there is likely to be an interval of a few years when the mother and her children have a lower income; and a few years can be a long time in the life of a child.

The breakup of a marriage also can cause emotional troubles for children. Observers agree that the experience of a parental divorce is initially traumatizing for nearly all children involved. But most children appear to recover eventually and resume normal emotional and cognitive development.[16] National surveys suggest that the long-term effects are relatively modest for most children, although more severe for children whose parents divorce when they are quite young.[17] Only a minority of children appear to suffer long-term negative emotional consequences from divorce.

Does the fact of having an employed mother harm the development of children? Hundreds of studies have succeeded mainly in demonstrating how difficult it is to give a simple answer to this question. The studies suggest that the effects, if any, depend on a host of factors, such as social class, race, whether the mother wants to work, and the age and sex of the child. Moreover, there still are few studies of the effects of various day care arrangements on children. Researchers agree on a few important characteristics by which to judge day care programs: the level of training or experience of the care givers, the number of children per care giver, and the stability of the arrangements. But beyond these factors, themselves not well understood, there is little agreement about what does and does not constitute satisfactory child care.

The conclusion of a National Academy of Sciences panel that reviewed the research on maternal employment was that no consistent negative or positive effects on children's well-being could be found. In some specific circumstances, the panel reported, there is evidence of beneficial effects (for example, on poor, minority children and possibly on girls); in other circumstances there is evidence of harmful effects (possibly on boys from middle-class families); and in many circumstances there is no evidence of any substantial effects one way or the other.[18] Overall, the research to date, although far from satisfactory or definitive, does not show pervasive, harmful effects on children. Thus there is little basis for lumping the employment of mothers with other family behaviors that nearly always produce short-term, if not long-term, stress for children, such as divorce, teenage childbearing, and family violence.

In other measures of children's well-being, the trends appear mixed. American children are healthier than ever, but the rate of improvement in health has slowed in recent years.[19] The infant mortality rate (the proportion of children who die before their first birthday) has declined steadily from about 30 per 1,000 births in the late 1940s to about 10 per 1,000 currently. And the death rate for children ages one to fourteen continued to fall over the past decade to about 34 per 1,000 children. Moreover, parents are better educated: In 1969 there were 3.7 births to women with less than twelve years of schooling for every birth to a college-educated woman; by 1984 the ratio had fallen to 1.3 births to women with less than twelve years of schooling for every birth to college-educated women. Children seem to benefit intellectually from having better-educated parents and from having fewer siblings with whom to divide parental attention.[20]

Still, there have been some disturbing trends in other domains. As is well known, the average scores of college-bound high school students on the Scholastic Aptitude Test declined substantially between the 1960s and the 1980s. But it is not at all clear that this decline can be linked to family change. According to the leading study, "two-thirds to three-quarters" of the initial decline between 1963 and about 1970 was a compositional effect caused by a more diverse college applicant pool—that is, larger proportions of students were taking the test, thus diluting the quality.[21] After 1970, however, compositional effects accounted for only about one-fourth of the continuing decline. The report speculates that the rest of the fall could stem from a number of factors, including a reduced emphasis on competence in reading and writing and a diminished "seriousness of purpose" in the schools, the effect of television—and changes in the family.

As for trends in the social behavior of children and adolescents, there is no question that a number of indicators worsened between the early 1960s and the mid-1970s, but it is also important to note that most of the trends have leveled or reversed since the mid-1970s. For example, juvenile arrest rates increased 41 percent between 1965 and 1975 but since then have remained stable or declined slightly. Suicide rates among young people between the ages of fifteen and nineteen more than doubled between 1960 and the late 1970s but have not risen much since. A similar pattern is evident for marijuana use and premarital sexual activity. In general, these indicators of antisocial or potentially self-injurious behavior show that although levels are higher now than in the early 1960s, nearly all the increases had occurred by the late 1970s.[22]

In any assessment of the causes of these trends, it is important to consider their timing. In a widely quoted 1986 article, demographers Peter Uhlenberg and David Eggebeen described these trends in adolescent well-being and hypothesized that the deterioration was due to the increased participation of mothers in the labor force and to the increase in marital instability.[23] But they presented no direct evidence linking trends in adolescent behavior to mothers' employment or divorce. In a forthcoming Urban Institute book, Frank F. Furstenberg, Jr., and Gretchen Condran argue that this explanation for the trends does not fit the facts.[24] Consider the labor force participation rates of mothers with children ages six to seventeen. Between 1965 and 1975, while indicators of adolescent well-being were deteriorating, the labor force participation rate for this group of women rose from 42 to 52 percent. So far, so good for the Uhlenberg-Eggebeen hypothesis. But between 1975 and 1985, when the rate rose from 52 to 67 percent, the indicators remained stable or improved. Moreover, during the quiescent 1950s, the rate rose from 27 to 39 percent. It is difficult to see how this steady increase in mothers' employment since World War II could have caused a decline in adolescent well-being only during one fifteen-year period but not before or since. Thus, the evidence linking an increase in employed mothers to declining adolescent well-being is weak.[25]

Although it is plausible that changes in the family have had adverse effects on the well-being of children, there is little convincing evidence to support this proposition. To be sure, such links are difficult to substantiate. Moreover, the emotional trauma and frequent income losses that occur in the immediate aftermath of a parental divorce must be at least temporarily detrimental to children. And the existence of child care arrangements of low quality—a standard that is hard to define—may be harmful to an unknown number. But with these important caveats, the case against the family has not been proved. It appears that the effects of divorce on children's emotional and cognitive well-being may be less serious than had been feared. And it appears likely that for many children—possibly for most children—having a mother who works outside the home is not detrimental.

## Women's Lives

The movement of married women into the labor force and the trends in marriage, divorce, and fertility have certainly altered the lives of American women. The most common status for American women with children under age eighteen in the 1980s is to be both married and working outside the home.[26] There were 13.8 million such women in 1985. But housewives have not disappeared: 10.2 million married mothers of children under age eighteen were not working outside the home in 1985.

There were also 6 million women with children under age eighteen who were maintaining their own families in 1985. About one out of ten was widowed and two out of ten had never married; but most—about seven out of ten—were separated or divorced.[27] The increase in marital dissolution since the 1960s means that it is quite common for women to live for a time as a separated or divorced single parent. As already noted, many women—especially older, middle-class women—experience declining standards of living at least temporarily after the dissolution of a marriage. Yet it must also be said that the greater freedom to end an unhappy marriage undoubtedly has been beneficial to some women, such as those whose husbands were physically abusive. For younger mothers with employment experience, a divorce is not necessarily an economic disaster, and it may have psychological benefits that compensate for any economic loss.

Nearly two-thirds of all mothers (including the married and the unmarried) with children under age eighteen are employed outside the home.[28] The most tangible benefit of work outside the home is, of course, the additional income it provides. For white, married couples in 1985, the median income was $25,307 when the wife was a full-time homemaker compared with $36,992 when she was in the labor force. The comparable figures for black couples were $15,129 and $30,502.[29]

Beyond income, employment can also bring greater self-esteem and self-confidence, although it can also bring increased feelings of pressure and anxiety. The rapidly growing research literature suggests that whether the net contribution of employment to women's psychological well-being is positive or negative depends on two factors: whether the woman wants to work outside the home and whether she receives adequate support from her family, her employer, and other institutions.

For example, sociologists who interviewed a national sample of married women in 1978 reported that the least depressed women were of two kinds: those who were employed and preferred to be and those who were not employed and preferred not to be. Wives who were employed but did not want to be were significantly more depressed, and the most depressed of all were those who were not employed but wanted to be.[30] As the preference for employment increases among women,[31] working outside the home would be expected to become a source of improved well-being for more women. But the second factor, support from others, is still problematic. In a 1976 national sample of white, married couples, sociologists compared indicators of mental health among employed wives and nonemployed wives. They found that employed wives whose husbands shared the child care tasks at least equally showed better levels of mental health than nonemployed wives, whereas employed wives who still did more of the child care showed worse levels of mental health.[32]

Most studies still find that the husbands of employed women spend only slightly more time on family care than do the husbands of stay-at-home wives. This situation leaves many employed wives (and most single mothers) facing the so-called double burden of work and family responsibilities. Although employed women tend to reduce the time they spend on child care and housework, their total time spent on obligatory activities increases. In a sample of families with children in metropolitan Toronto in 1980, wives who had full-time jobs and children age three or younger spent more than ten hours a day, on average, on paid work, child care, and housework combined. In contrast, similar wives who were not employed spent about eight-and-one-half hours a day on all tasks. The extra effort came out of the leisure time of employed wives: they spent an hour and a half a day, on average, on leisure pursuits, while wives who were not employed averaged more than two-and-one-half hours on leisure. Nor did the husbands of employed women contribute much more than those of nonemployed women. Consistent with other studies, the husbands of women who were employed full-time averaged fifty-seven minutes a day of housework, a minimal increase over the forty-three-minute average for husbands whose wives did not work outside the home.[33]

Evidence such as this led the author of a recent book to argue that the lack of assistance by husbands, employers, and government has resulted in "a lesser life" for women who combine working and rearing children.[34] But these tensions are not inevitable; rather, they reflect the persistence of social norms and social institutions that were established when the majority of mothers stayed home.[35] Most husbands still leave most of the family chores to their wives, and most employers still run their businesses on the assumption that someone is available to deal with family responsibilities—leading to the refrain that what every employed woman needs most is a wife. If the current set of social arrangements were altered—and there are indications that changes are occurring slowly[36] —it might become less stressful for women to combine work and family roles. The large number of mothers, both married and single, who are employed—about 17.5 million in 1985—suggests why combining employment and family responsibilities has become a central family issue of the 1980s. The implications for public policy are discussed later.

## Men's Lives

The behavior of American fathers is a paradox. On the one hand, men are feeling freer to involve themselves emotionally in fatherhood. This was strikingly confirmed in 1986 with the publication of *Fatherhood*, a slim volume by entertainer-educator Bill Cosby, which sold more than 2 million copies in hard cover and became the fastest-selling general nonfiction book in the history of U.S. publishing. Cosby's book, and the many others like it, serve to legitimate fatherhood as a role in which men can take pride. "Just what *is* a father's role today?" asks Cosby. And after listing some tasks that most fathers can't do well, like cooking, he continues: "The answer, of course, is that no matter how hopeless or copeless a father may be, his role is simply to *be* there, sharing all the chores with his wife. Let her *have* the babies, but after that, try to share every job around."[37]

On the other hand, as noted earlier, few fathers share every job around, even when their wives work outside the home. The amount of work men do in the home has been slow to increase. And the statistics on child support already mentioned suggest that a large number of divorced men are failing to support their children. One national survey found that half of the teenagers living with their divorced mothers had not seen their fathers in the past year; only one-sixth saw their fathers as often as once a week on the average.[38] Moreover, more men than women remarry, so that many men migrate from one family to another.[39]

What we have seen, then, is the emergence of two contrasting visions of fatherhood, what Frank F. Furstenberg, Jr., calls the "good dad/bad dad complex."[40] Fathers feel freer to be involved with their children, and some are; they also feel freer to leave, and many do. The emergence of this dual pattern may be rooted in the declining division of labor in the home. The separation of the workplace from the home, which occurred during industrialization, created a more rigid division of responsibilities. Fathers began to specialize almost exclusively on economic responsibilities, at the expense of their day-to-day contact with their children. But with the contemporary movement of married women into the labor force, the division of labor has become less rigid. Although fathers are encouraged to become equal partners at home, they are no longer the sole source of economic support and thus may feel freer to end their marriages.

To be sure, not all divorces are initiated by men. The improved labor market opportunities for women—especially for women with higher education and extensive work experience—have allowed more unhappy wives to leave their husbands.[41] (It is difficult to determine what proportion of divorces are initiated by men or by women; ex-spouses often develop contradictory accounts of the events that occurred.) Nevertheless, women are still more constrained by the economic risks of divorce, because most husbands have greater earning potential than their wives and because child support payments tend to be modest and irregularly paid.

Fatherhood, in essence, has become more of a voluntary activity. Fathers can choose to play a greater role or no role at all. In the 1950s, in contrast, strong social pressure forced men to accept the responsibility of supporting their wives and children (although these pressures also discouraged men from doing much child care).[42] Since then, the strictures have weakened, because of an ideology of personal liberation or the rising employment rates and wages of women.

Men are not necessarily better off because of these changes. To be sure, the "good dads" may benefit emotionally from closer ties to their children, and the "bad dads" may escape from financial responsibilities. But a number of studies suggest that the 1950s style marriages were good for men's health and well-being; married men lived longer, had fewer illnesses, and had a

greater sense of well-being than did unmarried men.[43] The question remains
as to whether marriage today is as good a deal for men as it was during the
heyday of the breadwinner-homemaker marriage. The gains from the easing
of the breadwinner burden have probably been more than offset by the increasing pressures to do more around the home and the loss of services and
support from busier working wives. Nonetheless, marriage still provides men
with an emotional anchor that they need—perhaps increasingly so, according
to one study.[44] Yet some men may be able to satisfy these emotional needs
from a series of two or three long-term relationships as well as they can from
a lifelong marriage.

## Family Change: Is There a Role for Government?

What should the public policy response be to the changes in the family
that have just been reviewed? The disturbing trends in the well-being of
children and adolescents appear to be only loosely connected to increasing
marital dissolution; yet it is clear that many children experience a sharply
lowered standard of living following a parental separation and that most
experience at least short-term emotional trauma. Children with adequate child
care arrangements appear unlikely to be harmed by having a mother who
works outside the home; but many children do not have adequate arrangements. And there is the strain on employed women who must maintain multiple
roles without much social or institutional support. These problems—the economic consequences of divorce, the adequacy of child care arrangements,
and the strain on employed mothers—are, at the least, worth public attention.
Some possible responses are examined in the following pages.

### Child Support Enforcement

The lack of compliance with court-ordered child support payments gives
strong justification for expanded efforts to compel absent fathers to pay adequate levels of support. Over the past several years a broad consensus has
emerged in favor of such efforts. Conservatives tend to see these measures
as enforcing traditional family obligations, whereas liberals tend to see them
as providing assistance to women and children. The widespread concern about
child support enforcement led to the passage of the Child Support Enforcement
Amendments of 1984 (42 U.S. Code Section 651), which will probably
improve the level of compliance with court-ordered child support payments.
The amendments require the states to establish procedures under which child
support payments are to be withheld from the wages of the noncustodial parent
if the payments are delinquent one month. The legislation also requires the

states to establish commissions that will set statewide standards for child support payments.

Moreover, the legislation authorized an experimental system in Wisconsin. Under this program, which began in July 1987, the amount of child support is determined as a simple percentage of the noncustodial parent's gross income: 17 percent for one child, and 25, 29, 31, and 34 percent for two, three, four, and five or more children, respectively. The obligation is automatically withheld from the noncustodial parent's paycheck, as is done with payroll taxes. In four Wisconsin counties, children are to receive either the amount paid by the noncustodial parent or an assured amount set by the state—whichever is larger.[45] Although such an approach is similar to current practice in several European countries,[46] it represents an innovation for the United States.

## Child Allowances

Beyond child support enforcement, there are few generally agreed upon proposals concerning family problems. Some believe that greater financial resources should be made available to all parents who are rearing children. To this end, they advocate raising the value of the personal tax exemption for dependent children only.[47] The value of the personal exemption has eroded substantially relative to the rise in real income over the past few decades. A 1986 Reagan administration report endorsed the goal of eventually raising the exemption from its current level of about $2,000 between $4,000 and $5,000.[48] This proposal is essentially a variation on the child allowances granted in most other Western countries. Because it would assist all families with children, it would help hard-pressed single-parent families and employed parents who cannot afford the cost of satisfactory child care. But because of its neutrality toward the employment of mothers, it appeals to people who believe that public policy ought to encourage—or at least not discourage—the formation of single-earner, breadwinner-homemaker families.

But child-allowance-like programs have some serious drawbacks. The first is cost. Because benefits are spread so broadly, the program would be expensive. According to an estimate by Espenshade and Minarik, doubling the personal exemption for dependent children from $2,000 to $4,000 would cost about $19 billion per year.[49] At a time of concern over budget deficits, the price tag alone could discourage enactment of such a program. In addition, there is no guarantee that the benefits would accrue to children. We can only assume that parents would spend their additional income in a way that would benefit the family as a whole. Moreover, because a tax exemption is worth more to wealthier families, who are taxed at a higher rate, much of the benefit would accrue to children from middle- and upper-income families.

## Child Care

Other proposals would provide support only for child care services provided by nonfamily members. These proposals lack the universality of a child allowance, in that no assistance is provided to parents who care for their own children. But they have the virtue of ensuring that the funds will be spent on the care of children.

**Current Policies.** The federal government currently funds several child care programs, but with the exception of the Dependent Care Tax Credit, all are restricted to children from low-income families. According to one estimate, expenditures for child care for low-income families totaled $2.1 billion in 1986, a 50 percent reduction from the amount spent in 1980.[50] Largely as a result of budget cuts in 1981, federal expenditures on care for children from low-income families failed to keep pace with inflation in the 1980s.

In contrast to the declining expenditures on low-income children, the cost of the Dependent Care Tax Credit increased from $956 million in 1980 to $3.4 billion in 1986.[51] The credit allows families to deduct part of their child care expenses from their income taxes, but the percentage that can be deducted is larger for low-income families. Nevertheless, all families can deduct at least 20 percent (up to maximum of $480 for one child and $960 for two or more children). More than 6 million families, about half of them with incomes under $25,000, are estimated to have used the credit in 1983.[52] However, low-income families with no tax liability—whose numbers have grown as a result of the 1986 tax reform—receive no benefit from the tax credit.

**Proposed Policies.** Some proposals would seek only to alter the flow of benefits under the Dependent Care Tax Credit. Such proposals would eliminate benefits to upper-income families, thus producing a savings to the Treasury which would then be made available to the states as child care vouchers for low- and moderate-income families.[53] This approach would provide assistance to poor families with no tax burden.

More ambitious proposals would seek to expand the supply of care givers, to improve the quality of care, and to subsidize the cost for low- to middle-income families at a price of several billion dollars in federal and state funds. In one current version, most of the funds would be provided to the states to help families with incomes below a cutoff point purchase child care. Each state could determine the method of assistance, which could include vouchers for parents or grants for providers; the rest of the funds would be used by

162 CHALLENGE TO LEADERSHIP

the states to pay administrative costs, to train child care workers, to establish information and referral services, and to bring child care centers and family day care homes up to federal standards.[54]

**Policy Issues.** In considering the more ambitious proposals, it is important to assess the current supply of child care services available to working parents. It is clear that the supply of day care centers and private nursery schools has increased substantially since the 1970s;[55] these facilities primarily serve children ages three to five. What is less clear is the supply of so-called family day care homes, in which a person (often a mother with her own children) cares for young children in her home. It is estimated that 60 to 90 percent of such homes are unlicensed and unregistered, thus constituting a vast gray market of possibly a million homes. Family day care is heavily used by parents of infants and one-year-olds—the very group of mothers whose labor force participation has increased most rapidly in the past decade. Yet the limited information that exists suggests that the growth in family day care homes has lagged behind the growth in centers and nursery schools. Thus there is a plausible case to be made that the supply of care givers for very young preschool children has not kept pace with the demand. The adequacy of the supply for older preschool children is harder to judge. There is also general concern about the quality of care provided in existing settings, particularly in family day care homes. Because of the lack of regulation, it is up to the parents to determine whether a potential care giver runs a safe, satisfactory home. Occasional newspaper stories about children who are killed in fires in unsafe, overcrowded homes—or abused—suggest that finding good care may be difficult. Nevertheless, beyond physical comfort and safety, there is little agreement or evidence, as already noted, about just what constitutes adequate care. Obviously, a higher ratio of care givers to children is preferable to a lower ratio, and a stable arrangement is preferable to a shifting series of settings. Other things being equal, trained, experienced care givers probably provide better care.

Difficult trade-offs exist among availability, quality, and cost. All proposals require that family day care providers register with the state in order to receive payments. And some would move quickly to bring all providers into compliance with existing regulations and eventually to enforce new, and presumably tougher, federal health and safety standards. Yet even the requirement that all providers be registered might in itself raise the price of care. It is suspected that much of the income earned by family day care providers is not reported to the Internal Revenue Service (IRS), an arrangement that holds down the price. Many of the newly registered providers might conclude that it is too risky to hide income from the IRS anymore. And stricter standards would probably raise the price further. In the absence of a substantial infusion of new funds, the supply of care givers might decline. A two-tiered system might evolve: a higher-priced, regulated market in which vouchers are accepted and a lower-priced, unregulated market in which only cash is accepted.

Similarly, it is well known that workers at licensed day care centers are hired at low wages, often the minimum wage. The low wages contribute to frequent staff turnover and to concern about the quality of the care givers. Some proposals would seek to increase salaries for child care workers. This goal would probably benefit children by improving the quality and stability of care. But it would also substantially raise costs in this labor-intensive enterprise, especially if coupled with stricter rules about staff-to-child ratios. The point of this discussion is not that care should be unregulated and wages low, but rather that the trade-offs need to be thought through carefully.

Another issue concerns the settings that should be used to provide child care. Currently a wide range of care situations exist: In a 1982 census survey of employed women with preschool-age children, 43 percent reported that they relied primarily on care by relatives, 22 percent reported that their child was cared for in a family day care home, and only 15 percent reported that their child attended a nursery school or day care center.[56] As already mentioned, many parents of very young children use family day care; so do many parents of school-age children who need after-school or vacation care. Center and nursery school care predominates for children ages three through five.[57] The widespread use of family day care for infants and toddlers appears to reflect, in part, the parents' preferences and, in part, constraints of availability (few centers will accept children under age two) and cost. But group care appears to be widely acceptable for children three and older.

There has been growing attention to the possibility of using public schools as the site for the care—and early education—of three- to five-year-olds as well as after-school care for older children. In the early nineteenth century, preschools were common in some states; in 1840, 40 to 50 percent of all three-year-olds in Massachusetts were enrolled in public or private school.[58] But in this century, there has been little interest in education for three- and four-year-olds until recently. Schools are attractive settings for several reasons: They are established, universal institutions, and their programs would probably be open to all children, regardless of the parents' employment status. They have existing physical plants that are becoming underutilized because of the decline in birthrates. They are the logical location for after-school programs and perhaps summer vacation programs as well. Moreover, most school funds are raised by state and local taxes. Presumably, any new initiatives would continue this mode of funding, thus making smaller demands on the federal budget than would be the case with a national program of vouchers and subsidies to parents and providers.

Nevertheless, school settings might pose some difficulties. The salaries of teachers and school custodians are far higher, on average, than those of day care workers; pressure to raise the salaries of the latter would probably increase. As noted, this pressure might have the salutary effect of raising the quality of care, but it might also raise the price substantially. In addition, a heavy reliance on school-based programs would do nothing to relieve the problems of the supply and quality of infant and toddler care, which may be more serious.

A final issue concerns who should pay the cost of any new child care programs. The use of public funds would result in a transfer from childless adults to those with children. The principle that education is a public good that everyone should pay for has long been accepted. But should people without children be asked to subsidize the care of preschool-age children as well? An argument could be made that the bearing and rearing of children is a public good, especially in an era of below-replacement birthrates, and that people who delay or forgo childbearing have a social responsibility to assist those who become parents.

A more difficult question is whether a married couple in which one partner has chosen to stay home with the children should subsidize the cost of care for the children of two-earner families. As noted in chapter 2, on average, two-earner families have higher incomes and have experienced more favorable income growth during the past several decades than have other families. Thus it is hard to argue that all such families should receive direct public subsidies for child care. A stronger case can be made for subsidizing two-earner families in the lower portion of the income distribution and single-parent families of modest means as well. It could be argued that their employment is necessary to give their children a decent standard of living and that their children ought not to suffer inadequate care as a result.

## The Responsive Workplace

Another set of programs and proposals seeks to alter the conditions of work, through efforts to be undertaken both by government and corporations, so that the workplace is more responsive to the family obligations of employees. Perhaps the best known of such innovations is flexible working hours, which were permitted for 14 percent of all nonfarm, wage and salary workers in the United States in 1985.[59] (In a metropolitan Toronto study, mothers who were working flexible hours reported feeling substantially less pressed for time.)[60] In addition to offering flexible hours, a small but growing number of firms in this country, probably about 2,000 to 3,000, offered their employees some kind of child care assistance in the mid-1980s. Most of this assistance took the form of information and referral services, modest discounts at selected local child care centers, or flexible benefit plans. Under the latter, employees can take part of their fringe benefits in child care assistance; in some versions, employees can set aside part of their salary in a fund that can be used to pay for child care in tax-free dollars.

Information services can make it easier for employees to find satisfactory child care, although such services do little to increase the supply of care or to help employees pay for it. The salary reduction and flexible benefit plans provide financial assistance at little cost to the employer; but such plans mainly assist higher-income workers, who can afford temporary reductions in take-home pay and who pay a higher marginal tax rate. Most workplace reforms are limited to large firms; small employers cannot or will not provide them. Overall, reforms initiated by firms can help employees to better integrate their work and family obligations, but expectations about the extent and effects of corporate reform should be modest. Few firms have on-site child care centers, and the reports on those that do are mixed.[61]

In part because corporate initiatives are likely to be modest, some advocates of change in the workplace look to government for action. One program being debated would provide employed parents with leave for infant care, some form of which is provided in most Western nations. Infant care leave might significantly ease the strain on new parents and their newborn children, but its implementation is not without difficulties. The length of the leave specified in one recent bill, eighteen weeks, seems to have arisen from political compromise rather than from studies of child development. An advisory panel of child development specialists and policy analysts convened by the Yale Bush Center in Child Development and Social Policy in 1985 recommended a six-month leave—and even their reports leave unclear why this exact length was chosen.[62] Moreover, even if the leave is to be unpaid, the costs of hiring replacements or making do with fewer workers are likely to be passed along in the form of higher prices, especially by small firms that cannot adjust easily to the loss of an employee. Some observers worry that employers will discriminate against women of childbearing age if parental leave is mandated. Others charge that only middle-class, married women will be able to take an unpaid leave. Thus, what looks at first like a straightforward way to help parents care for infants has become a controversial issue.

## Unintended Consequences

According to another school of thought, the government should do nothing about family problems because government action only makes social problems worse. A 1986 report on the family by a working group in the Reagan administration warned that "the indirect impact of government activity is often more important than its intended effect."[63] It cited the unanticipated economic consequences for women and children of the movement toward no-fault divorce, and it argued that "the fabric of family life has been frayed by the abrasive experiments of two liberal decades."[64]

What can be said about this argument with respect to the issues presented in this chapter? Should the unanticipated consequences of, say, expanded child care or parental leave programs be of concern here? Despite the warnings, it can be argued that fundamental family trends such as changes in divorce, marriage, and birthrates are little affected by government social or economic policies. For example, although no-fault divorce may have decreased wives' bargaining power in divorce settlements, a number of studies in the United States and Western Europe have demonstrated that the introduction of no-fault divorce laws did not increase the rate of divorce over what it otherwise would have been.[65] Rather, it appears that changes in the law ratified existing changes in people's attitudes and behavior.

One can also cite the experiences of East European nations such as Romania and Czechoslovakia, which have attempted to boost their low birthrates through providing substantial economic incentives and, in the case of Romania, outlawing nearly all forms of contraception and abortion. In 1966, the Romanian government banned abortion, restricted access to contraceptives, and instituted a whole range of special benefits and preferences for parents. The birthrate shot up temporarily in 1967, but it has since declined to pre-1967 levels. The Czechoslovak government has provided exceptional financial incentives; in 1981 a family with three children received family allowances that amounted to 53 percent of the average manufacturing wage. But the effect of these huge subsidies on the birthrate has been modest.[66] It seems reasonable to conclude that any feasible child care program or family allowance in the United States would be unlikely to influence the birthrate very much in either direction.

It is possible that there could be some further labor supply response to increased child care assistance. In two Census Bureau surveys, 13 to 17 percent of nonemployed women responded that they would look for work or return to work "if satisfactory child care were available at reasonable cost."[67] But it is hard to know what the phrases "satisfactory child care" and "reasonable cost" meant to the respondents. And as has been noted, married women's labor force participation has been increasing steadily and rapidly over the past few decades despite the lack of government child care programs that reach beyond the poor. This rise is rooted in basic changes in our society and hence is unlikely to be modified substantially by government action. Moreover, opinions differ about whether further increases of female workers would be detrimental: feminists and policymakers concerned about economic competitiveness and the size of the GNP might welcome a faster increase.

Mary Jo Bane and Paul A. Jargowski argue in a forthcoming Urban Institute volume that "family support policies such as day care and parental leave may well have substantial impacts on the lives of families and children. They may be well justified in terms of these benefits. The evidence suggests, however, that they should not be expected to bring about much change in family structure or behavior."[68] This conclusion is a double-edged sword. On the one hand, it implies that policymakers need not worry about the unintended consequences of potential programs. On the other hand, it implies that the direct effects on family trends are likely to be smaller than some advocates believe. For example, those who hope that expanded child care programs might help raise the U.S. birthrate will probably be disappointed.[69] Rather, what child care programs might do is provide a better environment for children and some relief to overburdened working mothers.

## Conclusions

All the policies discussed in this chapter—from tax exemptions to parental leave—are likely to be debated in the months and years ahead. Perhaps because the pace of change in families has finally slowed, we now seem ready as a society to make the necessary adjustments. As to just what these adjustments imply for government policy, reasonable people can and will disagree. However, here are a few general observations that seem to be broadly applicable to the current debate:

1. The reality is that large and increasing numbers of married women will probably remain at work outside the home. Whether this trend is welcomed as good for women and good for the economy or whether it is acknowledged with regrets about the passing of the breadwinner-homemaker family, its acceptance must be the cornerstone of any realistic family policy.

2. The benefits of family-oriented policies should not be overpromised or oversold. These policies are unlikely to solve problems such as antisocial and self-destructive behavior among adolescents, below-replacement birthrates, or the sluggish growth of labor productivity. They are even unlikely fully to solve the problems to which they are directly addressed, such as providing adequate child care and reducing the strain on employed mothers,

although they may make substantial progress toward easing these more limited problems.

3. The flip side of observation 2 is that the unanticipated consequences of government programs on the structure of American families are likely to be modest. Trends in marriage, divorce, childbearing, and women's labor force participation respond to long-term economic and cultural shifts and are unlikely to be altered significantly by any feasible programs of the type discussed in this chapter. It is more useful to focus attention instead on the direct, intended consequences of the policies under consideration.

4. Government can provide valuable symbolic leadership. One of the most important aspects of any child care, child allowance, or parental leave legislation would be to send a signal to corporate and community leaders that the needs of children (and of their parents) deserve more attention. Such a symbolic shift by political leaders would help legitimate these needs and would hasten the nongovernmental adjustments that must be made.

NOTES TO CHAPTER 5

1. Samuel H. Preston, "Children and the Elderly: Divergent Paths for America's Dependents," *Demography* 21 (1984):435-57. See also Samuel H. Preston, "Children and the Elderly in the United States," *Scientific American* 251 (1984): 44–49.
2. This rubric is meant to cover husband-wife families in which both partners work outside the home (the most common form for families with children), husband-wife families in which only one partner works, single-parent families (predominantly female-headed households), and families formed by first marriages or remarriages. A broad range of issues are relevant to all these family forms.
3. Andrew J. Cherlin, *Marriage, Divorce, Remarriage* (Cambridge, Mass.: Harvard University Press, 1981).
4. U.S. Bureau of the Census, "Marital Status and Living Arrangements: March 1984," *Current Population Reports*, Series P-20, no. 399 (Washington, D.C.: U.S. Government Printing Office, August 1985); and U.S. Bureau of the Census, *Historical Statistics of the United States, Colonial Times to 1970* (Washington, D.C.: U.S. Government Printing Office, 1975).
5. Cherlin, *Marriage, Divorce, Remarriage*; and David E. Bloom and Neil Bennett, "Marriage Patterns in the United States," Harvard Institute of Economic Research, Discussion Paper No. 1147, April 1985.
6. Cherlin, *Marriage, Divorce, Remarriage*.
7. Larry L. Bumpass, "Children and Marital Disruption: A Replication and Update," Demography 21 (1984): 71–82.
8. Nancy S. Barrett, "Women and the Economy," in Sara E. Rix, ed., *The American Woman 1987-88: A Report in Depth* (New York: W.W. Norton, 1987), 100–49; and U.S. President, *Economic Report of the President* (Washington, D.C.: U.S. Government Printing Office, January 1987).
9. U.S. President, *Economic Report*.
10. Ibid.
11. For a grudging acceptance, see Allan C. Carlson, "What Happened to the 'Family Wage'?", *The Public Interest* 83 (1986): 3–17.
12. Robert Haveman, Barbara Wolfe, Ross Finnie, and Edward Wolff, "The Well-Being of Children and Disparities among Them over Two Decades: 1962–1983," in John L. Palmer,

Timothy M. Smeeding, and Barbara B. Torrey, eds., *The Well-Being of the Aged and Children in the United States: Intertemporal and International Perspectives* (Washington, D.C.: The Urban Institute Press, forthcoming).

13. Greg J. Duncan and Saul D. Hoffman, "Economic Consequences of Marital Instability," in Martin David and Timothy Smeeding, eds., *Horizontal Equity, Uncertainty, and Economic Well-Being* (Chicago: University of Chicago Press, 1985).

14. Ibid.

15. U.S. Bureau of the Census, "Child Support and Alimony: 1985," *Current Population Reports*, Series P. 23, no. 152 (Washington, D.C.: U.S. Government Printing Office, August 1987).

16. Cherlin, *Marriage, Divorce, Remarriage.*

17. Frank F. Furstenberg, Jr., and Gretchen Condran, "Family Change and Adolescent Well-Being: A Reexamination of U.S. Trends," in Andrew J. Cherlin, ed., *Family Change and Public Policy* (Washington, D.C.: The Urban Institute Press, forthcoming).

18. Sheila B. Kamerman and Cheryl D. Hayes, eds., *Families that Work: Children in a Changing World* (Washington, D.C.: National Academy Press, 1982).

19. Nicholas Zill and Carolyn Rogers, "Recent Trends in the Well-Being of Children in the United States and their Implications for Public Policy," in Cherlin, *Family Change.*

20. Judith Blake, "Family Size and the Quality of Children," *Demography* 18 (1981): 42–142.

21. Advisory Panel on the Scholastic Aptitude Test Score Decline, "On Further Examination," New York, College Entrance Examination Board, 1977.

22. Zill and Rogers, "Recent Trends."

23. Peter Uhlenberg and David Eggebeen, "The Declining Well-Being of American Adolescents," *The Public Interest*, no. 82 (1986): 25–38.

24. Furstenberg and Condran, "Getting the Facts Straight," in Cherlin, *Family Change.*

25. Nevertheless, it is true that the period of deterioration in indicators of adolescent well-being, roughly the early 1960s to the mid-1970s, corresponded to the period in which the U.S. divorce rate increased sharply, as already described. But the effect on teenagers should have peaked several years after the rise in divorce because most divorces occur early in marriage. The very large number of young children who experienced parental divorce in the 1960s and early 1970s entered adolescence in the late 1970s and 1980s. Yet the indicators of well-being had leveled off by then.

26. Cherlin, "Women and the Family," in Sara E. Rix ed., *The American Women 1987–88: A Report in Depth* (New York: W.W. Norton, 1987), 67–99.

27. U.S. Bureau of the Census, "Household and Family Characteristics: March 1985," *Current Population Reports*, Series P-20, no. 411 (Washington, D.C.: U.S. Government Printing Office, 1986).

28. Cherlin, "Women and the Family."

29. U.S. Bureau of the Census, "Consumer Income," *Current Population Reports*, Series P-60, no. 156 (Washington, U.S. Government Printing Office, 1987).

30. Catherine E. Ross, John Mirowsky, and Joan Huber, "Dividing Work, Sharing Work, and In-Between: Marriage Patterns and Depression," *American Sociological Review* 48 (1983): 809–23.

31. Andrew Cherlin, "Postponing Marriage: The Influence of Young Women's Work Expectation," *Journal of Marriage and the Family* 42 (1980): 355–65.

32. Ronald C. Kessler and James A. McRae, Jr., "The Effect of Wives' Employment on the Mental Health of Married Men and Women," *American Sociological Review* 47 (1982): 216–27.

33. William M. Michelson, *From Sun to Sun: Daily Obligations and Community Structure in the Lives of Employed Women and Their Families* (Totowa, N.J.: Rowman and Allanheld, 1985).

34. Sylvia Ann Hewlett, *A Lesser Life: The Myth of Women's Liberation in America* (New York: William Morrow, 1986).

35. Cynthia Fuchs Epstein, "Towards a Family Policy: Changes in Mothers' Lives," in Cherlin, *Family Change*.

36. See Cherlin, "Women and the Family".

37. Bill Cosby, *Fatherhood* (New York: Doubleday, 1986), 61.

38. Frank F. Furstenberg, Jr., Christine Winquist Nord, James L. Peterson, and Nicholas Zill, "The Life Course of Children of Divorce: Marital Disruption and Parental Contact," *American Sociological Review* 48 (1983): 665–68.

39. Frank F. Furstenberg, Jr., "Good Dads/Bad Dads: Two Faces of Fatherhood," in Cherlin, *Family Change*.

40. Ibid.

41. For evidence linking higher earning potential for married women with higher probabilities of divorce, see Andrew Cherlin, "Work Life and Marital Dissolution," in George Levinger and Oliver C. Moles, eds., *Divorce and Separation: Context, Causes, and Consequences* (New York, Basic Books, 1979), 151–66; and Heather L. Ross and Isabel V. Sawhill, *Time of Transition: The Growth of Families Headed by Women* (Washington, D.C.: The Urban Institute Press, 1975).

42. Barbara Ehrenreich, *The Hearts of Men: American Dreams and the Flight from Commitment* (New York: Anchor Press, 1983).

43. Jessie Bernard, *The Future of Marriage* (New York: World Publishing Co., 1972).

44. Joseph Veroff, Elizabeth Douvan, and Richard A. Kulka, *The Inner American: A Self-Portrait from 1957 to 1976* (New York: Basic Books, 1981), especially 23–24.

45. Irwin Garfinkel and Sara S. McLanahan, *Single Mothers and Their Children: A New American Dilemma* (Washington, D.C.: The Urban Institute Press, 1986).

46. Mary Ann Glendon, *Abortion and Divorce in Western Law* (Cambridge, Mass.: Harvard University Press, 1987).

47. Carlson, "What Happened to the 'Family Wage'?"; and Allan C. Carlson, "Taxing Families into Poverty," *Journal of Family and Culture* 2 (1987): 7–15.

48. Gary L. Bauer, "The Family: Preserving America's Future," Report of the Working Group on the Family (Washington, D.C.: U.S. Department of Education, Office of the Under Secretary, November 1986).

49. Thomas J. Espenshade and Joseph J. Minarik, "Demographic Implications of the 1986 U.S. Tax Reform," *Population and Development Review* 13 (1987): 115–27.

50. Alfred J. Kahn and Sheila B. Kamerman, *Child Care: Facing the Hard Choices* (Dover, Mass.: Auburn House, 1987).

51. Ibid.

52. Ibid.

53. See, for example, the Child Care Act of 1987, introduced in the House of Representatives by Representative Nancy Johnson.

54. For example, legislation has been introduced on behalf of a coalition of nearly seventy national organizations, calling itself the Alliance for Better Child Care, which would authorize $2.5 billion in federal expenditures (with a matching 20 percent required of the states) and provide benefits to families with incomes below 115 percent of their state medians.

55. The information in this paragraph comes from Kahn and Kamerman, *Child Care*.

56. An additional 6 percent reported that their child was cared for by a nonrelative in their home; 9 percent reported that the mother cared for the child while working; and 5 percent provided no information. U.S. Bureau of the Census, "Child Care Arrangements of Working Mothers: June 1982," *Current Population Reports*, Series P-23, no. 129 (Washington, D.C.: U.S. Government Printing Office, November 1983), table A.

57. Kahn and Kamerman, *Child Care*.

58. Susan M. Juster and Maris A. Vinovskis, "Changing Perspectives on the American Family in the Past," *Annual Review of Sociology* 13 (1987): 193–216.

59. The information in this paragraph is taken from Sheila B. Kamerman and Alfred J. Kahn, *The Responsive Workplace: Employers and a Changing Labor Force* (New York: Columbia University Press, 1987).

60. Michelson, *From Sun to Sun*.

61. Kamerman and Kahn, *Responsive Workplace*.

62. Advisory Committee on Infant Care Leave, "Statement and Recommendations,"New Haven, Conn.: Yale Bush Center on Child Development and Social Policy, November 26, 1985; and Edward Zigler and Susan Muenchow, "Infant Day Care and Infant Care Leaves: A Policy Vacuum," *American Psychologist* 38 (1983): 91–4.

63. Bauer, "The Family," 7.

64. Ibid., 9.

65. Gerald C. Wright, Jr., and Dorothy N. Stetson, "The Impact of No-Fault Divorce Law Reform on Divorce in American States," *Journal of Marriage and the Family* 40 (1978): 575–80; and Jacques Commaille, Patrick Festy, Pierre Guibentif, Jean Kellerhals, Jean-Franois Perrin, and Louis Roussel, *Le Divorce en Europe Occidentale* (Paris: Institut National d'Etudes Demographiques, 1983).

66. Michael S. Teitelbaum and Jay M. Winter, *The Fear of Population Decline* (Orlando: Academic Press, 1985).

67. Harriet B. Presser and Wendy Baldwin, "Child Care as a Constraint on Employment: Prevalence, Correlates, and Bearing on the Work and Fertility Nexus," *American Journal of Sociology* 85 (1980): 1202-13; and Martin O'Connell and David E. Bloom, *Juggling Jobs and Babies: America's Child Care Challenge* (Washington, D.C.: Population Reference Bureau, Inc., February 1987).

68. Mary Jo Bane and Paul A. Jargowski, "The Length Between Government Policy and Family Structure: What Matters and What Doesn't," in Cherlin, *Family Change*.

69. See Ben J. Wattenberg, *The Birth Dearth* (New York: Pharos Books, 1987).

CHAPTER 6

# FINANCING HEALTH CARE AND RETIREMENT FOR THE AGED

John L. Palmer

Current demographic trends are producing a growing proportion of elderly households whose need to finance health care and retirement poses a major societal challenge. The purpose of this chapter is to document the ongoing changes that give rise to this challenge, to consider the particular issues they raise for public policies, and to discuss some of the concrete alternatives for dealing with them.

From the Social Security Act in 1935 through the mid-1970s, retirement and health care financing for the aged expanded rapidly, reflecting general agreement on the need for greater public spending for the aged and a tolerance for higher taxes on the working population. Since the mid-1970s, however, the foundations of this political consensus have been shaken by a number of developments, particularly the prolonged slowdown in economic growth, escalating health care costs, concern about the overall fiscal health of the federal government, and a growing public awareness of the greatly improved economic circumstances of the aged. Hence, proposals to further expand programs benefiting the elderly have stalled, and numerous steps have been

I want to thank Susan Hendrickson for research assistance, Stephanie Gould for editorial assistance, and Henry Aaron, Emily Andrews, Hugh Heclo, Bruce Jacobs, Jack Meyer, and Timothy Smeeding for comments on an earlier draft.

implemented to restrain the growth in public expenditures that previous measures had built in.

Present circumstances, however, are not sustainable. There is a growing mismatch between the actual problems the aged face in financing their retirement and health care and the current policies addressing these concerns. As a result, public pressure has been building once again to expand the federal role in a number of areas of concern to the elderly at the same time that there are strong fiscal pressures for further—and more drastic—federal budget cutbacks. Quite independent of the continuing search for means of reducing the federal deficit is the long-term prospect of a mushrooming financial burden on the working population simply to maintain spending under current policies for a rapidly growing aged population.

The overall conclusion of the chapter is that current federal policies in support of the aged must be significantly modified to encompass both carefully targeted expansions of financial support for some purposes and contractions for others—although in neither case as extreme as many people are advocating. Future policies will also have to focus more sharply on encouraging the further development of private as well as public sources of financing. The task of forging political consensus around these policies will prove formidable, and discussion of it lies outside the scope of this chapter. But, as discussed later, this task will be substantially eased if policies toward the elderly are formulated in the context of two large, societywide concerns: promotion of long-term economic growth and control of spiraling overall health care costs. In the absence of progress on these two fronts, it is hard to imagine any satisfactory resolution of the thorny issues examined here.

The body of the chapter has four major sections followed by conclusions. Because the aged population's current and prospective claim on overall economic resources is at the heart of much of the present concern, the first section explores the fiscal implications of current policies. The second section discusses the desirability of, and scope for, modifications in these policies in light of the changing needs of the aged. The third and fourth sections assess some of the concrete measures these policy modifications might entail—first, ones that would improve the economic security of the aged, and then, ones that would result in fiscal savings relative to current policies.

## Changing Numbers

The fiscal pressures that attend the aging of the U.S. population will be determined primarily by changing demography and public policies, and by the future course of the economy and health care costs.

The contribution of demographic change per se is attributable not simply to the growing numbers of Americans age sixty-five and over, but also to major shifts in the age distribution of the population—among the young, working-age, and aged, and within the aged population itself (see figures 6.1 and 6.2).[1] Over the next two decades the share of the aged within the total population is projected to continue to rise moderately, with the share of the very old (those eighty-five or older) advancing much more rapidly. In contrast, the share of the population under age twenty is expected to decline moderately. The net result of these two trends will be a small rise in the share of the working-age population. During the subsequent twenty years (roughly 2010 to 2030), the expected combination of continued low fertility rates, declining mortality rates, and the retirement of the baby boom generation will produce a much more dramatic shift. While the proportion of the population under age twenty will decline marginally, the aged population will grow much faster as the baby boom generation reaches retirement age, expanding considerably the potentially dependent population in comparison with the working population. Finally, unless the long-term downward trend in fertility rates substantially reverses early in the next century, this big change in the age structure of population will be more or less consolidated.[2]

Concern about the longer-term fiscal pressures resulting from the aging of the population stems primarily from the consequences of these demographic changes for spending under public programs for the aged. From being largely the concern of families and charities, the support of the aged has increasingly become a public or collective concern, underwritten by programs such as Social Security, Medicare, Medicaid, and public assistance (and tax subsidies to promote private savings and pensions). Until recently, legislation has successively expanded the coverage and benefits under this set of programs. As a result, the bulk of all transfers of resources between the working and the aged populations now occurs through the public sector—in particular, through the federal government. (Federal expenditures for the aged amount to about 7 percent of the gross national product [GNP], whereas state and local expenditures are less than 1 percent.) Moreover, almost all the programs are entitlements, for which all aged members of households with low incomes and assets, or aged ex-workers (and their dependents), are eligible. And program benefit levels are now automatically adjusted upward to reflect not only the rising costs of health care and other consumer goods but also (in the case of Social Security) the higher lifetime earnings of each new group of retirees.

These developments, in concert with the changing demographic picture, have resulted in a massive transfer of resources from the working population to the elderly and have been responsible for much of the growth in federal

FIGURE 6.1

AGE COMPOSITION OF THE TOTAL POPULATION, 1950–2050

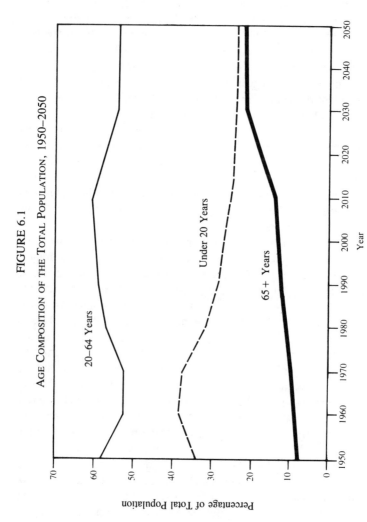

20–64 Years

Under 20 Years

65 + Years

Percentage of Total Population

Year

SOURCE: 1987 Annual Report of the Board of Trustees of the Federal Old Age, Survivors Insurance, and Disability Insurance (OASDI) Trust Funds.

NOTE: Projections are based on the Social Security Administration Actuaries' intermediate demographic assumptions.

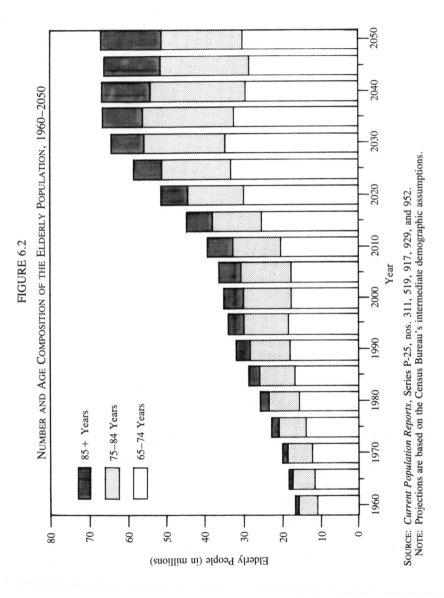

FIGURE 6.2

NUMBER AND AGE COMPOSITION OF THE ELDERLY POPULATION, 1960–2050

SOURCE: *Current Population Reports*, Series P-25, nos. 311, 519, 917, 929, and 952.
NOTE: Projections are based on the Census Bureau's intermediate demographic assumptions.

expenditures relative to GNP over the past several decades. Moreover, these developments ensure that, despite recent measures to slow their rate of growth, aggregate public expenditures for the aged under current policies will once again grow faster than the economy as the next century approaches.

Awareness that simply maintaining the present degree of support would require greater taxation of the working population in the future has prompted many people to argue for further major cutbacks in the current federal commitment to the aged. It has also stimulated concern about heightened competition for potentially dwindling public resources between the aged and other dependent groups, namely, children and the nonaged poor. At the same time it appears likely that many of the aged will need more public resources to cope with the problems associated with their greater longevity. All this potentially adds up to quite a strain on the public purse.

Just how much of a strain is difficult to quantify, because it will depend not only on future adjustments in public policies but also on the uncertain course of the economy and health care costs. One rough measure of the magnitude of the problem can be derived from projections of future expenditures for Social Security and Medicare under the policies now in effect, because these two programs currently account for more than four-fifths of all federal spending for the aged (as well as 48 percent of all domestic program spending and 29 percent of all federal outlays).[3] Some current-policy fiscal projections (and historical data) are displayed in table 6.1 using both the "intermediate" and "pessimistic" assumptions usually employed for the two programs. Obviously, they are not hard forecasts, because the assumptions on which they are based will undoubtedly change; but they at least provide some basis for thinking about the future.

Under the intermediate assumptions, the combined outlays for pension and health care financing creep up only marginally as a percentage of GNP over the next twenty years but then rise substantially (about four percentage points) as the baby boom generation retires, before becoming relatively stable once again. But although Social Security outlays fluctuate—going down and then rising—over the next forty years, Medicare outlays climb steadily throughout the period, greatly increasing in relative importance. (The initial decline in Social Security is attributable to the 1983 amendments to the Social Security legislation, which provided for, among other things, a significant reduction in benefits relative to most retiree's prior earnings, which is scheduled to phase in gradually early next century. Eventually though, the dampening influence of these amendments is far overshadowed by the retirement of the baby boom generation.) The continuously faster-than-GNP growth of Medicare outlays is attributable to two factors. The first is demography, including not only the general increase in the share of the aged population but also the

TABLE 6.1

CURRENT POLICY PROJECTIONS OF SOCIAL SECURITY AND MEDICARE EXPENDITURES
AS A PERCENTAGE OF GNP, 1990–2050

| | Social Security | Medicare[a] | Total |
|---|---|---|---|
| Historical data | | | |
| 1965 | 2.4 | (b) | 2.4 |
| 1970 | 2.9 | 0.7 | 3.6 |
| 1975 | 4.0 | 0.9 | 4.9 |
| 1980 | 4.3 | 1.2 | 5.5 |
| 1985 | 4.7 | 1.7 | 6.4 |
| Projections | | | |
| Intermediate assumptions | | | |
| 1990 | 4.7 | 2.1 | 6.8 |
| 1995 | 4.7 | 2.3 | 7.0 |
| 2000 | 4.4 | 2.5 | 6.9 |
| 2005 | 4.2 | 2.8 | 7.0 |
| 2010 | 4.4 | 3.0 | 7.4 |
| 2015 | 4.9 | 3.2 | 8.1 |
| 2020 | 5.6 | 3.7 | 9.3 |
| 2025 | 6.2 | 4.2 | 10.4 |
| 2030 | 6.5 | 4.5 | 11.0 |
| 2035 | 6.5 | 4.8 | 11.3 |
| 2040 | 6.4 | 4.8 | 11.2 |
| 2045 | 6.3 | 4.8 | 11.1 |
| 2050 | 6.2 | 4.8 | 11.0 |
| Pessimistic assumptions | | | |
| 1990 | 5.2 | 2.3 | 7.5 |
| 1995 | 5.2 | 2.8 | 8.0 |
| 2000 | 4.9 | 3.3 | 8.2 |
| 2005 | 4.8 | 3.8 | 8.6 |
| 2010 | 5.0 | 4.5 | 9.5 |
| 2015 | 5.6 | 5.3 | 10.9 |
| 2020 | 6.5 | 6.3 | 12.8 |
| 2025 | 7.3 | 7.6 | 14.9 |
| 2030 | 8.0 | 8.5 | 16.5 |
| 2035 | 8.3 | 9.0 | 17.3 |
| 2040 | 8.5 | 9.1 | 17.6 |
| 2045 | 8.7 | 9.1 | 17.8 |
| 2050 | 9.0 | 9.0 | 18.0 |

SOURCES: For 1965–1985, Historical Tables of the Federal Budget; for 1990–2050, 1987 Annual Report of the Social Security Board of Trustees of the Federal OASDI Trust Funds.
   a. This includes both the Hospital Insurance (HI) and Supplemental Medical Insurance (SMI) components of Medicare. Long-term projections are provided by the Medicare actuaries only for HI. SMI outlays are assumed to rise from 63 percent of HI outlays in 1990 to 66 percent in 1992 (as in the Congressional Budget Office's five-year projections) and then to remain a constant 66 percent of the HI outlays.
   b. Medicare was not implemented until the late 1960s.

increase within that population of the very old, who have relatively higher medical expenses. The second is increases in general health care costs per capita, which for years have greatly exceeded the rate of general inflation and are assumed to continue to do so, but by a much narrower margin.

Although the intermediate assumptions supposedly reflect the current "best guess," they are more likely than not to prove optimistic, particularly with regard to real rates of growth in the economy and of health care costs.[4] Different assumptions about these two and other relevant variables can dramatically alter the outlay projections. As shown in table 6.1 the pessimistic assumptions yield a far different fiscal outlook: combined Social Security and Medicare outlays climb rapidly over the entire projection period, increasing by ten percentage points of GNP by the end of the retirement of the baby boom generation. This pessimistic projection series merits attention not because it portrays a likely outcome, but because it illustrates the sensitivity of estimates of the future fiscal burden to variations in the assumed trajectories of key variables. However, given the rosiness of the intermediate assumptions, the outlay trends they yield under current policies are clearly on the optimistic side.[5]

Although rapid growth in the elderly population is a major contributor to the rising costs of current policies as projected in table 6.1, there is another dimension of the changing composition of the population that should serve to moderate the fiscal severity of the picture portrayed there. As shown in figure 6.1, youth's share of the total population is expected to fall by an amount equal to about half of the increase in the aged's share by the end of the retirement of the baby boom generation. However, per capita public expenditures for the pre-working-age population are only one-fourth to one-third those for the aged; and because these expenditures are much more a state and local responsibility, this relative shrinkage in the youth population will have only a minor effect on projected federal spending under current policies. Nevertheless, the total tax burden on the working-age population (and the strain on their private resources) should be relieved somewhat by this development.

Even granting this mitigating development, however, if the current public commitment to financial support for the aged is not scaled back, the working population appears to be facing major tax increases to pay for this support before long. In a display of unusual foresight, Congress attempted to provide at least partially for this contingency in the 1983 amendments to the Social Security Act. In addition to measures designed to avert the pending bankruptcy of the program's trust funds and to reduce long-term benefit commitments, the amendments included provisions for increasing Social Security's future revenues sufficiently to put the program on a sound financial basis well into next century. Most important, the earmarked payroll tax paid equally by employers and employees on Social Security-covered earnings was scheduled to increase by one percentage point between 1988 and 1990 (from a combined level of 11.4 to 12.4). And, in a significant departure from past practice, half of Social Security benefits for persons with adjusted gross incomes in excess of $25,000 ($32,000 for couples) were subjected to income taxation, with the proceeds also destined for the Social Security trust fund. These steps were designed to produce large annual surpluses that would accumulate as sizable reserves in the Social Security trust fund over the next two to three decades (possibly exceeding $2 trillion) and could then be drawn down to pay for the retirement of the baby boom (figure 6.3).

The intention is admirable, but the execution has been problematic so far and threatens to worsen. Although projected outlays and income for Social Security are in actuarial balance over the next fifty or so years under the intermediate assumptions, this does not necessarily mean that the total economic resources available to the population during the retirement of the baby boom generation will be any larger than they would have been in the absence of this build-up of reserves. If the reserves in the Social Security trust funds are to be of any real benefit in easing the financial burden of the retirement of the baby boom, they must be used to enhance economic growth in the interim. This will be the case only if the Social Security surpluses, which are a form of public savings, result in higher overall national savings and investment than would otherwise occur. But they cannot have this effect if they are used simply to offset deficits in other federal accounts. Unfortunately, this is what is already occurring.[6] In this era of Gramm-Rudman budgetary politics, no political leader is advocating balancing the federal budget exclusive of Social Security. The annual Social Security surpluses—which are expected to total $70 billion (more than 1 percent of GNP) by 1992 and still growing—are being used to avoid the need for even larger politically painful deficit reductions.

If general deficit reduction does not continue to supply sufficient temptation, yet another threat to the Social Security surpluses is looming a little further down the road. Unlike the action on Social Security, no provision has yet been made even on paper for the financing of Medicare's projected faster-than-GNP growth over the next twenty years, let alone the retirement of the baby boom. Medicare has two components. The larger one, Hospital Insurance (HI), accounts for about 60 percent of total program outlays and is financed by a 2.9 percent (combined employer-employee) payroll tax on Social Security-covered earnings. In the early 1990s HI will begin to run annual deficits that, even under the intermediate assumptions, will deplete its trust fund around the turn of the century and will exceed 1.6 percent of GNP (3 percent

FIGURE 6.3

ANNUAL COST AND INCOME RATES FOR SOCIAL SECURITY AND MEDICARE HOSPITAL
INSURANCE UNDER CURRENT POLICIES AND THE INTERMEDIATE ASSUMPTIONS,
1987–2050

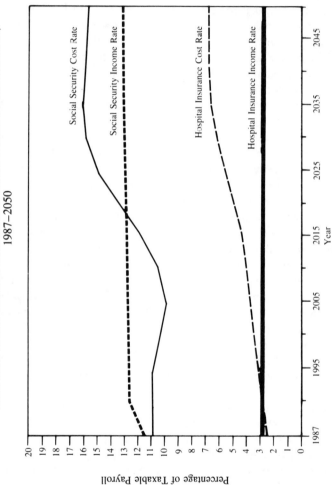

SOURCE: 1987 Annual Report of the Board of Trustees of the Federal OASDI Trust Funds.

of payroll) once the baby boom generation is retired (see figure 6.3). Medicare's other component, Supplemental Medical Insurance (SMI), which covers physician and outpatient services, is financed one-quarter from enrollee premiums and three-quarters from general revenues. Consequently, under this arrangement, as SMI outlays continue to rise relative to GNP, so, too, will the tap on general revenues required to finance the program. Under these conditions, it will be politically tempting to reallocate the Social Security surpluses in order to postpone Medicare's day of reckoning or to finance new health care benefits for the aged.

In sum, the interaction of an aging population, public policies, and rising health care costs has resulted in a substantial increase in the share of total economic resources being devoted to the support of the aged population over the past several decades, and this share undoubtedly will continue to increase over the foreseeable future. By how much is difficult to predict, because the amount will depend on the uncertain course of the economy and health care costs, among other things, as well as on future adjustments in public policies in support of the aged. However, it appears likely that the revenues necessary to finance projected expenditures *under current policies* would have to increase modestly over the next two decades and by at least 5 percent of GNP by the end of the retirement of the baby boom—with the bulk of the increase earmarked for health care. How burdensome such an increase would be on future working generations is discussed further in the concluding section.

The next section deals with the needs of the aged. The same factors that have altered the fiscal outlook are also contributing to major changes in circumstances among the elderly, and it is important to understand the nature of these changes in considering possible shifts in public policies that are responsive to the evolving needs of the aged and to overall fiscal concerns.

## Changing Needs

Over the past several decades the sizable expansion of federal programs, as well as general economic growth, has led to one of the greatest success stories of public policy—an overall major improvement in both the absolute and relative economic status of the aged. This improvement is clearly reflected in aggregate income statistics. Between the late 1960s and the mid-1980s, the median per capita income of the aged population rose by 50 percent, from three-quarters to over nine-tenths of that of the nonaged population. The poverty rate among the aged also declined, from well above the rate for the nonaged (28.5 percent vs. 13.3 percent in 1966) to somewhat below (12.4 percent vs. 13.7 percent in 1986).

This general story of substantial improvement in the economic status of the aged appears to hold true even when simple income measures are adjusted for numerous other differences in the circumstances of the aged and nonaged. For example, the aged receive greater amounts of in-kind assistance (such as Medicare), pay proportionately less in taxes, have lower consumption needs (because of lower caloric intake requirements and fewer work-related expenses), and have greater net worth (as a result of a lifetime of savings). Conversely, the aged have greater health care needs and are less able to take advantage of the economies of scale available to the nonaged, who typically live in larger households. Several studies, using various methodologies, have tried to adjust for these kinds of differences.[7] The general conclusion they reach is that the economic status of the aged *as a group* is more or less on a par with that of the nonaged and such that they can maintain in retirement the standard of living achieved in their middle-age working years.

Even these adjusted measures of the economic status of the aged fail to capture the full extent of the improvement in the well-being of this group. The gains have been realized despite a major reduction in the labor force participation of the aged. (Participation of elderly men has been declining for several decades, dropping from 46 percent in 1950 to 16 percent in 1986, with a corresponding decline in the share that earnings represent in the total income of aged households from more than one-third in 1950 to about one-seventh today.) Rising pension and asset income and rapidly expanding Social Security benefits have made retirement a more economically viable alternative to continued employment among the aged, and many have responded by taking a large portion of their rising standard of living in the form of leisure. (The same phenomenon is also prevalent among men ages fifty-five to sixty-four, who have increasingly opted for early retirement.) Further testimony to the improved well-being of the aged is their increasing ability to live independently—a preference which they and their children have consistently and strongly registered in surveys over this period. The big gains in such independent living came in the 1950s, but they have continued since then. Between 1960 and 1984 the percentage of all persons age sixty-five and over who were household heads or spouses of heads increased from 80 to 91 percent, and the share of single, aged persons with no live-in relatives rose from 40 to 70 percent.[8]

Although it is commonplace to present data on the aged as a group, averages by no means tell the whole story. Rather, they mask an extremely (and increasingly) heterogeneous population which spans more than thirty years of age and has highly disparate economic, demographic, and health conditions. For example, aged persons who live alone, are very old, or are minorities are the most likely to be poor. Poverty rates ranged in 1984 from as low as 5 percent for younger, married elderly persons to as high as 41 percent for older single women (see table 6.2).[9] Because of the combination of their high poverty rates and large share of the total aged population (due to their greater longevity), single women account for nearly two-thirds of all aged poor persons.

In general, the economic status among the aged is more unequal than among the nonaged.[10] Despite their lower overall poverty rate, a much higher proportion of the aged than the nonaged have below-average incomes. For example, in 1984 nearly one-third of the aged, in contrast to less than a fifth of the nonaged, had incomes between only one and two times the poverty level. At the other end of the distribution, net wealth is extremely concentrated among aged households; the top 5 percent account for well over half of the total. The only important form of wealth that is widespread among lower- and middle-income aged households is home equity.

The aged also manifest quite different exposure to economic insecurity over their remaining lifetimes. Despite the past rapid expansion of Medicare and Social Security, many elderly persons are still very vulnerable to certain financial exigencies—most notably, medical expenses or the death of a spouse and concomitant loss of income—that can overstrain their resources and, for many, result in a precipitous decline in their standard of living. Medicare pays less than half of the health care costs of the aged and covers neither long-term care nor many acute-care needs (such as prescription drugs). And the availability of private insurance covering either long-term care or extraordinarily high acute-care costs is extremely limited. The portion of the annual income of the noninstitutionalized aged that is currently devoted to health care averages about 14 percent and is rising.[11] However, these expenses range from well above an average of 20 percent of income for the low-income aged to below 5 percent for those with per capita income above $20,000. And within all income groups, these health expenses are heavily concentrated among the aged in any given year who require extensive hospitalization. Moreover, nursing home costs ($20,000 to $30,000 a year) are a further burden to many of the aged. Only about 5 percent of the aged are now in nursing homes, but the lifetime risk of such institutionalization exceeds 40 percent, with its likelihood increasing markedly with age.

The aged facing the greatest economic insecurity are the half to two-thirds who are in the broadly defined lower-middle income class.[12] Medicaid covers most health care costs, including nursing homes, for the poorest aged; and the more affluent generally have sufficient income and assets or supplementary medical coverage to cover most contingencies. But people in between these groups are largely dependent on Medicare and have to "spend down" their income and assets to poverty or below-poverty levels before they become

TABLE 6.2

POVERTY AMONG DEMOGRAPHIC SUBGROUPS OF THE ELDERLY IN 1984

| Demographic Subgroup | All Elderly | | | | White | | | Black | | |
|---|---|---|---|---|---|---|---|---|---|---|
| | Number (In thousands) | Percentage Below Poverty Line | Percentage Below 125% of Poverty Line | Percentage of Total Elderly Poor Persons[a] | Number (In thousands) | Percentage Below Poverty Line | Percentage Below 125% of Poverty Line | Number (In thousands) | Percentage Below Poverty Line | Percentage Below 125% of Poverty Line |
| All elderly | | | | | | | | | | |
| 65–74 | 12,027 | 17 | 26 | 47.7 | NA | NA | NA | NA | NA | NA |
| 75–84 | 6,878 | 24 | 38 | 37.8 | NA | NA | NA | NA | NA | NA |
| 85+ | 1,886 | 34 | 51 | 13.9 | NA | NA | NA | NA | NA | NA |
| Total | 20,791 | 21 | 32 | 100.0 | 18,590 | 18 | 29 | 1,888 | 48 | 61 |
| Married couples | | | | | | | | | | |
| 65–74 | 5,757 | 5 | 9 | 11.8 | NA | NA | NA | NA | NA | NA |
| 75–84 | 2,177 | 9 | 15 | 8.0 | NA | NA | NA | NA | NA | NA |
| 85+ | 355 | 11 | 20 | 1.6 | NA | NA | NA | NA | NA | NA |
| Total | 8,289 | 7 | 11 | 22.6 | 7,665 | 6 | 10 | 508 | 20 | 28 |
| Nonmarried persons | | | | | | | | | | |
| Men | | | | | | | | | | |
| 65–74 | 1,530 | 21 | 34 | 6.6 | NA | NA | NA | NA | NA | NA |
| 75–84 | 909 | 27 | 40 | 5.0 | NA | NA | NA | NA | NA | NA |
| 85+ | 315 | 33 | 49 | 2.1 | NA | NA | NA | NA | NA | NA |
| Total | 2,754 | 24 | 38 | 13.7 | 2,303 | 20 | 30 | 388 | 48 | 60 |
| Women | | | | | | | | | | |
| 65–74 | 4,740 | 30 | 43 | 29.1 | NA | NA | NA | NA | NA | NA |
| 75–84 | 3,791 | 32 | 50 | 24.8 | NA | NA | NA | NA | NA | NA |
| 85+ | 1,215 | 41 | 60 | 10.2 | NA | NA | NA | NA | NA | NA |
| Total | 9,746 | 32 | 48 | 64.1 | 8,621 | 28 | 45 | 992 | 62 | 77 |

SOURCE: "Income of the Population 55 and over, 1984," Social Security Administration Publication 13-11871.

NA: Not available.

NOTE: Numbers include noninstitutionalized population only. Entries may not add to total because of rounding.

a. Based on person weights. Data in all other rows are based on household weights.

eligible for Medicaid. They are also the most likely to be dependent on modest earnings or pension income, in addition to Social Security, to maintain their prior standard of living, and these sources of income often cease with the disability or death of a spouse.

What of the future? How are the circumstances of the aged likely to evolve in the absence of any major policy changes? Any answer to this question must, of course, be speculative, because it depends on many factors that cannot be predicted with any certainty. Nevertheless, a few observations seem warranted.

There is little doubt that the economic status of successive new groups of aged persons will continue to improve on average. Far less clear is what the rate of that improvement is likely to be and, in particular, whether the economic status of the aged will continue to rise faster than that of the nonaged. Past improvements in the overall relative economic status of the aged have largely been the result of public pensions and health care financing programs, whose coverage greatly expanded and whose average benefits increased far more rapidly than earnings. Both these trends have largely ceased. Indeed, the fact that Social Security benefits for new retirees are scheduled to grow more slowly than earnings in the next century and that the aged will live longer will tend to reduce the relative economic status of the aged as a group. But private incomes of the newly aged are likely to rise faster than workers' earnings over the next several decades because of the greatly expanded coverage of the labor force by employer-based pensions from the 1940s through the 1970s as well as major improvements in pension vesting and portability and in tax incentives for individual retirement savings since the mid-1970s. In addition, the generation that will reach retirement age over the next two decades will probably be favored by relatively high net worth.[13]

Leaving aside the matter of averages, there is a strong possibility of increased disparities in the future economic status of the aged. Unfortunately, the public sources of income that will be growing less rapidly are far more important to the lower- and moderate-income aged (particularly the very old) than the private sources that are likely to be growing more rapidly (see table 6.3). Social Security and other public cash assistance account for 55 to 85 percent of the total income of aged persons in the bottom three quintiles of the income distribution, whereas the top income quintile of aged persons receive more than 80 percent of their income from assets, private pensions, and earnings. (The importance of Social Security to the lower-middle-income aged is underscored by the fact that nearly half of the aged would be poor without Social Security benefits.) As a result of these factors and the greater longevity of the aged, it appears likely that there will be more pulling apart of the "haves" and the "have nots" among the aged in the future—with the

TABLE 6.3

PERCENTAGE DISTRIBUTION OF INCOME BY SOURCE FOR THE ELDERLY BY INCOME
QUINTILES, 1984

*Elderly Couples*[a]

| Income Source | All Income Groups | Income Quintiles by Dollar Range | | | | |
|---|---|---|---|---|---|---|
| | | Less than $10,100 | $10,100– $14,449 | $14,450– $20,099 | $20,100– $30,099 | $30,100+ |
| Social Security | 37.6 | 82.2 | 69.2 | 55.5 | 37.4 | 17.8 |
| Pension income | 16.2 | 4.7 | 12.4 | 17.2 | 20.4 | 16.6 |
| Income from assets | 27.6 | 6.1 | 10.4 | 17.9 | 26.7 | 38.4 |
| Earnings | 16.9 | 2.2 | 6.0 | 7.9 | 14.7 | 25.7 |
| Means-tested cash transfers | 0.3 | 3.3 | 0.6 | 0.1 | 0.0 | 0.0 |
| Other income | 1.3 | 1.5 | 1.4 | 1.4 | 0.8 | 1.5 |
| Total | 100.0 | 100.0 | 100.0 | 100.0 | 100.0 | 100.0 |

*Elderly Individuals*[a]

| Income Source | All Income Groups | Income Quintiles by Dollar Range | | | | |
|---|---|---|---|---|---|---|
| | | Less Than $4,200 | $4,200– $5,799 | $5,800– $8,049 | $8,050– $13,699 | $13,700+ |
| Social Security | 44.5 | 75.0 | 81.6 | 74.2 | 52.9 | 21.7 |
| Pension income | 12.5 | 1.0 | 2.1 | 7.8 | 15.3 | 16.1 |
| Income from assets | 30.6 | 3.5 | 4.7 | 10.0 | 21.6 | 48.5 |
| Earnings | 8.1 | 0.6 | 1.3 | 2.5 | 7.1 | 12.3 |
| Means-tested cash transfers | 2.3 | 17.8 | 7.2 | 3.1 | 0.2 | 0.0 |
| Other income | 2.1 | 2.1 | 3.1 | 2.4 | 2.9 | 1.4 |
| Total | 100.0 | 100.0 | 100.0 | 100.0 | 100.0 | 100.0 |

SOURCE: Congressional Budget Office calculations based on the March 1985 *Current Population Survey*. Entries may not add to totals because of rounding.

a. Elderly couples include those in which the older spouse is age sixty-five or older and the younger spouse is age sixty-two or older. Elderly individuals include all unmarried people age sixty-five or older. The institutionalized population is not included.

economic status of those at lower income levels declining in the future relative to the status of nonaged people, and the status of the well-to-do continuing to gain.[14]

Although the overall financial resources of the aged will increase over time, so, too, it appears, will the financial burdens associated with health care, especially long-term care. Projections of the future health status of the aged are especially problematic in view of the considerable uncertainty surrounding advances in medical technology and their consequences for morbidity (illness), disability, and mortality rates. However, in the past, general medical advances against the predominant causes of ill health among the aged have been offset by our increasing ability to keep alive many of the least healthy members of the population. Hence the general health status of the senior citizens of any given age remains roughly unchanged—and there is no reason to expect a major future shift in this pattern.[15] Thus, as the aged become increasingly numerous and long-lived, the economic insecurity engendered by extensive long-term care needs will become far more widespread. As evidence of this, simple extrapolations based on current population projections and age-specific institutionalization rates indicate an approximate doubling of the nursing home population over the next thirty years and quadrupling over the next fifty years.

This overview of the changing circumstances of the aged suggests two general conclusions. First, despite the dramatic overall improvement in their economic status, the aged still have several important current (and prospective) needs for economic security. Second, because of this improvement, some of the aged have a greatly enhanced (and growing) capability for directly shouldering more of the burden for their own economic security. In short, there is a growing mismatch between the needs of the aged and the policies now in place. The need for a more discriminating set of public policies seems obvious.

The major needs of the elderly now are much more particular than general. If the United States is to address these needs in a fiscally responsible way, as well as address the growing fiscal gap under current policies, policymakers must develop a set of policies that (1) will increase the direct responsibility of the well-off aged persons for their own economic security without unduly undermining the important gains thus far achieved by the aged as a group and (2) will make more efficient use of both public and private resources. The two sections that follow first explore the primary options for filling gaps in current policies with regard to income security and health care financing and then survey the prospects for achieving savings in public programs in ways that are consistent with these objectives.

## Improving the Economic Security Of the Aged

As is evident from the previous discussion, a major economic security need of the aged is protection against catastrophic expenses for acute and, especially, long-term care. In addition, poverty continues to be a reality for a significant minority of the aged, and a much larger group still has inadequate private resources after retirement with which to supplement Social Security and meet the more routine expenses of daily living. Although these concerns confront all demographic subgroups of the aged to some degree, very old people and divorced or widowed single women are especially vulnerable.

## Income Security

The most promising approaches for addressing the income security needs identified earlier are expanding private pensions and individual retirement annuities, facilitating reverse-annuity mortgages, implementing some form of so-called earnings sharing under Social Security, and liberalizing the Supplemental Security Income (SSI) program.

**Expanding Pensions and Individual Retirement Annuities.** As already noted, the importance of employment-based pension income for the aged is expected to continue to grow over the next several decades. The gains will be particularly widespread and dramatic for women, because of their greatly increased labor force participation since World War II.[16] However, less than 60 percent of the labor force currently has pension coverage, and this percentage is not expected to change significantly under current policies.[17] This means that pension recipiency rates will cease to rise once all those workers who entered the labor force during the period of greatly expanding coverage have retired. Thus, a sizable portion of the lower-middle-income aged population will still be left with little or no pension income to supplement Social Security benefits at a time when the share of past earnings replaced by these benefits will be declining for those who retire before age sixty-seven. Because most of these aged people will be the same ones who will have found it difficult to accumulate other forms of liquid wealth during their working years, it would be desirable to increase the availability of pension and annuity income in their retirement.

The most obvious way to address this concern is to mandate some basic coverage for all employers above some minimal size for their employees who meet certain conditions with respect to age, hours worked, and, possibly, job tenure (as was recommended in the 1981 report of the President's Commission on Pension Policy). However, such a step raises a number of concerns, particularly regarding the potential economic costs to the newly covered workers and their employers. In view of the potential negative impact on profitability and employment in small firms (for whom pension coverage is currently much lower and the per capita costs of administering a plan much higher than for larger firms), more study and refinement of mandated pension systems are clearly called for before legislation is considered.

In the interim the federal government could consider taking several more modest steps that could expand somewhat the expected pension and annuity income of lower-middle-income retirees who would otherwise have little or none. Three of these steps appear particularly meritorious, because they would be minimally disruptive of the current private pension system and entail relatively small private and public costs. First, the provision of a tax credit to smaller employers to offset their higher administrative costs should encourage many more to offer pension plans.[18] Second, much more stringent penalties or restrictions could be imposed on workers for using tax-sheltered retirement savings in IRAs and employer-based pensions to finance either early retirement or current consumption in their preretirement years, which is now common practice among workers with such sources of wealth. And, third, tax incentives could be increased for IRA contributions by lower-middle-income workers and their spouses, whose current use of this form of retirement savings is quite low.[19]

**Facilitating Reverse-Annuity Mortgages.**[20] About 40 percent, or an estimated $700 billion, of the total net worth of the aged population is currently held in the form of home equity. Nearly three-quarters of aged households are homeowners and more than four-fifths of these homes are unencumbered by a mortgage. Although high levels of home equity are concentrated among higher-income households, home equity is not uncommon among lower- and middle-income households.[21] Heretofore, aged homeowners have not generally been able to convert their home equity into available income without selling their houses and moving to rental property or new homes that cost considerably less than their equity in their prior home. Recently, however, variants of innovative financial instruments—popularly called "reverse-annuity mortgages"—have emerged for translating equity into income. Their potential benefits are particularly attractive for very old persons, whose shorter expected life span would enable them to obtain higher monthly payments for any given amount of equity.[22]

Unfortunately, for a complex number of reasons, markets for reverse mortgages have been slow to develop: banking laws and regulations effectively prohibit them in some states; there are inadequate protections for both lenders and borrowers if the homeowners' actual life span greatly exceeds their expected life span; insurance is generally unavailable to spread the risk of default (in contrast to the case with conventional mortgage insurance); homeowners face the possibility that the liquidation of home equity will affect their program eligibility and benefit levels under public assistance programs; and potential borrowers are generally reluctant to take on new debt and often lack the sophistication to assess the advantages and disadvantages of doing so. Some of these problems are now being addressed, but more aggressive action by the federal government, as well as by state and local governments, will be necessary to overcome the barriers.

**Implementing Earnings Sharing under Social Security.** The Social Security program itself offers obvious opportunities for greater targeting of cash assistance on particularly needy aged. As noted earlier, the dramatic improvement in the economic status of the aged population in recent decades has been primarily a result of the rapid expansion of Social Security as a source of retirement income. But further general increases in Social Security would be extremely expensive and, in any event, would only hit the desired target on the periphery. In contrast, several proposals that have surfaced in recent years for some form of sharing of earnings records between spouses for purposes of determining individual benefits could hit the target more directly for a politically feasible price. The proposals vary considerably in the complexity of their design and consequences, depending on the relative weight given to different possible objectives. But, for the purposes here it is necessary only to note that, among other things, they can be structured to provide significantly higher benefits than under current law to the remaining spouse of a married couple (typically the wife) with the lower (or no) history of Social Security covered earnings in the event of divorce or death of the spouse.

Several prototypical incremental earnings-sharing plans, which do not disadvantage any current or future Social Security beneficiaries, have been analyzed by the Congressional Budget Office.[23] They would increase average benefits to widows and divorcees about 10 percent, with an eventual (during the retirement of the baby boom) annual cost of about 4 percent of currently projected Social Security outlays. (Four percent of Social Security outlays in 1988 would be $8 billion.) Moreover, this increase in benefits would be distributed in a highly progressive manner, ranging in excess of 20 percent for low-benefit recipients to under 2 percent for high-benefit recipients. The cost of full implementation of any of these incremental plans would be less than 2 percent of total Social Security outlays. A phase-in for new beneficiaries only, or immediate implementation of only some of the several potential changes involved, could reduce the costs even more. Also, more full-blown earnings-sharing plans have been designed which could be implemented at little or no long-run cost, because they would naturally result in reduction of benefits (relative to current law) for certain classes of recipients (particularly divorced men).[24]

**Liberalizing SSI benefits.**[25] None of the previous three categories of possible measures to improve the income security of the aged are directly targeted on poverty per se. And, although all would eventually contribute to further reductions in aged poverty, their effects would take several decades to be fully felt. Fortunately, there is also a direct and relatively inexpensive way to achieve a substantial and immediate effect on aged poverty rates—liberalizing SSI benefits.

The federal means-tested SSI program currently provides an inflation-indexed income guarantee at 77 percent of the poverty level for aged individuals and 91 percent for aged couples. Many states supplement these benefits, but few do so to the poverty level, and the real value of these supplements has eroded by more than half since the program was instituted in the mid-1970s. Raising the federal income guarantee to the poverty level for individuals and couples would reduce poverty among the aged by a third, at an annual cost of about $5 billion. Moreover, this reduction would be concentrated among the aged with the highest rates of poverty. (For example, the poverty rate among the oldest single women would decline by half or more.)

There are two reasons why raising the SSI income guarantee to the poverty level would not entirely eliminate poverty among the aged. Many of the aged who qualify for SSI benefits on the basis of their incomes are excluded from eligibility by the program's limitation on liquid assets (scheduled to be $2,000 for an individual and $3,000 for a couple in 1989). In addition, more than a third of the people who are eligible do not participate because of their unwillingness "to be on welfare," the small size of the benefit they would receive, or lack of knowledge about the program. Liberalization of the assets test, greater efforts at program outreach, and an income guarantee higher than the poverty level—all would improve the antipoverty effectiveness of the program for a cost of a few billion dollars beyond that of simply raising the guarantee to the poverty level.

## Health Care Financing

Greater assistance in financing catastrophic health care expenses is probably the most pressing economic security need for the aged. But, although a consensus on the public role in catastrophic acute care now (in November 1987) appears imminent, public debate about how to proceed on financing of long-term care has barely begun.

**Catastrophic Acute Care.** Numerous alternative approaches to providing the elderly improved Medicare protection against catastrophic acute-care expenses have been analyzed or proposed.[26] Depending on the specifics of design, many of the improvements could be made relatively inexpensively. For example, the legislation proposed in early 1987 by the Reagan administration to limit annual expenses for acute-care services covered by Medicare to $2,000 (excluding prescription drugs) would add less than $3 billion to annual Medicare expenditures in 1988 and would be totally self-financed by an across-the-board increase in the SMI premium of under $60 a year (from its otherwise expected level of $300). However, a package of benefit expansions for acute-care costs that would substantially reduce beneficiary cost sharing (copayments and deductibles), limit beneficiary expenses to $1,000, and add a prescription drug benefit could cost upwards of $10 billion a year.[27]

At the time of this writing, congressional passage and administration acceptance of a catastrophic acute-care bill that would provide coverage between these two extremes seems highly likely. Although the details are unclear, it appears that the final bill would modestly reduce beneficiary cost sharing, cap beneficiary expenses for Medicare-covered services at somewhat less than $2,000 in 1988 (an amount that would automatically increase in line with an appropriate cost index in future years), and add a separate upper limit to expenses for prescription drugs—along with several other minor changes. It also appears that the new benefits would be entirely self-financed by SMI enrollees through a mix of a small increase in the current flat-rate SMI premium and the institution of a new income-related supplemental premium collected through the tax system. If such modifications are made to the Medicare program, they would substantially ease the financial burdens of acute-care costs for many aged Americans, although they would do little to help those lower-income aged whose expenses are under the caps but still high relative to their incomes.

**Long-term Care.** As a nation, we currently spend about 1 percent of GNP ($45 to $50 billion) on long-term care for the functionally limited aged population through a highly fragmented payment and delivery system. Approximately half of this spending is public and half private, with Medicaid accounting for about three-quarters of the public share and direct out-of-pocket spending (as opposed to insurance) accounting for virtually all the private share. The great bulk of both public and private spending for long-term care is for the 1.3 million aged in nursing homes. The remainder is spent on a wide range of personal and medical services in support of the much larger (5 million) noninstitutionalized disabled elderly population. This formal (paid-for) noninstitutional care, however, meets only a small part of the needs of the disabled aged people living in the community. More than four-fifths of such assistance is provided by family members (primarily spouses and daughters), who average twenty-six hours a week in care giving.[28]

As the proportion of the very old markedly increases in the population, so inevitably will the share of GNP devoted to long-term care. Advances in medical technology and a more efficient delivery system that encourages noninstitutional care to the extent practicable could somewhat slow this increase. But, in addition to the increase in the sheer number of disabled aged, there will be upward pressure from health care cost inflation and a declining pool of informal care givers (because of lower birthrates, higher divorce rates, and increased labor force participation of the primary care givers, middle-aged women). Thus, the major public policy issue is not *whether* we are going to devote a substantially larger share of our GNP to long-term care but, rather, *how* we are going to do it—through what mix of public and private means.

Two extremes for this public-private mix are conceivable. One would entail a fully comprehensive long-term benefit with minimal cost sharing under Medicare. Under this approach, Medicaid's role would be limited to picking up any remaining out-of-pocket costs for the poorest aged persons. This would mean, in effect, public social insurance financing for the vast majority of all long-term care. The additional public costs for such a scheme cannot be precisely estimated, but they would probably be upwards of 2 percent of GNP or more within several decades (depending on the degrees of accompanying utilization and payment controls and of substitution of formal for informal care). Alternatively, Medicare coverage could be limited to acute care with Medicaid serving as a last resort, as now, and private sector mechanisms could be relied on to meet the needs of the nonpoor aged insofar as possible. Each of these extremes is a potentially feasible outcome for long-term care policies in this country. But given the current public fiscal outlook and the continuing American preference for private sector approaches where feasible, on the one hand, and the growing public concern about the inadequacies of current financing mechanisms for long-term care, on the other hand, some less-extreme approach involving the expansion of the roles of both the public and private sectors seems both likely and desirable.

Just what is the potential for the expansion of more attractive private sector financing mechanisms for long-term care? Until recently there had been essentially no systematic analysis of this subject. However, in the past year or two, several studies have been completed (with numerous others in progress) that may shed some light on the matter.[29] One major study analyzed the likely overall consequences thirty years from now of a wide range of private sector financing mechanisms under what the authors characterize as fairly optimistic assumptions both about the possibility for their development and about improvements in the economic status of the aged in the interim. The mechanisms considered were private insurance, continuing care retirement communities, reverse-annuity mortgages, tax incentives for individual retirement annuity (IRA) types of accounts for long-term care, and the extension of the health maintenance organization (HMO) concept to include long-term care services. The conclusion reached was that

> with the exception of home equity conversions, only a minority of the elderly could afford private sector financing mechanisms. Moreover, [as a

whole] private sector approaches are very unlikely to finance more than a modest proportion of nursing home and home care expenditures and will have only a small impact on . . . the number of people who [would otherwise have to] impoverish themselves down to Medicaid financial eligibility limits.[30]

Other studies are somewhat more optimistic about the potential of private sector financing mechanisms.[31] However, even they indicate that, although these mechanisms could eventually play a major role, a sizable expansion of public program expenditures also will still be necessary if tomorrow's aged are to be protected against widespread hardship from catastrophic long-term care expenses. In any event, the challenge to public policymakers will be to design this public program expansion prudently, while also fostering the development of the most promising complementary private sector mechanisms. (The two such mechanisms that appear to have the potential for the widest effects are reverse-annuity mortgages and long-term care insurance.)

Such a moderate expansion of direct public financing could be sensibly built into Medicaid and Medicare along either of two separate lines.[32] The first approach would be limited to Medicaid. Its eligibility for long-term care could be extended so that the descent into abject poverty, which now must precede any coverage, would be cushioned with graduated subsidies and more asset protection. Medicaid coverage is currently governed by a complex set of determinations involving SSI eligibility, stringent income and asset limitations, and spend-down provisions that vary considerably from state to state and even exclude the majority of aged persons with incomes below poverty level. The measures to expand SSI discussed earlier would improve Medicaid coverage of the poor aged.[33] Complete, uniform, national coverage of the poor aged would cost a few billion dollars more; costs would rise rapidly if coverage were extended further up the income and assets ladder.

The other approach to a moderate expansion of direct public financing for long-term care would involve reforming Medicare to provide a measure of protection against catastrophic expenses for all the aged. This could be done either as an alternative to a major, or a complement to a minor, liberalization of Medicaid. In either event, it would involve adding to Medicare a long-term care benefit for aged persons with rather serious functional impairment; the benefit would include a waiting period for eligibility, a substantial deductible, and possibly other cost sharing.[34]

Such a Medicare approach would have three main advantages. First, far fewer middle-income aged households would have to spend down into poverty or near poverty to obtain coverage for long-term care. Second, this level of public protection against expenses for catastrophic long-term care could reduce many of the barriers to private sector financing mechanisms and generally encourage rather than substitute for their development.[35] Finally, the added public costs could be kept to under 0.5 percent of GNP.[36]

## Achieving Savings in Public Programs

The steps considered in the foregoing section would target additional public and private resources on the priority needs for income security of today's and tomorrow's aged. But financing any such expansions in public programs without adding to the deficit will require additional revenues or reductions in other budgetary commitments. So, too, will bridging the projected long-term fiscal gap under current federal policies assisting the aged. In addition, because of their large share of the budget, cutbacks in the Medicare and Social Security programs are often advocated as one means of achieving overall deficit reduction in the near term. It was pointed out earlier that the improving economic status of the aged provides scope for some of them to shoulder more of the burden for financing their retirement and health care without undermining the improvements in economic security already achieved. This section considers various approaches that at least partially address the fiscal needs just mentioned through changes in the Medicare and Social Security programs.

### General Considerations

There are numerous ways of effectively increasing the burden on the aged for the financing of their retirement and health care while still preserving the essential functioning of the current social insurance system (i.e., Social Security and Medicare). It is important to note at the outset, however, that the desirability of preserving that system has been increasingly called into question in recent years. Numerous proposals (politically unthinkable a decade ago) have cropped up for replacing the current system with private provision ("privatization") for retirement and health care for the vast majority of the aged, accompanied by expanded provision of means-tested benefits (as in Medicaid and SSI) to cushion the consequences for the less fortunate. At the very least, proponents of privatization argue, the current working generation ought to be given the choice of opting out of the social insurance system. Such partial or total privatization, it is alleged, not only is more in keeping with the American ideology of individualism and free markets, but also would reduce taxes on the working population and solve the fiscal problem posed by rapid aging of the population.

The issues raised by various proposals for privatization and means testing are too complex to discuss fully here.[37] But it is worth noting the major opposing arguments, because they are sufficiently compelling to justify the focus here on less extreme adjustments to current policies. Briefly, these arguments are as follows.

First, it is true that switching from our present social insurance system for the aged to a system much more oriented to the private sector could eventually permit a sizable reduction or elimination of the current sources of taxation supporting Medicare and Social Security. But because of the present reliance on pay-as-you-go financing, unless social insurance benefits were abruptly terminated (which would be neither politically feasible nor socially fair), the current and near-future generations of working taxpayers would have to finance two systems: the current public one for the aged and near-aged populations and another one financed through added private savings for themselves.[38] This would approximately double the expenditures for these purposes for these households.

A second argument against privatization is that private insurance markets are generally unable to provide actuarially fair policies. The primary reason for this is that the risk of adverse selection—the ability of low-risk persons to opt out of insurance—means that actuarially fair insurance markets simply do not exist, except where participation is compulsory (as for Social Security and Medicare). Furthermore, the private market—unlike the public one—cannot guarantee a steady flow of real income during retirement (for any given amount of savings over the working years) because of the uncertainties posed by fluctuations in inflation and interest rates.

Beyond these two arguments is the overriding fact that, in contrast to many public programs, Social Security and Medicare have been extremely successful in accomplishing their objectives and have earned unusually strong and widespread support among Americans of all ages. They were created and have thrived because the alternatives were unacceptable to the overwhelming majority of the public. These programs are particularly popular among the broad middle class, many of whom would otherwise experience substantial hardship in their middle years from supporting their parents and to whom the prospect of having to rely on their own children or "demeaning" means-tested public programs in their own old age is fearsome indeed. Surveys as recently as the mid-1980s have shown that, despite some lack of confidence in the future ability of the system to provide for their retirement, two-thirds of young adults thought that Social Security taxes were fair and that their level was about right or too low.[39] In short, some modifications in our social insurance system for the aged appear to be needed to respond to changing circumstances, but privatization as a solution looks like another case of the proverbial baby and bath water.

What, then, are the most promising ways to alter social insurance programs to increase the burden on the aged for the financing of their retirement and health care while still preserving the essential functioning of the current social insurance system? Several are detailed here, but they all share certain general characteristics. The wide array of options boils down to two fundamental approaches: the burden can be increased in a way that either is or is not related to income. Refinements come into play over the implementation of these approaches. The increased burden can be achieved directly, through explicit reductions in benefits, or indirectly, through measures such as taxation of benefits or increased premiums in the case of Medicare. Also, timing is important: changes could affect the aged of today or only those after some future date.

The advantages of income-related approaches are obvious in light of our earlier evidence about the heterogeneity of the economic status of the elderly population. In particular, income-related approaches can minimize the adverse consequences for the lower- to middle-income aged, who currently are highly dependent on Social Security and Medicare to maintain their prior standards of living and avoid poverty. But income-related approaches are not without their disadvantages. One problem is the potential for administrative complexity. The implementation of non-income-related approaches requires no new information about recipients, whereas income-related approaches require information about the income not only of recipients, but also of their households. Neither type of income information is currently collected by Medicare or Social Security, and instituting any mechanism to do so would be a complex and costly undertaking for the government and an undesirable imposition on recipients and their families. For these reasons, use of the tax system to accomplish the income-relating process is vastly preferable, even though some precision in targeting might be lost by less-than-ideal definitions of income or family unit.

A second disadvantage of income-related approaches is their potential for undermining political support for the programs. This erosion of support could be widespread—because of a generally perceived violation of the "earned right" concept underpinning social insurance—or it could be concentrated among higher-income recipients, who might increasingly perceive social insurance as a bad deal for them, because their added burden would be much larger. (Non-income-related approaches obviously also have this potential, but to a lesser degree.) Although this concern is legitimate, there are several mitigating factors. The first is that the sine qua non of our social insurance system—universal eligibility for all workers (and their dependents, where relevant) with covered earnings—would be retained. The "earned right" would still be there; only the net benefit ultimately derived would be affected. Second, to the extent that taxation of benefits is the chosen instrument, benefits would simply be treated on a comparable basis with other sources of income, such as private pensions, that are currently included in the tax base, in accordance with our collective notion of what constitutes ability to pay. Finally, when all is said and done, our current system of social insurance constitutes a "good deal" even for prospective higher-income recipients. By virtue of being in on the early stages of a pay-as-you-go system, retirees at all income levels are currently receiving benefits of value far beyond what they contributed. And although the "windfall" component of benefits for new retirees is now declining rapidly with the maturation of the social insurance system and changing demography, it has a long way to go before calculations of self-interest should become problematic.[40]

So far only the abstract merits of broad approaches to changes in our social insurance system that would increase the burden of aged persons for the financing of their retirement and health care have been considered. The next sections consider some of the concrete measures that might be taken to reduce benefits for, or raise revenues from, Social Security and Medicare recipients.

## Social Security

Three general classes of options for Social Security are most often suggested. These are listed in table 6.4, along with estimates of the fiscal effects of variants of each.

First, the annual Social Security cost-of-living adjustments (COLA) to benefits could be restricted. Eliminating the COLA for one year would amount to an immediate and identical percentage cut (equal to the prevailing rate of inflation) in real benefits for all current recipients. Limiting it to, say, two percentage points less than the rate of inflation for five years would amount to a 10 percent cut in real benefit levels by the end of that period for all recipients. (Recipients also participating in SSI would receive offsetting increases in SSI benefits.) If the formula for calculating benefits for new retirees were similarly adjusted downward, in order to eliminate the disparities that would then otherwise exist between their treatment when they began to receive benefits and the treatment of the already retired, these COLA restrictions would reduce the cost of Social Security over the long run by roughly the same percentage as in the short run.

Second, more of Social Security benefits could be subject to income taxation. The current adjusted gross income (AGI) thresholds could be lowered or eliminated and more than 50 percent of benefits included in income (on

TABLE 6.4

OPTIONS FOR REDUCING OR TAXING SOCIAL SECURITY BENEFITS

| Option | Program Savings or Revenue Increase When Fully Implemented |
|---|---|
| | *In billions of 1990 dollars* |
| Restrictions on the cost-of-living adjustment (COLA) | |
| Eliminate the COLA for one year[a] | 9 |
| Limit the COLA to the CPI minus two percentage points for five years[b] | 13 |
| Taxation of benefits | |
| Lower or eliminate current thresholds for taxation of 50 percent of benefits[c] | 3–7 |
| Tax 85 percent of benefits with lower or no thresholds[c] | 9–17 |
| | *As a percentage of GNP in the long run* |
| Phased-in benefit reductions | |
| Raise age of eligibility for full benefits above 67[d] | 0.4 (for each year raised) |
| Reduce benefits proportionately across the board[d] | 0.6 (for each 10 percent reduction) |
| Reduce benefits progressively across the board[d] | 0.6 (for each 10 percent total reduction) |
| Addendum: | |
| *Estimates for 1990 of:* | *In billions of 1990 dollars* |
| GNP | 5,380 |
| Outlays for Social Security under current policies | 255 |

SOURCE: Author's estimates based on Congressional Budget Office and Social Security Trustees Report data.

a. The expected savings of eliminating the COLA for 1990.

b. The expected annual savings in 1993 of limiting the COLA to the Consumer Price Index minus two percentage points beginning in 1988 and going through 1992.

c. The lower revenue estimate assumes that the current adjusted gross income thresholds of $25,000/$32,000 are lowered to $12,000/$18,000. The upper estimate assumes that the thresholds are entirely eliminated.

d. These are the approximate annual average savings during the retirement of the baby boom generation based on the intermediate assumptions. If the aged were to work more in response to the changes, the savings would be greater.

the rationale that the windfall currently far exceeds that proportion of benefits). The revenue yield of any such measure would increase over time with the income of the aged. However, lower-income aged persons would still have no income tax liability because of the zero bracket amount and personal exemptions (which are indexed for inflation under the 1986 tax reform), and only the highest-income aged would face a marginal tax rate on Social Security benefits above 15 percent.

Third, benefits could be constrained to grow less rapidly than earnings more or less across the board for future retirees. The previous two steps discussed would have sizable immediate, as well as long-term, fiscal consequences. In contrast, numerous other measures have been proposed which would not have any immediate fiscal impact, because they would only affect new retirees at some future time. Depending on how these reductions are structured, they could place more of this future burden of this future on workers who retire early rather than later, and on workers with higher rather than lower earnings. They also would ensure future retirees of real benefit levels at least as high as those of their predecessors.[41]

## Medicare

Because of the complexity of the Medicare program, with its two separate components, multiple sources of revenues, and several types of cost sharing, an enormous variety of measures could be employed to increase the financial burden on beneficiaries of Medicare-covered services. All such measures that do not affect reimbursement rates to providers (discussed later), however, will fall into one of five basic categories. Table 6.5 shows the fiscal impact of some illustrative approaches for each category based on the structure of the program in 1987 (that is, before any modifications as a result of possible passage of a catastrophic acute-care bill).

First, cost sharing that is tied to utilization (deductibles and copayments) could be increased. The greatest strength of such an approach is that it might discourage unnecessary care, and the greatest weakness is that it would increase the costs for precisely those beneficiaries who are the heaviest users (generally for necessary care) and therefore already have the greatest financial liability. With a new catastrophic benefit for acute care, this liability would be capped, but the burden of the increase in cost sharing would still fall on the heaviest users across all income groups (except for those covered by Medicaid).

Second, the current flat premium paid by all SMI enrollees could be raised to cover more than 25 percent of total costs, or a similar premium could be instituted for HI. The added dollar costs would be identical for all

TABLE 6.5

<small>OPTIONS FOR INCREASING THE FINANCIAL BURDEN ON MEDICARE ENROLLEES</small>

| Option | Program Savings or Revenue Increase in 1990 (Billions of dollars) |
|---|---|
| Increased cost sharing | |
| Increase HI copayments[a] | 3 |
| Increase SMI copayments[b] | 3 |
| Raise SMI deductible[c] | 2 |
| Increased non-income-related premiums | |
| Raise the SMI premium above 25 percent of costs | 3 (for each 5 percent increase) |
| Institute an HI premium | 7 (for each 10 percent of program costs covered) |
| Taxation of a portion of benefits[d] | 4–7 |
| Institution of an income-related premium through the tax system[e] | 4–10 |
| Increase in age of eligibility to 67[f] | 7 |
| Addendum: | |
| *Estimates for 1990 of:* | *In billions of 1990 dollars* |
| HI outlays | 68.7 |
| SMI outlays | 44.8 |
| GNP | 5,380 |

SOURCE: Author's estimates based on Congressional Budget Office data.

a. Involves eliminating the current structure of copayments in favor of copayments of 10 percent of the deductible for the second through the thirtieth annual hospital days.

b. Involves raising the SMI coinsurance from 20 to 25 percent.

c. Involves raising the SMI deductible from $75 to $200 in 1988 and indexing thereafter to the Consumer Price Index.

d. Involves taxing the portions of SMI (75 percent) and HI (50 percent) not financed by employees or enrollees. The lower estimate assumes the same adjusted gross income thresholds currently applying to Social Security benefits, whereas the upper estimate assumes no thresholds.

e. Involves adding a constant percentage tax on the taxable income of enrollees, with the total liability for each person capped at 75 percent of the insurance value of SMI and 50 percent of the insurance value of HI. The amount of revenue raised will depend on whether the tax is applied to both SMI or HI or to only one and what rate (ranging from 1 to 5 percent) is imposed on the aged persons (currently about 40 percent of the total) who have taxable incomes.

f. This is the amount that could be saved in 1990 if the age of eligibility were immediately raised to 67. However, if it were phased in along with the change in Social Security as discussed in the text, there would be no savings from this measure this century. The savings would gradually increase early in the next century, reaching a maximum in 2020, after which they would amount to 6 or 7 percent of currently projected annual program costs.

Medicare enrollees. Such a step would be entirely consistent with the historical method of financing SMI, because enrollees paid premiums equal to 50 percent of costs when the program was first instituted.[42] However, it would be a major departure for the HI program, which heretofore has been financed exclusively through a payroll tax.

Third, the insurance value of a portion of Medicare benefits could be subject to income taxation, with consequences similar to those discussed earlier in connection with fuller taxation of Social Security benefits. Such a step would also raise the issue of parallel treatment of employer-based health insurance, for which employer contributions are currently nontaxable. Taxation of some portion of this fringe benefit is often advocated as a means of broadening the income and payroll tax base and raising revenues.

Fourth, as an alternative to taxation of benefits, an income-related premium could be instituted through the tax system. Doing so for HI would represent a major departure for the program, just as would a flat-rate premium. In contrast, the political precedent for an income-related premium for SMI already has been established in congressional consideration of a possible new catastrophic acute-care benefit. However, passage of a catastrophic bill with such a financing feature would greatly limit the potential for further raising beneficiary costs through an income-related premium for general cost-saving purposes.

Fifth, the age of eligibility for Medicare could be raised above sixty-five early next century, as will be the case for eligibility for full Social Security benefits under the 1983 amendments. However, the distributional effects of this measure for Medicare would be very different from those caused by the change in Social Security. The Social Security change will essentially amount to a partial benefit reduction relative to the prior law for all workers who retire before age seventy, with the degree of reduction depending on the precise age at retirement.[43] In the case of Medicare, no benefits would be provided to sixty-five- or sixty-six-year-olds, who would then have to rely fully on private individual and employer-based insurance; the status of people once they turn sixty-seven would be the same as now.

All the preceding measures would directly increase the costs to Medicare enrollees for health care services currently covered by the program. But the potential fiscal impacts of all these measures are small compared with Medicare's long-term fiscal problems under current policies. For this reason, changes in Medicare's reimbursement policies also are often advocated. Although these would most directly affect health care providers, they could also have important consequences for Medicare enrollees and raise important broader issues about health care in this country.

Recently enacted reform of the Medicare system for hospital payment reflected the widespread belief that the previous system of cost-based reimbursement encouraged increasingly expensive and inefficient modes of care. With the implementation of a prospective payment system based on diagnostic-related groupings beginning in 1984, Medicare substantially changed the cost incentives facing hospitals, shifting the determinants of future rates of growth in hospital payments per admission from a professional medical judgment to a budgetary one. On budgetary grounds, the first years of the program appear to have been successful. Medicare admissions, length of stay, and increases in rates of expenditure for hospital care have all declined significantly relative to past trends. But there is ample reason to doubt that budgetary savings on the order of those experienced thus far—and carried forward by the current projections—can be sustained, let alone further ones achieved.[44] Concerns about such phenomena as premature discharges of patients, "dumping" of other uninsured patients, and cost shifting on the part of hospitals are already prevalent. Over time these concerns are likely to intensify and new ones to emerge about the consequences of the new hospital reimbursement policy for the coverage of newly developing services and technologies.[45] Similarly, there is undoubtedly some scope for new savings through the adoption of more stringent reimbursement procedures for physician services. However, these savings, too, must be quite limited, if they are not to reduce the kind and quality of care available to at least a substantial portion of the aged.

These complex issues cannot be discussed in any detail here.[46] But the heart of the matter is that rapidly rising health care costs are endemic to the entire health care system and not just to public programs, and that attempts to deal with them that are largely constrained to public program payment systems will ultimately undermine these programs' objectives, as well as have other undesirable consequences.[47] As one noted analyst has observed:

> All developed nations face a profound dilemma—to bear the rapidly increasing costs of providing ever more sophisticated care to aging populations or, alternatively, to ration care, and in doing so deny some potential benefits to some patients. Some savings, possibly large in absolute amount, can be achieved by eliminating services such as unnecessary hospitalization or idle equipment that provide no medical benefits at all and by improving the efficiencies with which beneficial services are provided. But these savings can be achieved only once. After they have been reaped, the source of the rising trend in medical outlays—the technological transformation of medical care—will reassert itself. At that point the dilemma—pay the bill or ration services—will have to be faced.[48]

So far the United States is unique among Western industrialized democracies in its overwhelming reliance on the marketplace to accomplish whatever rationing is done, and the aged have been shielded from the consequences of this choice. If this country continues to rely primarily on the marketplace, the government will have to continue to "pay the bill" for the aged, or tolerate even greater variation in access, by income, to mainstream health care among the aged than now exists. Of course, continuing to pay this bill on current terms threatens to skew the overall distribution of health care resources even more toward sick and dying old people in the future than is now the case. If Americans want to have their health care cake (i.e., achieve reasonably equal access to mainstream health care across all age and income groups) and still be able to afford their dinner (i.e., slow the rise in the share of GNP devoted to health care), this country must adopt far more drastic changes in its health care system than policymakers have heretofore been willing to consider.[49] Even so, Americans will have to expect some continued increases in the share of the nation's GNP devoted to health care as a result of population aging and advancing technology.

## Conclusions

This chapter has dealt with two issues: (1) the growing mismatch between the problems the aged face in financing their retirement and health care and the current policies that relate to these concerns, and (2) the growing gap between projected public expenditures for the aged and the share of GNP currently devoted to supporting such expenditures. Substantial adjustments in current policies are both desirable and inevitable. Just how substantial is impossible to specify with any precision, because the answer depends in part on the uncertain size of the fiscal gap and future economic gains of the aged. However, even under the relatively optimistic intermediate assumptions about economic growth and health care costs (among other things), expenditures for current commitments for Medicare are projected to rise by well over 1 percent of GNP over the next twenty years, and for Medicare and Social Security combined by another 4 percent during the retirement of the baby boom.

Thus, one clear lesson to be drawn is that population aging should further compel policymakers to deal with two issues that presumably would be high on their agenda in any event—the promotion of long-term economic growth and the control of cost inflation in health care. Treatment of these issues is beyond the scope of this paper, but it is worth underscoring two points made earlier: (1) If the Social Security surpluses are to make a meaningful contribution easing the fiscal burden attendant to population aging, they must not be used to offset deficits in other areas of the federal budget.[50] (2) Because escalating real health care costs are not limited to Medicare or the aged, any approach to restraining those costs that will be both effective and capable of sustaining public support in the long run will have to go far beyond changes in Medicare reimbursement to more fundamental changes in the way in the nation organizes and finances the provision of health care in general.

Although it is impossible to specify the extent to which the current policies for financing the retirement and health care of the aged will eventually need to be adjusted, the preceding pages have provided pointers for the directions that adjustment should take.[51] The chapter contains a menu of possible expansions in public policies that, both directly and indirectly (through the leveraging of private resources), would respond to the current and prospective needs of the aged for greater economic security. These are by no means the only possibilities, but they do satisfy the criteria of being politically both feasible and fruitful. Although many of the measures would require little or no new commitment of additional public funds, implementing all of them would entail annual public costs on the order of 0.5 percent of GNP over the next decade or two and 1 percent of GNP during the retirement years of the baby boom generation, if the public financing of long-term care were only moderately expanded.[52]

It is not the intent here to weigh the relative merits of such new public expenditures for the aged vis à vis other competing claims on the public purse, but it is important to reiterate that any such expenditures should be carefully aimed at the changing needs of an increasingly heterogeneous aged population discussed earlier. Furthermore, it can be argued that policymakers should vigorously pursue the measures that require no significant new resources. Also, among the measures that do require much more government money, policymakers should give priority to the ones providing the greatest assistance to the low-income aged.

The chapter has also considered various approaches to modifying Medicare and Social Security in line with the growing capability among some of the aged to shoulder more of the burden for the financing of their retirement and health care. In the immediate future these measures could be used to finance any expansion in assistance to the aged or to contribute to general deficit reduction. Eventually they could at least partially alleviate the increased pressures on the public purse that will attend the retirement of the baby boom.

Here there are clear grounds for establishing priorities among the measures discussed. Income-related approaches that operate through the tax system are strongly preferable. They would concentrate the added burden on those among the aged who are in the best position to bear it. Of course, as noted earlier, there are limits to how far income-related approaches can be pushed before they become widely viewed as inequitable to higher-income aged people. Thus, depending on how much of the growing fiscal burden is ultimately borne by the aged rather than by the working population (through higher taxes), some across-the-board measures might eventually be considered desirable. However, across-the-board measures will be less problematic if they apply only to future groups of the aged, because even the lower-income members of these groups would have the advantage of greater overall financial resources and a longer lead time with which to adjust.

The desirability of such a lead time for adjustment is only one of several reasons why the nation needs to focus now on the kind of policy adjustments discussed in this chapter. Pressures for general deficit reduction and selective expansion of benefits will continue to motivate more immediate changes in social insurance and other programs serving the aged, and actions to greatly improve Medicare's fiscal outlook will be required in the next decade. Furthermore, whereas Social Security, per se, may be on sound financial footing for the next few decades, its rapidly accumulating reserves are already generating strongly conflicting views on their desirable disposition. A coherent longer-range vision of how our society wants to finance retirement and health care for the aged is needed, so that any potential changes in public policies can be assessed on the basis of their consistency with such a vision and appropriate adjustments in the behavior of individuals and private institutions can be fostered. Otherwise the country may have to make more wrenching and less palatable changes in public policies and private circumstances in the future.

Many analysts tend to pose the issue as one of inevitable conflict between the aged and nonaged populations. Although the focus of this chapter is on the consequences of policy changes for the aged, changes in taxes on the working-age population also will have to be part of the equation. But it is important to keep two points in mind concerning the trade-off between relatively lower benefits for the aged and higher tax burdens on the nonaged.

First, today's working-age population will be tomorrow's aged population. Thus, in the longer run, the issue is not "us" versus "them" but the role all Americans would like to see public policies play in promoting economic security over their lifetimes. Less consumption when people are working will increase the economic resources available later and vice versa. The overall structure of taxes and public benefits will be an important determinant of the prevailing lifetime pattern of resource usage.

Second, Americans of tomorrow in all age groups will almost certainly have a much higher level of material well-being than Americans in similar age groups have today. In the four decades following World War II, per capita real GNP increased at an average annual rate of nearly 2 percent, leading to more than a doubling of the overall standard of living. Even if this rate of growth were to slow to, say, 1.5 percent annually (about that assumed in the intermediate projections in table 6.1), per capita real GNP would double once again by the time the baby boom generation is fully retired. Under these circumstances, closing a fiscal gap of 5 or even more percent of GNP certainly need not entail an onerous burden from today's perspective—so long as this burden is distributed reasonably equitably both between *and within* the aged and nonaged populations. Developing consensus on just what constitutes equitable distribution will be an arduous task for political leadership. But if the task is pursued in the context of policies to enhance long-term economic growth and constrain cost inflation in health care, it need not prove herculean.

NOTES TO CHAPTER 6

1. For general purposes, changes in the size of the group between the ages of twenty and sixty-four serve as a reasonable proxy for changes in the size of the labor force. Of course, labor force participation trends within this group are subject to change as well. In particular, the labor force participation rate of men ages fifty-five to seventy has been declining for the past several decades and is expected to continue to do so for several more, although at a more moderate pace; but this decline is likely to be more than offset by continuing—also moderating—increases in the labor force participation of women under age sixty-five.

2. The baby boom aside, the total fertility rate (the average number of births over a woman's lifetime) has been declining in the United States (and all Western industrialized societies) since the Industrial Revolution. Recently this rate has stabilized at about 1.8, although there is some evidence of a slight upward creep. The replacement rate—the rate of total fertility that will yield an indigenous population of more or less constant size in the long run—is 2.1. The "best guess" demographic assumptions underlying figures 6.1 and 6.2 assume that fertility rates will creep up toward this level but not exceed it. If this is the case, then only a major shift in expected trends in mortality or net immigration rates could alter the basic picture shown in figure 6.1 for the first half of the next century.

3. Other major federal programs that serve the aged are veterans' health care and pensions, housing assistance, Medicaid, Supplemental Security Income, and federal workers' retirement pensions. However, no one of them accounts for more than 5 percent of total federal spending for the aged and most account for far less. Furthermore, their overall share of total benefits for the aged is expected to decline over time, even though Medicaid outlays will increase substantially with growing long-term care needs.

4. Even the pessimistic projections assume that the performance of both variables over the long run will be considerably better than it has been during the past fifteen years. For example, labor productivity has increased at an average annual rate of about 1 percent since 1973, but the assumed long-run increase in the pessimistic projection series is 1.5 percent and in the intermediate series 1.7 percent. (These rates bracket the average for the past three decades. See chapter 3 for a discussion of the causes of the productivity slowdown since 1973 and the prospects for its revival.) Trends in real health care costs and the prospects for their slowing as much as is assumed in the intermediate series are discussed near the end of this chapter. The key demographic differences underlying the two projection series are with respect to fertility and death rates. The intermediate series uses basically the same assumptions reflected in figures 6.1 and 6.2, which assume a modest rise in fertility rates and a slowdown in the rate of decline of mortality rates relative to the recent past. The pessimistic series assumes a somewhat faster rate of population aging resulting from both a continuing rapid decline in mortality rates and a modest decline in fertility rates.

5. The Social Security Administration actuaries also publish projections for an "optimistic" set of economic and demographic assumptions (not shown in table 6.1), which show a modest decline in combined Social Security-Medicare outlays as a percentage of GNP over the next twenty years, followed by an increase to a peak after the retirement of the baby boom that is about two percentage points higher than today's level. These projections are not included because the assumptions appear unduly optimistic.

6. This subject is too complex for discussion here. See chapters 3 and 9 for further explanation and discussion. It is also true that under the pessimistic assumptions the Social Security program itself is substantially underfinanced over the projection period. However, given the uncertainties involved in such long-term projections, it seems reasonable to rely for now on the intermediate assumptions for planning purposes. But the shortfall under the pessimistic assumptions is indicative of a possible need for further steps within the next two decades to ensure Social Security's fiscal health during the retirement of the baby boom generation.

7. See, for example, Timothy Smeeding, "Full Income Estimates of the Relative Well-Being of the Elderly and Nonelderly," in *Research in Economic Inequality*, vol. 1, edited by Daniel Slottje and David Bloom (Amsterdam: JAI Press, forthcoming).

8. Bruce Jacobs, "The Elderly: How Do They Fare?" in *Understanding Poverty and Dependence*, edited by Douglas Besharov and Leslie Lenkowsky (New York: Free Press, forthcoming). Some of these increases in independent living may not be voluntary and could reflect diminished well-being. But as the previous sentence in the text indicated, they generally appear to be consistent with the preferences of the aged.

9. The source of the data for table 6.2 does not permit a full cross-classification by age, race, sex and marital status. Other sources indicate that the poverty rate for very old black women is in excess of 65 percent.

10. Joseph F. Quinn, "The Economic Status of the Elderly: Beware the Mean," *Review of Income and Wealth* (March 1987): 63–82.

11. This share is about the same as that prevailing before the implementation of Medicare; it had dropped considerably in Medicare's early years, but continuously escalating health care costs and recent increases in Medicare cost sharing resulted in its increase.

12. Timothy Smeeding, "Nonmoney Income and the Elderly: The Case of the Tweeners," *Journal of Policy Analysis and Management* 5, no. 4, (1986): 707–24.

13. This age group has had the good fortune to be in their prime working years during the high earnings growth of the 1960s, to find the value of their homes soaring during the housing inflation of the 1970s, and to be in the maximum liquid asset position to capitalize on the high real interest rates and stock boom of the 1980s. Marilyn Moon and Timothy Smeeding, "Can the Elderly Really Afford Long Term Care?" (Washington, D.C.: American Enterprise Institute, forthcoming in a book to be published as a part of the "Encouraging the Expansion of Personal Resources for Retirement"project supported by the Commonwealth Fund).

14. This situation will be further reinforced by the gross disparities in wealth among the aged, particularly as a result of the schism between tomorrow's elderly who will have benefited (either directly or indirectly through inheritance) from the great escalation in housing prices and those who will not have.

15. James Poterba and Lawrence Summers, "Public Policy Implications of Declining Old Age Mortality," in *Work, Health and Income Among the Elderly*, edited by Gary Burtless (Washington, D.C.: Brookings Institution, 1987), 19–58.

16. Whereas the proportions of the aged who received pensions in the early 1980s ranged from less than one-tenth for unmarried women to about one-third for married couples, these proportions are projected under current policies to exceed one-third for unmarried women and to approach two-thirds for married couples who will retire in the next five to fifteen years and, for retired baby boomers, to exceed one-half for unmarried women and approach three-quarters for married couples. Emily Andrews, "Changing Pension Policy and the Aging of America," *Contemporary Policy Issues* 5, no. 2, (1987): 84–97.

17. After growing rapidly for decades, pension coverage of the work force leveled off in the late 1970s at about 60 percent. Since then, it has declined moderately, because of slow

economic growth and the continued shift in employment away from jobs that typically provide pension coverage to those for whom coverage is less likely. Although substantial continued deterioration of pension coverage is not expected, neither are sizable increases. See ibid.

18. In the most recent survey year (1983), more than two-thirds of uncovered workers between the ages of twenty-five and sixty-four who worked at least half-time were in firms of less than 100 employees. Also, 35 percent had earnings of less than $10,000, and 88 percent had earnings of less than $25,000. See table IV.2 in Emily Andrews, *The Changing Profile of Pensions* (Washington, D.C.: Employee Benefit Research Institute, 1985).

19. As a result of the 1986 tax reform, the tax savings from the $2,000 deductible IRA contribution to low- and moderate-income workers will range from zero to a maximum of only $300 (because they will be in either the zero or the 15 percent marginal tax bracket). There are numerous ways in which the incentives restricted to these workers to contribute to IRAs could be increased through the use of higher deductions or refundable tax credits.

20. The discussion in this subsection is largely based on Bruce Jacobs, "The National Potential of Home Equity Conversion," *Gerontologist* 26, no. 5, (1986): 496–504; and Jacobs, "The Elderly."

21. For example, more than one-quarter of those with incomes below 150 percent of the poverty level have home equity of $50,000 or more. Jacobs, "The National Potential of the Home Equity Conversion," table 1.

22. The home equity loans that have become so popular recently are not useful for the purposes being discussed here, because they are amortized over relatively short periods and require monthly payments not easily affordable on a limited budget. Reverse-annuity mortgages, in contrast, require no monthly payments and are amortized over a longer period.

23. Congressional Budget Office, *Earnings Sharing Options for the Social Security System* (Washington, D.C.: U.S. Government Printing Office, 1986).

24. However, because it might be desirable to phase in the increases in benefits inherent in such plans more quickly than the reductions (to protect current beneficiaries and persons near retirement from cuts in their benefits), the annual costs could be significant for a substantial transition period.

25. This discussion of SSI, including the cost and poverty impact estimates, is based on Sheila Zedlewski and Jack Meyer, "Toward Ending Poverty Among the Elderly and Disabled: Policy and Financing Options," Project Report, (Washington, D.C.: The Urban Institute, 1987).

26. See, for example, *Congressional Budget Office, Changing the Structure of Medicare Benefits: Issues and Options* (Washington, D.C.: U.S. Government Printing Office, 1983); K. Davis and D. Rowland, *Medicare Policy* (Baltimore: Johns Hopkins University Press, 1986); U.S. Department of Health and Human Services, *Catastrophic Illness Expenses* (Washington, D.C.: U.S. Government Printing Office, 1986); and Harvard Medicare Project, *Medicare: Coming Of Age. A Proposal for Reform* (Cambridge, Mass.: Harvard University Press, 1986).

27. As noted earlier, Medicare does not cover all acute-care services, including routine preventive care and prescription drugs. Also, it has a quite complex cost-sharing formula for those services that are covered. For each hospitalization, beneficiaries are responsible for a first hospital day deductible ($520 in 1987) as well as copayments that apply to expenses for days 90 through 150 of extended hospital stays. SMI also has a deductible ($75 in 1987) followed by 20 percent copayments, without limit. Out-of-pocket expenses for services not covered by Medicare would not count toward the catastrophic limits of the various proposals discussed in this section. But they would result in Medicare's reimbursing beneficiaries for all expenses for covered services above the limit, whether or not such services were also covered by private insurance.

28. Although many disabled elderly persons in the community are only moderately impaired, about one-third are limited in three or more of the activities of daily living that are commonly used to define the degree of functional limitation (for example, getting in and out of bed, eating, dressing, getting around indoors, going to the toilet, bathing). In fact, there are two elderly persons in the community for every one nursing home resident with the same level of disability. Most husbands, wives, and children provide home care for their disabled spouses and parents

for as long as is possible for them. See Korbin Liu, Kenneth Manton, and Barbara Marzetta Liu, "Home Care Expenses for the Disabled Elderly," *Health Care Financing Review* 7, no. 2, (1985): 51–58.

29. See, for example, ICF Incorporated, *Private Financing of Long-term Care: Current Methods and Resources* (Washington, D.C.: ICF Incorporated, 1985); Mark R. Meiners and Jay N. Greenberg, "Improving the Role of Private Markets in Financing Long-term Care Services" (New York: New York University, Committee for Economic Development, 1987), processed; Moon and Smeeding, "Can the Elderly Really Afford Long-term Care?"; and Joshua M. Weiner, Ray Harley, Denise Spence, and Sheila Murray, "Financing and Organizational Options for Long-term Care" (Washington, D.C.: Brookings Institution, 1987) processed.

30. Weiner et al., "Financing and Organizational Options," 17. According to the authors, there are basically two reasons why private sector financing mechanisms do not have a bigger effect. First, they are too expensive for most of the aged to afford. Second, they offer limited financial protection. (For example, most private insurance plans have prior hospitalization requirements and exclusions for prior conditions.) The essential problem is that improving insurance protection raises the costs and reduces still further the number of people who can afford it.

31. See especially Meiners and Greenberg, "Improving the Role of Private Markets," and ICF, *Private Financing*.

32. Jack Meyer, "Medicare and Medicaid: An Agenda for Reform" (Washington, D.C.: American Enterprise Institute, forthcoming in a book to be published as a part of the "Encouraging the Expansion of Personal Resources for Retirement" project supported by the Commonwealth Fund).

33. There are also indications that—as part of any legislation adding a catastrophic acute-care benefit to Medicare—Congress may also liberalize somewhat the Medicaid asset limitations and spend-down provisions that apply to the spouse of someone who is in a nursing home.

34. For example, premiums could be charged starting at age sixty-five but eligibility could begin at age seventy, could be restricted to those needing assistance in three or more activities of daily living, and could exclude coverage for the first six months of nursing home care.

35. According to Meyer, "Medicare and Medicaid," if Medicare offered this kind of "back-end" catastrophic protection, private insurers and prepaid plans would be more willing to enter the long-term care financing market by providing coverage at the front-end and in the middle in new insurance and delivery packages because their exposure could be limited. Similarly, there is a greater chance that the types of restrictions built into current private insurance mentioned in note 30, above, would be relaxed.

36. According to one expert, "a moderately comprehensive" plan would cost between $12 and $15 billion annually in 1990, and "a more ambitious" plan from $20 to $30 billion (excluding the costs of any liberalization of Medicaid). Karen Davis, "Medicare Financing and Beneficiary Income" (Baltimore: Johns Hopkins University, 1987), processed.

37. For more background on this discussion, see Michael J. Boskin, *Too Many Promises: The Uncertain Future of Social Security* (Homewood, Ill.: Dow Jones-Irwin, 1986).

38. A modest reduction in scheduled payroll taxes and future benefit commitments to the Social Security could be achieved without reducing the expected benefits of current retirees and near retirees by simply forgoing the projected surpluses over the next several decades. However, doing so would add to the overall federal deficit.

39. Hugh Heclo, "Generational Politics," in *The Changing Well-Being of Children and the Elderly* (working title), edited by John L. Palmer, Timothy Smeeding, and Barbara B. Torrey (Washington, D.C.: The Urban Institute Press, forthcoming).

40. Assessing just how good a deal Social Security is for current and prospective elderly persons is an extremely complex matter. The assessment is highly dependent on the specific circumstances of individuals (for example, their age at retirement, their position in the income distribution, their life expectancy, whether or not they receive dependents' benefits), the assumptions made about the future course of the economy (especially real interest rates), whether only payroll taxes paid by workers or those paid by both workers and their employers are

considered, and the value placed on such things as Social Security's ability to guarantee a steady flow of real income during retirement (which, as noted earlier in the text, cannot be done by private annuities). The numerous studies that have been done vary considerably in the way they deal with these matters and, therefore, in the conclusion they reach. See, for example, Geoffrey Kollman, "Social Security: The Relationship of Taxes and Benefits for Future Retirees" (Washington, D.C.: Congressional Research Service, March 9, 1987), Report No. 87-103 EPW, processed; Michael J. Boskin, Lawrence J. Kotlikoff, Douglas J. Puffert, and John B. Shoven, "Social Security: A Financial Appraisal Across and Within Generations," Working Paper No. 1891 (Cambridge, Mass.: National Bureau of Economic Research, Inc., 1986); Robert J. Myers and Bruce D. Schobel, "A Money's-Worth Analysis of Social Security Retirement Benefits," *Transactions*, Society of Actuaries, 1983; Anthony J. Pellechio and Gordon P. Goodfellow, *Individual Gains and Losses Before and After the 1983 Social Security Amendments* (San Francisco: Cato Institute, 1983). They agree (1) that all current retirees, especially those with high earnings histories, receive benefits from Social Security far in excess of any contributions made over their working lifetimes and (2) that this excess value will be declining over time for successive future groups of retirees, with the net redistributive effects of Social Security among these groups becoming more progressive. However, it is impossible to arrive at any definitive answer to the question of just how good (or bad) a deal Social Security will prove to be for today's youth or young workers, based on these analyses.

41. The Social Security benefit formula is now structured so that the typical worker in each successive new group of retirees receives a benefit that is a constant proportion of his or her covered earnings. Because real wages tend to rise over time, this means that the average benefit level of successive groups of new retirees also rises over time in line with the average increase in earnings. Thus, the reductions in Social Security benefits affecting future retirees as discussed in this option need not result in those new retirees' receiving lower real benefits than previous groups of retirees. Rather, the real benefit levels of successive groups of new retirees would simply grow more slowly than under current law or be held constant.

42. In the early years of the program, the Medicare law provided for automatic annual increases in the SMI premium in line with the general rate of inflation. Because medical cost inflation was consistently much higher than general inflation, the portion of total SMI expenditures covered by premiums gradually declined (and that covered by general revenues gradually increased) over time. Several years ago Congress amended the law, effective through 1988, to fix the premium at the level deemed necessary to cover 25 percent of expected total SMI expenditures. Unless that provision is extended, the calculation of automatic SMI premium increases will revert to the former basis in 1989. All fiscal projections based on current policies in this chapter assume that the premium will be set at levels in the future necessary to continue to cover 25 percent of projected total SMI expenditures.

43. The degree of reduction will vary inversely with the age at retirement and amount to a maximum of about 12 percent for workers who retire at age sixty-two, the earliest age of eligibility for old-age benefits under Social Security. Thus this measure would contribute to overall deficit reduction and strengthen the financing of both Medicare and Social Security.

44. The assumption of a continuing, similarly stringent hospital reimbursement policy has led to a major decline in previously projected long-term HI expenditures, which is already reflected in figure 6.3 and table 6.1. For example, in 1983 and 1984, Medicare actuaries were projecting that HI expenditures would eventually rise to well in excess of 9 percent of taxable payroll during the retirement of the baby boom, as opposed to only 6 + percent for taxable payroll costs shown in the more recent projections in figure 6.3.

45. Age- and sex-adjusted per capita health care costs have risen much more rapidly than the general price level for the past several decades, primarily because of increases in the services provided (for example, greater number of, and more sophisticated, diagnostic tests) per day of hospital stay or per physician visit. Average annual increases in measures of "services intensity" exceeded 3 percent over this period. In the past, Medicare essentially paid prevailing rates for whatever services were provided. The allowable increase (that is, what Medicare will pay for)

in service intensity is a policy variable under the new hospital reimbursement system for HI and is assumed to grow at an average annual rate of only 0.25 percent in the future.

46. For background and further discussion, see John Holahan and John L. Palmer, "Medicare's Fiscal Problems: An Imperative for Reform," *Journal of Health Policy, Politics, and Law* (forthcoming).

47. Despite some slowdown in the growth of real expenditures for Medicare and Medicaid in the 1980s in response to more restrictive provider reimbursement and other program cutbacks, cost inflation in overall health care has not slowed in real terms from its high level of the 1970s. Restraint of Medicare provider reimbursement to below-market levels is a primary source of the problems alluded to here.

48. Henry Aaron, "When Is a Burden Not a Burden? The Elderly in America," *Brookings Review* (Summer 1986).

49. The share of our GNP devoted to health care is currently over 11 percent and still rising rapidly (having doubled since the early 1960s). This percentage is higher than that of other Western industrialized countries, virtually all of which have comprehensive national health insurance systems with comprehensive cost controls and substantial nonmarket rationing.

50. This would be of less concern if other measures were taken to increase the national savings rate commensurately. As Henry Aaron has pointed out ("When Is A Burden Not a Burden?"), larger groups of aged need not impose a larger fiscal burden on the rest of the population if these larger groups save enough more than the previously smaller groups during their working years. However, the political prospects look dim for generating large, net, public savings through any means but the Social Security surpluses in the foreseeable future, and our private savings rate has remained remarkably stable over time despite large shifts in the age distribution of the population and major changes in public policies that might have been expected to affect it.

51. Many other adjustments to public policies and private practices beyond those focused upon in this chapter also may be desirable (for example, increasing immigration quotas and reducing incentives for early retirement in order to expand the future size of the labor force relative to the retired population). For a general discussion of these matters, see John L. Palmer and Stephanie G. Gould, "The Economic Consequences of an Aging Society," *Daedalus* 115, no. 1 (Winter 1986).

52. These added costs would probably run 2 to 3 percent of GNP under a very generous approach to public financing of long-term care.

# CHAPTER 7

# POVERTY AND THE UNDERCLASS

Isabel V. Sawhill

Poverty has been surprisingly persistent in the United States. Despite considerable efforts to reduce it, the incidence of poverty in 1986 was as high as it had been in the late 1960s. It was also higher than the rate in most other industrial countries for which comparable data are available. This much poverty in one of the world's wealthiest democracies invites notice.

The persistence of poverty in the United States has raised questions about the ability of government to solve the problem and has even led to complaints that government is the cause of the problem. Arguments that welfare and other programs that aid the poor cause the breakup of families, undermine the work ethic, and create a syndrome of dependency have become commonplace in recent years. Although such arguments are not necessarily consistent with the evidence, they have shifted the terms of the debate and put liberal scholars and activists on the defensive. As President Reagan puts it, in the War on Poverty, poverty won. The persistence of poverty over the past twenty years would seem to support this view. Unless this history can be reevaluated in a more favorable light and the lessons it suggests incorporated into current thinking, it will be difficult to proceed with confidence that any new government effort to reduce poverty will work. This chapter therefore attempts to evaluate the effectiveness of earlier efforts.

The author would like to thank Michael Fix, Robert Haveman, Susan Hendrickson, Ronald Mincy, Raymond Struyk, and Timothy Smeeding for their comments or assistance.

215

Not only has poverty not declined significantly over the past twenty years, but the composition of the poverty population has shifted toward groups about whom the public feels ambivalent if not downright disapproving. When the typical poor person was an elderly widow rather than an unwed mother, it was easier for society to act compassionately, and providing income seemed the obvious solution. Now, with the perception that a rising proportion of the poor are concentrated in inner-city areas where crime, teenage pregnancies, and welfare dependency are common, there is talk of a growing underclass in American society. New data presented in this chapter confirm that the underclass is indeed growing rapidly.

The next generation of antipoverty policies is likely to be strongly influenced by this development. Whereas the older War on Poverty relied heavily (if unintentionally) on providing income to the poor and succeeded in substantially reducing poverty among groups such as the elderly and disabled, it did little to stem the growth of chronic poverty among the able-bodied, nonelderly population or to prevent the spread of antisocial behavior within this group. This chapter argues that the major challenge for the next decade will be to integrate this growing underclass back into the mainstream by strengthening family responsibilities, putting people to work, and breaking the intergenerational cycle of poverty through education. The shape of these new, nonwelfare strategies—and the extent to which they are likely to succeed—is the focus of much of this chapter.

## Dimensions of the Problem

In 1986, 32.4 million people—13.6 percent of the population—lived in households that had incomes below the poverty level. The poverty level itself varies with family size and, in 1986, was equal to $5,255 for an elderly person, $11,203 for a four-person family, and $22,497 for a nine-person family.[1] Although these federally established poverty lines are now widely accepted as the appropriate yardstick for measuring poverty, they are inherently subjective. Any change in the poverty thresholds would alter the poverty rate. Thus, a better way to assess the current dimensions of the problem may be by making comparisons with other countries or with our own recent history.[2] The data needed for making international comparisons have only recently become available. What they reveal is that, with one exception (Australia), the United States has a higher poverty rate than any other industrialized country for which comparable data exist (see table 7.1). The lower incidence of poverty in other countries appears to result from their more equal distribution of earnings and their higher levels of social welfare spending relative to the United States.

TABLE 7.1

THE INCIDENCE OF POVERTY FOR SELECTED COUNTRIES, 1979, 1981, AND 1982

| Country (year) | Absolute Poverty Rate[a] | Relative Poverty Rate[b] |
|---|---|---|
| Australia (1981) | 13.2 | 12.2 |
| Britain (1979) | 11.8 | 9.7 |
| Canada (1981) | 7.4 | 12.6 |
| Norway (1979) | 8.6 | 5.2 |
| Sweden (1981) | 5.6 | 5.3 |
| Switzerland (1982) | 5.8 | 8.5 |
| United States (1979) | 12.7 | 17.1 |
| West Germany (1981) | 8.3 | 5.6 |

SOURCE: These data are from the Luxembourg Income Study data base; see Timothy Smeeding, Barbara Boyle Torrey, and Martin Rein, "Patterns of Income and Poverty: The Economic Status of the Young and the Old in Eight Countries," in *The Changing Well-Being of the Aged and Children in the United States*, edited by John L. Palmer, Timothy Smeeding, and Barbara Boyle Torrey (Washington, D.C.: The Urban Institute Press, forthcoming).

a. Absolute poverty includes all persons with after-tax disposable income below the official U.S. government poverty line in the appropriate year, converted to other currencies using Organization for Economic Cooperation and Development (OECD) purchasing-power parities. Poverty is calculated by adjusting family incomes using the U.S. poverty line equivalence scales so that they are normalized to the income of a three-person-family. Adjusted incomes are then compared with the U.S. three-person-family poverty line.

b. Relative low income includes all persons with family-size adjusted disposable incomes below half the median adjusted national income.

The higher rates of poverty in the United States are particularly evident when poverty is measured in relative terms. A far higher proportion of the population has incomes that are less than one-half the typical family's income in the United States than in other countries. But even when an absolute, or fixed income, standard is used, other countries—including a country like Britain, where average incomes are nearly one-third lower than those in the United States—do a better job of keeping people out of poverty (as it is defined in the United States).

Recent trends in poverty within the United States also are discouraging. Measured in relative terms, poverty has increased over the past two decades; that is, a higher fraction of the population had incomes below one-half the median income in the mid-1980s than in the 1960s. Measured in absolute terms, poverty is almost as high now as it was two decades ago (figure 7.1). It declined sharply during the 1960s, then leveled off at around 11 or 12 percent in the 1970s, and increased again in the early 1980s as the result of two back-to-back recessions and the Reagan budget cuts (which were about equally responsible for the rise). As unemployment rates have fallen over the

## FIGURE 7.1

### TREND IN THE OFFICIAL POVERTY RATE, 1960–86

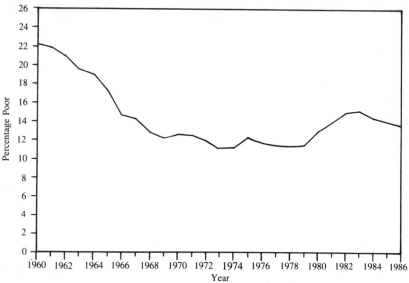

Year

SOURCE: U.S. Bureau of the Census, "Money Income and Poverty Status of Families and Persons in the United States: 1984," *Current Population Reports*, Series P-60, no. 149 (Washington, D.C.: U.S. Government Printing Office, 1985), U.S. Bureau of the Census, "Money, Income, and Poverty Status of Families and Persons in the United States: 1986," *Current Population Reports*, Series P-60, no. 157 (Washington, D.C.: U.S. Government Printing Office, 1987); U.S. Council of Economic Advisers, *Economic Report of the President, 1985* (Washington, D.C.: U.S. Government Printing Office, 1986) for the years 1961–64 and 1967–68.

past few years, the incidence of poverty has dropped as well, and this progress should continue as long as the economy continues to improve. However, even if economic growth continues, projections suggest that, for the remainder of this decade at least—assuming no new program spending on the poor—the poverty rate will not again achieve the low levels reached in the 1970s.[3]

In one important respect, the official poverty data are misleading: they exclude the value of noncash benefits such as food, housing, and medical care. Primarily because of the growth of Medicaid and Medicare, these benefits more than doubled in real terms between 1970 and 1985. Currently, they represent almost two-thirds of total government assistance going to the poor. Adding these noncash benefits to people's incomes reduces the current poverty rate by two to five percentage points and makes the trends appear more favorable.[4] However, in view of the fact that most noncash benefits come in the form of medical insurance, which cannot be used to here buy other goods and services, it is not clear that such an adjustment is warranted. The poor clearly have greater access to health care than they used to have and are better off for this reason alone; but income poverty has not declined since the late 1960s.

The persistence of poverty in the United States over the past several decades and its high levels relative to the levels that prevail in other industrialized countries are a challenge to a nation that prides itself on being a relatively classless society. In addition to being a challenge, these facts are also a puzzle. If the nation is to do better in the future, it will need to understand what lies behind these numbers, beginning first with the reasons why poverty has been so persistent.

## Why Has Poverty Been So Persistent in the United States?

In 1984, Charles Murray published a controversial but widely cited book in which he argued that social policy in the United States had been a failure.[5] The War on Poverty, in his view, was not simply ineffective, it was counterproductive. The welfare system produced financial incentives that discouraged people from working or marrying. In addition, the entire social policy establishment sent a message to the poor that poverty was a societal and not an individual problem, thereby excusing them from taking responsibility for their own lives. The predictable result, in Murray's view, was an increase in various antisocial behaviors such as crime, out-of-wedlock childbearing, and poor performance in school. Although Murray's book has been criticized for its misuse of data and its one-dimensional explanation of the trends,[6] it nevertheless raises an important question: Why, indeed, after the expenditure of so much effort and so many dollars, has there not been greater progress? If the programs did not fail, what did go wrong?

Reasonable people looking at the same facts can disagree about how to interpret them and researchers are still searching for better answers. However, a review of currently available evidence produces the following picture for the 1967-85 period:

1. The poverty rate was about the same at the end as at the beginning of the period.

2. Two factors were clearly pushing up the poverty rate: demographic changes and the poor performance of the economy.

3. At the same time, antipoverty policies were working to reduce the poverty rate. Even after adjusting for their possibly negative effects on work and family stability, these policies played a positive role. If spending on social welfare programs had not increased, the poverty rate would now be considerably higher—an estimated two to five percentage points higher. Put differently, in the absence of increased spending on the poor, an additional 5 to 12 million people would now be poor; and many of those who remain poor would be far worse off. The rest of this section elaborates on this summary.[7]

## Demographic Trends

The post-World War II period has seen a sharp increase in the proportion of households headed by women with children and by younger or older persons living alone. Because these are the groups most susceptible to poverty, these shifts have tended to increase the overall poverty rate. Indeed, some evidence suggests that this trend has been pushing up the poverty rate about one percentage point per decade.[8]

As described in chapter 5, these demographic trends are the result of a number of factors. Greater affluence has permitted young people and the elderly to live more independently, and greater economic opportunities for women have contributed to higher divorce rates and thus to the growth of families headed by women. The explosive growth of such families has also been attributed to the welfare system. However, the literature on the relationship between the welfare system and the growth of female-headed families suggests that welfare can account for no more than 15 to 25 percent of the growth in the incidence of women heading families over this period, or—at most—for a 0.4 percentage-point increase in the poverty rate.[9]

## Economic Trends

It has long been argued that economic growth is the single most powerful weapon in the battle to raise the incomes of the poor. The Reagan administration's emphasis on supply-side economics with its "trickle down" benefits for the poor was very much in this tradition. However, the growth of real incomes since the mid-1960s has not had the expected effect. The poverty rate among the working-age population (measured before the receipt of cash transfers) was higher in 1985 than at any time since the late 1960s (see figure 7.2). There appear to be two reasons for this upward trend: the high unemployment rates of recent years and the growing inequality in earned incomes.

Cyclical downturns or periods of sustained high unemployment are especially harmful to people at or near the poverty level. When jobs are scarce, the heads of low-income families are more likely than other household heads to lose their jobs, less likely to be able to find steady work, and less likely to move up the occupational ladder. As a result, when the overall unemployment rate rises, the relative income losses suffered by the working heads of (normally) poor families are about three times as great as the losses suffered by middle-income families.[10] Thus, economic growth notwithstanding, it should not be surprising that poverty was as high in the first half of the 1980s, when unemployment averaged 8.2 percent, as it was in the latter half of the 1960s, when unemployment averaged 3.7 percent. If the poverty rate is adjusted for the demographic shifts that have occurred since 1967 and the rise in unemployment rates, a clear downward trend in the adjusted rate emerges. Specifically, these two changes are estimated to have increased the poverty rate by between four and five percentage points over the past two decades.[11]

As discussed in chapter 2, another factor that has been at work is the growing inequality in the distribution of earned incomes.[12] For example, the proportion of working-age men with weekly earnings below $244 per week (1986 dollars)—roughly the poverty line for a family of four—grew from 13.5 percent in 1967 to 15.2 percent in 1978 at the same time that average (real) earnings were increasing.[13] This trend does not go away when the figures are adjusted for factors such as the business cycle, the depressing effects of the baby boom on wage rates, and the shift from high-wage manufacturing to low-wage service jobs over this period. Whatever the causes of this trend toward greater inequality in earnings, its results are clear: a rising tide can no longer be assumed to lift all the boats, and work is no longer so sure a route out of poverty as it once may have been.

## Government Policies

When poverty was publicly discovered in the United States in the mid-1960s, the country launched a War on Poverty that created many of the programs we know today. These included preschool education for the children

FIGURE 7.2

TREND IN THE POVERTY RATE AMONG NONELDERLY, EXCLUDING CASH TRANSFERS,
1967–85

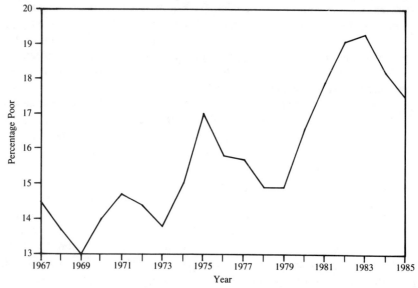

SOURCE:   Christine Ross, "Trends in Poverty, 1965–1984: Tables from the Current Population
          Survey," November 1984, Institute for Research on Poverty, as background for the
          conference, "Poverty and Policy: Retrospect and Prospects." As revised February
          1987 by George Slotsve.

of the poor (Head Start), compensatory education for grade-school children (now funded under Chapter One of the Education Consolidation and Improvement Act), training for high school dropouts (the Job Corps), and employment and training for disadvantaged adults (currently funded under the Job Training Partnership Act). Overall, the federal government spent roughly $281 billion (1986 dollars) on targeted education and training programs between 1963 and 1985. The figure would be larger if health programs were included. Expenditures on Medicaid alone approached $444 billion (1986 dollars) between 1966 and 1984.

Such investments were intended to help people earn their way out of poverty, to give them a hand up and not a hand-out. Consider the following statement from the 1964 report of the Council of Economic Advisers (CEA):

> Conquest of poverty is well within our power. About $11 billion a year would bring all poor families up to the $3,000 income level we have taken to be the minimum for a decent life. The majority of the Nation could simply tax themselves enough to provide the necessary income supplements to their less fortunate citizens.... But this "solution" would leave untouched most of the roots of poverty. Americans want to earn the American standard of living by their own efforts and contributions. It will be far better, even if more difficult, to equip and to permit the poor of the Nation to produce and to earn the additional $11 billion, and more.[14]

It was a commendable plan, but did it work? As we have seen, the proportion of people earning less than a poverty level income has actually *increased* since the mid-1960s. However, as already noted, adjusted for demographic shifts and rising unemployment, the poverty rate has fallen, a trend that is at least consistent with the idea that there was some payoff from these investments. When this indirect evidence is combined with the positive results found in evaluations of some specific education and training programs, there is room for cautious optimism. Certainly not everything that was tried worked, but programs such as the Job Corps, Head Start, and employment and training assistance for women on welfare (discussed in some detail later in this chapter) all appear to have been successful. As previously noted, the poor also have better access to health care. The extent to which this access has translated into better health is not entirely clear, but the assumption is that it has, and the sharp drop in overall and infant mortality rates since the late 1960s, especially among blacks, supports the assumption.

If the payoff from investing in the human capital of the poor was not larger and more obvious, it may be because so much was being tried for the first time, subjected to intense political pressures, and continuously modified, with all the attendant implications for administrative efficiency. It may also be because programs that prepare people for work are not likely to be very effective when overall jobs are scarce. Finally, it is possible that much education goes on within the family and that remedial education and training have little hope of offsetting the powerful influence of home environment, especially when, as has often been the case, the programs end up investing "too little, too late."

Although it was originally thought that the War on Poverty would be won by helping people earn their way out of poverty rather than by putting them "on the dole," the fact is that spending on income maintenance programs has grown enormously since the mid-1960s. However, most of this growth occurred in social insurance programs, such as Social Security and Medicare, rather than in means-tested programs, such as Aid to Families with Dependent Children (AFDC), food stamps, and Medicaid, which are directly targeted on the poor (table 7.2). Indeed, real outlays for means-tested cash assistance have declined since the mid-1970s. In AFDC—the program most people have in mind when they think of "welfare"—average real benefits for a family of four (with no other income) fell by one-third between 1970 and 1987. Still, over this entire period, cash transfers grew substantially (table 7.2).

This growth in income transfers has reduced the poverty rate. The estimate of just how large the reduction has been depends on the assumptions that are made. If it is assumed that the provision of aid to the poor has not also undermined their work ethic or destabilized families, the poverty rate was about three percentage points lower in 1985 than it would have been in the absence of the growth of cash transfers.[15] Most of this reduction in poverty has been concentrated among the elderly, reflecting the large and growing expenditures for Social Security over this period. In fact, the growth of transfers reduced the poverty rate for the elderly by almost twelve percentage points but reduced the rate for the nonelderly population by only one percentage point.

Alternatively, if it is assumed that the growth of welfare programs has caused fewer people to seek jobs or has contributed to the growth of female-headed families—both of which can themselves lead to poverty—the net contribution of income transfers to reducing poverty has been more modest. However, no study has produced findings suggesting that income transfers have increased rather than reduced poverty, and most studies suggest that the positive effects just discussed have been only modestly attenuated by the indirect effects of transfers on work and family decisions. Nevertheless, such indirect effects are real, and they increase the costs of solving the poverty problem by transferring income from one group to another. They are one reason why spending on the poor does not lead to a dollar-for-dollar reduction in the poverty gap as implied by the CEA's statement in 1964, and they

TABLE 7.2

SOCIAL WELFARE EXPENDITURES, 1960–84

| Expenditure | In Billions of 1986 Dollars | | | | | | Percentage Change 1960–84 | Percentage Change Since 1975 |
|---|---|---|---|---|---|---|---|---|
| | 1960 | 1965 | 1970 | 1975 | 1980 | 1984 | | |
| Total means-tested | 16.2 | 22.2 | 45.0 | 84.2 | 93.3 | 100.4 | 521.1 | 19.3 |
| Cash[a] | 13.1 | 15.6 | 24.1 | 35.3 | 31.1 | 30.4 | 132.3 | −13.9 |
| In-kind[b] | 3.1 | 6.6 | 20.9 | 48.8 | 62.2 | 70.0 | 2,173.3 | 43.4 |
| Total social insurance | 81.7 | 110.0 | 167.2 | 263.8 | 319.8 | 375.4 | 359.3 | 42.3 |
| Cash[c] | 81.7 | 110.0 | 147.1 | 233.6 | 273.2 | 309.2 | 278.3 | 32.3 |
| In-Kind[d] | 0.0 | 0.0 | 20.1 | 30.1 | 46.5 | 66.2 | 229.0 | 119.7 |
| Total | 97.9 | 132.2 | 212.2 | 347.9 | 413.1 | 475.8 | 386.0 | 36.8 |
| Cash | 94.8 | 125.6 | 171.2 | 269.0 | 304.4 | 339.6 | 258.1 | 26.3 |
| In-kind | 3.1 | 6.6 | 41.0 | 79.0 | 108.7 | 136.2 | 4,323.6 | 72.5 |
| Per capita (dollars per person) | 542 | 681 | 1,035 | 1,610 | 1,814 | 2,007 | 270.2 | 24.6 |
| Total as a percentage of GNP | 5.2 | 5.5 | 7.6 | 11.0 | 11.8 | 13.4 | 157.1 | 21.5 |

SOURCES: U.S. Department of Health and Human Services, Social Security Administration, "Public Social Welfare Expenditures, FY 1984," *Social Security Bulletin* 50, no. 6 (June 1987); and United States Department of Agriculture, Office of Government Affairs, "Information Package," revised April 1987. Entries may not add to totals because of rounding.

a. Includes Aid to Families with Dependent Children, General Assistance, and Supplemental Security Income.

b. Includes Medicaid, food stamps, school lunch, public housing, and social services.

c. Includes Old-Age, Survivors, and Disability Insurance (OASDI), Railroad Retirement, Unemployment Insurance, Workers' Compensation, Government Employment Pensions, Veterans' Pension and Compensation.

d. Includes Medicare.

further reinforce the importance of helping the poor earn their way out of poverty.

## Conclusions

The problem of poverty in the United States has been far more difficult to eradicate than the architects of the War on Poverty envisaged. Poverty has declined dramatically among the elderly, largely as the result of the growth of social insurance programs, but it has remained stubbornly high among working-age household heads and their dependents. It is not that human capital investments and income transfers have not improved the well-being of younger households. They have. But programs for the nonelderly were less generously funded to begin with, provided many of their benefits in kind rather than in cash, and have been curtailed in recent years. Most important, they have had to swim against the tide of higher unemployment and the general breakdown in the American family over the past twenty years.

One result of these trends is that a much higher proportion of the poverty population now consists of working-age adults, especially women heading families with children. In addition, poverty is increasingly an urban rather than a rural phenomenon, with the poor somewhat more clustered than previously in low-income neighborhoods within the nation's cities.[16] These changes have raised concerns about whether a permanent underclass is emerging in the United States—an issue that will be explored at greater length after data on the characteristics of the current poverty population have been reviewed.

## A Profile of the Poor

The 32 million poor people in the United States are a diverse group. One way to characterize the poverty population is to divide it into five mutually exclusive groups according to the major reason for the low income of the head of the household in which these people live (as reported to the census). The first group is the elderly and disabled, a set of people who are not generally able to work and for whom direct income assistance is probably the most appropriate form of aid. The second group is single parents, most of them women, whose child care responsibilities make it difficult for them to work, especially full-time. The third group is the "underemployed poor," those who report that they are poor because they are unemployed or unable to find sufficient work. The fourth group is "the hardworking poor," those who work all year at a full-time job but still do not earn enough to escape from poverty. The fifth group is a residual that includes students, early retirees, and homemakers (without minor children). Because all the members of this last group are able-bodied and do not report having any difficulty finding work, it seems likely that they are only temporarily poor or that they represent statistical anomalies.

As indicated in figure 7.3, approximately one in three poor households is headed by someone who is elderly or disabled, one in seven by a single parent, one in six by someone who is underemployed, one in twelve by a low-wage full-time worker, and almost one in four by someone in the residual category.[17]

Ideally, it would be helpful to know, in addition to why people are poor, how long they remain poor. Not all the people who report themselves as poor to the census have chronically low incomes. Indeed, considerable turnover is evident within the poverty population. Many people suffer temporary drops in income because of the loss of a job, a divorce, or a period of illness, and then later regain their previous standard of living. As a result, only about one-half of the census poor who are not elderly are likely to remain poor for eight years or more.[18]

Still a third way to characterize the poor is by where they live. A little over half live in a big city, where they tend to be concentrated in downtown rather than suburban areas. Very few live in what might be called urban slums. In 1980, 7 percent lived in big-city neighborhoods where the poverty rate was 40 percent or higher.

In sum, the poverty population—defined by annual income alone—is large and diverse. About one-third are elderly and disabled. Another one-third are likely to remain poor only temporarily. The remaining one-third might be called the "hard-core" poor—those working-age, able-bodied family heads and their dependents who have chronically low incomes. If there is an underclass in this country, it is drawn from this third group.

## Is There an Underclass In the United States?

Recent journalistic accounts paint a picture that leaves little doubt that an underclass exists. This picture includes young men who father children with little or no expectation of supporting them. It includes unmarried women on welfare, raising children at taxpayers' expense and passing a life of poverty on to the next generation. It includes men who spurn regular work in favor of more lucrative but less legitimate or conventional means of earning a living, and alienated teenagers who drop out of school and remain semiliterate into their adult years. And whatever its contents, the picture is usually framed by a depressed urban landscape, and most of the faces are black.

FIGURE 7.3

A PROFILE OF THE POOR

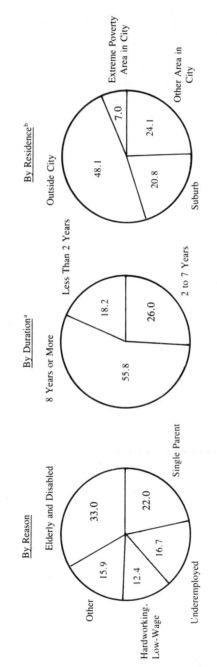

SOURCES: Urban Institute tabulations from the March 1987 *Current Population Survey*; U.S. Bureau of the Census, "Money Income, and Poverty Status for Families and Persons in the United States: 1985," *Current Population Reports*, P-60, no. 154, tables 19 and 20; Mary Jo Bane and David T. Ellwood, "Slipping Into and Out of Poverty: The Dynamics of Spells," *Journal of Human Resources* 21, no. 1 (Winter 1983): 1–23, table 2; and U.S. Bureau of the Census, *Poverty Areas in Large Cities*, vol. 2, Subject Reports, PC80-2-8D, February 1985.

a. Includes nonelderly poor only.
b. City refers to one of the 100 largest standard metropolitan statistical areas.

Research confirms that there is an urban underclass in the United States and that it is growing. Estimates of the size of the underclass vary with the definition chosen to describe it. Some researchers have equated the underclass with the able-bodied, persistently poor, a group estimated to number around 8 million people in the mid-1980s.[19] Others have defined the underclass as people living in areas of concentrated poverty, a definition that yields considerably lower estimates. For example, in 1980, 2.4 million poor people lived in neighborhoods where the poverty rate was above 40 percent.[20]

Recent work at The Urban Institute has taken still another approach, focusing on behavior rather than income as the distinguishing characteristic of the underclass. In this work, the underclass is defined as people who live in neighborhoods where welfare dependency, female-headed families, male joblessness, and dropping out of high school are all common occurrences.[21] Although not all the people in these neighborhoods are poor (in part, because some obtain income illegally and in part because many are employed, albeit erratically), given the environment in which they live, they are all at risk of being dragged into the underclass.

The size of this "at risk" group was 2.5 million people in 1980, of which 1.1 million also had poverty-level incomes. The group is disproportionately concentrated in large northeastern or midwestern cities such as New York or Chicago. A majority of the residents of these neighborhoods are black or Hispanic, and more than three-fifths of the adults have less than a high school education. In addition, the majority of men in these communities are not regularly employed, three-fifths of the households are headed by women, and about a third of the households are dependent on public assistance (table 7.3). Although the problems in these neighborhoods are serious, the proportion of the total poverty population living in such areas is only 4 percent (1.1 million divided by a total of 26.1 million poor in 1980). And although 59 percent of the underclass is black according to these estimates, stereotypes that imply that being black and being a member of the underclass are synonymous are clearly misleading. Less than 6 percent of the black population and less than one-fifth of the black poverty population live in such areas.

The substantial attention paid to the underclass, despite its small size, undoubtedly reflects the serious social consequences that most people attach to its existence and possible continued growth. Such growth is disturbing and raises compelling questions about the dynamics of the process. It may be that some inner-city areas become so devoid of stable families, well-functioning schools, and employed adults that they make "escape" into the middle-class extremely difficult and thereby become breeding grounds for another generation of poor people with little hope of becoming part of the mainstream. The limited evidence that exists suggests that this group, though small, is

TABLE 7.3

ESTIMATED SIZE AND COMPOSITION OF THE UNDERCLASS, 1980

| | Living in: | |
|---|---|---|
| Characteristic | Underclass Areas | United States |
| Total population | 2,483,676 | 226,545,805 |
| Total poverty population | 1,065,952 | 26,072,000 |
| Proportion[a] of total population that is | | |
| Urban | .99 | .77 |
| In Northeast | .36 | .25 |
| In North Central | .27 | .24 |
| In South | .26 | .30 |
| In West | .11 | .21 |
| White | .28 | .82 |
| Black | .59 | .12 |
| Hispanic | .10 | .03 |
| Children (under age 19) | .34 | .30 |
| Adults with less than a high school education | .63 | .31 |
| Ratio of women to men | 1.20 | 1.05 |
| Families headed by women, with children | .60 | .19 |
| High school dropouts, ages 16 to 19 | .36 | .13 |
| Adult men not regularly employed | .56 | .31 |
| Families with public assistance income | .34 | .08 |

SOURCE: Urban Institute analysis of the 1980 census.

a. Proportions are from unpublished data and do not include untracted areas in either the numerator or denominator.

growing quite rapidly. Between 1970 and 1980, although the overall population grew by one-third, the number of people living in underclass areas grew from 592,000 to 2,484,000—319 percent—according to preliminary Urban Institute estimates.[22] Although neighborhood-level data are available only from the decennial censuses, making it difficult to know what has happened since 1980, a good guess is that this group has continued to expand.

In summary, the underclass, broadly defined, is the approximately 8 million people living in households headed by able-bodied, chronically poor adults. More narrowly defined, it is the 2 to 3 million people living in neighborhoods where mainstream behavior patterns and life-styles have all but disappeared. Any definition, like the definition of poverty itself, is inherently arbitrary, and it is perhaps best to think in terms of a continuum of disadvantages defined in terms of income, behavior, and neighborhood environment.

## Priorities for the Next Decade

The recognition that the needs and circumstances of the poor vary is likely to be one factor that distinguishes the policies of the future from the policies of the past. Whereas it was once argued that a negative income tax was the appropriate response to all forms of poverty, there is now far greater sensitivity to the fact that poverty is not one problem but many problems and that policies should be designed to reflect this diversity. Some of the poor (such as those who have lost a job) need only temporary income support to help them through difficult times. The traditional safety net programs such as unemployment insurance, food stamps, and AFDC were designed for this purpose. Some of the poor (such as the elderly and disabled) need a more permanent safety net, such as that provided by Social Security or the Supplemental Security Income program. (These are further discussed in chapter 6). And some (such as the able-bodied, chronically poor, or the underclass) need to be helped to become productive and respected members of society. In this last case, because reducing dependency is an important objective, income transfers cannot be viewed as an appropriate long-term solution.

Although all these groups need help, it will be argued here that the nation's top priority should be to stem the growth of chronic poverty and the underclass. The costs of allowing the underclass to grow unchecked include more crime, greater welfare dependency, and lower productivity among the working-age population. Children growing up in chronically poor families, and especially those living in troubled neighborhoods, may—in the absence of intervention—be doomed to repeat their parents' lives. And the emergence of such a permanent underclass damages the social fabric. That damage is compounded when a majority of this population consists of minorities who are not being effectively integrated into the larger society.

The objective of moving this group of chronically poor, able-bodied adults toward self-sufficiency will not be easy to achieve but is probably best advanced through policies that strengthen parents' responsibility for their children, encourage work, and improve education, as described in the remainder of this chapter.

## Reestablishing Parents' Responsibility for Their Children

The incidence of poverty among female-headed families with children has always been very high. Roughly half of them are poor, and this statistic has changed little over the past half-century. However, fifty years ago there were far fewer such women, many more of them were widows, and they were generally not expected to work. Under the circumstances, public support for poor women and their children was neither very expensive nor particularly controversial. Today, in contrast, as the result of higher divorce rates and more out-of-wedlock childbearing, more than one in every five children lives in a female-headed family, up from one in ten in 1960. In nine out of ten cases, these children have a living, if absent, father who can be presumed capable of providing some support to his children. Moreover, virtually all the parents of these children came of age during a period when effective contraception was widely available and most middle-class couples were limiting the size of their families as one means of maintaining their standard of living. Finally, employment has become commonplace for women.

Less early widowhood, more control over family size, and more employment opportunities for women might have been expected to reduce the dependency of children on government assistance. Yet the proportion of all children under age eighteen dependent on AFDC rose from around 3 percent in 1960 to approximately 11 percent in 1985.[23] These developments have produced a new interest in reestablishing the primacy of parental financial responsibility for children. This overall objective can be furthered in three ways: first, by discouraging childbearing among people not yet prepared to take on this responsibility (usually teenagers); second, by requiring that absent parents (usually fathers) contribute to the support of children already born; and third, by requiring or encouraging welfare mothers to work. As indicated in table 7.4, these three factors together are potentially responsible for most of the poverty among female-headed families with children. Thirty-seven

TABLE 7.4

POOR FEMALE-HEADED FAMILIES, BY REASONS FOR THEIR LOW INCOMES, 1986

| Category | Number | Percentage of All Poor Female-Headed Families |
|---|---|---|
| Total, poor female-headed families | 2,039,171 | 100.0 |
| Mother bore first child as a teenager | 754,276 | 37.0 |
| Father does not provide support | 1,608,574 | 78.9 |
| Mother is not employed | 689,700 | 33.8 |
| All three problems[a] | 182,172 | 8.9 |
| None of above problems[b] | 198,449 | 9.7 |

SOURCE: Urban Institute tabulations from the March 1987 *Current Population Survey*.

a. Poor female-headed families in which the mother bore children as a teenager, the father does not pay child support, and the mother does not work.

b. Poor female-headed families in which the mother delayed childbearing, the mother is employed, and the father pays child support.

percent of these mothers had their first child as a teenager, 79 percent are receiving no assistance from the child's father, and 34 percent are not themselves contributing to the financial support of the family. The proportion of female-headed families who have poverty-level incomes despite the facts that they delayed childbearing and that both parents contribute something to the support of their children is only 10 percent.

**Preventing Early Childbearing.**[24] Teenage pregnancy rates have increased about 20 percent since 1972 in the United States—the only developed country to have experienced such a rise. The rate of births to teenagers has actually fallen somewhat over this same period, because a rising proportion of all adolescent pregnancies (almost half in recent years) are terminated by abortion. Research has shown that the life chances of teenage mothers and their children are severely limited; that about two-thirds of them spend some time on welfare; that they are responsible for at least half of total AFDC expenditures; and that they cost the nation an estimated $17 billion a year in welfare, food stamps, and Medicaid benefits.[25]

Solutions to this problem remain elusive in part because of deeply held views on such questions as sexuality, family planning, and abortion—and in part because we do not know much about the motivations of teenagers or ways to affect them. However, research on adolescent pregnancy and childbearing indicates some areas that could be addressed in formulating more effective policies:[26]

- Sex education has been found to be associated with lower pregnancy rates. Although sex education courses are widely available in large city schools, most districts do not introduce the most relevant or essential information early enough (i.e., before the ninth grade).

- The availability of family-planning services in a community is associated with lower teenage birthrates. A promising, though controversial, new approach is school-based health clinics that provide both information and access to contraceptives.

- Providing family-planning services to teenagers who are already mothers *may* help to prevent second or third births (the evidence is mixed).

- The potential role of the media in affecting the attitudes and contraceptive behavior of teenagers has not been exploited. Teenagers watch approximately twenty-four hours of TV each week and listen to the radio eighteen hours a week.[27]

- The availability of abortion is currently preventing about 675,000 first births among unmarried women each year in the United States. If access to legal abortion were restricted by, say, a constitutional amendment, some of these women would undoubtedly take greater precautions to avoid pregnancy and some would marry the child's father or put the baby up for adoption. But the available evidence suggests that the majority would simply resort to illegal abortions and that a significant minority—probably the most disadvantaged—would become unwed mothers. One estimate puts the additional growth in such families that would be occasioned by a constitutional amendment at roughly 80,000 a year.[28] Because the number of female-headed families with children has been growing, on average, at a rate of 113,000 a year since 1980, a restriction on legal abortion would mean an estimated 70 percent increase in the number of such families being formed each year.

Much of the literature on teenage pregnancies has suggested that such pregnancies are, for the most part, unintended. But there is also evidence that in some low-income communities where few alternative opportunities exist for young women or men, some teenagers may deliberately choose early parenthood. To the extent that this is the case, the solution lies in improving education and labor market opportunities for both sexes.

Nevertheless, the aforementioned approaches are unquestionably a cost-effective way of reducing long-term poverty and welfare dependency among women and their children. How widely they are adopted will depend on forging a new consensus concerning their appropriateness.

**Collecting Child Support.** Teenage pregnancy is only one of the reasons for the high incidence of poverty among single-parent families. Another important reason is that the children in such families are receiving inadequate levels of support from their fathers. As we have seen, four-fifths of poor mothers heading families from which the father is absent receive no help from their children's fathers.[29] Although it is often assumed that absent parents either cannot afford to support their children or cannot be identified or located, what information is available (and it is inadequate) suggests that these may be false assumptions. Specifically:

- Divorced and separated fathers do not appear to have lower incomes than other men.

- Several studies of the fathers of AFDC children show that they have average incomes of between $13,986 and $18,143 (1986 dollars).[30]

- A survey of a matched sample of 203 custodial and noncustodial parents in Florida and Ohio found that the median income of the noncustodial parents was $13,394, whereas the median income of the custodial parents was $7,411 (1986 dollars).[31] The incidence of poverty was 31 percent among the noncustodial parents and 57 percent among the custodial parents.

- Although many young men father a child when they are still in school or unemployed, this does not mean that they will have no income to contribute to their children for eighteen years. Furthermore, in cases where the age of the father is known, 70 percent of the babies born to teenage mothers were fathered by men over the age of twenty. Men of all ages may take a greater interest in pregnancy prevention if they know there are future financial consequences.

- About one-fifth of all women eligible to receive child support have never been married, and this group is growing far more rapidly than the ever-married group. These women are much less likely to receive child support than ever-married women, in part because the establishment of paternity in the case of out-of-wedlock births has not been vigorously pursued. In 1981 only about one-quarter of women who gave birth out of wedlock had paternity adjudicated.[32] The technical means to do so exists, and other countries have far better records.[33] In Sweden, for example, paternity is established in more than 90 percent of cases. The best approach appears to be through the health care system—that is, securing voluntary acknowledgment of paternity at the time of birth.

- In a pretest of a national survey of absent parents, researchers at The Urban Institute and the National Opinion Research Center were able to locate 84 percent of all absent parents, a far higher proportion than had been anticipated.

Numerous recent studies show that if child support awards were more prevalent, more generous, or better enforced, poverty and welfare costs could be substantially reduced.[34] For example, it is estimated that the kind of child support system now being tested in Wisconsin (described below) could reduce the amount of poverty among female-headed families with children by about 40 percent and AFDC caseloads by nearly 50 percent, with savings to the government of over $2 billion a year.[35] Although these estimates are probably too optimistic, because they assume 100 percent compliance with the relatively generous Wisconsin standard, they underscore the potential of this strategy and suggest that it is particularly important to review current and proposed policies in this area.

The 1984 Child Support Enforcement Amendments were an important step in the right direction. Under this law, states are required to withhold child support payments from an absent parent's wages after one month of delinquency, are encouraged to establish statewide child support standards, and are given financial incentives to collect support on behalf of non-AFDC as well as AFDC mothers. Because the law has been in effect only since late 1985, it is too early to tell what effects it will have. However, the Census Bureau estimates that only $7 billion out of the $10 billion of child support currently due is being collected, and a number of studies indicate that tougher enforcement at the state level increases the amount collected.[36]

Although better enforcement of existing awards is important, the potentially most significant feature of the 1984 law is the encouragement provided to the states to establish more adequate child support standards. Some research suggests that it is higher standards, rather than better enforcement alone, that are most likely to reduce poverty and welfare dependency.

Of particular interest in this connection is the experiment currently under way in Wisconsin. As of July 1, 1987, courts in Wisconsin were required to use a percentage-of-income standard for establishing support obligations, except where individual circumstances clearly dictate an exception. The formula to be used is 17 percent of the absent parent's pretax income for one child, rising gradually to 34 percent for five or more children. A percentage-of-income standard not only creates a system firmly based on ability to pay but also ensures that awards are indexed for inflation or for increases in a parent's earnings over time. In addition, Wisconsin plans to institute automatic wage withholding of amounts obligated for support and to supplement this support (at public expense) when both parents' resources are insufficient to provide a minimum level of income to the children. Eligibility for this benefit requires only that the custodial parent cooperate in securing child support payments; it is independent of the welfare system. The state estimates that there will be little or no net cost associated with the system. The publicly provided child support benefit for very poor families is, in effect, financed by higher child support payments from fathers who can afford to pay. Thus, even the children of fathers who have little or no ability to pay can benefit from an improved child support collection system. And by firmly establishing the principle of parents' financial responsibility for their children, such a system might eventually reduce the incidence of out-of-wedlock childbearing in underclass communities.

**Expecting Welfare Mothers to Work.** According to the new social contract, it is not only fathers that should be asked to help support their children but mothers as well. Now that 67 percent of all mothers in the United States are employed, almost half of them year-round and full-time, the right of poor mothers to stay home with their children at taxpayers' expense is being questioned.[37] Somewhat surprisingly, a similarly high proportion of poor women are employed, although fewer work full-time. Only one-third are not employed at all. However, a large proportion (64 percent) of these nonemployed mothers are dependent on public assistance.[38]

Studies of welfare recipients suggest that they want to work,[39] but they apparently need more encouragement and assistance in preparing for and finding jobs as well as help with child care. Where such assistance has been provided, as in some earlier federal jobs programs and in many of the programs initiated by the states since 1981, the results have been somewhat encouraging.[40]

In evaluating employment programs for welfare recipients in San Diego, Baltimore, Arkansas, Virginia, and West Virginia recently, the Manpower Demonstration Research Corporation found that these programs increase the employment and earnings of participants and reduce welfare costs for taxpayers. Employment rates for participants in the programs were three to six percentage points higher than for other welfare recipients, and the proportion of the participants receiving any AFDC declined by one to five percentage points.[41] Thus, the effects, although positive, are generally small. Extrapolating to the nation as a whole, at best, employment rates among women on welfare might increase from 52 to 58 percent, and the proportion of poor female-headed households dependent on welfare might decline from 46 to 41 percent.

It is not yet clear what mix of program services or work requirements best achieves these results. However, job search assistance and training probably need to be part of the package. Workfare alone (that is, requiring people to perform unpaid work in entry-level clerical, maintenance, and human service jobs in the community in return for their welfare benefits) may not be sufficient.[42] Workfare does provide useful public services. In West Virginia, the productivity of workfare participants was judged to be higher, on average, than that of regular workers doing the same jobs, and the state was able to provide some public services that it otherwise could not have afforded. Moreover, working for one's benefits may be deemed an appropriate obligation by taxpayers and welfare recipients alike. Surveys of workfare participants indicate that the great majority of them consider a work requirement fair. However, at present, there is no evidence that workfare discourages people from applying for welfare or helps them to move toward greater self-sufficiency.

Assuming job search assistance, training, education, child care, and other services are required to move welfare recipients into regular jobs, an up-front investment will be needed to accomplish this goal. The hope is that, over the longer run, these investments will more than pay for themselves by reducing welfare and related public assistance costs and increasing revenues as more people are productively employed. In the five demonstration programs mentioned earlier, the costs of the up-front investment varied from $200 to $1,000 per participant. Thus, a program that attempted to serve all welfare mothers with no children under six could cost between $78 million and $388 million per year. The evaluations of the demonstration programs suggest that such an investment would pay for itself within five years. However, these estimates are based on a variety of assumptions about the extent to which any earnings and employment gains persist into the future and the extent to which welfare recipients displace other workers in the job market, thereby decreasing the latter's net contribution to public revenues.[43]

A program that failed to pay for itself in narrow fiscal terms would not necessarily be a bad investment for society as a whole. To the extent that more people were productively employed, that they felt better about themselves, and that their children were not harmed in the process, it would have been a worthwhile effort.

## Encouraging Work: The Broader Challenge

The recent interest in substituting work for welfare among single parents is understandable given the drain of AFDC outlays on public treasuries, the persistence of poverty among this group, and the evidence that they can be helped by work-related programs. In other respects, however, the emphasis may be misplaced. First, nonemployed women on welfare represent only 15 percent of all those working-age, able-bodied household heads who are poor because they are not working enough. Targeting exclusively on welfare recipients may put them in competition with other poor people for existing jobs, leading to a reshuffling of the poverty population that penalizes poor people who have not applied for welfare. Second, such proposals—by focusing almost exclusively on unemployed women while ignoring unemployed men—may contribute to the growth of female-headed families and the poverty that is associated with it.

These considerations suggest that work-related programs for welfare recipients, although potentially valuable, must be seen not as the centerpiece of efforts to reduce poverty and dependency but as one potentially valuable element in a broader strategy of moving people toward self-support. Doing this will require both increasing employment and rewarding work more adequately.

**Increasing Employment.** A large number of the heads of poor households are not working or are working irregularly, and they report that the reason is their inability to find work (see figure 7.3, presented earlier). These data are hard to interpret and support no easy generalizations. In particular, it is hard to distinguish the extent to which jobs are really unavailable and the extent to which people are using this answer as a socially acceptable cover for their own lack of interest in working—at least in the kinds of jobs that are available to them.

It *is* clear that when the overall unemployment rate drops, so does the incidence of poverty, especially the proportion of the poverty population that consists of household heads looking for work. The reason is that the total number of vacancies rises relative to the number of people seeking work, making it easier for those with the fewest skills or the weakest attachment to the labor force to obtain jobs. Employers may lower their hiring standards, bid up wages, or cast a broader (and less discriminating) net in their search for employees.

Even when the economy has enough jobs for everybody, there may be a mismatch between the skills or location of jobs and job seekers. Some evidence suggests that this mismatch is particularly serious in the large cities of the Northeast and Midwest. These cities have many people with little education; recall that 63 percent of the adults in "underclass areas" have less than a high school education. These people typically do not qualify for jobs in the growing service and information-based sectors of the nation's major metropolitan centers. For example, between 1970 and 1984, the number of jobs in New York City that required less than a high school education declined by 34 percent, while those requiring some higher education increased by 24 percent. Similar figures apply to other northern cities.[44]

The fact that jobs are more difficult to get when unemployment is high or when the structure of the economy changes does not mean that there are no jobs available. Help-wanted signs, the classified ads, the flow of immigrants into the U.S. labor market, and the large increase in total employment over the past decade all testify to the contrary. Even the most disadvantaged may have some job opportunities. A 1979-80 survey of young black men living in poverty areas in Boston, Chicago, and Philadelphia found that 71 percent of nonemployed, out-of-school youths thought they could obtain a minimum-wage job either very or somewhat easily.[45] Alternative sources of income such as crime or hustling may keep these young men from accepting very low-paid jobs, and alternative sources of labor such as women and immigrants may keep employers from offering higher pay.

Other workers, with fewer disadvantages than those associated with inner-city black youths, may be unemployed for similar reasons—their inability to quickly locate a job that meets their requirements in terms of wages, location, and type of work. Whether these requirements are viewed as reasonable is debatable. The reality is that a low-paid job is no guarantee of escape from poverty, that community norms about what is and is not "acceptable work'' matter to most people, and that a temporary bout of joblessness and poverty may be the price of holding out for a job that promises better long-term prospects. In some cases, child care or transportation expenses may loom large relative to prospective wages. And negotiating a labor market as large and complex as that found in most large cities may be a daunting experience for people with little education, few personal contacts, and low self-esteem. The difficulty of evaluating these more subjective barriers to employment, along with clear evidence that jobs are available, has made the public generally unsympathetic to people who are poor because "they cannot find work."

At the same time it would be a mistake to conclude that all unemployment is "voluntary." Even middle-class job seekers know that a job vacancy does not always translate into a job offer and that there may be little scope for bargaining over wage levels or anything else if a job applicant is not what the employer is looking for. This problem is magnified greatly for groups such as disadvantaged minority youths who are believed by employers— correctly or incorrectly—to make poor employees. For example, one study of young, unemployed men found that the black youths had lower employment rates than white youths largely because of the black youths' inability to generate job offers when applying directly for a job. The racial difference in the ability to generate a job offer persisted even after adjusting for differences in age, education, urban residence, local unemployment rates, and family background, suggesting that discrimination remains a problem.[46] Even more striking is evidence from an experiment conducted in the late 1970s. Employers in two cities were offered a 100 percent wage subsidy if they would hire low-income, largely minority youths, but only 18 percent were willing to participate. The remaining 82 percent did not want to hire these youths even at a zero wage. The youths themselves were willing to take the minimum-wage jobs that were created for them, mostly in the public sector, with the result that the black youth employment rate in the seventeen sites where the program operated increased from 25 to 65 percent. Evaluations of the program also suggested that these youths performed adequately on the job.[47]

These and other studies suggest that some people are not able to generate job offers even at low wages. Such evidence of involuntary unemployment has led to proposals to guarantee minimum-wage or sub-minimum-wage jobs to the unemployed.[48] A demonstration program that did so would provide better evidence not only about the feasibility and cost of such an effort but also about the extent of true "involuntary" unemployment. Targeting such a program on male and female heads of households living in underclass neighborhoods might complement the current emphasis on employment programs for women on welfare.

In conclusion, much poverty is related to unemployment. That some of this unemployment is temporary and most of it "voluntary" in the sense that job vacancies do exist is also undeniable. The quantity, location, and wage levels of available jobs and the ability of some job seekers to generate actual offers of employment appear to be the issue. Recent macroeconomic and structural changes in the economy have exacerbated the shortage of jobs for unskilled workers. The longer-run remedies will need to include a healthier economy, better mechanisms for helping the unemployed locate and obtain available jobs, and (as discussed in more detail later) more intensive investments in the education and training of the most disadvantaged to help them qualify for these jobs. In the meantime, before these investments pay off, a society that expects the able-bodied poor to work may need to create low-wage jobs of last resort for its least employable members. The alternatives could be greater welfare dependence and more crime.

**Rewarding Work.** Moving unemployed people into jobs is no guarantee that poverty will be ended. As indicated in figure 7.3, the number of people who are poor despite rather strenuous efforts to earn a living is not large; but the significance of this group probably should not be judged by its size alone (and it would be larger if employed single parents were included). The failure of this group to earn adequate incomes may send a signal to other people that hard work does not pay off. Indeed, it is likely that many of those who report that they are unable to find work are people who, in effect, are discouraged not just by a lack of jobs but by their inability to earn enough to climb out of poverty combined with the availability of other options.

In 1987, a full-time, year-round, minimum-wage job produced an income of just under $7,000 a year. Although this is enough income to move a single person above the poverty line, it is not enough for an adult with even one dependent. (It is also lower than the combined AFDC and food stamp benefits available to a mother and two children in fifteen states. In addition, unlike most low-paid jobs, welfare automatically provides health care benefits through Medicaid and involves no payroll taxes and no child care or other work-related expenses.) Two adults, one working full-time and the other half-time, can earn $10,500 a year—still not enough to support a couple with two children above the poverty line. Thus, for young people who do not yet have any dependents, working at a minimum wage job is not a disaster. But for adults with family responsibilities, it is a recipe for poverty.

The best long-term strategy for the "hardworking" poor is more schooling to prepare them for higher-paying jobs. (Some promising approaches in this area are described in the next section.) In the interim—and for those whose productivity may always be low—the options include raising the minimum wage, or supplementing the earnings of the poor through wage subsidies or refundable tax credits (a variant of a negative income tax).

The minimum wage, currently $3.35 per hour, has not been raised since 1981; as a result, its real purchasing power has declined by 27 percent. In 1986, about 7 percent of all workers earned the minimum wage or less. An additional 6 percent earned above the minimum but less than $4.00 an hour. However, 20 percent of minimum-wage workers live in poor families.

An increase of $1.00 an hour in the minimum wage would compensate for the dollar's loss of purchasing power since 1981 and help to restore the minimum wage to its traditional level—50 percent of the average hourly wage for nonsupervisory workers. Although some workers—teenagers in particular—would have fewer employment opportunities as the result of a higher minimum, most low-wage workers would gain substantially. On balance, the aggregate earned income of the poor would rise.[49]

Higher wage costs would, of course, create inflationary pressures and might undermine U.S. competitiveness in world markets. In addition, since four-fifths of minimum-wage workers do not live in poor families, raising the minimum wage is a rather blunt instrument for reducing poverty.

For these reasons, other more targeted and less inflationary alternatives for raising the incomes of the working poor should also be considered, even though these alternatives are more administratively complex and would require additional public outlays to finance them.

One alternative would be to provide a direct wage subsidy to workers with very low earnings. For example, any family heads earning less than $7.00 per hour could be eligible to receive a subsidy equal to one-half the difference between their actual wage and $7.00. This would provide a subsidy of $3,650 to full-time, minimum-wage workers and provide their families with an income of $10,650 per year. The largest subsidies would go to persons who worked the longest hours, thereby rewarding those who made the greatest efforts.

Another alternative would be to make the Earned Income Tax Credit (EITC) more generous. The EITC, introduced in 1975 and amended most recently as part of the Tax Reform Act of 1986, provides a refundable tax credit to low-income families with children.[50] Although the EITC has the potential to serve as a negative income tax for the working poor, at present its main function is to offset the payroll taxes paid by this group.[51] Thus, proposals have been made to increase the generosity of the credit, to adjust it for family size, or to extend it to families without children.

Other changes that might benefit the working poor include allowing welfare recipients with inadequate earnings to keep a larger portion of their grant, making the tax credit for child care and dependent care refundable, raising state income tax thresholds above the poverty line (as was done for federal income tax thresholds in 1986) and extending health care protection to the working poor so that they will not be worse off than welfare recipients who automatically qualify for Medicaid. (In 1984, roughly three-quarters of workers from poor families worked in jobs that did not offer group health insurance.) None of these policies is cheap, but all are designed to make work more attractive than welfare and to reward the efforts of people who are trying to support themselves and their families by working at relatively low-paid jobs.[52]

## Investing in Education

Although efforts to strengthen family responsibilities and make people self-supporting through work are important, they do not tackle one of the root causes of poverty: a lack of education or basic skills. In 1986, half of the heads of poor families had less than a high school education compared with about a quarter of all family heads.[53] Equally striking is the association between deficiencies in basic skills and such problems as becoming an unwed parent, dropping out of school, welfare dependency, unemployment, and crime (table 7.5).

Education has always been the route to upward social mobility in the United States. Although education is one vehicle by which relatively advan-

TABLE 7.5

PERCENTAGE OF PERSONS 18 TO 23 YEARS OLD IN BOTTOM FIFTH OF BASIC SKILLS
DISTRIBUTION

| Category[a] | Percentage |
|---|---|
| All persons 18 to 23 years old | 20 |
| In a poor household | 46 |
| Unwed parent | 59 |
| Welfare dependent | 53 |
| School dropout | 52 |
| Not working | 40 |
| Arrested | 37 |

SOURCE: Gordon Berlin, and Andrew Sum, "Toward a More Perfect Union: Basic Skills, Poor Families, and Our Economic Future," based on a speech delivered by Gordon Berlin at a Conference of School and Employment and Training Officials sponsored by the National Governors' Association and the Chief State School Officers, December 1986.

NOTE: Based on scores on the Armed Forces Qualification test, which measures reading and mathematical skills and has been administered to a representative national sample of youth, interviewed annually from 1979 to 1985 as part of the National Longitudinal Survey of Youth Labor Market Experience.

a. All categories except the first exclude persons attending college from the base used to calculate percentage.

taged parents pass on these advantages to their children, it is also the chief way to break the cycle of poverty between generations. The correlation between the lifetime earnings of parents and children found in a variety of studies of the U.S. population is about 0.25.[54] In a complete meritocracy this correlation would be zero and in a society with no mobility it would be 1.0, so the 0.25 figure suggests that the United States is much closer to being an open than a closed society. Children from low-income families are more likely to end up poor as adults than are children from high-income families; but more than half of those whose families were in the bottom one-fifth of the income distribution when they were growing up end up in a higher income group after establishing their own households.[55] The evidence also suggests that overall social mobility has increased since the early 1960s.[56] It is less clear whether these findings extend to people with the most disadvantaged backgrounds, such as children being raised in "underclass areas" where poor schools and a high incidence of crime and drug abuse make learning difficult and where racial discrimination compounds the problems. Indeed, the very growth of the underclass could be interpreted as suggesting that upward mobility for children born into chronically poor families living in distressed neighborhoods has all but ceased.

In other respects, this conclusion is too pessimistic. Intergenerational mobility is a long-term process. Thus, even if social mobility were to have improved for the generations born after the civil rights revolution and the start of the War on Poverty, we would not yet have seen it in the data, because these children are only now entering adulthood. The more direct evidence on their educational experiences is encouraging. Overall educational attainment has gone up, and the gap between minority and nonminority students has narrowed substantially. Moreover, contrary to popular impression, average test scores for persons born after the mid-1960s have improved—with the gains being particularly large for minorities, students from schools in disadvantaged urban communities, and those whose parents did not graduate from high school.[57] For example, the proportion of blacks, ages twenty-two to twenty-four, who were high school dropouts declined from 38 percent in 1970 to 18 percent in 1985 (versus a decline from 16.3 to 13.3 percent for whites). At the same time, the mean reading proficiency scores of black seventeen-year-olds increased by 10 percent (versus a 1 percent improvement for whites). In general, whether the test scores are examined by race, by parents' education, or by type of school attended, the differences have narrowed over this period. Thus, clear progress has been made in reducing the dependence of education on race, family background, or neighborhood and in improving educational outcomes for those most at risk of being poor.

Despite this progress, an educational underclass remains. In 1985, one-fifth of Americans twenty-one to twenty-five years old (and almost half of the blacks this age) were reading below the eighth-grade level.[58] Large gaps in schooling and test scores remain between students from different backgrounds. The reading scores of seventeen-year-olds who are black, come from disadvantaged urban communities, or have parents without a high school degree are no higher than the reading scores of thirteen-year-olds who are white, come from advantaged urban communities, or have parents with at least some college education.[59]

These educational deficiencies are interacting with an economy that increasingly demands or requires higher levels of literacy. Currently, 18 percent of all jobs require less than a high school education, but it is conservatively estimated that not more than 14 percent of the jobs created between now and the year 2000 will fall into this category. Furthermore, according to detailed analysis by the U.S. Department of Labor, the most rapidly growing occupations are those that require the highest levels of language, math, and reasoning skills.[60]

What can be done to raise the levels of education and literacy among children from poor families, thereby breaking the cycle of poverty? A number of existing programs aimed at accomplishing this objective have proved reasonably successful and would seem to be candidates for further expansion: Head Start for disadvantaged preschoolers, compensatory education under Chapter One of the Education Consolidation and Improvement Act for grade-school youth, and the Jobs Corps for school dropouts.

Preschool programs appear to have been especially effective. Early childhood education has an immediate, positive effect on a child's intellectual performance, and although the gains in IQ fade after a few years, the programs have a more lasting effect on school performance. The most plausible interpretation of these results is that the programs give children the confidence that they can succeed. Success in the early years then has a cumulative impact, establishing the basis for further learning at each stage in the educational process. The best programs typically work with parents as well as children, thereby changing the entire family's attitudes toward education. In the Perry Preschool program of Ypsilanti, Michigan, where 123 children were randomly assigned either to an experimental or to a control group in the early 1960s, and their progress was followed until they were age nineteen, quite dramatic findings have been reported. The group attending preschool was much more likely to be employed, to have graduated from high school, and to be enrolled in further education or training. They were also less likely to have become pregnant or to have been arrested. For each dollar invested in the program,

$4.75 was saved because of lower costs for special education, public assistance, and crime.[61] Although it is not clear that such high-quality programs can be replicated nationally, the attempt to do so would appear to be extremely worthwhile. Currently, less than one-fifth of the children eligible for Head Start are enrolled in the program.

Compensatory education programs at the grade-school level also improve the reading and math scores of children enrolled in the program. However, the gains are small and do not appear to be maintained over time.[62] Currently, about half of the children who need compensatory education are receiving it.

The Job Corps is another successful, largely residential program for extremely disadvantaged out-of-school youths, ages fourteen to twenty-one. Virtually all enrollees are from poor or welfare-dependent families, and the average participant enters the program reading at about the sixth-grade level. The program provides a range of services including remedial education, vocational training, and health care; the cost can be as high as $15,000 per person per year. However, careful evaluations of the program indicate that it improves health and educational outcomes and increases annual earnings by about 28 percent, an increase that is sustained for at least four years after the end of the program. And despite the high cost of the program, its estimated social benefits exceed its costs by 46 percent.[63]

The results achieved from these and similar education and training programs—along with the post-1960s gains in educational attainment and test scores cited earlier—suggest that intergenerational mobility and equality of opportunity can be enhanced by investments in children. Early, intensive interventions that involve parents as well as children, and build self-esteem as well as skills, appear to be the most promising approaches.

## Conclusions

The debate about how much poverty exists in the United States and what to do about it will undoubtedly continue. Conservatives will emphasize the responsibility of the poor for their own fate, and liberals will bemoan the shortcomings of our social and economic system. Although these ideological differences will never be fully resolved, there are signs of an emerging maturity in our public debates, one that accepts that both systemic and individual factors play a role, often interacting with one another in complex ways.

Accompanying this more balanced, less simplistic view of the causes of poverty may be a new realism about the role of government in responding to the problem. If it was naive to believe that antipoverty programs would accomplish as much as some of the architects of the War on Poverty had hoped, it is equally naive to believe that these programs have been as counterproductive as some conservatives have recently argued. The nation seems to be groping for a new middle ground, one based on a compassion tempered by concern about the willingness of the poor to help themselves, the cost of any new effort, and its likely effectiveness. This chapter has argued for precisely this kind of tough-minded compassion.

Compassion should not be limited to particular groups of the poor, but tough-mindedness means setting priorities. Thus this chapter has argued that particular attention be paid to the growing underclass in American society. Should this group continue to grow, it could impose large costs on society, threaten our sense of social cohesion, and exacerbate racial tensions.

The objective must be to integrate this group into the mainstream more effectively through a renewed emphasis on parents' responsibility for their children, work, and education. A number of specific strategies that might be used to accomplish this objective over the next decade have been detailed in this chapter. Some targeting of policy on those inner-city neighborhoods where chronic poverty and antisocial behaviors are commonplace may be appropriate. In addition, policies that work on several fronts at once are likely to be more effective than those that deal with one problem at a time. Without education, people will not be prepared to take the jobs that are available. Without jobs at the end of the process, education and training may be a cruel hoax. And without stronger families, education may have to carry too big a burden.

Making progress against persistent poverty is likely to be a long, difficult, and expensive process. It would be far easier to treat the symptoms than to cure the disease. But this chapter has argued for a strategy that goes after root causes: weak families, substantial joblessness, and poor education. Although there should be no expectation of early success, a society that does not even try to reduce poverty and bring members of the underclass back into the mainstream cannot feel very good about itself.

NOTES TO CHAPTER 7

1. Poverty levels for different kinds of households in the mid-1960s were established as multiples of the cost of a minimally adequate diet. Since that time they have been adjusted for inflation but not for the fact that real incomes have also grown. As a result, the poverty line for a family of four which stood at $3,223 in 1965 had increased to $11,203 by 1986, but as a proportion of the median income of a four-person family, it had fallen from 46 percent in 1965 to 32 percent in 1986.

2. In making these comparisons, two different yardsticks can be used: an absolute measure of poverty or a relative measure. An absolute measure takes the official poverty lines for the United States and adjusts them only for differences in purchasing power between countries or between years. A relative measure uses poverty lines that vary with average family income for a particular country or year. The first yardstick is based on the notion that poverty consists of having less than a fixed subsistence level of income, whereas the second yardstick recognizes

that what may be considered a sufficient income in one time or place might be considered less than adequate in another.

3. These projections are based on models that predict the poverty rate based on factors such as economic growth, unemployment, and spending on income transfers. See, for example, Peter Gottschalk and Sheldon Danziger, "Macroeconomic Conditions, Income Transfers, and the Trends in Poverty," in *The Social Contract Revisited*, edited by D. Lee Bawden (Washington, D.C.: The Urban Institute Press, 1984), 185–215.

4. Another factor that makes recent trends appear somewhat more favorable is the use of an alternative measure of inflation, corrected for the upward bias in the official Consumer Price Index (CPI) during the late 1970s. Working in the opposite direction have been rising payroll and income tax burdens over this period, a trend that is also not reflected in the official poverty measure (which is based on pretax income).

5. Charles Murray, *Losing Ground: American Social Policy, 1950-1980* (New York: Basic Books, 1984).

6. For an excellent review and critique of Murray's book, see Sara McLanahan, Glen Cain, Michael Olneck, Irving Piliavin, Sheldon Danziger, and Peter Gottschalk, "Losing Ground: A Critique," Institute for Research on Poverty, University of Wisconsin, Special Report No. 38, August 1985.

7. The section that follows is based on a more detailed review of the evidence in Isabel V. Sawhill, "Poverty in the U.S.: Why Is It So Persistent?" *Journal of Economic Literature* (forthcoming).

8. Gottschalk and Danziger, "Macroeconomic Conditions, Income Transfers, and Trends in Poverty."

9. Irwin Garfinkel and Sara McLanahan, *Single-Mother Families and Public Policy: A New American Dilemma* (Washington, D.C.: The Urban Institute Press, 1986).

10. Edward M. Gramlich and Deborah S. Laren, "How Widespread Are Income Losses in a Recession?" in Bawden, *The Social Contract Revisited*, 157–84.

11. This estimate is derived by using regression analysis to estimate unemployment's effect on the pretransfer poverty rate for four demographic groups, by using the regressions to simulate the trend in the poverty rate for each group holding unemployment constant, and by holding demographic change constant using base-year weights for the four different groups (the elderly, male heads of households with children, female heads of households with children, and all other households).

12. For a review of the evidence, see Sawhill, "Poverty in the U.S."; and Peter Gottschalk and Sheldon Danziger, "Do Rising Tides Lift All Boats? The Impact of Secular and Cyclical Changes on Poverty," *American Economic Review 76*, no. 2 (May 1986): 405–10.

13. Martin Dooley and Peter Gottschalk, "The Increasing Proportion of Men with Low Earnings in the United States," *Demography 22*, no. 11 (February 1985): 25–34.

14. U.S. Council of Economic Advisers, *Economic Report of the President, 1964* (Washington, D.C.: U.S. Government Printing Office, 1964), 77.

15. The effects would be even larger if it had not been for the budgetary retrenchments of the early 1980s, which accounted for about 40 percent of the increase in poverty between 1980 and 1983, according to the Institute for Research on Poverty. The effects would also be larger if noncash benefits were included in the measurement of income.

16. According to the *Current Population Survey*, between 1966 and 1986, the share of the poverty population that consisted of elderly persons dropped from 18 to 11 percent, while the share that consisted of working-age adults increased from 43 to 55 percent. At the same time, the proportion of the poor living in female-headed families increased from 36 to 52 percent. Between 1967 and 1986, the share of the poor living in urban as opposed to rural areas rose from 50 to 70 percent. Within metropolitan areas, the poor are somewhat more likely now than previously to live in low-income neighborhoods. See, for example, Robert D. Reischauer, "The Geographic Concentration of Poverty: What Do We Know?" (Washington, D.C.: Brookings Institution, 1987), processed.

17. One final group could be mentioned: the homeless. This group is not even included in official counts of poverty, because income data come from household surveys conducted by the Census Bureau, and the homeless by definition are not part of a household. Special surveys of this group provide only rough estimates of its size but suggest that it is smaller than some popular reports indicate and probably runs between 250,000 and 500,000 nationwide. Although the homeless are a particularly visible and troubled population, they are only the tip of the iceberg; for every homeless person there are somewhere in the neighborhood of one hundred poor people in the United States. See Felicia Kornbluh, "Homelessness: What Are the Facts and What Can We Do?" (Washington, D.C.: The Urban Institute, 1987).

18. Mary Jo Bane and David T. Ellwood, "Slipping Into and Out of Poverty: The Dynamics of Spells," *Journal of Human Resources* 21, no. 1 (Winter 1983): 1–23.

19. Patricia Ruggles and William P. Marton, *Measuring the Size and Characteristics of the Underclass: How Much Do We Know?*, paper prepared for the Rockefeller Foundation (Washington, D.C.: The Urban Institute, December 1986); and Robert D. Reischauer, "The Size and Characteristics of the Underclass" (Washington, D.C.: Brookings Institution, 1987), processed. Both these sources come up with estimates of around 8 million using a persistence-based measure and excluding the elderly and disabled.

20. This estimate is from an Urban Institute analysis of the 1980 census. A similar approach to measuring the underclass is taken by William Julius Wilson, *The Truly Disadvantaged* (Chicago: University of Chicago Press, 1987), and by Mary Jo Bane and Paul Jargowsky, "Urban Poverty and the Underclass: Basic Questions," Center for Health and Human Resources Policy, John F. Kennedy School of Government, Harvard University, 1987, paper presented at the Association for Public Policy Analysis and Management 1987 conference. Their estimates are based on published data for the largest cities only, whereas The Urban Institute data are for the entire country.

21. "Common" here means that the incidence of each of these behaviors was one standard deviation above the mean for the country as a whole. Erol R. Ricketts and Isabel V. Sawhill, "Defining and Measuring the Underclass," *Journal of Policy Analysis and Management* (forthcoming).

22. Erol Ricketts and Ronald Mincy, "Growth of the Underclass: 1970–1980," Urban Institute Discussion Paper, 1987.

23. U.S. House of Representatives, Committee on Ways and Means, *Background Material and Data on Programs within the Jurisdiction of the Committee on Ways and Means* (Washington, D.C.: U.S. Government Printing Office, March 6, 1987).

24. The discussion in this section and the next draws heavily on Isabel V. Sawhill, "Anti-Poverty Strategies for the Next Decade," *Work and Welfare: The Case for New Directions in National Policy* (Washington, D.C.: Center for National Policy, 1987).

25. Kristin A. Moore and Martha R. Burt, *Private Crisis, Public Cost* (Washington, D.C.: The Urban Institute Press, 1982); Richard F. Wertheimer and Kristin A. Moore, *Teenage Childbearing: Public Sector Costs—Final Report* (Washington, D.C.: The Urban Institute Press, December 1982); and Martha R. Burt, "Estimating the Public Cost of Teenage Childbearing," *Family Planning Perspectives* 18, no. 5 (September-October 1986).

26. This review of the family-planning literature draws heavily on Freya L. Sonenstein, "Pregnancy among Teenagers: What Can Be Done?" (Washington, D.C.: The Urban Institute, 1986), processed. Also, see National Academy of Sciences, *Risking the Future: Adolescent Sexuality, Pregnancy and Childbearing* (Washington, D.C.: National Academy Press, 1987).

27. 1984 National Audience Demographics, A. C. Nielson Company, Inc., New York, 1984; and Radar, Radio Advisory Board Research Report No. 33, "Summary on National Radio Listening Habits," conducted by Statistics Research, Inc., Radio Advisory Board, New York, Spring 1986.

28. Garfinkel and McLanahan, *Single-Mother Families and Public Policy*.

29. For additional data, see U.S. Bureau of the Census, *Child Support and Alimony: 1983*, *Current Population Reports*, Series P-23, no. 141 (Washington, D.C.: U.S. Government Printing Office, 1985).

30. Ron Haskins, Andrew E. Dobelstein, John S. Akin, and J. Brad Schwartz, *Estimates of National Child Support Collections Potential and the Income Security of Female-Headed Families*, Final Report, Grant 18-P-00259-4-01 (Washington, D.C.: Social Security Administration, Office of Child Support Enforcement, April 1, 1985).

31. Income and poverty status were measured after the transfer of child support (if any was paid) to the custodial parent. The sample was drawn about equally from recently divorced couples and those involved in a child support enforcement program in the state; as a result, the sample is somewhat younger and poorer than a cross section of parents who do not live with their children. However, it does not include divorce cases in which no child support order exists and out-of-wedlock cases in which paternity has not been established. Freya L. Sonenstein and Charles A. Calhoun, *Survey of Absent Parents: Pilot Results* (Washington, D.C.: The Urban Institute Press, June 1987).

32. Esther Wattenberg, "Protecting the Rights of the Minor Child of Unmarried Minor Parents; Toward a Rational Policy," paper presented to the Child Support Enforcement Research Workshop of the Office of Child Support Enforcement, Washington, D.C., 1984.

33. Most teenagers have only one sex partner at a time and even in disputed cases, blood tests permit accurate identification with an error rate of less than one in a billion cases.

34. See, for example, Isabel V. Sawhill, "Developing Normative Standards for Child Support Payments," in *The Parental Child-Support Obligations*, edited by Judith Cassetty (Lexington, Mass.: Lexington Books, 1983); Barbara R. Bergmann and Mark Roberts, "Work and the Single Parent," in *Gender in the Workplace*, edited by Clair Brown and Joseph Pechman (Washington, D.C.: Brookings Institution, 1987); Donald Oellerich and Irwin Garfinkel, "Distributional Impact of Existing and Alternative Child Support Systems," *Policy Studies Journal* 12, no. 1 (September 1983): 119–30; Philip K. Robins, "Child Support, Welfare Dependency, and Poverty," *American Economic Review* 76, no. 4 (1986): 768–88.

35. Garfinkel and McLanahan, *Single-Mother Families and Public Policy*.

36. Reviewed in Sonenstein and Calhoun, *Survey of Absent Parents*.

37. Data for all mothers from Congressional Budget Office (CBO), *Work-Related Programs for Welfare Recipients* (Washington, D.C.: Congressional Budget Office, April 1987).

38. Based on Urban Institute calculations from the March 1987 *Current Population Survey*.

39. Leonard Goodwin, *Do the Poor Want to Work? A Social-Psychological Study of Work Orientations* (Washington, D.C.: Brookings Institution, 1972).

40. Laurie Bassi and Orley Ashenfelter, "The Effect of Direct Job Creation and Training Progams on Low-Skilled Workers," in *Fighting Poverty: What Works and What Doesn't*, edited by Sheldon Danziger and Daniel Weinberg (Cambridge, Mass.: Harvard University Press, 1986), 133–51; and Judith M. Gueron, *Work Initiatives for Welfare Recipients* (New York: Manpower Demonstration Research Corporation, March 1986).

41. CBO, *Work-Related Programs for Welfare Recipients*.

42. In West Virginia, for example, a depressed rural area, a relatively large proportion of the welfare recipients were assigned to workfare projects, but the program had no impact on their employment and earnings relative to those of welfare recipients who were not assigned.

43. For a more extended discussion, see CBO, *Work-Related Programs for Welfare Recipients*.

44. J. D. Kasarda, "The Regional and Urban Redistribution of People and Jobs in the U.S.," paper prepared for the National Research Council Committee on National Urban Policy, National Academy of Sciences, Washington, D.C., 1986, as adapted by William Julius Wilson, "Social Policy and Minority Groups: What Might Have Been and What Might We See in the Future?," paper prepared for an Institute for Research on Poverty conference on Poverty and Social Policy: The Minority Experience, at Airlie, Va., November 5–7, 1986.

45. Richard B. Freeman and Harry J. Holzer, eds., *The Black Youth Employment Crisis* (Chicago: University of Chicago Press, 1986).

46. Harry J. Holzer, *Informal Job Search and Black Youth Unemployment, Working Paper No. 1860* (Cambridge, Mass.: National Bureau of Economic Research, Inc., March 1986).

47. Bernard Anderson, "Rethinking Youth Employment Policy," in *Work and Welfare: The Case for New Directions in National Policy*, Alternatives for the 1980s, no. 22 (Washington,

D.C.: Center for National Policy, 1987); and George Farkas, Randall Olsen, Ernst W. Stroms-dorfer, L. Sharpe, F. Skidmore, D. Smith, S. Merrill, and Abt Associates, Inc., *Post-Program Impacts of the Youth Incentive Entitlement Pilot Projects* (New York: Manpower Demonstration Research Corporation, June 1984).

48. Isabel V. Sawhill, "Jobs for the Truly Unemployed" (Washington, D.C.: The Urban Institute, 1985); Mickey Kaus, "The Work Ethic State," *New Republic* (July 1986): 22–33; and Paul Simon, *Let's Put America Back to Work* (Chicago: Bonus Books, 1987).

49. Preliminary estimates suggest that the poverty gap for working poor families would decline by an estimated 13 percent, and the number of working poor families would decrease by an estimated 9 percent if everyone were covered by a minimum wage that was $1.00 higher than the current one. Ronald Mincy, "Minimum Wage Increases and the Working Poor," Urban Institute Discussion Paper, Washington, D.C., forthcoming.

50. The credit is 14 percent of earned income up to $6,214 in 1988, yielding a maximum credit of $870. The credit is then reduced by 10 cents for each dollar by which income exceeds $9,840, phasing out entirely at an income of $18,540.

51. Maximum eligible earnings as a proportion of the poverty thresholds for a family of four declined from 73 percent in 1975 to 51 percent in 1988. Eugene Steuerle and Paul Wilson, *Focus* 10, no. 1 (1987): 1–8.

52. For further discussion of policies for the working poor, see Robert D. Reischauer, "Welfare Reform and the Working Poor," and Robert Greenstein, "Welfare Reform Issues Affecting Families with Children—What Can Be Done in the 100th Congress?" in *Work and Welfare: The Case for New Directions in National Policy*, Alternatives for the 1980s, no. 22 (Washington, D.C.: Center for National Policy, March 1987).

53. U.S. Bureau of the Census, *Money Income and Poverty Status of Families and Persons in the United States: 1985 (Advance Data from the March 1986 Current Population Survey)*, Series P-60, no. 154 (Washington, D.C.: U.S. Government Printing Office, 1986).

54. Paul Taubman, *Income Distribution and Redistribution* (Reading, Mass.: Addison-Wesley, 1978).

55. Martha Hill, Sue Augustyniak, Greg Duncan, Gerald Gurin, Patricia Gurin, Jeffrey Liker, James Morgan, and Michael Ponza, "Motivation and Economic Mobility," Research Report Series, The Institute for Social Research, University of Michigan, Ann Arbor, 1985.

56. For a review of the literature, see Robert Haveman, *Poverty Policy and Social Research: The Poverty War and the Social Sciences* (Madison: University of Wisconsin Press, 1987); for evidence on changes in social mobility, see D. L. Featherman and R.M. Hauser, *Opportunity and Change* (New York: Academic Press, 1978).

57. Gordon Berlin and Andrew Sum, "Toward a More Perfect Union: Basic Skills, Poor Families, and Our Economic Future," based on a speech delivered by Gordon Berlin at a Conference of School and Employment and Training Officials sponsored by the National Gov-ernors' Association and the Chief State School Officers, December 1986; Congressional Budget Office, *Trends in Educational Achievement* (Washington, D.C.: Congressional Budget Office, April 1986). The well-publicized decline in test scores ended with the cohorts of children born around 1962 or 1963 who entered grade school in the late 1960s and were taking SATs and other widely publicized tests for high-school-age youth in 1980.

58. U.S. Bureau of the Census, *Statistical Abstract of the United States: 1987* (107th edition) (Washington, D.C.: U.S. Government Printing Office, 1986); and Carol Jusenius Romero, "Past is Prologue; Educational Deficiencies and the Youth Labor Market Problem," Monograph Series 1, no. 3, National Commission for Employment Policy, Washington, D.C., April 1987.

59. Berlin and Sum, "Toward a More Perfect Union."

60. William B. Johnston, *Workforce 2000: Work and Workers for the 21st Century* (Indi-anapolis: Hudson Institute, June 1987).

61. Irving Lazar and Richard B. Darlington, "Lasting Effects After Preschool," DHEW Publication No. 79-30178, U.S. Department of Health, Education, and Welfare (Washington, D.C.: U.S. Government Printing Office, October 1978); and John R. Berrueta-Clement, Law-rence J. Schweinhart, W. Steven Barnett, Ann S. Epstein, and David Weiker, *Changed Lives:*

*The Effects of Preschool Program of Youths Through Age 19*, Monographs of the High/Scope Educational Research Foundation, no. 8 (Ypsilanti, Mich.: The High/School Press, 1984).

62. Stephen P. Mullin and Anita A. Summers, "Is More Better? The Effectiveness of Spending on Compensatory Education," *Phi Delta Kappa* 64, no. 5 (January 1983): 339–47.

63. Charles L. Betsey, Robinson G. Hollister, Jr., and Mary R. Papegeorgiou, eds., *Youth Employment and Training Programs: The YEDPA Years* (Washington, D.C.: National Academy Press, 1985).

# CHAPTER 8

# LIFE, LIBERTY, OR THE PURSUIT OF HAPPINESS

Thomas C. Schelling

The history of individual liberty in the United States is a history of triumphant, if uneven, progress. Whether measured by individual dignity, access to the marketplace, or access to the political system, the signs of that progress are everywhere.

Furthermore, the practical results of most of these advances in individual liberty are as welcome as the improvements in human rights. Most of us not only believe in the principle that ethnic minorities should not be discriminated against in the workplace, but also like to see them earn more, participate more, and raise healthier families. Most of us probably want contraceptive information available not only because suppressing it is intolerant but because we believe that people should be able to plan and limit their pregnancies.

But social objectives and civil liberties are not always in tune. Preventive detention can reduce crime but reduces freedom; wire tapping can identify terrorists but invades privacy; control of handguns may reduce accidental deaths and homicides but only by denying a right that some people believe is guaranteed by the Constitution. These are straightforward conflicts; a person calculates a trade-off and picks a side or selects a compromise.

Not all the conflicts are straightforward. Individual rights clash not only with social goals but, increasingly, with one another. The constitutional protection of pornography has recently been alleged to violate the rights of women. The rights of parents to decide on medical treatment for seriously defective newborns conflict with the rights of newborns to be protected from their parents' decisions, and even with the rights of physicians and nurses to practice medicine in accordance with their consciences. The right of a person to decide in advance, while mentally competent, what treatment may or may not be administered when the person has later become incompetent conflicts intertemporally with the person's subsequent right to choose, however incompetently, the person's own treatment. Abortion confronts a fetus's right to be born with a woman's right to control the functioning of her body and the size of her family (and even, in some interpretations, the same fetus's right *not* to be born).

Moral and religious values collide with civil rights in the issues of abortion, euthanasia, nonviable births, and the several new technologies for conceiving and bearing a child. In 1983 a California judge ruled against a quadriplegic woman who wished to die and had asked a hospital's help in starving herself to death. The judge ordered force-feeding, with the comment, "Our society values life." Any right to die apparently conflicts with, and even was overruled by, a value attributed by the judge to our society; it conflicts with deeply held religious values, and these in turn conflict with such social objectives as reducing, for terminally ill people, and for some who can only wish their illness were terminal, the pain, the horror, the loss of dignity, and even the medical expense.

Social objectives, individual rights, and moral and religious values are all involved in the question of whether contraceptive education should be provided in junior high school. The right of children to have knowledge conflicts with the right of parents to deny knowledge or to provide the knowledge in their own fashion; the moral issues in abetting premature sex conflict, for many Americans, with the social objectives of reducing schoolgirl pregnancies, controlling venereal disease, and, most recently, protecting individual children against acquired immune deficiency syndrome (AIDS) and the entire population against an epidemic. And, as is often the case, people disagree about the social objectives themselves or about the efficacy of the proposed program: some believe, or claim to believe, that safer sex—safer against pregnancy, against traditional venereal disease, and against AIDS— may so increase sexual activity as to aggravate, on balance, what the sex education was supposed to ameliorate.

To explore some of the ways that rights, values, and social objectives conflict with one another, this chapter has to be arbitarily selective. Potential candidates for examination are as diverse as genetic engineering, markets for human organs, surrogate motherhood, the terminally ill, homosexual marriage, capital punishment, animal experimentation, and the burning of cigarettes in public. Each raises a different cluster of issues, problems, and values.

This chapter concentrates on just two topics, AIDS and the right to die. AIDS, besides being a hideous contagion, is a case study that generates a stunning set of conflicts among personal rights, moral values, and urgent social objectives: life, health, and medical care; privacy, discrimination, quarantine, and segregation; drug abuse, prostitution, and sexual behavior; and personal and legal obligations to spouses and other sexual partners, to the child that a woman may bear, to schoolmates, and to colleagues at work. Some of these conflicts are quite unfamiliar and unprecedented. The many uncertainties about the origin, nature, and future course of this disease and the rapidity with which popular and expert understanding are changing might be thought to make AIDS an unripe candidate for treatment; alternatively, these characteristics can be construed as one more dimension adding richness to the case.

The right to die is one of the many conflictual issues brought recently into prominence and near-universal interest as a side effect of spectacular advances in medical technology, and by the consequent drastically changing demographic profile of our population. Pneumonia and other violent infections used to perform an often welcome euthanasia that ran afoul of nobody's values or the laws of any state; now the paralyzed victim of stroke can stare vacantly at the ceiling indefinitely with antibiotics and nasal and intravenous tubing to keep that fatal infection at bay. This issue, like syphilis until the *Reader's Digest* lifted the rug off it fifty years ago, is ineluctably going to preoccupy more and more Americans not only as a political, social, and moral issue but as a matter of intimate personal involvement.

## HIV and AIDS

It is hard to imagine a more mischievous, dreadful contagion than the human immunodeficiency virus (HIV). When first diagnosed, the disease was AIDS, and its symptoms were malignancies, infections, and brain damage. Since discovery of the virus—and there may be several forms of the virus—it has made more and more sense to think of the disease as infection with the virus, a condition that is asymptomatic for at least months and usually some years, and to think of AIDS as a fatal end stage of that disease.

The fraction of the HIV-infected population that will eventually manifest AIDS is not yet reliably known, but with every passing year the epidemiological data become more alarming; current estimating procedures indicate that something between 30 percent and 100 percent of HIV infections will ultimately terminate in AIDS. AIDS is not the manifestation of a single disease but a complex of malignancies and infections to which the breakdown of the immune system subjects the victim; but from the time symptoms occur and are diagnosed until the patient dies, there is invariably, besides the awful demoralization that accompanies any terminal illness, a period, often of several months, of exceedingly disagreeable symptoms. Most victims so far have been young, and it is too early in the history of this new disease to know whether aging patients will have a different symptomatic experience or whether those (if there are any) who become infected while young and appear free of symptoms for some decades may display different neurological and immunological disorders as they age.

It is an astounding coincidence that this monstrous virus should appear apparently for the first time in the human race just when two decades of extraordinary scientific progress in genetics and the human immune system have made it possible to identify the nature of the disease and probably to do something about it. Had the disease arrived thirty years in the future it might not have become the threat it is, at least not in the United States; and had it come thirty years ago it could only have stupefied medical scientists, not stimulated them.

The characteristics of the disease, its arrival so recently with unknown origins, and the nature of the virus itself would make HIV medically unique. What makes the disease unique in its proliferation of conflicting rights is a number of insidious characteristics, most but not all of which are probably familiar to the reader:

1. The principal method of transmission of the disease in this country is one or another mode of sexual intercourse.

2. The most effective way to guard against infection during intercourse is to use a condom, which is also a principal way, especially among young people, to guard against pregnancy.

3. For reasons that have to do with the nature of their sexual acts, their high rate of sexual activity, and the multiplicity of sexual partners among certain parts of male homosexual society, the most numerous and prominent victims of AIDS in this country are male homosexuals. That fact has from the outset been widely publicized.

4. The second most prominent mode of transmission is the use of infected secondhand needles; and, in the United States, such use is almost exclusively the intravenous abuse of drugs, mainly heroin.

5. Because of their high rate of sexual activity and multiplicity of partners and because of the prevalence of drug abuse among them, female prostitutes are not only a population at high risk of infection, with a significant infection rate in some parts of the United States, but a population with relatively great capacity for infecting others.

6. The incidence of AIDS among blacks and Hispanics in the United States is significantly higher than among whites, especially for women. (The difference may be due to the greater prevalence of intravenous drug abuse among heterosexual blacks and possibly Hispanics.)

7. Because of the alleged high prevalence not only of sexual activity but of homosexual rape in prison populations, a prevalence that correctional authorities usually prefer not to acknowledge, some convicted criminals are not only at high risk of infection but at risk of forcible infection.

8. Infants born to symptomless mothers infected with HIV are estimated to have a 50 percent likelihood of dying of AIDS not long after birth.

9. Carriers of the virus have no way of knowing their infected status during the protracted period before symptoms are diagnosed unless they undergo laboratory tests (or give birth to a child that shows symptoms).

10. Laboratory tests are imperfect. False *negatives* are especially likely for a few months after infection because the test is for antibodies that are not present in detectable amounts for two or three months after infection. The rate of false *positives*, though perhaps only a fraction of 1 percent, will be for some time large in relation to the true incidence in most of the heterosexual population; at the current estimated prevalence of the virus outside the high-risk groups, one-third of the positive indications of the virus might be erroneous.

11. Among some groups in some parts of the country, there has been an almost hysterical, if understandable, fear of contracting the virus through otherwise innocuous contact with infected people—between dental technicians and their patients, in contact sports, from common tools in the workplace, from toilet seats. The recommendation of the U.S. Public Health Service that dentists and dental technicians wear gloves when they put their fingers in people's mouths is the kind of good advice that will continually sensitize people to the hazards of associating with carriers of the virus.[1]

The incidence of AIDS—the part of the disease that is diagnosable and reportable—has been doubling in not much more than a year, and a projection of that growth rate through just one more decade would suggest a devastating epidemic. There are uncertainty and controversy about how quickly the growing prevalence of the virus in the U.S. population may slow down once the high-risk populations have been saturated, after which a much lower rate of growth among the more heterosexual and monogamous populations will occur, with the possibility of vaccines or cures before the second wave reaches plaguelike proportions. But even so, the number of carriers of the virus in this country is already estimated at a million or two; so even if the growth slows, the inventory of ultimate fatal illness that has already accumulated guarantees not only a dreadful burden of medical costs and human tragedy but a potential for self-defensive panic in large parts of the population.

The potential for discrimination, segregation, privation, and even punishment inherent in this disease and in some popular attitudes toward it has already been manifested: allegations or conjectures of some religious leaders, including black religious leaders, that AIDS is sent by God to punish people who engage in morally despicable practices;[2] reports of public officials (including police) who would willingly see the addicts and the homosexuals (whom they would call by other names) wiped out before the disease is contained; a proposed, but rejected, referendum in California that would have required testing of people in health care, food handling, teaching, and several other occupations and their legal proscription from continued employment if tested positive (and that contained what some observers construed as a veiled authorization to separate them physically, like lepers in earlier times).

To a degree that is hard yet to determine, some countries in Europe and Asia are selectively requiring the testing of tourists and immigrants for AIDS virus. Nations of central Africa have officially complained of discrimination against travelers from that continent. (The incidence of HIV in central Africa has been estimated as high as in the tens of millions and growing rapidly because of a number of blood-contaminating practices that do not occur on the other continents and because of high rates of skin and genital lesions.) The U.S. Public Health Service issued rules, on August 28, 1987, for the testing of immigrants and of any illegal aliens or refugees who desire legal status as citizens, and the denial of such status to all who test positive.

And given the characteristics of the high-risk populations mentioned earlier—homosexuals, prostitutes, drug abusers, blacks, and Hispanics—it is hard to imagine any illness or condition with more abundant potential for discriminatory action. Some of the forms that discrimination may take will presently be examined, partly to identify those that may be socially necessary and even in the interest of carriers of the virus. But besides discrimination there are other invasions or compromises of individual rights that may be on the AIDS agenda.

## Testing

One issue is testing. It is easy to see that there is a collective interest in helping high-risk potential carriers know whether they are carriers, in the expectation that most of those who are will wish to avoid infecting others. A special case is pregnant women; the incidence of AIDS among the offspring of HIV-infected women is being reported at around 30 to 50 percent.

Mandatory testing can be of two kinds. The most benign in terms of individual rights, but unlikely, is mandatory testing with the results available only to the tested persons. Mandatory testing of, say, prison populations, would surely be for the purpose of segregating the carriers from the virus-free.[3] Mandatory testing of military service personnel would almost certainly be for monitoring or limiting the nature of their military service. Mandatory testing of hospital and clinical personnel, licensed dentists, and dental technicians, to say nothing of convicted prostitutes and users of heroin, would almost certainly be for the imposition of restrictions, even if, in some cases, the restrictions might only be suggested for self-imposition.

The question of who gets test results arises even with voluntary testing. Test results may be worth money to employers and others who have legitimate or illegitimate access to the test results. A sensitive issue is whether the spouse of someone who tests positive has a right, or should have a right provided by law, to be informed by the physician or laboratory.

Testing is complicated by the fact, mentioned earlier, that the tests in current use can produce false positives; in populations not especially at risk, false positives is probably a large part of all positive tests. (It is important to keep in mind that in this context "positive" means the presence of HIV antibodies, not that one has "passed" the test.)

Discrimination against, or limits placed on, people who test positive, whether because they are presumed infected or because they are presumed to be homosexuals or drug addicts, while perhaps equally tragic for the infected and for the uninfected, will be a poignantly unjust burden on the latter. Perhaps a worse burden would be just the belief that one were infected; there has been serious controversy over whether American military recruits, subject to mandatory testing, should be informed of the results of their tests. (Obviously there is no way to give the good news to all the negatives and be blandly noncommittal to all positives.)[4]

Understanding the epidemiology of AIDS is severely impaired by lack of evidence about the prevalence of HIV in the population as a whole and in demographic subgroups. Whether the number currently infected is a half-million or upwards of 3 million; whether the current rate of increase is 20 percent or 50 percent per year; whether the increase in the heterosexual population is similar to that in homosexual populations or lower by one or two orders of magnitude; whether the incubation period for AIDS itself differs by age, by sex, by health status, or by medical history; and whether the susceptibility of newborns to infected mothers depends on the progress of the disease in the mothers—all these questions would be much better understood if there could be some HIV counterpart to the National Health Interview Surveys conducted by the National Center for Health Statistics. Just as the federal government can, in principle, require citizens and residents to submit to a decennial census, the government might imaginably draw periodic samples of the population for AIDS testing. The benefits in improved epidemiological understanding of the disease would be immense.

Certainly an important side effect of mandatory testing of any large population, like young men and women being inducted into the military services, especially populations that were not markedly different from the entire population in characteristics pertinent to HIV infection, would be a vast improvement in data about the disease itself and its transmission. There should be no technical difficulty in guaranteeing anonymity of the blood samples if the testing were done for this research purpose. In fact, as has been done for economic reasons with hepatitis at blood donation centers, blood samples could be mixed in batches from several donors and the incidence of HIV estimated fairly accurately from the frequency of HIV-free batches in relation to the number of blood samples per batch.

## Needles

In many states, notably New York, syringes and needles are not for sale to the public. That restriction was intended to frustrate intravenous drug abuse. Needles are durable, easily shared, and needed only briefly when borrowed; and heroin injection is often an activity of pairs and small groups. The principal effect of the ban on fresh needles has probably therefore been the sharing of needles. And until AIDS came along, the danger of hepatitis and a few other diseases transmitted through exchange of blood was probably insufficient to induce great care in the sterilization of needles before each use. Little if anything is known yet about whether shared needles are now, with the danger of AIDS, being regularly sterilized; informed opinion seems to doubt it.

Needles are cheap, and new needles would remove any doubt about sterility compared with needles that may have been flushed or boiled hastily by an impatient addict. So a policy question does arise—and specifically has arisen as a proposed experiment in New York—whether to reestablish the market in needles (or even to distribute needles free!) to facilitate the sterile injection of addictive drugs into a user's veins in order to protect against the transmission of AIDS. This question is something like whether an addict has a right to guard against a lethal infection by consuming the kind of needles that used to be freely available in the marketplace. Like the paraquat that was dumped on Mexican marijuana to spoil the crops and that threatened consumers of any marijuana so treated with lung damage, the denial of clean needles may somewhat impede drug abuse while increasing, perhaps drastically, the hazard to drug abusers.

But, of course, the consequences do not stop there. People who can dredge up no sympathy for a junkie who feeds his habit on stolen goods and who do not even care if the junkie, after becoming infected, infects another one, have to consider that through a concatenation of sexual contacts the larger population has an interest in keeping all these junkies clean.

## Prostitutes

The same issue arises with prostitutes. The two issues overlap, prostitutes having a high incidence of intravenous drug abuse that, because most of their customers are heterosexual, may be their primary connection to the disease. Nevada decided half a century ago to compromise with prostitution—to legalize and regulate it—in the control of venereal disease. A case is now undoubtedly building to permit voluntary testing of prostitutes who can be certified clean or to require testing of prostitutes with certification of cleanliness for those who test negative and harassment of those who test positive.

It will not be easy to put the seal of approval on serum-negative prostitutes without appearing to license their practicing their trade free from harassment. And of course, as with the drug abusers just mentioned, everyone has an interest in the ability of healthy prostitutes to compete against infected prostitutes. The young man who returns home after four years of military service will be the more welcome, the more confident his home town can be that if, as may be likely, he has visited prostitutes near military bases, they were in an HIV-free regime of license and control. But for many among us, this action is compromising a moral principle.

## Safer Sex

A similar moral compromise is involved in combating transmission of HIV by encouraging the practice of safer sex among young people. The objection to teaching safer sex and dispensing condoms in junior high schools in order to limit teenage pregnancy may seem equally applicable to the prevention of teenage HIV infection. Admittedly, there is a danger of overselling the condom, inducing youngsters who might in horror of AIDS have completely abstained from sexual activity to engage freely in "safer sex" that is not completely safe. But if it is decided that promoting condoms among school children is an effective part of the campaign to curtail an HIV epidemic, we have that clash of social policy with moral principles, *both* the moral objection to facilitating teenage sex and the moral objection to the denial of lifesaving information through the schools and through whatever other media may reach the children.

## The Media

The media, print and electronic, are proud of their role in a free society and resist secrecy, censorship, and libel actions, not just in pursuit of their professions but on behalf of the citizens' right to know. The major TV networks have admitted publicly that, in the interest of not offending their family viewers, they refuse to accept condom advertisements or even public service films promoting condoms. When one reflects on the vitality and imagination that have gone into the portrayal of underarm perspiration as a substance capable of devastating social and sexual relations and on how the faithful, fastidious use of deodorants has become so nearly universal, it is wondrous how little has been done to represent teenage pregnancy as capable of devastating the high school careers of young women and to promote the regular and conscientious use of contraceptives. It is similarly remarkable how little has been done— substantially nothing on the major TV channels— to portray AIDS as being worse than underarm perspiration, and condoms as meriting a higher priority in a youngster's budget than deodorant. The First Amendment is for everyone's benefit, not just for the benefit of publishers and broadcasters, who have not been meeting their obligations to us.

## Discrimination

We can distinguish among the different forms that discrimination can take, the different populations that may be the objects of discrimination, and the different populations that may practice the discrimination. And it is important not to assume that discrimination is always "against" its subjects. Giving pregnant women priority in an HIV testing program so that they can abort a doomed fetus, and among pregnant women giving preference to blacks, and among blacks giving preference to drug abusers, can hardly be considered discrimination "against" the target populations. Testing prison populations and segregating the HIV-infected from the uninfected can benefit the uninfected without causing any hardship, inherent in segregation per se, to the infected.

It is too early to assess whether—by publicizing the less fastidious behaviors of particular homosexual communities and making these people appear not only different but dangerous—AIDS will ultimately have reversed the recent progress toward greater acceptance of homosexuals as normal citizens and neighbors and workmates and toward the greater popular interest in defending their civil rights. But at least the potential for reversal of the recent progress is there, and organized homosexuals have at times appeared more concerned to avoid discriminatory action that may be taken against them than to cooperate in the control of AIDS. Attempts to close bathhouses in San Francisco can be interpreted as public health measures to protect the homosexual community or as harassment in the guise of public health.

Homosexuals now have to fear not only the traditional discrimination against homosexuals but also discrimination against people presumed to be carriers of HIV. Because of the prevalence of HIV among homosexuals, proposals for universal testing or even testing of designated populations can be interpreted as precursors to the denial of certain rights of persons found infected. And homosexuals, without testing, can assume that they are statistically much more likely to be identified as targets of whatever action may appeal to anti-AIDS zealots. This leads to the issue of discrimination against people who carry a disease from which they will eventually die.

There is certainly one kind of discrimination toward known carriers of the virus that we can condone. Everyone is better off if the infected and the uninfected abstain from sexual contact with each other, or at least abstain from sex without the most careful safeguards and avoid sexual practices that enhance the risk. Everyone wants the epidemic contained. For the purpose of disease control, the fewer sexual contacts between carriers and noncarriers the better. Even the carriers, for whom it is too late to be saved by segregated sexual contact, know and love people who are not carriers and whom they wish protected from this awful disease. So virtually everybody, carrier and noncarrier, wants to minimize transmission. (Not every infected person will necessarily care enough to forgo all sexual contact with uninfected partners; nevertheless, all can be interested in insulating their not-yet-infected friends and family from infectious contact.)

The general public therefore has an interest in everybody's knowing his or her status, so that the uninfected can confine their sexual relations to other uninfected people or use extreme caution in sexual contact with infected spouses and other partners, and so that the carriers of the virus can confine their sexual contacts as much as is feasible to others who are already carriers and therefore in less or no further danger. (It is not certain whether further harm is done by reinfecting a person who is already carrying HIV.)

It is difficult to think of any experience that prepares us for understanding a segregation as intimate as this. It is redolent, without necessarily having the racist aroma, of the taboos against miscegenation. (And the greater prevalence of HIV among blacks may generate that racist aroma.)

The possibility of mandatory testing of selected populations and regulation of the behavior of those who test positive has been mentioned. That would be official discrimination, and it might be designed and carried out considerately and prudently and in the spirit of good public health practice, somewhat the way children were quarantined with scarlet fever in earlier times. It could also be done exaggeratedly, stridently, inconsiderately, and in a way that added stigma to restrictions.

It is easy to foresee the possibility of unofficial restrictions imposed by pressure from clients, customers, and employers. Dentists and doctors, who normally have diplomas and licenses of all kinds on their office walls, might add in public view a certification of a negative HIV test dated as recently as six months, with similar diplomas for nurses and technicians. If such practice became widespread, the clients might come to expect such displays of HIV-free certification, gradually coercing other dentists and physicians not only to produce documentation of tests but to declare and document that all employees have been tested and found negative. (And doing that would mean that those not found negative had been dismissed.) Barber shops might ostentatiously disinfect scissors, clippers, and razor blades, and, going a step further, announce the availability of documentation for the HIV-negative status of all the barbers. Nursery schools, whose staff may treat minor wounds in which blood contact is possible, may come to find that their customers expect HIV-free documentation. This process will be influenced by the eagerness with which people in such professions and occupations exploit their HIV-free status.

Employers, if not legally free to make a negative test a condition of employment, may let it be understood that they will not ask for test results but will accept them if proffered; they may find excuses to decline to employ anyone who does not volunteer such evidence.

According to press reports, some HIV-free clubs have been formed, members of which carry certified HIV-free IDs used in dating when "exchange of body fluids" is contemplated. There are problems of counterfeit and the limitation that, with current testing, antibodies do not show up in the test for two or three months after infection, so that the most up-to-date negative results only indicate probable absence of infection three months earlier.

## Insurance

The status of HIV testing for purposes of health and life insurance is in a turmoil. Insurance companies argue that with the life insurance or health insurance premiums currently in effect they will lose large amounts of money on terminal care for AIDS patients or early death for the life-insured, unless they can discriminate either by rejecting HIV carriers or by excluding benefits when AIDS is responsible for medical treatment or death.

If everyone were equally at risk of dying prematurely of AIDS and none of us had any way of finding out who was already infected with HIV, the insurance industry could simply adapt to shorter life expectancies and higher terminal-care costs. But what the insurance companies foresee is that people who believe themselves at risk and get tested and test positive will have reason to take out million-dollar life insurance policies. If this happens on a large scale, the problem will be not merely that insurance premiums rise because of higher medical costs and shorter life spans, but that a few million "inside traders" will exploit the system for extravagant policies and short premiums.

As background to this sharply divisive issue of insurance discrimination toward HIV carriers, and AIDS victims, it should be noticed that there is a constitutional issue in relation to insurance discrimination, one that has recently been in flux. The issue is what kind of discrimination insurance companies can legitimately exercise in deciding whom to insure and whom not, what contingencies they can treat as uninsurable and excluded from the contract, and what premiums they can charge different policyholders. The issue arises in two forms, by individual and by class. For the individual it arises in whether one has a history of heart attack, has installed smoke detectors in his house, or has a special lock on the ignition and hood of his Toyota. At the class level it arises in whether one can be denied auto insurance because he is a male driver under twenty-five, whether a woman can be charged less than men of the same age for life insurance (because of women's greater life expectancy), whether people can be denied burglary insurance because they live in a black neighborhood, or whether either a man or a woman can be charged more for life insurance than a person of the same sex five years younger.

Rarely if ever does anyone contest the economic necessity of graduating life insurance premiums with respect to age. The courts have recently determined that retirement annuities, which always discriminate by age, may not discriminate by sex despite the incontrovertible evidence that in this country women on average live much longer than men and that their current mortality statistics reflect this greater life expectancy. Whether or not the legal status of sex discrimination has been finally settled in the courts, evidently sex has recently been treated as a "suspect" criterion, and it is simply improper to discriminate by sex in retirement income. This decision seems independent of whether the annuity rates that did discriminate were actuarially sound: women in the aggregate presumably collected as much retirement income, discounted back to the date of retirement, as the men because they lived longer. The animus against insurance discrimination is bolstered by the strict regulation of insurance in most states and a regulatory philosophy that converts commercial private insurance for some purposes into social insurance.

The philosophy of insurance discrimination went into total uproar as AIDS entered its second half-decade. Insurance commissioners in several states and the District of Columbia ruled that testing for HIV could not be made a condition for life insurance, and a number of companies discontinued selling policies in those jurisdictions. (The clients' "right to be insured" was matched by the companies' "right to go out of business.") In one state the commissioner of insurance resigned in a public dispute with the secretary for health and human resources over the issue of HIV testing for life insurance. Commissioners were struggling with the decision whether or not to let companies write insurance contracts with a clause that excluded death diagnosed as due to AIDS or (as is usually done with suicide) death due to AIDS within some specified short period of years.

The medical or hospice costs of treating AIDS patients, currently estimated at some tens of thousands of dollars per patient, could, of course, be declared a federal responsibility. Obliging health care insurers to enroll people without testing or to accept people who test positive would be an indirect way of putting the financial burden on the insured population, through higher premiums. It would also be exceedingly uneven in that the prevalence of HIV is so much higher in particular localities, like New York, Miami, and San Francisco, than in the rest of the country. (A large part of the currently infected population is in socioeconomic classes that ordinarily are not insured.)

Life insurance is different. Even if federal financing for AIDS victims included some provision for dependents, life insurance companies would probably insist successfully that new policies, especially with large face values, be issued only on HIV documentation (or contingent on a negative test three months after the policy date, to cover the testing lag) or that new policies be issued with an exclusion for death due to AIDS.

Such discrimination has to be considered legitimate, even if one believes there is an overriding social interest in asserting everybody's "right to insure," perhaps at public expense.

Of doubtful legitimacy is the kind of discrimination that insurers (and others who consider themselves especially threatened by HIV carriers) might practice if direct evidence of HIV status were denied. That would be to decline to offer insurance (or employment, or housing, or whatever) to people who appear to belong to any of the highly publicized high-risk populations. There are certain occupations in certain cities in which homosexuals are widely believed, probably correctly, to be heavily represented. With billions of dollars of insurance at stake, extensive investigation into occupational and other correlates of HIV risk would be indicated. Hairdressers, for example, may find it difficult to get life insurance; and to avoid legally the appearance of overt discrimination, insurers might not even accept evidence of heterosexuality. Employers might learn to discriminate in the same way. Thus direct discrimination on the basis of testing may ultimately provide more attractive even—or especially—to the people in high-risk populations than the alternative, covert discrimination against personal qualities associated with a high risk of HIV (particularly where, as in New York, race is a strong correlate of seropositivity).

## Summary

Children with AIDS, denied the right to go to school with their class-mates, regained the right; and telephone workers, refusing to work alongside someone with AIDS, were eventually quieted through authoritative reassurance that ordinary in-school or on-the-job contact would not transmit the disease. Avoidance of physical contact or proximity, up to the point of ostracism, can nevertheless occur.[5]

There is still some mystery in the ways that the disease may be transmitted; not all the cases that have been identified and studied can be explained by sexual contact, needles, contaminated instruments that puncture skin, transfusion of infected blood, or the handling of AIDS patients with open wounds. It is not considered out of the question that other modes of transmission may be discovered; and even if sources of infection yet to be discovered prove to account for only a small percentage of cases, their absolute significance will increase as the seropositive population grows. (A far-fetched hypothesis that has not yet been ruled out, for example, is that head lice, not uncommon among schoolchildren, may move from host to host with infectious blood on their mouth parts.) If the assurances that have been received from reputable sources, like the Centers for Disease Control, should have to be qualified or reversed sometime in the future, there may be a loss of confidence that the authorities know what they are talking about and are telling the truth. People may just not want their infant children near the intensive care unit where an infant born to a woman with AIDS is being monitored; and maybe no reassurance will be acceptable.

There is hope that the rapid spread of HIV that has been observed has mainly been through high-risk populations, that the increase will decelerate as the supply of uninfected in those populations is exhausted, and that further spread will be at the much lower rates of transmission believed likely among the large majority of the population not believed to be particularly at risk. And it is possible that vaccines or therapies may be developed in time to prevent the infection of more than a small proportion of the population in the United States. But if the exponential growth of AIDS should continue, reaching 100,000 new cases per year a few years from now, 200,000 a few years from then, 400,000 a few years from then, and if no wholly reliable vaccine becomes available, large parts of the public may be willing to tolerate—may even demand—the public health equivalent of martial law to cope with the menace.

Mandatory testing of the entire population, holograph ID cards bearing the test results,[6] registries of test results where anyone's status can be ascertained, and the ultimate obscenity—indelible tattoos—might be only the beginning. If the current demographics of AIDS continues, clamor for such identification and the inevitable separation and segregation may be seen as aimed especially at homosexuals and at the black and Hispanic populations.

## The Right To Die

When the hindquarters of my fourteen-year-old dog could no longer support his body, I took him to a veterinarian who injected a couple of CCs of something into his foreleg. Nothing happened for about for about five seconds and the doctor explained that circulation is slow in the elderly. The dog then shuddered, relaxed, and was dead. I suffered no trauma, only envy.

The astonishing advances in medical technology that have, in the past few decades, made it increasingly easy (and costly) to keep people alive in discomfort, indignity, and despair have been paralleled by increasing attention—in the courts, the legislatures, and the press; among professional ethicists; and among patients and their families—to the questions whether, in what circumstances, and by whose decision these life-extending medical procedures might be eschewed. The questions arise similarly but not identically for patients at the beginning of life and for patients who are, or who hope they are, near the end of life.

Everyone who reads this book recognizes the name Karen Ann Quinlan and most will read about more than one judicial decision on the subject within the year. Many older readers have already signed, before witnesses, a "living will." Ten years ago no state had passed any form of living-will legislation; by now more than three-quarters of the states and the District of Columbia have provided some statutory recognition of this modest instrument, endorsing some limited and qualified "right to die."

In order to draw the line, or even to identify the line, that circumscribes this limited right not to be kept alive against one's wishes, it is useful to identify the spectrum of circumstances in which the issue arises and the kinds of acts and omissions that may fall within or beyond the lines. I shall try to list them in increasing order of moral complexity or ambiguity.

## The Dead, the Unconscious, and the Incompetent

The most primitive case involves the question of what constitutes death. Whether a *body* can survive after the *patient* has died is a metaphysical question as well as scientific one. The patient at that stage is no longer concerned, but the patient's "interests" may still be a legitimate consideration—publicity, organ donation, and especially the stress on family members for whom no funeral ceremony can yet help them begin to get over their grief, to say nothing of the expense if the costs are not fully covered. By moving the definition from one of heartbeat and respiration to one of brain activity, some of the patients who might have preferred to claim a right to die in these circumstances can simply be declared already dead.

The next situation worth distinguishing is that of a patient permanently in coma. By no reasonable definition is the patient dead, although many of us in that condition might be happy to be treated as though dead—not fed, not respirated, not administered antibiotics. This is one of the borderline areas that the courts have been struggling with; two crucial aspects have been who has the right or obligation to decide, and how one establishes the wishes of the patient who cannot communicate.

The third stage has been the most difficult of all in this country: that of the patient who is alive but incompetent, neurologically unable to speak or, if able to speak, unable to comprehend, or physically unable to see or to hear or to speak or to write. Unlike comatose patients, these people suffer and their suffering can be terminated only by death. (If they do not manifestly suffer pain and frustration, the question of letting them die does not arise.)

Unlike the comatose, these people can be presumed to have preferences in the matter, although it may be hard to define what "preferences" mean for a person who has thoughts and feelings but perhaps no comprehension of any alternatives. But getting at what the patient would answer if the patient could give an answer; what the patient would decide if he or she could understand the choice; whose testimony counts in that inquiry; and whether the patient's prior testimony as expressed to family, physician, attorney, or pastor, possibly in a signed statement with witnesses, should be determining— these are the questions that have occupied the courts and the professional witnesses who appear in court and those who write on the subject in journals devoted to medicine and ethics.

A question that cannot be pursued here, but one that has been raised by legal and ethical scholars, is whether a formal and unambiguous instruction signed before witnesses and issued to all who may be eventually concerned should be binding. That is, should a competent person have the right to decide in advance for when he or she will be incompetent? Or instead is the right to decide for oneself a right that can never be relinquished? Do prior instructions have only the status of evidence for deciding what the patient in his or her present state would choose if the patient could choose?

## The Competent Patient Who Cannot Die

The fourth stage worth distinguishing is that of the competent patient who would rather die than go on living but cannot die without the passive or active help of people who have been keeping him or her alive. Courts have been of several minds about this in recent years, some ruling that patients have a right not to be "artificially" kept alive by extraordinary and heroic means but that they must be provided nourishment, respiration, and drugs, at least the drugs that do no great violence.

Complications arise, of course, in determining just how competent a patient is; some participants in debate on this subject go so far as to assert that a desire to terminate one's own life is itself evidence of incompetence. The hardest cases are probably those patients who continually express preferences but whose preferences change. Sometimes they plead to be disconnected from life support, other times they appear to welcome it. Sometimes they attempt, when one preference governs, to discredit the contrary expressions that issue from time to time. And even if the patient is unwavering in requesting to bc allowed to die, the people who are reluctant to permit it can always propose that if the ultimate decision is postponed the patient may yet undergo a change of mind.

Court decisions in recent years have been more sympathetic to these patients' wishes, allowing patients the right to be unfed and unrespirated while being treated for terminal pain and discomfort.

To this point the patients discussed are those incapable of taking their own lives. Some of them can try, by yanking tubes from veins and nasal passages, but they are usually at the mercy of people who can immediately replace them. What the patients can request, or what can be requested on their behalf—the removal of some essential part of a life support system—is at the borderline between what is sometimes called "passive euthanasia" and "active euthanasia." The former is usually taken to mean the omission of some life-extending act, the latter the commission of some life-shortening act. The removal or withdrawal of life support is sometimes construed as the commission of a life-shortening act, sometimes as merely a reversion to the nonadministration of life support and identified with omission rather than commission. (It is letting the patient die "naturally," not accelerating death.)

## Unrequested Euthanasia

Euthanasia ("the action of inducing the painless death of a person for reasons assumed to be merciful") that is neither requested by the patient nor otherwise known to be desired is not considered here. Whatever the merits and moral values of painlessly killing someone who wants to stay alive, even if the person clings to life only out of sheer horror of dying itself, there are legal and other practical reasons for leaving this case outside the realm considered here. It deserves and receives attention (and an actual case of a man who shot and killed his hopelessly ailing wife was featured on network television), but euthanasia at the initiative of the killer is better treated here as extenuated homicide and left at that.

## Assisted Suicide and Euthanasia

Finally we come to two actions or circumstances that have to be discussed together. One is euthanasia of the active kind, provided on request; the other is assisted suicide. They have to be discussed together because they are sometimes indistinguishable. (Unassisted suicide in this country is no longer subject to any legal sanction, the "right" being freely exercisable, except in a few important special cases that will be treated later.)

Active euthanasia is exemplified by what my dog experienced. In this country when such an injection is administered to human beings it is murder. It is murder whether or not the patient requests it. Laws could be changed to specify conditions and procedures that would make such euthanasia the legal practice of medicine. Bills are under consideration in a few states that would accomplish this.

The only country in the world in which a terminally ill competent patient can request and receive a physician's assistance in dying is the Netherlands. In that country there are formal procedures intended to assure that the decision is the patient's and that the patient is adequately informed of the nature and prognosis of his illness. The procedure can be done in hospital or at home. And the death-inducing medical procedure can be almost as simple as what my dog received.[7]

Hopelessly ill patients are often incapable of performing their own intravenous injections, but in principle a physician could hand the syringe to the patient who would administer it to himself; or the physician could write a prescription that the spouse could have filled; or the physician could simply advise on a combination of drugs and the best procedures for administration; or the physician could write a column in the health section of a newspaper providing the pertinent information. There is thus a progression from active euthanasia through "assisted suicide" to medically informed but unassisted suicide.

So far only the physical or technological dimension of euthanasia and suicide has been considered. Equally important, though less susceptible to legal restraint and specification, are the several kinds of moral and psychological assistance that patients may need to reach a responsible and informed decision with which they are comfortable, to arrange their affairs with decency and dignity, to reduce the psychological trauma to family and friends, to minimize feelings of guilt among those who participate in the decision, and to protect them from suspicion or accusation of duress or precipitate action.

Because of the criminal sanctions and possible malpractice suits, physicians are exceedingly uneasy about, and usually reluctant to be accomplices in, mercy-suicides, and they are almost always unwilling to acknowledge publicly that they play a role or how they do it. Courts in most jurisdictions have not explored the line that may separate medical advice from complicity in suicide. It is generally assumed that many physicians do try to be of help but discreetly, indirectly, noncommittally.

In the United States, recipes for painless suicide can be published and distributed through the mails. This has been done by the National Hemlock Society. In Britain a similar book by a similar society was not allowed to be commercially sold but could legally be distributed to members of the society upon payment of the society's initiation fee. In France, bootleg copies of such a book have circulated illegally, publication not being allowed.

What has been published in this country makes clear that the direct services of a physician can be important in selecting the drugs to be used. The patient's medical history, including drug history, is pertinent to the selection of appropriate drugs—often a combination of drugs for prompt unconsciousness and drugs for timely death.

There has been remarkably little public discussion of these issues in the United States. What the public thinks about it is interesting. A Roper Poll taken in 1986 inquired whether or not doctors should be allowed by law to end the life of a suffering, terminally ill patient if the patient requests it. The results are surprising! Ten percent of the Americans polled did not know or gave no answer; among the ninety percent who stated that such help should be or should not be allowed, favorable answers outnumbered unfavorable answers by more than two to one, 62 percent answering yes, 27 percent answering no. When the answers were categorized by the religion of the respondent—Protestant, Catholic, Jewish, other, none—the responses in every category were preponderantly favorable, even Catholics favoring such assistance by 59 to 31 percent, 10 percent not answering or not knowing.

Education made little difference: the range of answers from college graduates to respondents who had not finished high school was narrow and more than two to one in favor for each category. Democrats, Republicans, and Independents differed by minuscule amounts, as did "conservatives," "moderates," and "liberals." Responses in the four major geographic areas of the country differed hardly at all. Male and female answers were virtually identical. Least in favor were blacks with 46 percent in favor to 39 percent against and 15 percent expressing no preference. Age made no difference. Income made some difference, respondents with high incomes being more than three to one in favor and those with the lowest incomes not quite two to one in favor. The occupational category in which the responses were least favorable was blue-collar, but even people in that category were more than two to one in favor.[8]

This is a stunning finding—a silent majority that is unlikely to remain silent much longer.

As mentioned earlier, states have been increasingly adopting varying forms of living-will legislation over the past few years. Standard forms for living wills have been available for many years; they have been freely available from Concern for Dying. Living wills and the surrounding issues have been discussed frequently in *The Hastings Center Report*. The typical key statement in such a document is something like the following:

> If the time comes when I can no longer take part in decisions for my own future, let this statement stand as an expression of my wishes and directions, while I am still of sound mind. If at such a time the situation should arise in which there is no reasonable expectation of my recovery from extreme physical or mental disability, I direct that I be allowed to die and not be kept alive by medications, artificial means, or "heroic measures." I do, however, ask that medication be mercifully administered to me to alleviate suffering even though this may shorten my remaining life.

The statement is signed, dated, and witnessed by two persons not of the immediate family. The document may append a list of treatments to be specifically excluded, and may appoint someone to make decisions—a kind of executor.

In most jurisdictions, courts have been responsive to living wills or equivalent prior expressions on the subject by people who are no longer competent. What, then, does the legislation add? Clearly, the legislation gives moral support to those who will be responsible for not administering the proscribed procedures. Legislation can reassure attending physicians and nurses and hospital authorities fearful of damage suits. And a few technical issues, like the applicability of suicide clauses in life insurance policies, can be taken care of by statute. The most important effect, however, is to build an impressive nationwide legislative record in favor of a right to die, a record that will probably encourage efforts to liberalize rights to more active assistance on the part of physicians under appropriate safeguards.

Except for institutionalized persons, the right to unassisted suicide is freely exercised. But as in the case of physician assistance, ambiguity—partly legal, partly moral—surrounds what constitutes illegitimate complicity in suicide. Providing ten grams of Barbital with a chaser of alcohol and Valium to a person who is awake and knows exactly what he or she is drinking and for what purpose may feel to the provider like a merciful assistance to suicide;

injecting an equivalent substance intravenously, especially while the patient sleeps, after full and conclusive discussion by the patient with all appropriately interested parties, may feel more like killing. The difference in feeling may be even more stark when the alternatives are between procuring a handgun and ammunition that the patient can fire into his or her own head, after the helping person has left the room, and firing the shot when the patient lacks the physical strength or dexterity to handle the weapon or, more tantalizingly, lacks the nerve.

## The Institutionalized

When people are arrested and jailed, they typically surrender anything with which they could hang or cut themselves, even their eyeglass lenses. The law does not recognize the prisoners' right to die by suicide. The justification is unclear, aside from the avoidance of embarrassment to the custodians (or accusations of murder). But nationwide the incidence of suicide in jail is high, and for many people the psychological trauma of sudden incarceration might be feared to produce a transient despondency that could lead to an act of suicide that, were it prevented, the prisoner would ultimately be glad to have been spared.

A final important category of patients whose "right to die" is typically not acknowledged is one so complex that it can be only mentioned briefly here. I once asked the dean of a school of public health which classes of medical patients—emphysema, bone cancer, phantom limb syndrome, stroke-induced paralysis—he thought the most wretched and the best candidates for assisted easy termination of life. His answer was prompt and unequivocal—people in state mental institutions. Some of these people are "incompetent" in the full sense, unable to hang or cut themselves or even to appreciate that a suicide option might be available. Others are sufficiently competent to cut, strangle, or bash themselves to death without assistance, as long as they are not restrained or denied the simple instruments for taking their lives. To prevent exactly that they are denied cords or belts or pointed or sharp-edged instruments of any kind; sometimes they are physically restrained and sometimes they are kept in padded rooms. In a legal sense it has been determined that they are incompetent to make the decisions for themselves, even if they are competent to carry out those decisions.

And what most starkly distinguishes these patients from the ones to whom living wills are typically applicable, or from those whose expressed preferences for death may be acknowledged, is that they are *not* terminally ill. Wretched, hopeless, they can be kept alive for decades by the most ordinary means. These institutions may ultimately be the ugliest and most difficult arena in which to attempt to define an appropriate right to die.

## Guns and Doctors

A poignant statistic relates the right to die to the right to bear arms. A study of 743 deaths from gunshot in the Seattle area of Kings County, Washington, from 1978 to 1983, found that 333 of these deaths were suicides.[9] In the nation as a whole, according to Joseph Fletcher, 57 percent of suicides are accomplished by gunshot. According to Fletcher,

> The plain fact is that those who plan self-deliverance, usually for reasons of broken health, find that it is often extremely difficult to get drugs in lethal forms or quantities, and that suffocation may be awkward and too open to interference (for example, monoxide in closed garages). Gunshot, on the other hand, is quick, solitary, simple. Booklets advising people of ways and means to self-deliverance by methods other than gunshot have been published...but the average run of people, at least to date, have found their recommendations sophisticated and difficult to carry out. Guns, especially pistols, are much more familiar and available.[10]

Dr. Pieter V. Admiraal, who has participated in patient-requested euthanasia in the Netherlands, once closed an address with the words:

> Let me then end here, by submitting to you my sincere hope that already the next generation will be profoundly puzzled by the length of time our generation has taken to come to the unconditional acceptance of euthanasia as a recognized, natural human right.[11]

The argument is powerful but not absolutely compelling. The Netherlands is not the United States. There are strategic considerations that need to be carefully examined.

Some rights bring responsibilities and verge on obligations. The "right" of seventeen-year-olds to volunteer in wartime can subject them to a sense of obligation. The right to early retirement can be construed as an obligation of older workers to get out and clear the way for younger people. The right to depart this world at least raises the question for dying persons whether the decent thing to do might be to discontinue being a burden, an annoyance, an expense, and a source of anxiety to the people caring for the dying person. One's terminal disability is a burden shared with one's spouse as long as no alternative is available; it is a burden of which the spouse can be relieved if the option of dying is known to be available. And it is an option that can preoccupy both of them, whether or not there is any immediate intention of taking advantage of it.

If a man could die and relieve his wife of the burden and the expense, how could the wife persuade him she truly wanted him to live? Saying so, repeatedly, may only demonstrate awareness of the option and remind him of it. If the man's survival gains him a few years of life of exceedingly low quality and condemns his wife to the same when she could have been free had he exercised his right to go, and a friend feels this keenly, how does the friend perceive the obligation to the wife, including the obligation to respect what the wife believes to be her own obligations? How does the man manage his guilt upon awakening every morning, knowing he is spoiling another day of her life? And how does he evaluate the guilt she will feel if he takes his life for her sake?

These are real, not just rhetorical questions. Procedures and safeguards will have to be devised, and the medical conditions in which assisted dying is a legitimate option appropriately circumscribed, so that these nagging questions can be dealt with.

The issues are not only legal and strategic, they are psychological and political. Legislative efforts to replace a fuzzy area in which some right to die is ambiguously perceived by a clear line that deliberately enlarges the area may only push that fuzzy borderline farther outward. Thoughts and feelings on the subject may be pushed various distances in different directions in ways that are hard to foretell.

The line between abortion and infanticide may exist primarily in people's minds and feelings, not just in the science of neurology or in court-interpreted statutes. The same may be true of the line between freely undertaken, mercifully assisted suicide and something that invites an uglier name.

NOTES TO CHAPTER 8

1. In a Louis Harris poll, 31 percent of respondents thought a child could get the disease by sitting in a classroom with an AIDS victim; 31 percent thought it could be caught by eating in a restaurant where an AIDS victim was also eating; 30 percent thought it could be contracted by breathing too close to an AIDS victim; 35 percent thought it could be transmitted by being in the same hospital with an AIDS victim; 37 percent thought it could be contracted by working side by side with someone with AIDS; 45 percent thought it could be transmitted by inhaling the air expelled by sneezes and coughs of an AIDS victim; and 44 percent thought it could be caught by living in the same house with an AIDS victim. Harris emphasizes the nearly two-to-one majority that did not believe these things and concluded, "the essentially sober reaction and lack of panic among the public was reflected in the 80 to 17 percent majority who firmly said that AIDS victims should *not* be treated as lepers." (Emphasis in the original.) I am appalled that a full 17 percent apparently believed that AIDS victims *should* be treated as lepers. Louis Harris, *Inside America* (New York: Vintage Books, 1987).

2. Forty-two percent of the respondents to a Gallup Poll agreed with the statement, "I sometimes think that AIDS is a punishment for the decline in moral standards" (*New York Times*, National Edition, August 30, 1987, 12.)

3. The Associated Press (AP) reported October 23, 1987, that the Bureau of Prisons would immediately begin segregating federal inmates who tested positive for the AIDS virus and who displayed "predatory or promiscuous behavior," as announced by the Justice Department the day before. That announcement coincided, according to the AP, with the bureau's release of

statistics showing that nearly 500 prison inmates, about 3 percent of those tested under a pilot program in the federal prison system, had tested positive for the AIDS virus.

4. The problem of what are known as Type One and Type Two errors, false positives and false negatives, is a general one. In medicine the "sensitivity" of any test for the presence of some infection is measured by the relative infrequency of false negatives among the infected population, and the "specificity" by the infrequency of false positives in the uninfected population. In many contexts the possibility of false positives or false negatives is of serious concern aside from the mere "error" involved, and often the consequences of false negatives and false positives are quite asymmetrical. Courtroom and jury procedures have to reflect a compromise between the twin errors of convicting an innocent person and letting the guilty go free. In the recent controversy over the use of polygraphs in business and government, objections to delving into a person's mind and memory have rested not only on the invasion of privacy itself but on the damage that can be done to a person who is wrongly accused, wrongly judged, wrongly labeled, and wrongly denied employment. The victim of a polygraph false positive may suffer both denial and stigma; the victim of an AIDS false positive may suffer denial, stigma, and the appalling possibility that the test result may be true.

5. Three HIV-infected hemophiliac youngsters, ages eight, nine, and ten, were barred from school by the school board of Arcadia, Florida; separate rooms were proposed but refused; a suit by the parents led to a court order to admit the boys. There ensued a school boycott, bomb threats, and a fire that consumed the children's home and all its contents and severely injured a member of the family who, with help, escaped. (*New York Times*, August 31, 1987, 1.)

6. Sixty percent of the respondents in a Gallup Poll agreed with the statement, "People with the AIDS virus should be made to carry a card to this effect"; 24 percent disagreed. (An implication is that everyone should be tested.) (*New York Times*, National Edition, August 30, 1987, 12.)

7. Dr. Pieter V. Admiraal, "Active Voluntary Euthanasia," *Hemlock Quarterly*, no. 21 (October 1985):3–6.

8. *Hemlock Quarterly*, no. 24 (July 1986):2–3. Harris, *Inside America*, 154–58, reports similar responses to similar questions going back to 1973. On whether it was right "to give a patient who is terminally ill, with no cure in sight, the right to tell the patient's doctor to put the patient out of his or her misery," the percentage answering yes was only 37 in 1973 and was 61 by 1985. Those opposed declined from 53 to 36 percent over the twelve-year period.

9. Arthur L. Kellerman, M.D., and Donald T. Reay, M.D., "Protection or Peril," *New England Journal of Medicine* 314, no. 24 (June 12, 1986):1557–60.

10. Joseph Fletcher, "Guns and Suicide: A Personal Opinion," *Hemlock Quarterly*, no. 24 (July 1986):8.

11. Admiraal, "Active Voluntary Euthanasia," 6.

CHAPTER 9

# FISCAL CHOICES

Joseph J. Minarik
Rudolph G. Penner

The federal budget deficit is like a debilitating disease. It has weakened government's ability to undertake important initiatives, and it has inspired increased dishonesty in the budget process as policymakers resort to accounting tricks and off-budget initiatives to minimize the problem artificially. The inability to deal effectively with the deficit has shaken the confidence of Americans and foreign observers in the ability of the United States to manage its own affairs.

If left untreated, the deficit disease could become very painful. Thus far the pain has been mitigated by the willingness of international lenders to supply the United States with relatively low-cost credit to finance both a private spending binge and public dissaving. But in 1987 international investors became disenchanted with U.S. policy and demanded higher risk premiums for a smaller supply of funds. If this disenchantment grows into a capital flight from the United States, the shock to the U.S. economy could be severe indeed.

The problem is that the cure for the disease is also painful. Policymakers have already accepted considerable pain to contain deficit growth. Taxes have been raised significantly and nondefense spending has been constrained since 1981. But these actions, however courageous, were not sufficient to put the deficit on a rapid enough downward path, and there is much more to be done.

Choosing a future course of action necessarily involves subjective judgments. What government functions should be cut? Who should pay increased

279

taxes? What are the economic effects of spending cuts and tax increases of different types? In this chapter, the authors suggest a variety of cures for the problem, all involving pain. Even so, they do not yield the full amount of deficit reduction that is desired.

These cures will not be popular, and no one set of options is clearly superior to all others. But if these suggestions provoke further suggestions, the analysis will have succeeded. It is reasonable to demand, however, that the debate be carried out with considerable specificity. Generalized claims that the United States is overspending or is undertaxed are vapid without supporting detail. One statement can be made with assurance. There is no free lunch out there. Anyone making that claim should be viewed with extreme suspicion.

## Background

It is difficult to know where to begin in explaining the fiscal crisis of the 1980s. Obviously, the bulk of the damage was done in 1981 when the military build-up was accelerated, taxes were cut substantially, and neither the administration nor the Congress had detailed plans to cut nondefense spending sufficiently to compensate.

However, hints of problems to come can be found as soon as the late 1960s and early 1970s. At first sight, it appears paradoxical to start the analysis at that time. Between 1968 and 1973 total federal spending was cut relative to gross national product (GNP); and so was the deficit, because the total tax burden remained almost constant. But at that time the composition of spending and taxes changed significantly—and the effects have bedeviled the nation ever since. Spending for the Vietnam War peaked in 1968, when defense reached 9.6 percent of the GNP. It then fell rapidly, to 6 percent by 1973. Some of this peace dividend was used to cut the deficit from 3.0 to 1.2 percent of the GNP, but a significant proportion was indirectly used to finance a series of increases in Social Security benefits, culminating in a 20 percent increase in 1972 when benefits were also indexed for the first time, and to finance the growth of the relatively new Medicare program. Nominally, the growth in Social Security and Medicare was financed by increases in earmarked payroll taxes, but the overall tax burden was held relatively constant by cutting other taxes.

In essence, a massive long-term commitment of resources was made to the elderly and disabled, and this commitment was initially financed by cutting the military—a source of funds that was bound to disappear in short order. Defense spending reached its trough relative to GNP in fiscal 1979 at 4.7 percent. By the late 1970s, however, U.S. military readiness was widely believed to be inadequate, and President Carter responded to this broad consensus and to crises in Iran and Afghanistan by greatly expanding defense spending. The conflict between defense and the now solidly built-in growth of nondefense spending suddenly became more apparent than it had been earlier. The problem was resolved at first by allowing inflation to raise personal and corporate income taxes, through bracket creep and as a result of the erosion of depreciation deductions and the taxation of phantom capital gains on inventories. The federal tax burden neared 20 percent of the GNP by 1980, a level not seen since the Vietnam War surtax of the late 1960s.

In the late 1970s tax revolts broke out at the state and local levels, significantly influencing the 1980 presidential election. Both candidates promised tax cuts, but candidate Reagan promised cuts far exceeding those promised by Carter. Reagan also promised to accelerate the Carter defense build-up; and although Reagan asked for some domestic spending cuts, his additional promise of a balanced budget by 1984 could be satisfied only if the economy grew miraculously and if the Congress implemented further, as yet unspecified, domestic spending cuts in the future. With such economic growth and further spending cuts, the final Reagan plan in the spring of 1981 promised to balance the budget by 1984 with spending and receipts equal to 19 percent of the GNP.

Not only did the growth miracle not occur, but the nation confronted a deep recession in 1981–82. Inflation slowed much faster than most economists had expected, and some of the Reagan tax cuts that had been planned originally to prevent inflation-induced tax increases became real tax cuts instead. The combination of recession and deflation sent the nation's tax burden falling toward 17 percent of the GNP rather than the 19 percent that Reagan promised. Despite some small cuts in benefits, entitlement spending rose because of the depressed economy, and the resulting record-breaking deficits pushed the interest bill on the national debt from 2 percent of the GNP in 1980 to 3 percent by 1984 and 3.3 percent in 1986.

By late 1982, the deficit threatened to explode because of soaring debt-servicing costs. Over the next four years, the Congress struggled mightily to contain the problem, enacting four significant tax increases—the Tax Equity and Fiscal Responsibility Act of 1982 (largely a measure to broaden the income tax base), gas and payroll taxes in 1983, and the Deficit Reduction Act of 1984 (which further broadened the tax base). These major efforts brought the tax burden to 18.4 percent of the GNP in 1986, lower than the president's original goal of 19 percent for 1984. However, under current law, the burden should creep above 19 percent in 1987 and beyond.

The Congress also attacked the spending side of the budget. It cut nondefense discretionary spending from 5.8 percent of GNP in 1980 to 4.1 percent by 1986, a level not seen since the early 1960s. Reforms in welfare, Social Security, Medicare, Medicaid, and unemployment insurance trimmed these entitlements, but the built-in growth is such that the entitlements grew slightly faster than GNP, increasing from 10.5 percent of GNP in 1980 to a peak of 12.1 percent during the recession of 1982 and holding at 11 percent in 1986. Finally, the military build-up was halted in 1986, and that, too, greatly improved the spending outlook. Despite these efforts, 1986 ended with a record deficit of $221 billion.

The Congress and the administration negotiated a two-year budget-reduction package late in 1987. However, that package was designed at best to forestall the automatic sequestration process under the Gramm-Rudman-Hollings deficit-reduction legislation. Many of the outlay cuts and tax increases in the agreement involve asset transactions and changes in the timing of outlays and receipts, and so do not improve the deficit outlook in the longer run. The provisions that truly reduce the long-term deficit are woefully inadequate by the scale of the long-term deficit gap. Although the cumulative effect of the post-1981 legislation is to put the deficit on a slowly declining path, no one is satisfied with the outlook.

## The Budget Outlook

Estimates of future deficits are notoriously volatile. Of course, the deficit is not really what is forecast; two much larger numbers, outlays and receipts, are forecast, and the deficit is the difference. In 1988, pre-agreement outlays were expected to be $1,080 billion, receipts $897 billion, and the deficit $183 billion.[1] Thus, a 1 percent error in forecasting outlays plus an opposite 1 percent error in forecasting receipts implies more than a 10 percent error in forecasting the deficit. Errors of 1 percent in forecasting a year ahead are less than average, and so errors that economists consider to be statistically insignificant become matters of great importance to politicians and policymakers. Putting the matter another way, an underestimate of the 1988 deficit by $10 billion is trivial compared with the usual forecast error, but cutting programs or raising taxes by $10 billion is a significant political event and may make the difference between a politician's winning and losing an election. These errors grow geometrically as the forecast horizon is lengthened; and the opportunities for cheating expand, because it is impossible to say with certainty that an optimistic forecast will not materialize. The inability to forecast deficits with the accuracy required by politicians has been the Achilles' heel of the budget process. Still, rational planning requires a forecast, because without one there is no way of estimating future budget totals.

## Deficit Estimates

The CBO estimates of current policy revenues, outlays, and deficits through fiscal 1992 are shown in table 9.1.[2] The deficit estimates show a peculiar pattern. The deficit peaks at $192 billion in 1989 and then falls to approximately the 1987 level by 1992. These numbers obscure the true underlying budget trends—the 1987 deficit is not so good as it seems and the 1989 deficit is not so bad. The former has been artificially lowered by two factors. When confronted by the Gramm-Rudman-Hollings deficit goal for 1987, the Congress made some real efforts to comply but soon tired of virtue and resorted to accounting tricks to finish the job. For example, the military payday was shifted from the last day of fiscal 1987 to the first day of fiscal 1988. Tricks of this type, and one-time sales of government assets, accounted for $14 billion of "savings" in 1987, some of which will show up as higher outlays later. In addition, tax reform had the effect of pulling revenues forward, in part because taxpayers were encouraged to take capital gains in calendar 1986 before tax rates went up. The revenue surge related to tax reform is about $20 billion. If the figures were adjusted for tax reform and timing tricks, the true deficit would amount to about $192 billion in 1987, $172 billion in 1988, and $154 billion in 1992.

Thus the true deficit was higher than it seemed in 1987 but is on a slow downward path in the longer run. The true deficit in 1992 amounts to 2.5 percent of the GNP, a number that would have seemed very high in any peacetime growth year before the mid-1970s but is much lower than the average of 3.9 percent since that time.

The downward drift of the deficit is not surprising given the definition of current policy, which holds about 45 percent of spending constant in real terms (28 percent in defense and 17 percent in nondefense discretionary). The rest of the budget—entitlements and interest—is assumed to grow at about the rate of growth of the economy. Thus, the definition of current policy and the economic assumption of real growth guarantee that total spending

TABLE 9.1

CONGRESSIONAL BUDGET OFFICE CURRENT POLICY ESTIMATES,
FISCAL YEARS 1987–92

| Item | 1987 | 1988 | 1989 | 1990 | 1991 | 1992 |
|------|------|------|------|------|------|------|
| Revenues | 853 | 897 | 954 | 1,036 | 1,115 | 1,195 |
| Outlays | 1,010 | 1,080 | 1,146 | 1,212 | 1,280 | 1,345 |
| Deficit | 157 | 183 | 192 | 176 | 165 | 151 |

SOURCE: Congressional Budget Office, *The Economic and Budget Outlook: An Update* (Washington, D.C.: U.S. Government Printing Office, August 1987), 47.

must grow more slowly than the economy. Because under constant law revenues grow a bit faster than the economy (in part because of the progressive income tax), the deficit outlook cannot help improving.

Consequently, current policy estimates are highly artificial and cannot be considered to be a forecast, because actual policy is bound to deviate from what is assumed. The CBO projections therefore represent only a convenient starting point for a discussion of the effects of possible policy changes.

## The Sensitivity of the Estimates

The budget is highly sensitive to a host of economic and other variables (see table 9.2 for the economic assumptions underlying the forecast). The state of the economy determines the level of receipts, the interest bill on the debt, payments for welfare and unemployment insurance, cost-of-living adjustments (COLAs) in pension plans, and so on. Although the state of the economy may determine the number of people eligible for welfare or unemployment insurance, it is always difficult to forecast the proportion of persons eligible who will actually apply for benefits. Even if the economic forecast is correct, estimated agricultural subsidies may be quite wrong, for example, because the implicit weather forecast is incorrect—and the number of earthquakes must be forecast correctly if the estimate of disaster assistance payments is to be accurate.

The sensitivity of budget estimates to errors in economic forecasting is illustrated in table 9.3.[3] A major recession starting early in the projection period could easily push the deficit above $250 billion, whereas a return of

TABLE 9.2

CONGRESSIONAL BUDGET OFFICE ECONOMIC ASSUMPTIONS,
CALENDAR YEARS 1987–92

| Economic Assumption | Actual | Projections | | | | | |
|---|---|---|---|---|---|---|---|
| | 1986 | 1987 | 1988 | 1989 | 1990 | 1991 | 1992 |
| Nominal GNP | 4,235 | 4,486 | 4,797 | 5,119 | 5,464 | 5,843 | 6,234 |
| Real GNP change (%) | 2.9 | 2.6 | 2.7 | 2.6 | 2.7 | 2.7 | 2.7 |
| CPI-W[a] change (%) | 1.6 | 3.8 | 5.2 | 4.8 | 4.4 | 4.4 | 4.4 |
| Unemployment rate (civilian) | 7.0 | 6.3 | 6.1 | 6.0 | 5.9 | 5.8 | 5.7 |
| Three-month Treasury bill rate | 6.0 | 5.9 | 6.6 | 5.8 | 5.7 | 5.7 | 5.7 |

SOURCE: Congressional Budget Office, *Economic and Budget Outlook: An Update*, (Washington, D.C.: U.S. Government Printing Office, 1987), 38.
[a]This represents the Consumer Price Index for Urban Wage Earners and Clerical Workers.

TABLE 9.3

EFFECTS ON CONGRESSIONAL BUDGET OFFICE BASELINE BUDGET PROJECTIONS OF
SELECTED CHANGES IN ECONOMIC ASSUMPTIONS, FISCAL YEARS 1987–92

| *Economic Variable* | *1987* | *1988* | *1989* | *1990* | *1991* | *1992* |
|---|---|---|---|---|---|---|
| Real growth: effect of one percentage-point higher annual rate beginning January 1987 | | | | | | |
| Change in revenues | 4 | 14 | 27 | 43 | 61 | 83 |
| Change in outlays | −1 | −3 | −6 | −10 | −15 | −22 |
| Change in deficit | −5 | −16 | −33 | −52 | −76 | −105 |
| Unemployment: effect of one percentage-point lower annual rate beginning January 1987 | | | | | | |
| Change in revenues | 19 | 30 | 31 | 34 | 36 | 37 |
| Change in outlays | −3 | −6 | −8 | −11 | −14 | −17 |
| Change in deficit | −22 | −36 | −40 | −45 | −50 | −54 |
| Interest rates: effect of one percentage-point higher annual rates beginning January 1987 | | | | | | |
| Change in revenues | 0 | 0 | 0 | 0 | 0 | 0 |
| Change in outlays | 3 | 11 | 16 | 20 | 23 | 26 |
| Change in deficit | 3 | 11 | 16 | 20 | 23 | 26 |
| Inflation: effect of one percentage-point higher annual rate beginning January 1987 | | | | | | |
| Change in revenues | 5 | 14 | 27 | 39 | 53 | 70 |
| Change in outlays | 3 | 15 | 26 | 38 | 51 | 64 |
| Change in deficit | −2 | ([a]) | ([a]) | ([a]) | −2 | −6 |

SOURCE: Congressional Budget Office, *Economic and Budget Outlook: Fiscal Years 1988–1992.*
(Washington, D.C.: U.S. Government Printing Office, 1987), 53.
NOTE: Totals include Social Security, which is off-budget.
[a] Less than $500 million.

the growth rates experienced in the 1960s could provide a budget surplus by 1992.

Clearly the range of possibilities is very wide, but planning should be based on the most realistic scenario; and the CBO baseline probably provides the most useful starting point for thinking about the budget problem. By historical standards, it is almost certain that there will be a recession within the next five years, which is not explicitly recognized by the CBO baseline; but the recovery from that recession should proceed at a pace far greater than the average long-run growth rate assumed by CBO. Hence the average long-run current policy deficits estimated by CBO are likely to be more accurate than the estimate for any one year. Nevertheless, it must be remembered that the uncertainties are enormous.

## The Policy Impasse

CBO's deficit projections suggest that, given the tax increases and spending cuts of the last few years, it is now theoretically possible to grow our way out of the deficit problem if we wait long enough and never change any policies. But that is not practical. There will constantly be pressures for new spending and for new tax incentives. Moreover, the public debt that accumulates while we wait for growth to lower the deficit creates numerous economic risks—including the risk that the required growth will never materialize. The deficit has so far not reduced living standards as much as it might have because of our ability to borrow in international capital markets. But if international investors do not see evidence of future deficit reduction, they will demand higher and higher risk premiums for lending to the United States, and the consequent rise in U.S. interest rates will crowd out more domestic capital formation, thereby raising the cost of the deficit to future generations. If such a loss of confidence were sudden, interest rates might skyrocket, plunging the country into a recession. The higher interest rates would not only choke off economic growth, they would also drive up the deficit. The events of October 1987 make it easy to conjure up such a frightening scenario.

Furthermore, if no action is taken, there is little room for responding to either international or domestic crises. If a major defense spending increase were required, the deficit could again become explosive as the growing interest bill on the national debt began to feed upon itself. Similar results could ensue from a serious health crisis, such as the one that may be caused by acquired immune deficiency syndrome (AIDS), or by a hundred other contingencies. It is important that our budget policies provide some margin for maneuvering to contend with such eventualities. Thus, for both economic and policy reasons, the deficit should be reduced more rapidly than the CBO projections imply. There is a broad political consensus in favor of reduction, but there is no consensus about how it should be done.

On the surface, the political impasse appears to be between the president and the Congress, but that impasse has its roots in the ambivalent and somewhat inconsistent desires of the American electorate. There are clear signs that the political pendulum is beginning a slow leftward shift and the American people, although still quite conservative, are again beginning to demand a more activist government on domestic issues.[4] The administration has joined in by proposing a major expansion of Medicare, which has since been broadened in the House of Representatives. Public opinion polls show growing support for initiatives of this type as well as for increased spending on education and other domestic programs. At the state and local levels, which provided the first signs of the swing to the right with the tax revolts of the late 1970s, spending has been rising, and state and local tax burdens relative to GNP are back up to where they were before the tax revolts lowered them— and they will probably surpass those levels this year.

The public seems more and more sympathetic to increased nondefense spending but not yet antagonistic enough toward defense to reduce total spending. At the same time, there seems to be little willingness to pay higher taxes. It appears as though the public does not understand arithmetic, and that may be true, but more seriously, the public seems to lack understanding about where budget funds go and what sorts of actions would be required to correct the deficit problem. There is a widespread belief that the deficit can be cured by cutting programs that the public does not like, such as foreign aid, while avoiding tax increases and maintaining popular programs, such as Social Security. As cumbersome as they may be, however, our democratic procedures do seem to ensure that most of our money will be spent on popular programs, whereas more controversial expenditures, although not eliminated altogether, are severely constrained. Thus, foreign aid amounts to less than 1.5 percent of the budget (and therefore cannot provide much further help in curing the deficit), while Social Security amounts to 20 percent of outlays. The public must acquire more knowledge of the type of policy changes that can provide meaningful deficit reductions, and it is to that goal that the rest of this chapter is devoted.

## Choosing a Deficit Goal

For most of U.S. economic history there has been a strong belief that the budget should be balanced. That belief has acted as a restraint on government and, with exceptions during wars and recessions, the budget has been for the most part balanced or has run considerable surpluses. The Keynesian revolution of the 1930s removed the intellectual justification for a balanced budget; economic theory provided a rationale for using variations in surpluses or deficits to manipulate the economy in the short run. Then in the early 1980s, supply-side economists argued that tax rate cuts produced more, rather than less, revenue. Because deficits are politically easier to run than surpluses, there was a strong bias—for Keynesian or supply-side reasons— toward arguing that the economy required stimulation; and therefore there was a strong bias toward deficits.

Intellectual attitudes toward deficits in the long run also changed. Although an interest in stabilizing the economy led economists to call for short-run deficits and surpluses, an interest in long-run growth led some economists to argue for greater surpluses as one means of augmenting national savings. Others responded that future generations, who will be richer because of real economic growth, need no special sacrifice from current generations, who are correspondingly less well off. The issue was further confounded by those who pointed out that deficits are not measured correctly by government accounting techniques. Scholars have suggested adjustments for inflation, for government assets, for contingent liabilities represented by loan guarantees and pensions, and for a host of other variables.[5] Thus, a consensus grew among economists that balanced budgets, as we measure them, were rarely optimum, and so the government lost the disciplining force of the old balanced-budget myth.

Discipline could be restored if a widely supported deficit or surplus target could be defined under a specific set of circumstances, for then there would be strong political pressures to design tax and spending policy to fit that target. But although most economists might agree that a continually balanced budget is wrong, they do not agree at any specific time about what deficit or surplus is right. Consequently, government operates with no specific and widely accepted budget constraint, and the deficit has been on an upward trend since World War II.

There are, however, some general standards that would probably gain the support of the vast majority of economists. First, most would agree that current deficits are too high in view of the facts that the country is relatively prosperous and the world is relatively peaceful. Second, most also would agree that the deficit should not be reduced too fast for fear of pushing the economy into recession. The definition of "too fast" is controversial, but few would protest a reduction in the structural deficit equal to 1 percent of the GNP per year. Third, most economists would support reducing the deficit to a level that implies a declining debt-to-GNP ratio, so that, in the longer run, the interest bill absorbs a steadily lower share of our incomes. A significant decline would now require a deficit less than $130 billion—a target too ambitious to make in one year, but one that is certainly feasible in two years.

The new version of Gramm-Rudman-Hollings adopts the traditional goal of a balanced overall budget for the federal government by 1993. It is hoped that the discipline implied by that goal can restore fiscal sanity, although the intellectual justification for the goal has withered.

A strong intellectual case can be made for being more ambitious. The twenty-first century will bring a mass of new retirees, and, in preparation, government should be running a surplus to expand the economy's capacity to pay their retirement benefits. Indeed, the Social Security system is projected to run in surplus over the next thirty years or so, to accumulate reserves against its obligations after about the year 2020 (see chapter 6 of this volume). For that accumulation to have any economic meaning, the rest of the federal government must not run a deficit and thereby implicitly offset the Social Security surplus; in other words, the budget of the non-Social Security part of the government (that is, not including Social Security benefits or tax revenues) should be balanced. This argument implies that the projected Social Security surplus is somehow correct—which could only be true by accident— but the projected surplus may be useful as a crude indicator of where we should be heading. Hence, according to the CBO assumptions, the goal for 1992 should be an overall (Social Security plus the rest of the government) surplus of $69 billion (equal to the projected Social Security surplus), or 1.1 percent of the GNP—a swing of 3.6 percentage points from the deficit level implied by current policy. If carried out over five years, this change would pose no risk of disrupting the economy, but, as will become apparent later, it requires such dramatic changes on the spending and tax sides of the budget that most observers would consider the goal totally implausible politically.

It is, moreover, a net change. If any room is to be made for new initiatives, such as those suggested elsewhere in this volume, the combination of spending cuts or tax increases from current policy would have to exceed 3.6 percent of the GNP.

It should be reemphasized that the choice of a target is as much a function of political values as it is of economic theory; it is largely a decision on the allocation of resources among generations. Moreover, the method by which the target is reached is also important. Deficit reduction achieved by cutting public capital formation would not be long lasting, and therefore would not be very helpful. Conversely, reforms that slowed entitlement growth might look very attractive in the long run even though their short-run effect on the deficit was minute. Because the main reason for deficit reduction is to increase long-term growth, it is, obviously, undesirable to achieve it with tax increases or spending cuts that significantly impede economic growth.

## Budget Strategy

In attempting to reduce the deficit significantly by altering spending, it is crucial to recognize that most federal spending is for very few items. In fiscal 1987, defense accounted for 28 percent of net outlays. Social Security constituted about 20 percent of the budget, and other pensions—mainly military, civil service, and Supplemental Security Income (SSI)—about 6 percent.

(Roughly, one-half of military and civil service pensions were offset by employee contributions classified as offsetting receipts.) Medicare amounted to 8 percent of the budget and interest on the debt 13 percent. Because the net cost of these program categories constitutes approximately 70 percent of spending, it is hard to see a significant reduction in the spending path without program cuts in defense, Social Security, or Medicare. Interest is the result of other program decisions, and military and civil service pensions have so recently been reformed that further important changes in the next five years are unlikely.

On the tax side, more than 90 percent of receipts come from three sources—personal and corporate income taxes and payroll taxes. Inasmuch as payroll taxes (35 percent of the total) are determined largely by spending policy, it is hard to imagine significantly increasing the take from existing taxes without raising personal or corporate tax burdens. Of course, new tax sources could be considered, and that possibility is discussed later in detail.

An infinite variety of combinations of program cuts and revenue increases could be used to achieve any given deficit goal. Indeed, that is one of many barriers standing in the way of resolving the budget problem: there are so many choices that it is hard to get a majority behind any one of them. The authors have, in the following sections, selected only a small portion of the total universe of possible options for discussion. We recognize that the choices are largely value-laden, tempered only slightly by what we know about their economic effects. The intent is not to claim that our choice of deficit reductions is any better than any other citizen's. The goal is to illustrate that two economists not far from the center of the ideological spectrum can arrive at a balanced budget only with some fairly radical—and many people would say politically implausible—changes in tax and spending policy.

## Spending Options

**Defense.** Formulating the defense budget requires long-term planning. Weapons systems require a long development period, and the decisions made today have important implications for the nature of the U.S. military establishment in the first decade of the next century. Under these circumstances, planning would be much more efficient if the nation were willing to make a long-term commitment to a steady rate of growth of defense budget authority. Unfortunately, such a commitment is lacking, and defense spending seems to go through periodic phases of rapid expansion followed by sharp retrenchments.

It is, of course, natural for defense spending to soar during wars, as it did during the Korean and Vietnam wars, but there was also a rapid expansion during the Kennedy administration followed by a pre-Vietnam War cut; and more recently, the United States launched the most rapid expansion in its peacetime history, followed by absolute cuts in real spending in 1986 and 1987 (see figure 9.1).

Such feasts and famines tend to result in imbalanced forces. For example, equipment ordered during the build-up phase is now being delivered. That equipment has to be manned and maintained, and there are strong upward pressures on the operations and support budget just as the overall budget is cut. Defense policymakers have the choice between skimping on readiness or greatly reducing procurement. Because canceling weapons systems is always extremely difficult politically, the reduction of procurement means that the production of weapons is stretched out again and again to the point that economies of scale are lost and weapons are produced at highly uneconomic rates.

The instability in defense policy is partly the result of being unable to provide an objective answer to the question, How much is enough? At a superficial level, defense is often debated with reference to the rate of real growth of budget authority for defense or the share of GNP devoted to defense compared with the share at some earlier point in history. But neither measure can really indicate "adequate" or "inadequate" defense. President Carter was believed to have made a major defense commitment when, after the post-Vietnam War drought in spending, he along with the other NATO allies promised 3 percent real growth in defense spending. But it was not long before some experts argued that 5 percent was required. President Reagan and the Congress raised the ante further and enacted rates of growth of budget authority exceeding 9 percent per year in the 1981–84 period. In 1985, the build-up was slowed and in 1986 and 1987 it was reversed, bringing the average rate of growth close to 5 percent thus far in the Reagan administration (see figure 9.2).

Clearly, the threat to U.S. safety cannot have fluctuated so violently as U.S. attitudes toward defense spending have fluctuated thus far in the 1980s. But having said that, it is not easy to develop an analytic framework that would allow anybody to judge whether the initial build-up was misguided or whether the recent cuts are misguided.

The defense debate proceeds at different levels, and all are difficult to analyze. First, there is a contentious debate about what the U.S. foreign policy goals should be and about the nature of the threats facing the country. Second, even if the threats could be clearly described and analyzed, which they cannot be, it is clear that there is no practical level of spending that can guarantee complete strategic deterrence or absolute certainty that the United States would prevail in any conceivable conventional conflict. Consequently, it is necessary

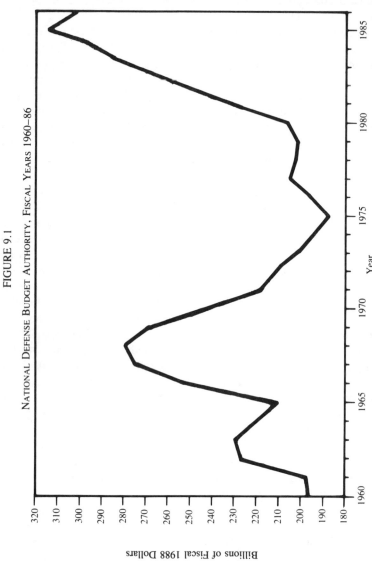

FIGURE 9.1

NATIONAL DEFENSE BUDGET AUTHORITY, FISCAL YEARS 1960–86

Billions of Fiscal 1988 Dollars

Year

SOURCE: Office of the Assistant Secretary of Defense (Comptroller), *National Defense Budget Estimates for Fiscal Year 1988–89* (Washington, D.C.: U.S. Government Printing Office, May 1987).

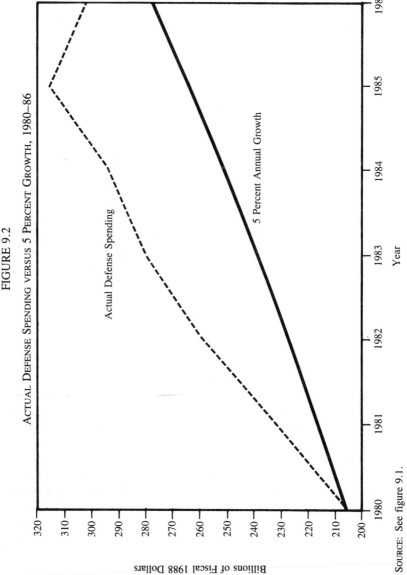

FIGURE 9.2

ACTUAL DEFENSE SPENDING VERSUS 5 PERCENT GROWTH, 1980–86

SOURCE: See figure 9.1.

to take risks, and even if everyone agrees on the nature of the threat, there can be profound disagreement about how much risk taking is wise. Third, there can be a vehement debate about whether any given level of defense spending is allocated efficiently to minimize risk or whether risk levels can be further reduced with a different allocation of spending.

This analysis starts by assuming that it is unrealistic to contemplate a significant change in U.S. foreign policy within the next five years. Given the number of lives at stake, it also would be undesirable to lower defense spending in a way that would, given U.S. foreign policy, significantly raise the risks of a nuclear exchange or a conventional war. The question then becomes whether it is possible to cut total defense spending while rearranging it in a way that would either leave current risk levels unchanged or actually lower them. Once the question is posed in this way, it is apparent that large percentage cuts in defense are ruled out, but, given the large size of the defense budget, small percentage cuts can imply significant deficit reduction or allow large percentage increases in other programs.

When the question is analyzed in this way, the problem of maintaining the current level of U.S. strategic deterrence is usually separated from the problem of reducing the risk of losing a conventional war, whether it is a major war in Europe with the Soviets or a minor war elsewhere against the Soviets, Soviet proxies, or some unrelated adversary. However, there is always a danger that the side that starts losing a conventional war will launch a nuclear attack. A deterrent must be designed to be effective under such crisis circumstances. This possibility is an additional good reason, if any more are required, for lowering the risk of a conventional war.

Although the development of highly accurate strategic weapons allows some planners to contemplate a limited nuclear exchange, U.S. forces must be designed to deter a massive attack. Strategic deterrence is based on the doctrine of mutually assured destruction. That means that if one side launched a first strike, the other would have enough surviving warheads to inflict an unacceptably devastating attack in return. The administration wants to modernize U.S. strategic forces by acquiring mobile Midgetman missiles, acquiring fifty rail-mounted MX missiles, deploying twenty Trident submarines equipped with Trident II or D-5 missiles, and by eventually producing a Stealth manned bomber and a Stealth cruise missile. Furthermore, it wishes to develop a defense against nuclear attack by spending rapidly growing amounts on research and development for its strategic defense initiative (SDI).

Many analysts argue that some or all of the costs of modernization are not necessary to maintain an effective deterrent. Indeed, some analysts go further and argue that some of the administration plans, notably the full development of SDI into a space-based defensive system, are destabilizing, in that the Soviets may be tempted to launch a first strike in a crisis because of the fear that the United States would have the capability greatly to diminish the power of a Soviet second strike.[6] Nevertheless, many analysts who worry about the vulnerability of U.S. ground-based missiles propose some modernization plus a ground-based SDI system designed to afford some protection against incoming missiles for vital U.S. installations. Such an approach would cost less than the administration's budget but would still achieve considerable modernization. For example, Joshua Epstein suggests canceling the Midgetman, freezing SDI spending at current levels, halting further MX procurement (and leaving the existing missiles in their silos, rather than pursuing a mobile basing system), slowing the development of the Stealth bomber, and canceling the antisatellite program.[7] This package would reduce the administration's request for budget authority by $8.3 billion in 1988 and $10.2 billion in 1989. Outlays would be reduced $2.2 billion in 1988 and $5.4 billion in 1989. The savings are relatively small because strategic forces absorb a relatively small portion of the defense budget, by some definitions less than 15 percent of the total.

Analyses of the current U.S. ability to wage a conventional war raise at least as many uncertainties as analyses of the U.S. strategic posture. Although considerable resources are devoted to preparing for contingencies around the world, such as the recent allocation of a large naval force to the Persian Gulf, the overriding long-run concern remains the possibility of a conventional Soviet attack on Western Europe.

Various experts disagree about where to start an analysis of this contingency because they disagree about how to assess the relative strengths of the adversaries at present. Generally, the question involves the Warsaw Pact's quantitative superiority versus NATO's qualitative superiority—plus the inherent advantages accruing to defensive as opposed to aggressor forces. But no one really knows whether the Soviet satellites would remain loyal in such a conflict, what the role of the French would be on the side of NATO, or how a thousand other contingencies would play out. Moreover, it is not necessary for either side to have overwhelming superiority in order to deter a conventional war. Suppose the Soviets thought that they had a 70 percent chance of winning. Would they take a 30 percent chance of losing? Would they take the chance that the war would go nuclear as NATO faced a conventional defeat?

Basically, there is a huge gray area that allows respectable experts to argue highly divergent positions. Some would like a huge build-up of conventional forces so that there is little doubt about NATO superiority. At the other extreme some think it safe to withdraw some NATO forces from Europe.

One important element in the complex crosscurrents in the debate, however, is the role of the navy. Its plan to have the capability to project power and to attack the Soviet homeland is particularly expensive, highly questionable, and perhaps very risky. If the navy took a more defensive posture and eliminated two carrier groups and other ships from the administration's request, it would be possible to make a meaningful increase in the less glamorous army defensive capabilities. Nonetheless, this approach would probably require curtailing naval deployments in peacetime, because the reduced number of carrier groups would allow fewer to be at sea at any one time.

Epstein has worked out the budget implications of such a strategy. He would strengthen NATO ground forces slightly by withdrawing resources from the pool devoted to non-European contingencies. He would weaken airlift capabilities and strengthen sealift. He would significantly cut navy procurement of ships and air force purchases of planes while strengthening low-tech defenses against tanks and planes within NATO. His package cuts the administration's request for budget authority for conventional forces by $13.9 billion in 1988 and by $14.9 billion in 1989. The resultant outlay savings in the two years are $4.8 and $9.4 billion.[8]

Putting Epstein's strategic and conventional recommendations together would cut real budget authority by 4.3 percent in 1988 but increase it by 2.5 percent in 1989 (as additional low-tech expenditures, including manpower, are authorized), leaving him only 2 percent below CBO's current policy amounts (which imply constant real budget authority) in the latter year. It is revealing and somewhat sobering that a fairly harsh critic of the Pentagon, although cutting the president's budget significantly, finds it so difficult to cut the current policy budget within the context of our current foreign policy and strategic stance.

Moreover, some experts reject Epstein's contention that his budget cuts and smaller program increases would actually reduce risks by making our forces more effective. Others who believe that the Soviet threat is greatly exaggerated might argue for considerably less modernization of our strategic and conventional forces. It is extremely difficult for nonexperts to judge the issue.

The Epstein critique of the president's budget focuses largely on the president's proposed investments in new weapons and modernization, but the operations and support budget may deserve a more thorough scrubbing. Military readiness and sustainability were so generally agreed to have reached a sorry state in the late 1970s that massive amounts were spent to correct the situation during our current build-up. The result might be considered one of the great successes of recent defense budgeting. There is no doubt that the quality of personnel and their morale have been greatly enhanced by higher pay and a well-managed recruiting effort. Although readiness and sustainability are much more difficult to measure, virtually all uniformed officers believe that the capability of the forces has been greatly enhanced in the 1980s. But did the country go too far in reaction to the situation in the late 1970s? Perhaps a somewhat lower quality of personnel is acceptable, and perhaps less could be spent on training, maintenance, and inventories of spare parts, weapons, and ammunition. Large amounts could be saved by reducing the size of the armed forces to 1982 levels, reducing the rate of pay increases, and reducing other readiness expenditures.

This line of argument is unlikely to gain much support from military experts. High-quality sophisticated weapons require high-quality people to operate them. If the issue in a European conflict is our quality versus Soviet quantity, it would seem risky to contemplate reductions in our quality. Although some reductions in operations and support may be possible, the authors, admittedly military amateurs, feel more comfortable searching for savings in the procurement budget. This leaves us with the type of approach advocated by Epstein and fairly modest reductions from current policy spending totals.

Clearly, it is very expensive to sustain the current U.S. foreign policy with commitments virtually around the globe. Policymakers frequently enunciate the hope the U.S. allies can be persuaded to share more of the burden, but the incentives are all wrong. As long as they are convinced that Americans believe that it is in the U.S. interest to defend Western Europe and the Western Pacific, countries such as West Germany, Japan, and South Korea will be reluctant to increase greatly their own commitment of national resources to defense. If the United States were so bold as to actually withdraw its forces— and doing that would save little or no money if they were maintained in the United States—other countries might step into the breach. But that possibility raises the more profound question as to whether long-run stability would be well served if there were several other major military powers in the world.

Another hope is strategic arms control, but it is difficult to negotiate an agreement that saves significant resources. A reduction in strategic arms will probably increase demands for conventional forces, and they are vastly more expensive. Moreover, it is difficult to negotiate a loophole-free agreement. For example, if a treaty treats bombers more leniently than missiles, there will be strong pressures for both sides to build more bombers. If the pressures to spend more on conventional forces and to exploit loopholes can be resisted, there could be substantial saving from the administration's request in that there would be fewer strategic forces to modernize; but the saving from current policy would be much less, because the current policy baseline does not allow for much modernization anyway, and because strategic expenditures are small relative to other expenditures.

If strategic arms limitations could be followed by a treaty limiting conventional arms, the prospects for significant savings would be much brighter. But, as our long-lasting discussions with the Soviets in Vienna illustrate, formidable problems face the negotiators. Nevertheless, it is something to hope for, even if it cannot be given high probability for the purposes of this analysis.

In assessing the defense budget, it is also necessary to admit that achieving optimization is extremely difficult. Long ago Eisenhower warned of the power of the special interest groups fostered by the military-industrial complex. That power is evident whenever there is an attempt to close an obsolete military base in the United States or to cancel a weapons system that shows signs of being ineffective. It is hard to admit that some waste is inevitable and obviously it should be fought with every device available, but in the end, perfection is likely to elude the policymaker, and military dollars will not be spent with utmost efficiency any more than civilian dollars will be so spent.

It is difficult to draw firm conclusions in this discussion. The horrors of nuclear war or even of modern conventional warfare are so extreme to contemplate that unemotional discussion seems almost impossible. Yet, it is essential to take a hard look at the dilemmas presented. All sides should be ready to agree that wild swings in the rate of growth of defense spending breed much inefficiency. A more stable commitment to a given defense effort is much to be desired. But at what level should that commitment be made?

Given the nature of the risks involved, it would be irresponsible casually to advocate substantial cuts. The Epstein budget projects spending at 2 percent below current policy budget authority in 1989. Epstein provides no detailed analysis of the implications of his strategy for the early 1990s, and, of course, any look that far ahead requires assumptions about the defense spending policies of potential adversaries. If no significant changes in their attitudes are assumed, it seems difficult to contemplate anything more than a 2 percent cut in budget authority by 1992 in the absence of significant reductions in manpower and the amorphous "readiness" category. Given that an Epstein type of strategy would focus cuts on investment in the intervening years, that approach might yield a 3 percent cut in outlays by that time. That does not sound like much, but it amounts to $10.4 billion—only 0.2 percent of the GNP, but more than 25 percent of the entire federal current policy budget for education, employment and training, and social services.

The budget agreement between the president and the Congress, signed on November 20, 1987, would result in a fiscal 1989 defense budget slightly lower than that implied by the Epstein strategy. However, the requisite cuts may, to some degree, involve a further stretching-out of procurement, or, in other words, may not involve a fundamental change in defense policy. Some of the spending cuts may, therefore, be susceptible to being reversed in future years.

**Social Security.** Social Security is undoubtedly one of the most politically popular programs ever invented by government. It is also, by no accident, the largest nondefense program—constituting almost 30 percent of nondefense spending.

Because Social Security is so popular, policymakers find it extremely difficult to advocate money-saving reforms. The possibility of cutting Social Security evokes the strongest of emotions, and people proposing the most minor changes are often accused of destroying the integrity of the system.

Moreover, there are constraints on reform other than emotional ones. While on average (as documented in chapter 6) the elderly are becoming rapidly more affluent and by some measures are now better off than the rest of the population, a considerable proportion are still below the poverty line and a disproportionate number are clustered just above the line. Concern for the poor and the near poor inhibits consideration of any across-the-board cuts. Even some elderly persons who are significantly above the poverty line feel highly insecure financially because of the risk of encountering expensive health problems. Those who are more secure financially have nevertheless considered Social Security an integral part of their retirement planning and would not look kindly on surprise cuts. Indeed, it might be argued that there is a moral contract to keep Social Security largely constant.

But moral contracts should be subject to renegotiation, just as ordinary contracts are when surprises create a need for change. The fall in birthrates and slower-than-expected economic growth created a need for reform in 1983, and it might be argued that further reform is essential in view of the financial plight of the federal government. It is true that the Social Security trust fund is experiencing surpluses, but that should not rule out consideration of reductions in benefits, perhaps comparable reductions in payroll tax rates and comparable increases in other taxes to reduce the deficit for the rest of the government.

Nevertheless, the existence of a moral contract suggests that any reform should be phased in gradually; as a result, the immediate deficit reduction will be very small. But if the burden implied by Social Security can be reduced in the long run, the case for immediate deficit reduction becomes less pressing.

Concern for the poor and near poor suggests that any reform should focus on changing the benefits received by the more affluent. As described in chapter 6 this can be accomplished by putting a higher proportion of benefits into the tax base or by lowering the replacement rate (the ratio of benefits to average real lifetime wages) for more affluent recipients.

The formula that determines benefits for newly retired workers provides replacement rates that fall as lifetime earnings enjoyed by the recipients rise. The indexing of the formula is designed to keep replacement rates constant over time for each successive cohort of retirees at the same *relative* point in the income distribution. For example, workers earning the average wage over their lifetime will enjoy the same replacement rate as the average worker retiring earlier, even though economic growth will have raised average lifetime earnings in the interim. Instead, Social Security might provide an absolute floor for retirement income: replacement rates could be allowed to fall as society became more affluent and more retirees surpassed that absolute floor. A compromise position would allow the average real benefit to rise, but not so fast as average living standards; that is, the average replacement rate would be allowed to fall very gradually. Because the benefit reduction would be gradual, active workers would have sufficient time to adjust their retirement planning; current retirees would not be affected at all, nor would the very poor who would continue to enjoy current replacement rates.

The slow phase-in, however, implies virtually no budget saving the first year, very little saving five years hence, but a budget saving that compounds through time and reaches massive proportions two and three decades in the future. Such a reform could be designed to save 0.6 percent of the GNP by the year 2020, while reducing real benefits by only about 10 percent. It could, however, be combined with increased taxation of benefits in the near term to save $15 billion or 0.2 percent of GNP by 1992.[9]

Much more radical reforms of Social Security have been suggested, but they seem totally implausible politically. Some analysts have suggested letting current workers opt out of the system but forcing them to save sufficient amounts to provide for their own retirement. This would either place a double burden on the current working population (who would still have to finance benefits for those currently retired while contributing to their own retirement) or it would greatly increase the budget deficit by leaving current benefits unfunded. Note that a slow reduction in replacement rates would partially achieve the same goal desired by proponents of this radical reform; lower replacement rates should induce future retirees to save more for their own retirement voluntarily.

**Medicare.** Medicare is also an extremely popular program. Because of the aging of the population and the increased relative price of health services, the costs of the program have far outrun the rate of growth of GNP over the past decade. Yet the program does not cover some health services of grave concern to the populace: a true medical catastrophe will exhaust Medicare benefits, and there is no coverage of nursing home costs. Medicaid will cover such items, but only after the recipients have spent their way into poverty.

But despite the difficulty of qualifying for Medicaid, a rapidly growing proportion of the Medicaid budget is being used for the elderly, and as this process continues, the nonelderly poor are bound to suffer.

Because the current situation is highly unsatisfactory, the administration has proposed increasing the coverage for catastrophic events; the Congress has expanded the administration's program to the point that the administration may veto it. However, neither the administration nor the Congress contemplates covering nursing home care because of the immense potential cost of such coverage. But demands for such coverage will intensify, and it is clear that political pressures over the next decade will be strongly in favor of increasing the total Medicare budget rather than reducing it.

It is still possible to consider reforms to reduce the federal cost of current coverage. Two basic strategies are available. The providers of health care can be paid less for their services, or recipients can be made to pay a higher share of total costs, either on a means-tested or non-means-tested basis. The two strategies are not totally unrelated. Reductions in the compensation of providers often lead to increases in the fees that recipients pay themselves. For example, a recent reform in the way that hospitals are paid—the diagnosis-related groups (DRG) system—hoped to improve the efficiency of providers by, among other things, shortening hospital stays. It seems to have been successful, but hospitals have, in response, found it necessary to increase their daily fee; and because the deductible under Medicare equals one day's fee, costs to recipients have gone up.

In support of further restraints on payments to providers, it can be noted that health care costs in general and the incomes of health care professionals in particular tend to be considerably higher in the United States than those in countries that have national health plans, such as Canada and Britain. The United States spends considerably more of its GNP on health costs, even though governments in those countries provide free services to a much higher proportion of their populations.

The Congressional Budget Office has described some options in the current Medicare program[10] that could save considerably more than $15 billion annually by 1992 by reducing provider payments and increasing recipient contributions. A target cut might be $15 billion, with $10 billion coming directly from providers and $5 billion from recipients. As noted previously, such a policy would undoubtedly raise recipients' costs more than $5 billion, because providers would be able to pass along some of their losses to patients.

Lowering hospital fees under the DRG system would reduce payments to providers by $6 billion. Such a reduction could be justified on the ground that hospitals have recently been operating with increased efficiency, but the government would thereby seem to be penalizing hospitals for becoming more efficient. About $3 billion could be saved by promulgating a fee schedule that would slow the growth in physicians' compensation. Another $1 billion could be saved by lowering federal subsidies for medical education and capital expenditures by hospitals.

About $5 billion could be raised from recipients by raising Supplemental Medical Insurance (SMI) premiums. Although premium increases could be income-related (and this might make the increase more politically palatable), it should be recalled that the previous section advocated income-related cuts in Social Security benefits. As one income-related reform is piled on another and the tax-transfer system becomes more and more progressive, the cumulative effect is to reduce incentives to save and to work.

**Other Entitlements.** Social Security and Medicare outlays constituted almost 60 percent of total entitlement payments in 1987, and their share is expected to grow to almost 65 percent by 1992. Means-tested or welfare programs absorbed 15 percent of total entitlement spending in 1987, and their share is expected to remain approximately constant through 1992. Such programs were cut somewhat in the early 1980s and although further plausible cuts could be identified,[11] their effects on budget totals would be so small that they are not discussed here.

About 10 percent of entitlement outlays goes to military and civil service pensions. Those programs have recently been significantly reformed, and there is a strong case for leaving them stable for the next five years. It should always be deemed permissible to reopen the public employees' implicit labor contract, but some reasonable limit should be placed on the frequency with which pension rights should be changed.

Farm price supports constitute less than 6 percent of total entitlement spending, and their share is expected to decline substantially by 1992 because of the lower price and income support payments implied by recent legislation. Both short- and long-term projections of subsidy costs are notoriously inaccurate, however, and it is possible that agricultural subsidies will be more expensive or considerably cheaper than implied by recent estimates.

The long-term outlook for American agriculture is not optimistic, particularly if countries such as China and the Soviet Union succeed in boosting productivity by providing their farmers with more reasonable economic incentives. Large subsidies paid to farmers in other Western countries also worsen the plight of the American farmer, just as our subsidies hurt their farmers in a mutually destructive competition.

The subsidy system cries out for reform. Hard bargaining is needed with U.S. competitors, particularly in the Common Market, to achieve a more rational system and to reduce the burden on taxpayers. In the United States, there are strong arguments for moving away from price supports and toward income support and adjustment assistance for the large number of farmers who will inevitably be forced out of agriculture in coming years. It can be argued that the government bears no special responsibility to the agricultural sector, especially in light of how generous government has been, and that, as the sector shrinks, participants should be left to rely on the same social insurance system provided for other displaced workers in our basically free-market system. But that course is impractical, given the disproportionate political power possessed by the farm sector. It may be somewhat immoral as well; because the government was primarily responsible for fostering overinvestment in agriculture; hence the government should ease the transition to a more rational system.

By intensely pursuing international bargaining, as difficult as it may be, and by moving the U.S. system away from price supports and toward income support and adjustment assistance, it should be possible to cut agricultural subsidies by about one-third by 1992. This would save about $6 billion or 0.1 percent of the GNP.

In dealing with agriculture, it is always tempting to resort to production controls. This moves costs off-budget, but, if successful, it imposes a severe burden on the consumer and necessitates a system of import controls and export subsidies. In the long run it is clearly the most inefficient and destructive approach to the farm problem.

**Nondefense Discretionary Spending.** Domestic discretionary spending accounted for 17 percent of net outlays in 1987 and has been most severely affected by the budgetary constraint of the 1980s. It peaked at 5.8 percent of the GNP in 1980 but by 1987 had fallen to 3.8 percent, lower than the levels prevailing in the early 1960s. Within this category, grants to state and local governments have been cut most severely. In real dollars, grants not related to entitlements were cut by one-third between 1978 and 1987.

Past stringency does not, of course, imply that there is no room for further cutting. In this era when there is great reluctance to contemplate federal tax increases, state and local taxpayers seem more prepared to shoulder a greater burden because of a greater trust in the operation of state and local governments.[12] Therefore, it may make considerable sense to continue to give state and local governments more financial responsibility for the services that they provide. State and local voters may be in a better position to decide whether the services are worth the tax burden that they impose. The disadvantage of this philosophy is that services in which there is a national interest may be underprovided. In our current grant system, however, the federal share of costs is often so high that it must exceed any conceivable national interest in the service being offered; in the usual case, most of the benefits of a program accrue to the residents of the jurisdiction managing it.

The problem can be approached in one of two ways: federal cost shares can be radically reduced, or the grant program can be ended altogether. In some cases such as water and transportation grants, states and localities could finance some of the added burden by levying user fees. Other grants that deserve critical examination include community development block grants, Economic Development Administration and urban development action grants (which often succeed only in helping localities compete against each other to attract businesses), sewage treatment grants, untargeted elementary and secondary education grants, and heat conservation grants.

A number of nongrant transportation-related activities—including the air traffic control system and the inland waterways—could be considered for privatization. If privatization is considered unthinkable, much greater reliance could be placed on user fees. Other activities such as subsidies to Amtrak could be considered for substantial cuts.

The rest of the nondefense discretionary category covers diverse activities ranging from space exploration to the agricultural extension service. It also includes some fundamental functions of government such as the maintenance of law and order, which even the most conservative observer would be reluctant to cut.

A draconian approach to the grants and other dubious federal government activities explicitly mentioned above might yield $10 billion in saving in 1992 or an amount equal to 0.2 percent of the GNP.

**Summary of Budget Cuts.** Many of the cuts just discussed will be considered politically implausible, and others may be viewed as unwise for substantive reasons. A few critics may believe that the measures proposed here are not tough enough and that much more could be done by radically altering the role of the federal government in American society. However, the goal here is to be as tough as possible without going beyond the bounds of mainstream thinking—as the authors understand it—in the Congress and in the public at large. It may be argued that any cut in Social Security violates mainstream thinking, but some unthinkable cuts must become thinkable, or the country is left with an unthinkable deficit or an unthinkable tax burden.

As it is, not much progress was made toward reducing the deficit by cutting the spending side of the budget. The cuts described earlier for 1992 amounted to $10 billion in defense, $15 billion in Social Security, $15 billion in Medicare, $6 billion in agriculture, and $10 billion in nondefense discretionary spending. The total is $56 billion. If these cuts were implemented, the deficit would be lower, less public debt would be issued, and the interest bill on the debt would be lowered. The exact amount of the savings in interest would depend on how the cuts were phased in over time, but if they were phased in fairly rapidly, indirect savings in interest could amount to about $15 billion. Then total outlays would be cut by $71 billion or by about 1.2 percent of the GNP. If nothing else were done and CBO economic assumptions proved accurate, the resulting deficit would amount to 1.3 percent of the GNP, which many people would find quite acceptable. But the deficit—excluding Social Security revenues and benefits—would be 2.4 percent of the GNP, an amount that would, in peacetime, have been viewed as fiscal irresponsibility during most of our economic history.

**The Off-Budget Problem.** As noted earlier, a comprehensive analysis of the deficit problem would focus on the problems related to measuring the deficit and correcting it for inflation, changes in the values of government assets, and contingent liabilities. This was not done here because such problems, although important, would have little effect on the theme of this analysis. However, there is a problem that requires discussion because it is likely to get much worse in the next few years under the pressures of budget stringency and legislation (such as Gramm-Rudman-Hollings) that sets rigid targets for "the deficit" as now defined: pressures to move government activities off-budget will increase.

Already, this tendency has manifested itself in the recent initiative to bail out the Federal Savings and Loan Insurance Corporation (FSLIC). That bail-out will be done by a nominally private shadow corporation whose borrowing activities will not be considered part of the deficit. In fact, its initial contributions to FSLIC will be counted as offsetting receipts, and in the very short run it will appear to reduce the deficit. The federal government will not bear any explicit responsibility for the shadow corporation's debt, but buyers of that debt will rightly assume that if the corporation gets into trouble, there is a high probability that the federal government will bail it out. Thus the liabilities of the corporation will be a good substitute for federal debt, and the activity will have economic effects similar to an increase in the measured deficit.

A somewhat different approach is being taken to bail out the farm credit system, but the end result will be similar. New debt will be issued that will be regarded as being similar to federal debt, although it will probably not be counted as such.

Other more subtle devices are likely to be considered. As already mentioned, there is some interest in reducing the budget costs of farm subsidies by imposing production controls, which would raise the prices for food to consumers. The added burden would not be defined as a tax in the government accounts, but the omission of the program from the budget would not lower its cost to the American economy.

Another initiative would mandate that employers provide health benefits to their workers not now covered by insurance. This requirement is like increasing the payroll tax, but, again, it will never appear as such in the budget.

To the extent that off-budget initiatives reduce private saving or increase the long-term contingent liabilities of the government, the target for deficit reduction should be made more ambitious but it is hard to forecast where such initiatives might lead, and it is often conceptually difficult to estimate their economic effects.

## Taxation

No politicians like to raise taxes, but given the imperative of bringing the budget into line, tax increases must provide what spending cuts do not. The spending cuts just discussed would seem draconian to many people, and yet they have failed to balance the overall budget. Unless even greater spending reductions can be found, significant tax increases will be necessary.

**Recent History.** Since the end of the Korean War, federal revenues have generally hovered around 18 percent of GNP, with perhaps a slight upward trend (see figure 9.3). Revenues were higher during the Vietnam War, when inflation accelerated and the president and the Congress sought to contain it with an income tax surtax, and again at the beginning of the 1980s, when rapid inflation pushed taxpayers into higher tax rate brackets and expanded revenues. Given the urgency of a war effort, the earlier peak was probably easier to accept, at least for a time. The level of taxation in 1980 appears to have been less acceptable, and had at least some influence on the outcome of the presidential election and the enactment of the large tax cuts in 1981. The resistance to a tax increase today may arise from a concern that the nation may again be climbing that 1981 peak.

A revealing breakdown of the trend in revenues is the split between Social Security and other taxes. As figure 9.3 also shows, the slight upward trend in total revenues is largely the result of a strong upward trend in revenues for Social Security. If Social Security is excluded, federal revenues have declined steadily from roughly 16 percent of GNP in the 1950s to about 12 percent (although the downward trend does show the same relative peaks in 1969 and 1981).

This distinction between Social Security and other revenues raises two important questions. If the Social Security system is really not a part of the

FIGURE 9.3

TAXES BY TYPE AS A PERCENTAGE OF GNP, 1955–87

SOURCE: *Historical Tables, Budget of the United States Government, 1988* (Washington, D.C.: U.S. Government Printing Office, 1987), table 15.3.

budget deficit problem, as many people (including the president) maintain, then should Social Security revenues not be separated from general revenues in deciding whether taxes are too high or too low and whether a tax increase would be appropriate? Should the distinct downward trend in revenues exclusive of Social Security lead to reconsideration of a tax increase at this time? Conversely, if increases in Social Security benefits and taxes reduce people's ability and willingness to pay other taxes, this question must be asked explicitly: What spending priorities other than those enumerated earlier should be sacrificed to make room for the continuous Social Security increases of recent years? And what further priorities should be cut in the early part of the next century, when Social Security will expand dramatically as a share of GNP? Must policymakers drastically rethink the role of the federal government in other areas to accommodate the inevitable expansion of Social Security?

There are some other distinct trends evident in figure 9.3. Corporate income taxes have declined dramatically, both because the law has changed and because corporate profits have declined relative to GNP. The relative decline in corporate profits stems mainly from rising interest rates and a shift in corporate finance toward more debt; as a result, interest liabilities have increased and taxable corporate profits have decreased. About one-third of the decline in corporate taxes since the mid-1950s will be reversed, however, as the Tax Reform Act of 1986 shifts tax liabilities from individuals to corporations. An equal percentage decline, though from a smaller base, has occurred in excise taxes (the peak in excise taxes in the late 1970s arose from the oil windfall profits tax, which was categorized as an excise). Another tax that has declined relative to GNP is the estate tax, which has been very small in recent decades and was cut again substantially by the 1981 tax law. It raises fewer dollars now than it did ten years ago—even ignoring the effect of inflation.

**Excise Taxes.** Excise taxes on products whose consumption is thought to impose costs on the rest of society have eroded substantially in recent years. This erosion might well have occurred largely by accident and so might be ripe for reversal. Excise taxes on alcohol and tobacco were once a far more significant burden than they are now. In 1951, for example, the excise tax on a gallon of hard liquor was $10.50—43 percent of the typical total purchase price, and equal to $44.32 in today's dollars. The tax was increased in 1985 to $12.50 per gallon—still well below the real 1951 level. Similarly, the excise tax on a six-pack of beer has not been increased since 1951, when it was $0.16—$0.68 in today's dollars. The excise tax on wine was in 1951, and still is today, $0.03 per fifth of a gallon. The excise tax on a pack of cigarettes in 1951 was $0.08, which was about 42 percent of the price and about $0.34 in today's dollars; the cigarette excise tax was increased to $0.16 in 1983, but that is only about 15 percent of the price and is still well below the real 1951 level.

Increasing the excise tax on cigarettes from $0.16 to $0.32 cents per pack, increasing the taxes on beer and wine to the alcohol equivalent of the current per year hard liquor rate, and doubling the tax on hard liquor would raise $8.5 billion by 1992. Revenues from these taxes would not grow substantially over time, but they would hold their own if the excise tax rates were indexed for subsequent inflation.

The excise tax on gasoline has also eroded in relative terms since the 1950s, and, even if state and local taxes are included, the burden on gasoline in the United States is far lower than in most Western countries. An increase in the tax could be considered a conservation measure that would reduce U.S. vulnerability to a disruption of oil imports. An increase would, however, be highly controversial. The proceeds of the existing gas tax have, to this point, been earmarked for highway and mass transit subsidies. Using a gas tax to enhance general revenues would represent a significant departure from past practice. Nevertheless, the revenue implications of a tax increase are substantial. Raising the motor fuels tax by $0.12 per gallon would raise $11 billion per year by 1992.

Some concern has been expressed that excise taxes are regressive and that increases in excises would therefore impose an excessive burden on the poor. Clearly, raising comparable revenues from an increase in income tax rates would be more progressive, but the burdens imposed on the poor by excise tax increases are often exaggerated.[13] Undesirable distributional consequences could be offset by adjustments in other federal programs.[14] Perfect compensation is impractical, of course, and any compensating increase in transfers would reduce the net yield of any tax increase.

**Broadening the Income Tax Base.** Tax reform greatly reduced the number of loopholes in the personal and corporate income taxes. Some remain, however, and attacking a portion of the list could raise substantial revenues without directly increasing marginal tax rates.

Repeal of different items among the remaining tax preferences will appeal to different people. Some provisions affect people with relatively modest incomes; repealing those provisions would serve to tax more equally people with equal incomes from different sources. Some provisions apply to "middle-class" tax subsidies. Still others affect income from capital, primarily the domain of the most well-to-do. Some people might argue against the provisions affecting modest-income taxpayers on grounds of fairness; others might view the middle-class tax preferences as politically invulnerable; still others might wish to retain tax preferences for income from capital on the ground that their repeal would reduce savings, investment, and economic growth. Still, the significant reduction of tax rates in the 1986 law might justify the elimination of even more tax preferences; and a balanced combination of preference repeals affecting many groups might be more politically palatable than a focused revenue increase.

The prime candidates for inclusion in a deficit-reduction package (including some that affect excise and payroll taxes as well) and their revenue implications for fiscal 1992 are enumerated in table 9.4.[15] These potential

TABLE 9.4

POTENTIAL TAX REFORMS

| Proposals | Estimated Revenue Savings (in $ billions) |
|---|---|
| 1. Eliminate the interest exemption on municipal bonds issued to finance private activities. | 2.5 |
| 2. Repeal the exemption from gasoline taxes provided for gasohol and buses. | 0.4 |
| 3. Repeal the tax credit now provided for the rehabilitation of older buildings. | 1.9 |
| 4. Tax credit unions as though they were thrift institutions. | 0.5 |
| 5. Repeal the remaining tax advantages of extractive industries. | 2.6 |
| 6. Include 30 percent of the capital gain on the sale of owner-occupied houses in the tax base. | 2.5 |
| 7. Cap the allowable mortgage interest deduction at $12,000 for single returns and at $20,000 for couples. | 1.4 |
| 8. Put workmen's compensation and black-lung benefits into the tax base as is now done with unemployment insurance. | 4.1 |
| 9. Tax some life insurance and private health insurance premiums, but leave some basic coverage tax free. | 30.2 |
| 10. Extend the coverage of Social Security and hospital insurance payroll taxes to state and local workers. | 4.9 |
| 11. Lower the business deduction for entertainment and meals to 50 percent of cost. | 3.6 |
| 12. Force large farms to use accrual accounting instead of cash accounting. | 0.5 |
| 13. Tax accrued capital gains at death. | 6.0 |
| 14. Decrease limits on contributions to pension plans. | 3.6 |
| 15. Repeal salary reduction plans including 401(k) plans, 403(b) plans, and Simplified Employer Plans. | 8.1 |

SOURCE: Congressional Budget Office, *Reducing the Deficit: Spending and Revenue Options* (Washington, D.C.: U.S. Government Printing Office, January 1987).

tax reforms along with increases in gasoline, cigarette, and alcohol excise taxes could raise about $90 billion in fiscal 1992.[16] Enacting the entire list, with the likely associated interest savings, would reduce the deficit by about $112 billion. Combined with the outlay savings enumerated earlier, these reforms would yield a total deficit reduction of $183 billion, still well short of the $220 billion required to balance the budget, exclusive of Social Security. Yet even this tax increase package would encounter extraordinary resistance. Most readers—not to mention politicians—will probably have strong feelings about several of these suggestions, and many policymakers would undoubtedly contend that a program that involves more revenue increases than spending cuts would not be politically viable.

For these reasons a working goal of raising $60 billion from the list might be established, and then some items could be eliminated or reduced in severity. For example, the tax treatment of pension savings could be left the same or modified in only minor ways if this particular inducement to saving was regarded as effective and valuable; or the black-lung benefits might be left untaxed if policymakers decided this proposal was untenable.[17] If the changes were implemented quickly, it should be possible to obtain another $17 billion in indirect savings on interest on the public debt. The total deficit reduction would then be $77 billion—about 5 percent of revenues under current law, 1.3 percent of the GNP. The resulting receipts to GNP ratio would be 20.4 percent under the unrealistic assumption that GNP would be the same as without a tax increase; this would be slightly in excess of the previous post-World War II record of 20.1 percent attained during the period of the Vietnam War surtax and again in 1981.

With the spending cuts described earlier, the tax options would reduce the deficit by 2.5 percent of the GNP. Given CBO assumptions, this would precisely balance the overall budget of the government, but would leave a non-Social Security deficit of 1.1 percent of the GNP.

Some of the changes (particularly those affecting fringe benefits) would indirectly affect payroll tax receipts. There is no need to increase the size of the Old Age, Survivors, and Disability Insurance surplus further. Hence the payroll tax rates could be reduced in response to the added revenues, and income tax rates could be raised comparably to finance the rest of government; or the exccss could be devoted to the Hospital Insurance trust fund, inasmuch as it is likely to be emptied around the turn of the century.

The tax strategy described thus far might be called a "cats and dogs" approach. To many people it may seem totally unrealistic. The loopholes on this list have proved that they have great staying power by the very fact that they survived the most vigorous attempt at base broadening in our history when tax reform was crafted in 1986. Increasing the tax burden on owner-occupied homes may seem particularly implausible, but there will be little reduction in future deficits unless a number of implausible actions are taken. It is also reassuring to remember that taxing Social Security or unemployment benefits seemed just as implausible a very few years ago, but now it is done.

Quite a different approach would be to cut back across the board (without repealing) any targeted tax benefits that remain after the 1986 reform. Variations on the theme could include reducing all itemized deductions and other preferences by 10 or 20 percent; allowing only itemized deductions in excess of (say) 10 percent of income for upper-income taxpayers; or allowing itemized deductions to reduce tax liability by no more than 15 cents on the dollar (taxpayers in the 28 percent bracket now save 28 cents for every additional dollar of itemized deductions). Depending on the precise formulation, this approach could raise between $7 billion and $22 billion per year by 1992— not enough by itself, but enough to replace other options that may be judged too painful.

**Income Tax Rates.** If base broadening fails, the only remaining tool for increasing income tax revenues is raising tax rates. Doing this seems to betray the promises made when tax reform was passed, and it increases the bias in the system against capital income and the incentive to tax avoidance and evasion. Almost $60 billion could be raised by increasing the lowest income tax rate from 15 to 16 percent and raising the highest rate from 28 to 32 percent while raising the corporate tax rate from 34 to 35 percent. Although this option would be distasteful, it would still maintain marginal rates of income taxation far below their levels prior to tax reform.

**Value-added Tax.** Some readers may remain skeptical about any such continuing reform of the existing tax system, so it may be necessary to contemplate a new tax source. The possibility of a value-added tax (VAT) is discussed most frequently. It would act as a deterrent to work effort, but because the variant usually contemplated taxes only consumption, it would not have a direct negative impact on saving and investment. It could be administered as a national retail sales tax, which would have the same economic effects as a VAT and might be easier to implement in the United States because sales taxes already exist in most states.

A 5 percent VAT, exempting food, housing, and medical care, would raise about $66 billion in 1992 or slightly less than the cats and dogs listed above. A brand new tax should not be undertaken lightly, however. The additional administrative and compliance costs would be enormous, probably as burdensome as those now associated with the corporate tax. Somewhere between 10,000 and 20,000 new revenue agents would have to be hired for a simple version of the tax, and if the Congress did not completely resist the temptation to impose different rates on different goods or if the list of exemptions was not severely restrained, the complexities and administrative difficulties would grow exponentially. About two years would be needed to set up this bureaucracy. A VAT less than 5 percent certainly would not be worth the effort; something larger would be more efficient in that a lower proportion of the proceeds would go for collection costs.

But if a VAT can be kept broad-based, it is a fairly efficient tax imposing minimal economic distortions relative to the revenue that it raises. Some conservatives fear it simply because it is such a prolific revenue raiser. They worry that it will be too easy to increase in order to finance an expansion of government activity. Liberals dislike its regressive nature and would prefer a more progressive tax source. Although the effects of a VAT on income distribution could theoretically be neutralized by altering other components of the tax-transfer system, that would be very hard to accomplish, given the complexity of the task and considerable disagreement as to precisely what would be needed.

A VAT is sometimes favored because it is levied on imports and rebated on exports—and hence it is thought to give the country a competitive advantage in international trade, compared with raising the same revenues by increasing income taxes. Although a VAT might stimulate exports, it is unlikely to affect the country's overall trade balance, which is largely determined by macro policies and by the balance between private saving and private investment in the United States. To the extent that a VAT pushed the trade balance in a way that was inconsistent with such factors, exchange rates or some other variable would change to neutralize its effects.

**Income Tax Compliance.** Noncompliance with the individual income tax laws has been growing in recent years, and estimates of the "tax gap" (taxes legally owed but not paid) are large. In 1981, for example, it has been estimated that the tax gap amounted to $75 billion on income earned legally by individuals and $6 billion on income of corporations.[18] Figures such as these are tantalizing to people concerned about the budget deficit; they suggest that merely collecting all taxes owed would erase the greater part of the problem.

Unfortunately, the tax gap must be approached with caution. First, the tax gap estimates themselves are subject to extraordinary uncertainty; a substantial part of the gap is not estimated directly but rather is extrapolated from evidence about other parts of the problem. And just as the size of the tax gap is uncertain, so is the payoff to pursuing it. It is probably optimistic to assume that the payoff to the next dollar's worth of Internal Revenue Service (IRS) enforcement will be equal to the last; the IRS has targeted its efforts on tax returns selected for their likelihood of underpayment of tax, and auditing more returns would necessarily take in those with a lower payoff. Thus, recent increases of expenditures for compliance have yet to show a substantial payoff.

One technique that has been effective in collecting delinquent taxes in some states has been a temporary amnesty. Here again, however, the prospects are easily exaggerated. Many of the states that have had the greatest success were those with the worst enforcement prior to the amnesty—meaning that they had more back taxes to collect than the federal government has. (IRS research has shown that many participants in state tax amnesties had complied with the federal income tax while evading state taxes, and that only 10 percent of participants in the state amnesties examined were unknown to the IRS.) Much of the revenue of some successful state amnesties has been from accounts receivable (back taxes already identified by the states but not yet paid) and from uncollected sales taxes (which, of course, are irrelevant for the federal government).[19] Furthermore, a federal amnesty might not be perceived as a one-time event, and taxpayers might evade further taxes in anticipation of a later amnesty.

The point is not that noncompliance should be ignored; collecting back taxes reduces the deficit and serves the honest taxpayer. However, pursuing the tax gap is an uncertain effort; relying on improved tax compliance to reduce the deficit, to the exclusion of other efforts, may prove to be nothing more than procrastination.

## Conclusion

Reducing the budget deficit is not easy. That is why the nation now faces a political impasse over budget issues. The options considered here imply a significant change in the role of the federal government and the federal tax system; they would impose much pain on individuals, and the economy as a whole would have considerable difficulty adjusting to them. For all that agony, the changes simply balance the overall government budget by altering current policy. Absolutely no room is created for new program initiatives. The more ambitious goal of balancing the non-Social Security budget was left unattained.

Yet, failure to act will create even more pain. The budget deficit is eroding our prospects for future economic growth. The erosion is slow, but inexorable. If allowed to persist, the process will diminish U.S. power relative to that of other nations and reduce future living standards. There is also the risk that the slow erosion will create crises along the way that make the transition to lower living standards more abrupt and, therefore, more acutely painful. That could happen, for example, if foreign lenders, who have been so helpful in directly and indirectly financing the deficit, lose confidence in our policies. The interest rates required to continue to attract their capital may be so high as to cause a recession.

The selection of deficit-reducing options in this paper to a large degree reflects the judgments of the authors about both the substance and the politics of deficit reduction. What is politically plausible and what is not must await the hard bargaining by the various ideological factions in the budget dispute. The nation faces a political impasse that must ultimately be resolved by politicians, with the urging of an informed and involved populace. The task is enormous. It should be started.

NOTES TO CHAPTER 9

1. These are the August 1987 estimates of the Congressional Budget Office (CBO). See Congressional Budget Office, *The Economic and Budget Outlook: An Update* (Washington, D.C.: U.S. Government Printing Office, August 1987), 49.

2. Official current policy budget estimates are made by both the CBO and the Office of Management and Budget (OMB). Generally, current policy is taken to imply no changes in current tax and entitlement laws and constant real future appropriations for discretionary programs. Although this definition seems simple enough, numerous minor ambiguities arise in implementing it. There is, however, one major difference between the definitions of CBO and OMB: OMB defines current policy in defense to imply approximately 3 percent real growth in budget authority per year, whereas CBO keeps defense constant in real terms. If OMB had used CBO's definition for defense, OMB's defense outlays would be $23 billion lower in 1992, and because the deficit would be lower, interest on the debt would be $4 to $5 billion lower as well.

But OMB's estimated deficit falls more quickly than CBO's, because OMB's economic assumptions are much more optimistic and some of the noneconomic assumptions are more optimistic as well. For example, OMB assumes a lower cost for existing farm subsidies.

Although the current state of the art of forecasting makes it impossible to rule out very optimistic forecasts, the OMB assumptions are so out of line with recent experience and the assumptions of most forecasters that it would be unwise to rely on them for planning purposes, even though there is a small chance that they might be right. The discussion here is, therefore, confined to the CBO estimates.

3. CBO did not provide sensitivity tables for its August estimates. The current numbers would be slightly less sensitive to forecast errors simply because they were calculated seven months closer to the fiscal year totals being estimated; there would be other minor changes as well, but none important enough to alter any major conclusions.

4. American Enterprise Institute, *Public Opinion* (March-April 1987): 21–37.

5. See chapter 3, note 24.

6. See, for example, Joshua Epstein, *The 1988 Defense Budget* (Washington, D.C.: Brookings Institution, 1987), 19–21.

7. Ibid., 31.

8. Ibid., 54. Note that most of the individual elements of this package have been discussed and priced by the Congressional Budget Office, *Reducing the Deficit: Spending and Revenue Options* (Washington, D.C.: U.S. Government Printing Office, January 1987), 13–62.

9. A reasonable change in the replacement rate would save only about $1 billion by 1992. Raising $14 billion in tax revenue at that time would require raising the proportion of benefits included in the tax base to 85 percent and reducing the threshold for taxation from the current adjusted gross income (AGI) of $25,000 for singles and $32,000 for married couples (chapter 6, table 6.4).

10. Congressional Budget Office, *Reducing the Deficit: Spending and Revenue Options* (Washington, D.C.: U.S. Government Printing Office, January 1987), 68–96.

11. Ibid., 105–13.

12. *Washington Post*, "Poll: Federal Government Esteemed Least," September 8, 1987, D-2.

13. Recent estimates are presented in Congressional Budget Office, "The Distributional Effects of an Increase in Selected Federal Excise Taxes," Staff Working Paper, January 1987. This paper provides very useful estimates, but the results require some clarification. For one thing, the statistical tables present results for "families" by income category, but the term "family" is used loosely to apply also to single persons living alone or in groups. In the Census Bureaus survey of the population in 1985, only 46 percent of all households with incomes of under $5,000 were families with or without children. Furthermore, the CBO figures indicate that households with incomes under $5,000 had average incomes of $2,311 but average total expenditures of $9,690. This suggests that this group is composed disproportionately of, for example, students receiving cash from their parents, or relatively wealthy families experiencing only temporary reductions in their incomes (in some cases, tax shelter losses). Including such households tends to exaggerate the actual regressivity of the excise taxes on truly poor families.

14. To the extent that prices are raised by excises, low-income recipients of indexed entitlements will see those entitlements automatically increase. To the extent that excise tax increases cannot be passed on to the consumer they will fall more or less equally on the labor and capital involved in the production process, and the result will be similar to that following an increase in a proportional tax. If it was expected that the entire excise tax burden would show up as price increases, unindexed programs such as Aid to Families with Dependent Children (AFDC) could be increased to compensate; some increase in the earned-income tax credit also could be considered.

15. A detailed description of the following options along with a discussion of their advantages and disadvantages can be found in Congressional Budget Office, *Reducing the Deficit*.

16. Extending the telephone excise tax beyond its currently scheduled expiration is another option for increasing revenues in future years.

17. Most of the figures provided for individual items are computed as though they represented the only changes in the tax code. Obviously, interactions occur among the items, and so adding them all up does not yield an absolutely correct total. However, because of the nature of the items chosen, the interactions are likely to be minor.

18. Department of the Treasury, Internal Revenue Service, *Income Tax Compliance Research: Estimates for 1973–81* (Washington, D.C.: U.S. Government Printing Office, July 1983), table I-1, p. 3.

19. John L. Mikesell, "Amnesties for State Tax Evaders: The Nature of and Response to Recent Programs," *National Tax Journal* 39, no. 4 (December 1986): 507–25.

# INDEX

Abortion, 10, 11, 27, 233–234, 254
Acquired Immune Deficiency Syndrome. *See* AIDS
AFDC. *See* Aid to Families with Dependent Children
Aged. *See* Elderly
Agriculture
  Export position, 122
  Productivity growth trend, 77, 120
  Protectionist policies and, 123
  Subsidies, 302–303, 305–306
AIDS
  Described, 255–258
  Discrimination, 258, 259, 262–264
    insurance, 264–267
  High-risk populations: blacks, 257, 262
    Hispanics, 257; homosexuals, 256,
    262–263, 266; infants, 257, 258,
    262; intravenous drug abusers, 256,
    257, 260–261; prisoners, 257;
    prostitutes, 256, 261
  Media and, 262
  Policy issues, 10, 11, 12, 27, 254, 255
  Public perceptions, 11, 12, 27, 257, 258
  Testing, 27, 257, 258–260; California
    referendum on, 258; for
    epidemiological data, 259–260; of
    immigrants, 258; mandatory, 259,
    260, 263–264; results issues, 259,
    263–264
  Transmission, 256, 257
AIDS Commission, 3
Aid to Families with Dependent Children
  (AFDC), 26, 53, 224, 231, 232, 233,
  236, 238, 241
Arms control agreements, 2, 5, 297–298

Balanced budget, 181, 287–288
Blacks
  AIDS and, 27, 257, 262
  Education, 244
  Employment, 239, 240
  Income, 39, 59, 60
  Underclass, 227, 229
BLS. *See* Bureau of Labor Statistics
Budget deficit, 28–29
  Background, 280–282

Capital formation and, 92–95
Defense and, 6, 290–298
Estimates, 282–286
Family income impact of, 47–48
Implications for future, 2, 6–8, 13–15, 21
Off-budget problem, 305–306
Policy issues and goals, 8, 28–29, 286–289, 314–315
Presidential constraints, 13
Reduction strategies, 8, 29, 289–290, 304–305; defense spending and, 290–298; discretionary spending and, 303–304; entitlements, 302–303; Medicare, 300–302; Social Security, 299–300; Social Security surpluses and, 181, 206, 289; Taxation, 306–314
Bureau of Labor Statistics (BLS), 113, 129

Capital, 87–95
  Budget deficit and, 76, 92–95, 289
  Economic growth, 72, 96
  Economic obsolescence, 74–76
  Tax policy and, 76, 89–92
Capital-to-labor ratio, 74, 75–76
Carter, Jimmy, 2, 281, 291
Catastrophic health insurance, 185, 189, 193–194, 196–197, 301
CBO. *See* Congressional Budget Office
CEA. *See* Council of Economic Advisers
CETA. *See* Comprehensive Employment and Training Act
Child care
  Characteristics of good, 153, 162
  Employer assistance, 164–165
  Government programs, 161
  Policy issues, 8, 24, 162–164
Child care tax credit, 161, 243
Children
  AIDS and, 257
  Divorce effects on, 152–153, 154
  Health trends, 153
  Maternal employment and, 149–150, 153, 154–155
  Parental responsibility for, 231–233, 234–238

317

# ABOUT THE AUTHORS

**Andrew Cherlin** is professor of sociology at Johns Hopkins University. He has published extensively on the topic of the contemporary American family, including *Marriage, Divorce, Remarriage* (1981) and (with Frank F. Furstenberg, Jr.) *The New American Grandparent* (1986).

**Joseph J. Minarik** is senior research associate at The Urban Institute, where he has investigated topics such as taxation, the distribution of income, poverty, income security policy, the consequences of inflation, and fiscal policy. From 1981 to 1984 he served as deputy assistant director in the Tax Analysis Division of the Congressional Budget Office. He is the author of *Making Tax Choices* (1985).

**John L. Palmer** is a senior fellow of The Urban Institute and codirector of the Changing Domestic Priorities project. His research interests are in economic and social policy. He has been an assistant professor at Stanford University, a senior fellow of the Brookings Institution, and an assistant secretary for the U.S. Department of Health and Human Services. His most recent book is *Perspectives on the Reagan Years* (1986).

**Rudolph G. Penner,** a senior fellow at The Urban Institute, is a former director of the Congressional Budget Office. He has also held government positions at the Council of Economic Advisers, the Department of Housing and Urban Development, and the Office of Management and Budget. He has published widely on tax and spending policy issues.

**Isabel V. Sawhill** is a senior fellow of The Urban Institute and codirector of the Changing Domestic Priorities project. Her areas of research include human resources and economic policy. She has directed several of the Institute's research programs and has held a number of government positions, including that of director of the National Commission for Employment Policy. She is coauthor of *The Reagan Record* (1984) and *Economic Policy in the Reagan Years* (1984).

**Thomas C. Schelling** is the Lucius N. Littauer Professor of Political Economy at Harvard's John F. Kennedy School of Government. His policy research interests have included national security, energy, health care, substance abuse, the environment, and ethics. His most recent book is *Choice and Consequence* (1984).

**Charles F. Stone** is an economist at the Federal Communications Commission and a former senior research associate at The Urban Institute, where his research was in the areas of macroeconomics and international trade. He is coauthor of *Economic Policy in the Reagan Years* (1984).